# The ARAB-ISRAELI Conflict

## A Timeless Struggle

Leanne Piggott

**Science Press**

First published by Science Press 2008
© Leanne Piggott 2008

Science Press
Private Bag 7023 Marrickville NSW 1475 Australia
Tel: (02) 9516 1122  Fax: (02) 9550 1915
sales@sciencepress.com.au
www.sciencepress.com.au

# Contents

# Abbreviations

| | |
|---|---|
| AH | After the Hijra |
| ALA | Arab Liberation Army |
| ALF | Arab Liberation Front |
| APG | All Palestine Government |
| BCE | Before the Common Era |
| CE | Common Era |
| DP | Displaced Person/s |
| DOP | Oslo Declaration of Principles |
| IJ | Islamic Jihad |
| IDF | Israel Defence Forces |
| PA | Palestinian National Authority |
| DFLP | The Democratic Front for the Liberation of Palestine |
| PFLP | The Popular Front for the Liberation of Palestine |
| PFLP-GC | The Popular Front for the Liberation of Palestine – General Command |
| PLA | Palestinian Liberation Army |
| PLF | Palestine Liberation Front |
| PLO | Palestine Liberation Organisation |
| PNC | Palestine National Council |
| SLA | South Lebanese Army |
| UN | United Nations |
| UNEF | United Nations Emergency Force |
| UNIFIL | United Nations Interim Force in Lebanon |
| UNLU | Unified National Leadership of the Uprising (al-Qiyada al-Wataniyya al-Muwahhida li'l-Intifada) |
| UNSCOP | United Nations Special Committee on Palestine |
| UNWRA | United Nations Relief and Works Agency for Palestine |
| US | United States of America |
| USSR | Union of Socialist Soviet Republics |
| WZO | World Zionist Organisation |

# 1 Introduction

The Arab-Israeli conflict is more than just a dispute over boundaries. It involves identity, aspirations, legitimacy, and history.

From ancient times to the present day, there has been a seemingly timeless struggle for control of the small strip of land located between the Jordan River and the Mediterranean Sea and in the Negev Desert to the south. The most recent chapter in this history is the Arab-Israeli conflict. At the heart of this conflict lie the competing claims of two peoples, Israelis and Palestinians, over the land that Palestinians call *Filastin* (Palestine) and Israelis call *Yisra'el* (Israel). Their political rivalry has continued unabated since the early 1880s.

Since 1948, the local conflict between Israelis and Palestinians has been exacerbated by a regional conflict between the State of Israel and its neighbouring Arab states. This interstate conflict has led to six major wars: the 1947-9 War that was fought over the establishment of Israel; the Suez War of 1956; the Six-Day War of 1967; the Israel-Egypt War of Attrition of 1969-70; the October War of 1973; and Israel's invasion of Lebanon in 1982. Between these major outbreaks, the conflict between Israel and the Arab states has also been played out in the diplomatic and economic arenas and in continual low-level violence through border clashes and armed incursions. To date, two Arab states have signed peace treaties with Israel: Egypt in 1979 and Jordan in 1994. However, tensions remain high due to the unresolved conflict between Israelis and Palestinians.

The aim of *A Timeless Struggle* is to examine the history of the Arab-Israeli conflict at these two principal levels: the local and the regional. A third level of analysis will focus on the role of international powers in the modern Middle East generally and on the Arab-Israeli conflict in particular. Key features, issues, individuals, groups, and events will be described and analysed, as will key forces and ideas that have contributed to change and continuity in the history of the conflict and in attempts to resolve it. More detailed personality studies of Golda Meir and Yasser Arafat are provided. Issues concerning historiography are also considered. Questions at the end of each chapter provide further opportunity to analyse and synthesise information from different types of sources, and to develop the skills of oral and written communication.

The purpose of this present chapter is to provide an introduction to the study of peace and conflict, and to the issues that have caused conflict in the modern Middle East generally, and between Arabs and Israelis in particular. The chapter will also highlight the importance of understanding the historical roots of the Arab-Israeli conflict in the light of the role that history plays in the contemporary narratives of each side.

Following World War I, the Arab lands that had been a part of the Ottoman Empire were divided by the League of Nations into 'Mandates', newly created territorial units placed under the administrative rule of Britain and France. Britain was given a Mandate over the territory of Palestine where there lived an Arab majority and a Jewish minority. Under the terms of the Mandate, Britain was required 'to establish a Jewish national home in Palestine', while respecting 'the civil and religious rights' of the Arab population. The Arabs rejected the Mandate as an injustice and a betrayal, and during the decades of British rule over Palestine, conflict between the Arabs and the Jews intensified. In 1947, the British Government turned the problem over to the newly established United Nations (UN). In November of that year, the UN General Assembly voted to partition the territory into two separate states, an Arab state and a Jewish state. For reasons detailed in Chapters 5 and 6, the Jewish State of Israel was established while the Arab State of Palestine was not. Today, the Palestinian Arabs remain a stateless people, the majority of whom live in the territories of the Gaza Strip and the West Bank.

### Israelis: Facts at a glance

At the end of 2005, Israel's population was 6.95 million. 76% of the population was Jewish (5.3 million), 20% Arab (1.4 million), and 4% 'others' (250 000). The Jewish population includes about 238 000 settlers living in the West Bank (Israel Bureau of Statistics).

### Palestinians: Facts at a glance

At the end of 2005, the Palestinian population in the Palestinian territories was estimated to be 3.8 million: 1.45 million in the Gaza Strip and 2.35 million in the occupied West Bank (Palestine Bureau of Statistics).

The land that forms the focus of the Arab-Israeli conflict can be divided into four geographic regions:

- the Coastal Plain
- the Central Hills
- the Rift (or Jordan) Valley
- the Negev Desert.

The area of Israel is 20 770 sq km. The area of the Palestinian territories is 6220 sq km: the West Bank is 5860 sq km while the Gaza Strip is 360 sq km.

**Figure 1.1** Aerial photograph of the land of Israel/Palestine.

# The study of peace and conflict

What is **peace**? Peace means different things in different contexts. Peace at home might mean quiet and tranquillity. Peace within a country might mean freedom from civil disorder. International peace, or peace within a particular geographical region, might mean freedom from, or the cessation of, war. In each case, peace would appear to be the opposite of conflict. Not surprisingly, therefore, the study of peace often includes the study of how conflict is resolved.

What, then, is **conflict**? Conflict occurs when there is antagonism between two or more parties producing mutual hostility. It may be expressed in a variety of non-violent ways or through violence which in the worst cases can take the form of all-out war between states.

The Irish academic John Darby has argued that 'conflict is neither good nor bad, but intrinsic in every social relationship from marriage to international diplomacy. Whenever two or more people are gathered, there is conflict or potential conflict'.[1] This is because social life involves groups with different norms, values, attitudes, interests and levels of power. Various groups struggle for power and resources and this can generate opposition, exclusion and hostility from other groups. Darby goes on to argue that if conflict is an inevitable part of society, the real issue is not the existence of conflict, 'but how it is handled'. In cases where conflict resolution is not possible in the short or medium term, what is important is how the conflict is managed.

In the international context, the idea of **conflict management** emphasises, first and foremost, the need to bring about a reduction in violence, particularly its worst manifestations. Once the positive effects of successful conflict management have taken root, and there has been a significant reduction in violence over a sustained period of time, prospects for the parties to resolve the conflict through negotiations are greatly improved.

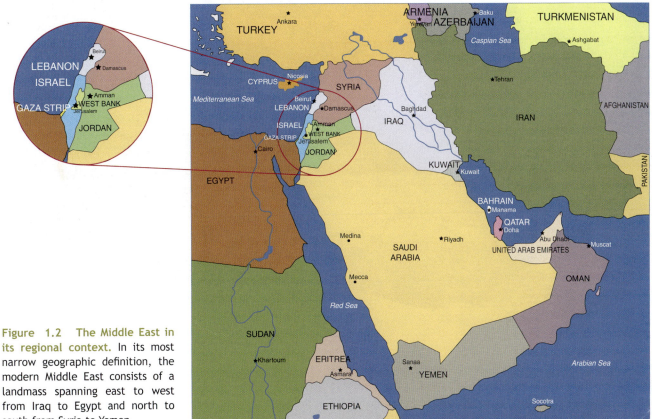

**Figure 1.2 The Middle East in its regional context.** In its most narrow geographic definition, the modern Middle East consists of a landmass spanning east to west from Iraq to Egypt and north to south from Syria to Yemen.

**Conflict resolution** means, in essence, an end to all hostilities between the parties. Often this will require a compromise on the underlying issues and a mutual relinquishment of the right to make further demands against each other – hence the formula: 'End of Claims, End of Conflict'. This means that each side, having agreed to a once-and-for-all-compromise to settle the issues driving the conflict, will have no outstanding claims against the other beyond the terms of settlement. Usually, neither party will regard the compromise as ideal, but rather one that they can each live with. They see the compromise as preferable to continuing the conflict. The resulting 'peace' may not necessarily produce warm and friendly relations between the former antagonists. It may mean nothing more than a mutual, legally binding commitment to 'live and let live'.

**Figure I.3 1990-91 Gulf War.** A damaged Iraqi tank sits abandoned in the Kuwaiti desert at the end of the 1990-91 Gulf War. In the distance Kuwaiti oil wells burn, ignited by Iraq's retreating forces.

# Conflict in the modern Middle East

**Figure 1.4** The Middle East in its global context.

There has been conflict in the Middle East from time immemorial. The causes have been numerous. So, too, have the forms that the conflicts have assumed, ranging from purely verbal 'slanging matches' to full-scale military combat. The players in these conflicts have also varied through the ages, although in some cases, contemporary conflicts in the Middle East are the result of age-old disputes that have simply been given a modern appearance.

In the modern history of the region, wars have been fought over issues such as natural resources (oil and water), territory and borders, navigation rights through waterways, nationalism, and religion. The first Gulf War, which was between Iraq and Iran (1980-88), involved most of these factors, and cost more than a million lives. It was followed by the second major war in the Gulf (1990-91) which began as a dispute between Iraq and Kuwait over natural resources and territory.

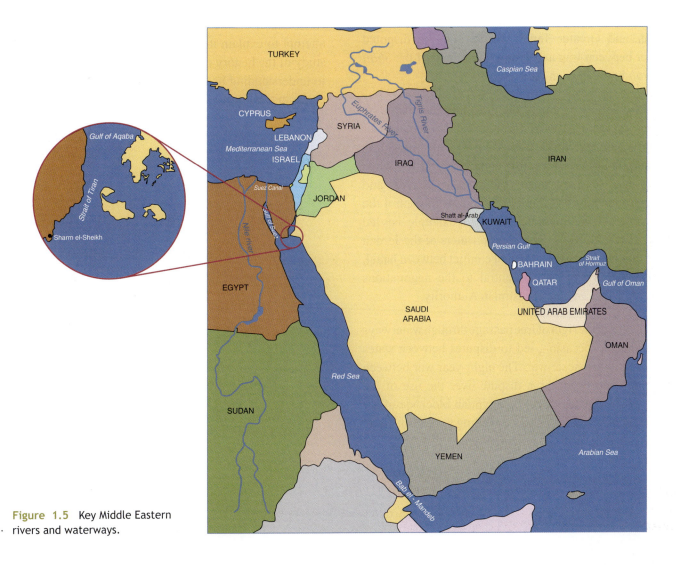

**Figure 1.5** Key Middle Eastern rivers and waterways.

It is not surprising that territorial disputes have been a major cause of conflict in the modern Middle East. Most of the countries in the region have only emerged as independent states with defined territories since the end of World War II. In some cases, border disputes between the new states resulted in armed conflict. The border between Saudi Arabia and Yemen, for example, was not agreed upon until 2000, at the end of 65 years of sporadic conflict. In this context, it is important to remember how many wars were fought between European states for the possession of territory, and how many lives were lost in those wars. The European order that came into being with the unification of Germany in 1871 was, as historian Michael Howard puts it, 'like all its predecessors, created by war.'

Territorial disputes that remain unresolved in the Middle East today include the Israeli-Palestinian conflict; the Israeli-Syrian conflict; the dispute between Iran and United Arab Emirates over Abu Musa Island and the Lesser and Greater Tanb Islands; and the disputed border between Iran and Iraq at the mouth of the *Shatt al-Arab* in the Persian Gulf.

The Middle East is one of the most arid regions in the world. In some parts of the region, the demand for water is approaching or surpassing annual supply. It is not surprising, therefore, that conflict has arisen when states need to share water resources from rivers and underground aquifers. Turkey's attempts to control the headwaters of the Euphrates River, for example, has led to conflict with Syria. Sharing the waters of the Jordan River has also been the source of conflict between Israel, Jordan and Syria, and is central to the negotiations between Israel and the Palestinian Authority.

Disputes over the right of free passage through waterways have also, on occasion, led to disputes between states and even to full-scale war. The eight-year war between Iran and Iraq began as a dispute over the use of the *Shatt al-Arab* waterway. The Egyptian blockade of the Straits of Tiran against ships travelling to or from Israel precipitated the 1967 Arab-Israeli War.

Competing ideologies and religions have been a further cause of conflict in the Middle East, both in ancient and modern times. In the modern period, ideologies of European origin, including nationalism and socialism, were introduced to the region with the arrival of western imperialism in the late 18th century. These concepts had a profound impact upon traditional Arab and Muslim society as centuries-old institutions, values and perceptions were undermined by the clash between tradition and modernity, religion and secularism. This friction remains a key feature of the contemporary politics and society of the modern Middle East.

Although conflict is a permanent part of the human condition, it is also important to appreciate that particular conflicts have their own distinctive character. Conflicts in the Middle East are especially complex because of the mixture of historical, religious and political components. All three factors are present in the Arab-Israeli conflict as is evident in the narratives that attempt to explain it, and in attempts to resolve it. The study of the history of this conflict is therefore essential to understanding its causes as well as the prospects for peace in the future.

# The Arab-Israeli conflict: The role of history and narrative

Historians study the past to attempt to make the present more intelligible. In his 1959 book, *Prelude to Israel*, the historian Alan R Taylor made another case for the importance of studying history. He argued that in order to find a resolution to a particular conflict, the process must begin with a sound understanding of its history. Taylor wrote the following about the Arab-Israeli conflict:

> Of primary importance in the peacemaking task is knowledge and understanding, a mature perspective which can show the way to possible avenues of approach ... The starting point of necessity is history. Perhaps the major cause of necessity is history. Perhaps the major cause of current confusion as to the real issues is ignorance of the problem's historical roots. The actual dimensions of the crisis cannot be grasped in terms of the more recent developments alone, for these reflect only claims and counterclaims, assaults and retaliations, without reference to the origins of the conflict and the deeper sources of causality.[2]

Taylor's advice regarding peacemaking is still relevant today. However, the study of history is seldom uncontroversial and the history of the Arab-Israeli conflict is no exception. From the very moment one begins to study this conflict, it becomes clear that it is not simply about 'facts and figures'; there are often emotionally-charged, competing narratives, giving rise to claims and counterclaims. Facts and figures are only part of a larger picture that includes the deepest aspirations and fundamental sense of identity of two different peoples.

This view is echoed by Dennis Ross, the US chief negotiator during Arab-Israeli peace negotiations between 1991 and 2000. In his 2004 book, *The Missing Peace*, Ross wrote the following:

> Peacemaking in the last decade emerged from a historical context of deep-seated grievances and desire for justice on both sides. Arabs and Israelis each have a narrative that tells their story and interprets their reality, and these narratives were lurking in every discussion. To understand these narratives, one needs to know what shaped them; how they evolved; and how particular historical developments affected attitudes and beliefs. Only then can one appreciate what we had to contend with in trying to promote peacemaking.[3]

Ross' experience bears witness to the important role that historical narrative plays in Arab and Israeli political and cultural discourse.

## The use of sources

Many scholarly works, too, are written to convince the reader about who is telling the 'real' history. Competing accounts about the past underpin conflicting ideas about what is required for a just resolution of the conflict. The writing of the history has thus become an ideological component of the conflict itself. Indeed, every historical work contains something of the author's subjective way of looking at the conflict and the world in general, for which the reader needs to be alert. For these reasons, the study of the Arab-Israeli conflict should also include a study of its historiography.

## What is 'historiography'?

The term 'historiography' is used to refer to the process of writing history and also to the products of that process. It is also commonly used to refer to an examination of the methods and approaches of the historian. Some of the basic questions considered in historiography are:

- Who is the author of the source (primary or secondary)?
- What were the author's perspectives when he or she created that source?
- Does the history attempt to provide a particular lesson or a neutral viewpoint?
- Who is or was the intended audience?
- Has there been a change in the way historians consider their subject or, in other words, have new ideas affected the writing of a particular history? If so, how did those new ideas come about?

Once the answers to these questions have been considered, it is possible to determine if there are any ulterior motives on the author's part. It is also possible to determine any processes of change that might have taken place in the wider realm of ideas of a particular society that have impacted on the world view of the historian/s.

Interestingly, a study of histories of the Arab-Israeli conflict written over the last 20 years reveals a clear debate even between historians within each 'camp'. Israeli historians are now divided between the older 'official' historians such as Martin Gilbert, Howard Sachar and Shabtai Teveth, and more recent authors who have had access to a broader range of primary sources. The latter group is divided between those such as Efraim Karsh who have supported the perspective of the earlier historians, and those in the so-called 'revisionist' school such as Baruch Kimmerling, Joel Migdal, Benny Morris, Ilan Pappe, Tom Segev, and Avi Shlaim who have sought to modify that perspective.

Although there are now competing versions of history written by Jewish and Israeli scholars, both groups have based their work on government archives that have progressively been released after 30 (or sometimes 50) years, as is the practice of Western governments.

The debate among Arab historians has not occurred to the same extent. This is partly due to the inaccessibility of Arab primary sources. While some archives of the Palestine Liberation Organisation (PLO) have been made available to a small number of historians, Arab government archives have not been opened to the public.

Nevertheless, some Arab historians have endeavoured to examine the events of the past beyond the 'official' Arab position. These include Adeed Dawisha, Albert Hourani, Rashid Khalidi, Walid Khalidi, Nur Masalha and Yezid Sayigh. Other important Arab writers on the Arab-Israeli conflict who are not historians include Ibrahim Abu' Lughod, Fouad Ajami, Mohamed Heikal and Edward Said. As is the case with Israeli writers, the perspectives of these authors often differ sharply.

This book attempts, through different types of sources, to allow both Israelis and Palestinians and other Arabs to recount their narratives in their own terms. This includes the writings of Arab and Israeli historians who have dealt with the new archival material relating to the events they are interpreting and takes into account their varying, and sometimes conflicting, conclusions. To the extent that the ideas of these historians clash, they reflect the reality that there are two distinct peoples, Arabs and Jews – Israelis and Palestinians – who have their own perspectives on history. Whether there is hope that one day their conflict of words and deeds might end, bringing peace to this land, will be contemplated in the final chapter.

As for the historical, religious, cultural and political connections that Israelis and Palestinians have to *Filastin/Yisra'el*, these will be examined in the following chapter.

# Review and research questions

1.  The majority of the states that make up the Middle East have an Arab-Muslim majority. Which states in the region do not? What ethnic or religious majority do these states have?

2.  Map exercise:

    (a)  Complete the table by linking the countries with their capital cities.

| Capital cities | |
| --- | --- |
| Manama | Cairo |
| Tehran | Kuwait City |
| Damascus | Beirut |
| Abu Dhabi | Muscat |
| Sana | Amman |
| Jerusalem | Baghdad |
| Riyadh | Doha |

| Country | Capital city |
| --- | --- |
| Egypt | |
| Israel | |
| Jordan | |
| Kuwait | |
| Yemen | |
| Bahrain | |
| Oman | |

| Country | Capital city |
| --- | --- |
| Iraq | |
| Lebanon | |
| Saudi Arabia | |
| Qatar | |
| United Arab Emirates | |
| Syria | |
| Iran | |

   (b)  Locate the countries and their capitals and the following waterways on the blank map (Figure 1.6) provided.

   Rivers: Nile, Tigris, Euphrates, Jordan

   International waterways:  Suez Canal; Straits of Tiran; Bal al-Mandeb; Persian (Arabian) Gulf

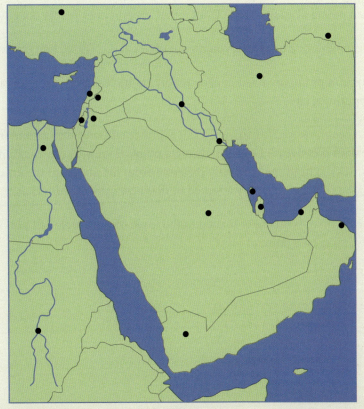

**Figure 1.6**

3. Media exercise: In the light of the important role that the media plays in shaping our understanding and knowledge of world events it is necessary to consider the nature of media coverage as a source for the study of the Arab-Israeli conflict.

The Arab-Israeli conflict is only one of several seemingly intractable conflicts in the Middle East today, although it is certainly the one that has attracted the most international media coverage. Saturation media coverage tends to distort reality by focusing our attention on certain issues to the exclusion of others.

The choice of issues that are covered, and the extent of the coverage, reflects the priorities of the relevant media outlet, including its editorial point of view, and not necessarily what is objectively significant. When studying the Arab-Israeli conflict, therefore, it is necessary to be aware of media perceptions and biases.

There are many ways to do this, for example, paying close attention to your local newspapers and television news broadcasts. To be more organised, try the following:

Begin a portfolio of articles collected from *two* different newspapers with opposing editorial views on the Arab-Israeli conflict. In the process, consider the following:

- Who owns the newspapers?
- What is the political orientation of the journalists who are their major contributors, or the agency which the newspaper uses for its articles?

In newspaper articles, there is a distinction between news reports, opinion pieces (Op Ed), and editorials. From each of the two newspapers you have selected, cut out news reports dealing with the same event in the Arab-Israeli conflict. Then consider the following questions and be aware of any differences in the way the two newspapers report on events and characters:

(a) Summarise the main points of each article. Does either report cover points not covered by the other?

(b) Are there any terms or abbreviations that you do not understand? If so, find out what they mean.

(c) What individuals or groups are involved in each report? Is it clear from each report what objectives these individuals or groups have?

(d) In either report, is a headline used? If so, is it a fair representation of the content of the article? If not, what message does it convey? Does it indicate a point of view of the 'headline writer'? (*Note*: The person who writes the headline is usually different from the author of the article.) Is the headline suggestive of the point of view generally adopted in that newspaper's editorials?

(e) Is a photograph used? If so, is it clearly related to the topic of the article? If not, what message does it convey? Does it also suggest a point of view?

(f) Does each article portray relevant individuals or groups as either 'positive', 'negative' or 'neutral'? Explain how this is expressed or implied and the techniques used.

(g) Who has written the article? Has the journalist previously written opinion pieces in support of either side in the conflict in that newspaper? Is the news report 'slanted' towards that opinion in any way?

(h) Consider generally how the two newspapers might be similar or different in the coverage of the topic/s.

(i) Critically assess whether each newspaper's reporting might be intended to influence public opinion about the Arab-Israeli conflict and if so, how? You might begin by thinking about whether it influences your opinion of the conflict. If so, how?

## Discussion questions

1. What causes conflict between different groups of people?

2. What 'causes' peace?

3. Why is history important when studying any conflict?

4. In the 14th century, the famous Muslim writer, Ibn Khaldun, who is often referred to as 'the founder and father of Sociology and Sciences of History', wrote in his work, the *Muqadimmah*, that 'all records, by their very nature, are liable to error'[4]. The reasons he gave are as follows:

(a) Partisanship towards a creed or opinion.

(b) Overconfidence in one's sources.

(c) The failure to understand what is intended.

(d) A mistaken belief in the truth of something that is wholly or partly untrue.

(e) The inability to place an event in its real context.

(f) The common desire to gain the favour of those of high rank, by praising them, by spreading their fame.

(g) Ignorance of the laws governing the transformation of human society.

Consider what Ibn Khaldun meant by these points and whether or not you agree with him.

# Part 1

## The Origins of the Arab-Israeli Conflict 1880s-1947

'The past isn't dead; it isn't even past.'

Nobel Prize-winning novelist William Faulkner

# 2 Setting the Scene

By the end of this chapter you will be familiar with the:

- central players in the Arab-Israeli conflict at the local and regional levels
- key historical and religious events as understood by individuals and groups involved in the Arab-Israeli conflict
- historical origin of the names *Filastin* (Palestine) and *Yisra'el* (Israel).

Although most historians date the origins of the Arab-Israeli conflict to the rise of Jewish and Arab nationalisms in the second half of the 19th century, some look for more ancient roots. One reason is to help explain why it was that during the 20th century, the Jewish people sought to establish a sovereign state in Palestine, a land where they were the minority and the Arabs were a majority, at a time when the majority of Jews lived in other parts of the world. Whilst the intensity of the historical and religious connection felt by the Jewish people to the land of Israel is seldom understood by other people, without it, the tenacity with which the Jews struggled to establish their state can not be fully explained. Similarly, the depth of Arab opposition to Jewish aspirations in Palestine cannot be understood without an appreciation of why Arabs regard this land as an integral part of a wider domain of Arab (and Islamic) sovereignty.

Although the Arab-Israeli conflict is not solely or even principally about religion, religious feelings help to explain why some Jews and Arabs see the conflict as the continuation of a struggle that dates back to ancient times. Some religious Jews, for example, trace the origins of the conflict to the Biblical story concerning Abraham over 3000 years ago and the rival claims of his two sons, Ishmael and Isaac, to be his legitimate heir. Ishmael and Isaac are identified as the patriarchs of the Arab and Jewish peoples respectively. Some Muslims view the contemporary conflict as the most recent chapter in an ongoing dispute between Jews and Muslims that began around 1300 years ago, as recorded in the Muslim holy book, the Koran.

In view of the role that history and religion play in the claims and counterclaims of both sides, the purpose of this chapter is to 'set the scene' by introducing the key peoples, their beliefs and some of the historical events that continue to inform their contemporary narratives. As will become evident, struggles for control of the land have been a feature of the region for millennia.

| Timeline | Event |
|---|---|
| c.1203 BCE | Earliest extra-Biblical record of a people called 'Israel' living in ancient Canaan. |
| c.1180 | The 'Sea People' (including Philistines) from Mycenae in Greece invade Canaan and settle along the coast in and around Gaza and Ashkelon. |
| c.1000 | King David unites the 12 tribes of Israel under one kingdom, Yisra'el (Israel), with Jerusalem (Zion) as its capital. |
| c.960 | King Solomon completes construction of the first Jewish Temple in Jerusalem. |
| 586 | Solomon's Temple is destroyed by the Babylonians. Many Jews exiled to Babylon. |
| 539 | The Jews in Babylon return to the Land of Israel and build the second Temple. |
| 165 | Hasmonean (Second) Jewish Kingdom established. |
| 63 | Romans conquer the Jewish Kingdom which becomes the Roman province of Judaea. |
| 66 to 70 CE | Jewish Revolt against the Romans. |
| 70 | Second Jewish Temple destroyed by the Romans. |
| 132 to 135 | Jews are defeated in their second revolt against Roman rule in Judaea and many expelled from the land. The land is renamed 'Syria-Palestina'. |
| 610 | Muhammad receives his first revelations from the Angel Gabriel. |
| 622 | Muhammad is invited to Medina, where he establishes the first Muslim community, marking the beginning of the Muslim calendar. |
| 630 | Muhammad's army conquers Mecca resulting in the rise of successive Arab Muslim empires. |
| 637 to 638 | Jerusalem is conquered by Arab Muslims. The land is renamed the province of Filastin (Palestine). |
| 687 to 691 | Dome of the Rock and Al-Aqsa Mosque are built on the ruins of the Jewish Temple. |
| 1095 | The first Christian Crusade establishes the Latin Kingdom of Jerusalem in 1099, which lasts until the fall of Acre in 1291. |
| 1517 | The Turkish Muslim (Ottoman) Empire conquers Palestine which remains under Ottoman administration until the end of World War I. |

# Israel/Palestine: Land, peoples and religions

In ancient times, the Middle East was the location of the rise and fall of a number of great civilisations, including those of the ancient Egyptians, Hittites, Assyrians, Babylonians, Canaanites, Israelites and other peoples of the biblical world. Here some of the earliest farms, cities, governments, legal codes, and alphabets were developed, spreading to all parts of the globe. For this reason, the region has been described as the 'Cradle of Civilisation'.

In the 7th century CE, another great civilisation arose in the region, that of the Arab Muslims. Various Arab empires dominated the region until the 16th century, when the Turkish Muslims defeated the Arabs and took control of the Middle East. The Ottoman Empire of the Turks remained in control until the Empire was dissolved following its defeat in World War I.

All of these civilisations and empires had at least one thing in common, namely, a connection with religion. Indeed, the Middle East is the birthplace of several great religions including **Judaism**, **Christianity**, and **Islam**. For the adherents of these faiths – **Jews**, **Christians** and **Muslims** – the region and its holy sites are a source of religious inspiration and emotional bonds with the land that have meaning regardless of where in the world they may live. For all three religions, Israel/Palestine is of special significance.

# Jews and Judaism, *Yisra'el*, Israelites and Jerusalem

**Judaism** is the religion of the Jewish people. It is the oldest of the three monotheistic religions, and arose during the 2nd millennium BCE, in the ancient land of *Yisra'el* (Israel), an area covering parts of the modern State of Israel and the area referred to in the Bible as Judaea and Samaria, known today as the West Bank.

However, the identity of the Jewish people is not only based on religion. Indeed, some Jews are agnostics or even atheists. Jewish identity is based, first and foremost, on belonging to a distinct and ancient nation, the Jewish people. The historical roots of the Jewish people are recorded in the Hebrew Bible (as distinct from the Christian Scriptures) and in non-Biblical records and archaeological material.

In the Biblical text, the story is told of the Hebrew patriarch Abraham and matriarch Sarah, whose descendants became a nation when they settled in a land called Cana'an (covering parts of modern day Israel, Gaza and the West Bank). It was the 12 sons of the third Hebrew patriarch, Israel (originally Jacob) who became the '12 tribes of Israel' or **B'nei Yisra'el** (the Children of Israel). This group became known as the **People of Israel**, or **Israelites** for short. The Biblical text also includes an account of a promise made to the Israelites by their God that the land of their origin would be theirs forever. The Biblical name for the land is **Eretz Yisra'el**, 'the **Land of Israel**'.

It must be remembered that the Bible is primarily a religious document rather than a historical study and so one cannot state definitively whether or when Biblical events occurred. Jewish tradition dates the earliest events to the 2nd millennium BCE.

## What is a 'nation'?

There is some debate as to the meaning of the term 'nation'. One reason for this is that 'nation', 'state' and 'country' are often used interchangeably. While 'state' and 'country' are both political entities, a 'nation' is a group of people who may or may not live in the same state or country.

Another difficulty in defining what or who is a nation is that definitions rely either on objective or subjective criteria, or on both. The more objective definitions point to the commonality of some particular trait among members of a group, such as: a sense of common identity, a history, a language, ethnic or racial origins (common descent), religion, a common economic life, a geographical location and a political base. While all nations encompass a measure of cultural, ethnic and racial diversity, these criteria and characteristics are often present in different degrees and combinations. Nations can exist, for example, without a distinct political base.

The more subjective definitions of what constitutes a 'nation' depend more on feelings and perceptions of the group, concluding that people belong to a nation if they feel they do.

Outside the Biblical text, the earliest record of a distinct people called Israel is found on an ancient Egyptian stele (block of stone used for inscriptions and carvings), which is devoted to the military campaigns of the Pharaoh Merneptah I, who reigned from about 1213 BCE to about 1203 BCE. The stele describes Merneptah's military victories over several Cana'anite city-states, and a nation in Cana'an called Israel, thus authoritatively dating the Israelite presence in the land to earlier than 1200 BCE.

Another ancient record of the same military campaign of Merneptah and of the nation of Israel is to be found in a pictorial relief in the ancient temple at Karnak in Egypt. This and other evidence places the Israelites in the land at the time of the ancient Cana'anites, depicting them as one of the indigenous peoples of Cana'an with whom they shared virtually the same language, clothing and hairstyles. The main differences between the Israelites and other Cana'anites, as evident from these ancient sources, were religious and socioeconomic.

**Figure 2.1 The Merneptah Stele.** This stele was discovered in Egypt in 1896 in Merneptah's Mortuary Temple in Thebes.

The period during which the Israelite tribes became settled farmers and villagers (c. 1225 BCE-1000 BCE) was one of great instability in Cana'an. In about 1180 BCE, the southern part of the coast of Cana'an (today Gaza) was invaded and occupied by a group referred to as the 'Sea Peoples'. These included the Philistines (*Pelishtim* in the Bible), who came from Mycenae in Greece. Their arrival and settlement in the area which came to be called 'Philistia' (today Gaza and Ashkelon), marked the beginning of a long period of conflict with the local inhabitants of Cana'an, including the Israelites.

By about 1000 BCE, the 12 tribes of Israel united to form the Kingdom of Israel, first under King Saul and then King David, a member of the tribe of Judah. David made Jerusalem, in the Judean hills, the Israelite capital. In Jewish tradition, another name for Jerusalem is *Zion*. It was here that David's son, Solomon, built the first Jewish Temple in about 960 BCE.

After King Solomon's death in about 930 BCE, Israel was divided into two separate kingdoms, one in the north, which continued to be called Israel, and one in south, with Jerusalem as its capital, called Judah. The northern Kingdom of Israel was destroyed by the Assyrians in 722 BCE. Large numbers of Israelites fled to the south and settled in Judah. The Kingdom of Judah, including Solomon's Temple in Jerusalem, was

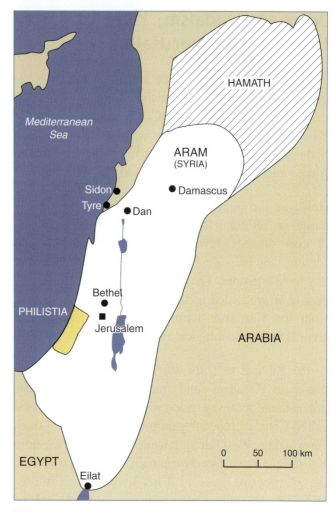

United Kingdom of Israel (c.1025-925 BCE)

Territory under control of King Solomon

**Figure 2.2** Maximum extent of Israel under David and Solomon c. 990-930 BCE.

destroyed by the Babylonians in 586 BCE. Judah's royal family and many of its people were taken into captivity in Babylon. From about 539 BCE they began to return, rebuilding the Temple in Jerusalem.

Over the centuries, the name Judah (in Hebrew *Yehuda*), as translated by the Persians, Greeks and Romans (and other ancient imperial powers) was used by these civilisations as the name of the central hill country around Jerusalem. The Roman name, *Judaea*, meaning 'the land of the Jews', is the Latin equivalent of the Hebrew *Yehuda*. Judaea is also the name for the land that appears throughout the Christian Scriptures.

During the period of Roman rule, the Jews continually rebelled, initially to protest against the Romans' attempts to impose pagan customs on them, and then in an effort to win freedom and independence. The most significant rebellion lasted from 66 CE until 70 CE, after which the Romans destroyed the Jerusalem Temple. Rome commemorated its victory by minting special coins bearing the inscriptions *'Judaea Capta'* (Judaea Captive) or *'Judaea Devicta'* (Judaea Defeated).

In 132 CE, the Jews again revolted to shake off Roman rule. After crushing the revolt in 135 CE, the Romans expelled the Jews and changed the name of the area from Judaea to *Syria-Palaestina*, the latter name referring to the Philistines, the Jews' former rivals.

Following their forced exile in 135 CE, no matter where they lived, Jews maintained their strong sense of attachment to their nationhood and to *Zion* – the Land of Israel and Jerusalem, the former Jewish capital. The Jews' desire to return to Zion and live as a sovereign people was captured in both their prayers and their secular literature. This dream began to be realised in the 19th century as a direct result of the rise of the modern Jewish nationalist movement called 'Zionism'. The reasons for this will be examined in the following chapter.

**Figure 2.3 Jews praying at the Kotel (Western Wall).** Today, the only visible remnant of the Second Jewish Temple in Jerusalem is *Har haBayit* (the Temple Mount) and its Western Wall, known in Hebrew as *haKotel haMa'aravi* or just the *Kotel*. The *Kotel* remains Judaism's most holy site and the direction to which all Jews face when praying.

## Zion

In Jewish literature throughout the ages, *Zion* is used as another name for Jerusalem, and sometimes as a synonym for the entire ancient Land of Israel, also called 'the Holy Land'. In particular, the word Zion is associated with the Jewish people's dream to return to Israel following their first exile by the Babylonians in the 6th century BCE, and their second exile by the Romans in the 2nd century CE. The famous Biblical Psalm 137 was written about 2500 years ago, after the Babylonian exile, and captures the longing of the Jewish people to return to their land:

> By the rivers of Babylon,
> There we sat down,
> Sat and wept,
> As we remembered Zion …
>
> If I forget you, O Jerusalem,
> Let my right hand wither;
> Let my tongue stick to my palate
> If I cease to think of you,
> If I do not keep Jerusalem in memory,
> Even at my happiest hour.

So central was the Jewish desire for and belief in an eventual return to Zion after their expulsion by the Romans in the 2nd century CE, that it became a part of the daily prayers of Judaism.

Today, there are approximately 13-14 million Jews living around the world of whom about 5.3 million live in Israel. Israel's population is made up of a widely diverse group of citizens from many ethnic, religious, cultural and social backgrounds. Israel's Jewish population consists of two main cultural groups, *Ashkenazim* (singular: *Ashkenazi*), and *Sephardim* (singular: *Sephardi*). The former term refers to Jews whose ancestors, following the exile from Judaea in the 1st and 2nd centuries CE, settled in Europe, and who eventually came under Christian rule. Sephardim refers to those Jews who settled in Spain and other countries which eventually came under Muslim rule.

Of the 20 per cent of Israel's non-Jewish population, most are Arab Muslims, of either Palestinian or Bedouin background. A small minority of Arab Israelis – about 2 per cent – are Christians. Small numbers of Israelis are Druze, who are Arabic-speakers but constitute a separate cultural, social and religious community; Circassians, who are Sunni Muslims but do not share either the Arab origin or the cultural background of the larger Islamic community; and others not classified by religion.

## Christianity, Christians and the Latin Kingdom of Jerusalem

Unlike Judaism, **Christianity** today is not the religion of a specific people. However, like Judaism, Christianity first arose among the Jewish people in the land of ancient Israel. The term **Christian** means 'follower of Christ', the name given by Christians to Jesus of Nazareth who was born and lived in Judaea in the 1st century CE. It is recorded in the Christian Scriptures that Jesus was born in Bethlehem in Judaea and was crucified and buried in Jerusalem where Christians believe he was resurrected (rose from the dead). Belief in the resurrection of Jesus is a central pillar of Christianity and Jerusalem is therefore considered to be a very holy place. It is here that Emperor Constantine built the Church of the Holy Sepulchre in 335 CE, marking the presumed site of Jesus' burial.

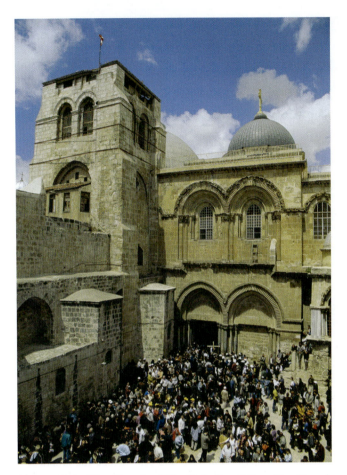

**Figure 2.4 The Church of the Holy Sepulchre.** The Church of the Holy Sepulchre, which contains the 'Tomb of Jesus', is believed by Christians to be built on the site of Jesus' last resting place after his body was removed from the cross.

During the Middle Ages, European Christians launched a series of nine wars called the Crusades, the stated purpose of which was to recover the Holy Land from Muslim control, especially the city of Jerusalem. The First Crusade (1095-1099) succeeded in establishing the **Latin Kingdom of Jerusalem** in what had been the Arab Muslim provinces of Syria and Palestine. Subsequent Crusades did not expand the kingdom; they were only able to fortify existing settlements and supply fresh troops for the garrisons.

Although the Crusades did not have a lasting impact on the region, they did help to shape later Muslim perceptions of Arab-European relations. In modern times, the memory of the Crusades has a powerful resonance throughout the Arab Muslim world, representing the triumph of Islam over the Western Christian invasion into Islam's heartland.

## Islam, Muslims, *al-Quds* and *Filastin*

**Islam** is the third great monotheistic religion to have risen in the Middle East. The followers of Islam are called **Muslims** who today number over 1 billion people. Whilst all of the prophets of the Hebrew Bible are venerated by Muslims, as is Jesus, Muslims believe that God's final revelation was given to Muhammad, 'the seal of the prophets'. They believe that these revelations came to Muhammad via the angel Gabriel and were recorded in the holy book of Islam, the Koran.

Muhammad was born in Makkah (Mecca) in the western part of the Arabian Peninsula (today Saudi Arabia) in 570 CE. As a young adult, he worked in the trading business of a woman named Khadija, whom Muhammad eventually married.

When not occupied with business matters, Muhammad was known as a gifted arbitrator of disputes. He also went on religious pilgrimages to the mountains for one month each year. It was on one of these that, according to Muslim tradition, Muhammad received his first revelation, in the year 610 CE. In 622 Muhammad journeyed to the town of Yathrib (renamed Medina, from the Arabic *Madinat an Nabi*, 'The Prophet's City'). Here Muhammad established the first *umma* (Muslim community), marking the beginning of the Islamic era and of Islam as a force in world history. Muhammad's move from Mecca to Medina is called in Arabic, the *hijra*, and its date begins the Muslim calendar. In Islam, each year is denoted as AH – 'After *Hijra*'.

For ten years after the *hijra*, Muhammad ruled over the Muslim community in both war and peace, and instructed it in the ways of Islam. In 630 Muhammad's army conquered Mecca. In Arabic the name for the city is *Makkah al-Mukarramah* which means 'Mecca the Blessed'. This is because it is the location of the holiest shrine of Islam, the *Ka'aba*, the centre of which marks the direction of the *qibla*, the focal point of Muslim prayer. This is the reason that Muslims face in the direction of Mecca when they pray.

**Figure 2.5 The Ka'aba and the Great Mosque of Mecca.** The Ka'aba is a large cubic stone structure, covered in a black cloth, which stands in the centre of the Great Mosque of Mecca. It is the place of worship which Muslims believe God commanded the Prophets Ibrahim and his son, Ishmael, to build.

Muhammad died in 632 CE. By this time, a Muslim state had already been established in a large part of the Arabian Peninsula. The popularity of Muhammad's message and the weakness of the Byzantine and Sasanian Empires to the north led to a series of Muslim conquests and the rapid expansion of *dar al-Islam*, 'the realm of Islam'.

Within 20 years of Muhammad's death, Arab Muslims had established an empire extending from Egypt in the west to Iran in the east. Muhammad's successors, known as caliphs, ruled first from Damascus (today Syria) as the capital of the Umayyad Caliphate, and then from Baghdad (today Iraq) as the capital of the Abbasid Caliphate. In addition to these two Arab empires, smaller Muslim dynasties arose, some of which were not ruled by Arabs such as the Safavid dynasty of Persia (today Iran).

At the end of the 7th century, early in the period of Islamic imperialism, the Arab Muslim armies conquered *al-Quds* (the Arabic name for Jerusalem) and its surrounding areas, which had been mostly under Byzantine (Christian) rule since the fall of the (western) Roman Empire. The area was divided into administrative units and *al-Quds* was located within the **Jund Filastin** (Province of **Palestine**). From this point on, with the exception of the period during the rule of the Crusaders (1099-1291), Palestine remained under Islamic rule until the end of World War I.

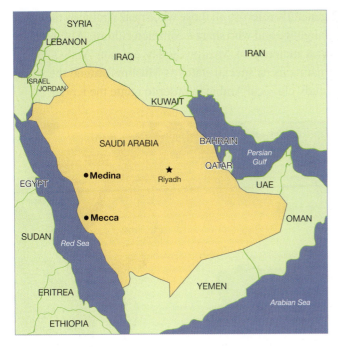

**Figure 2.6** The Arabian Peninsula today, showing the location of Mecca and Medina, the two holiest sites in Islam.

Control over Palestine was important to successive Muslim rulers because within its administrative borders is *al-Haram al-Sharif* (the Noble Precinct). Located upon the Jewish Temple Mount in Jerusalem, Muslims believe this was the site to which Muhammad came from Mecca, and ascended to God through the seven heavens. Muhammad's journey from Mecca to Jerusalem is called *al-Isra*, and his ascension is called *al-Mi'raj*. Together they are referred to as the 'Night Journey'. In the 8th century, Muslims built the *Qubbat as-Sakhrah*, (Dome of the Rock) and *Masjid al-Aqsa* (al-Aqsa Mosque) to mark the location of *al-Mi'raj*.

Jerusalem was also the original *qibla* of Muslims, before it was replaced with Mecca. For these reasons, Jerusalem is holy to Muslims and is Islam's third holiest site, after Mecca and Medina. The names for Jerusalem in Arabic are *Bayt al-Maqdis*, meaning the 'House of Sanctity', and *al-Quds al-Sharif*,' the 'Noble Sanctuary'.

**Figure 2.7** *Al-Haram al-Sharif* (the Noble Precinct).

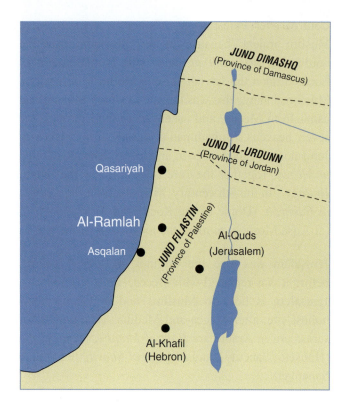

**Figure 2.8** The *Jund Filastin* (Province of Palestine) under Arab rule.

# Arabs

Islam today, like Christianity, is not the religion of a specific people, although it first arose among the **Arabs** of the Arabian Peninsula. The first known written record of the word *Aribi* (Arab in English) appears in an inscription of the Assyrian King Shalmaneser III in 853 BCE, which announces the king's victory over a group of Bedouin tribes of the Arabian Desert. One of the chieftains mentioned is 'Gindibu the Arab'. The place-name 'Arabia' occurs for the first time in the writing of the Greek historian Herodotus (484-425 BCE). Later Greek and Roman writers used the terms Arabia and Arab to refer to the entire peninsula and its inhabitants, including the Yeminis of the south-west.

From the 7th century CE on, the term Arab began to acquire a broader meaning. As Muslim influence expanded throughout the region, Arabic became the language of Muslim prayer, and often also the spoken language of those who converted to Islam. Initially, these converts were not considered as Arabs. Over time this distinction disappeared so that today the term Arab

generally refers to all those who speak Arabic as their first language and who share a common culture. Although the vast majority of Muslims today are non-Arabs, Arabic maintains its special status as Muslims around the world study classical Arabic in order to recite the Koran.

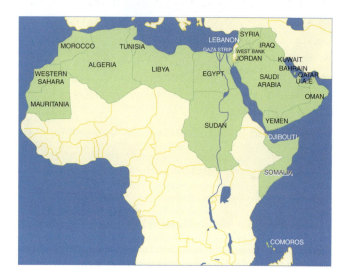

**Figure 2.9 The Arab world today.** Around 285 million people live in the countries that make up the Arab world. These are represented at the League of Arab States established in 1945. The 22 members of the Arab League are: Algeria, Bahrain, Comoros, Djibouti, Egypt, Iraq, Jordan, Kuwait, Lebanon, Libya, Mauritania, Morocco, Oman, Palestine, Qatar, Saudi Arabia, Somalia, Sudan, Syria, Tunisia, United Arab Emirates, Yemen. In 2003, Eritrea joined the Arab League as an observer.

By the 10th century, the majority of the population in Palestine had adopted Arabic culture and language, and had converted to Islam, although some of the population continued to adhere to Christianity and small Jewish communities also continued to live in Jerusalem, Hebron, Safed, Tiberias and elsewhere.

## Palestine and Palestinians

The name 'Palestine' is derived from the ancient Philistines, one of the Sea Peoples from Greece who crossed the Mediterranean Sea and settled in the area which became known in ancient times as *Philistia* and today covers the area of the Gaza Strip and the southern parts of Israel.

In 604-603 BCE, the Philistines were attacked by Nebuchadnezzar II of Babylon. Their cities, Ashkelon and Gaza, were laid waste and their inhabitants taken into captivity in Babylon. Although the Philistines as

a distinct people ceased to exist, the area where they had settled was sometimes referred to as *Philistia* or *Palestina*. The Romans adopted the name *Syria-Palaestina* to replace Judaea in the 2nd century CE.

When the Arabs conquered the area in the 7th century CE and it became a predominantly Arab and Islamic country, they referred to it using the Arabic equivalent of *Palaestina*, which is *Filastin*. In the light of the religious significance of Jerusalem, *Filastin* – Palestine – became known throughout the entire Muslim world. In his book, *The Question of Palestine*, Palestinian writer Edward Said recounts a 10th century description of the land:

> Filastin is the westernmost of the provinces of Syria. In its greatest length from Rafah to the boundary of Al Lajjun (Legio) it would take a rider two days to travel over; and the like time to cross the province in its breadth from Yaffa (Jaffa) to Riha (Jericho) ...
>
> Filastin is watered by the rains and the dew. Its trees and its ploughed lands do not need artificial irrigation … Its capital and largest town is Ar Ramlah, but the Holy City [of Jerusalem] comes very near this last in size. In the province of Filastin, despite its small extent, there are about twenty mosques, with pulpits for the Friday prayer.[1]

In 1517, the former *Jund Filastin* became a province of the Turkish Ottoman Empire. While the northern part of the country fell within the *Vilayet* (province) of Beirut, the area to the south around Jerusalem was administered separately as the *Mutasarriflik* of Jerusalem.

Although Turkish names were used in official Ottoman circles, the English word **Palestine**, derived from the Latin *Palaestina*, was used in English sources. It appears throughout English travel literature of the 18th and 19th centuries and was the name adopted by the League of Nations for the British Mandate established in 1922. It was at this point that Palestine, as an area designated by the English name for the land, acquired its modern boundaries.

The **Palestinians**, both Muslim and Christian alike, are an Arab people whose homeland was once part of the British Mandate of Palestine (according to the 1922 borders). These points are enshrined in the 1968 Charter of the Palestine National Council, the governing body of the Palestine Liberation Organisation:

> Article 1: Palestine is the homeland of the Arab Palestinian people: it is an indivisible part of the Arab homeland, and the Palestinian people are an integral part of the Arab nation.
>
> Article 2: Palestine, with the boundaries it had during the British Mandate, is an indivisible territorial unit …
>
> Article 5: The Palestinians are those Arab nationals who, until 1947, normally resided in Palestine regardless of whether they were evicted from it or have stayed there. Anyone born, after that date, of a Palestinian father – whether inside Palestine or outside it – is also a Palestinian.

## The Ottoman Empire

The Ottoman Empire was founded in the late 13th century by the Turkish ruler Osman I (in Arabic *Uthmān*). In 1453, the Turks captured the city of Constantinople, the seat of government of the (Christian) Eastern Roman Empire. The Ottomans made it their capital city – called Istanbul in Turkish – after which Islam became its predominant religion.

The Ottoman Empire reached its height in the 16th century under Sultan Suleiman the Magnificent, when it stretched from the Persian Gulf in the east to Hungary in the north-west, and from Egypt in the south to the Caucasus in the north. After suffering defeat at the Battle of Vienna in 1683, the Ottoman Empire began a slow decline, culminating in its defeat and dismantlement by the Allies at the end of World War I.

Today there are an estimated 10 million Palestinians living around the world, divided into three main subgroups: Palestinians who live in the territories of the Gaza Strip and the West Bank (3.8 million); those who live inside Israel and hold Israeli citizenship w(1.4 million); and those who live in the diaspora, including about 3 million in Jordan. According to the records of the United Nations Relief and Works Agency (UNRWA), some 4 232 510 Palestinians live in refugee camps in neighbouring Arab countries (Jordan, Lebanon and Syria). This includes the children, grandchildren and great grandchildren of refugees. Beyond the Arab world, many Palestinians also live in North America and Europe.

# Summary

At the heart of the Arab-Israeli conflict is the struggle between two people, Israelis and Palestinians, for control of the land of *Filastin/Yisra'el*. Both Arabs and Jews have long historical and religious connections to this land, and knowledge of these connections and the emotions to which they give rise is essential to understanding the nature of their dispute.

Religion has always played a role in the seemingly timeless struggle for the 'Holy Land' and continues to be a problem in the contemporary conflict between Israelis and Palestinians. As will be seen in later chapters, in the latter decades of the 20th century, exclusive claims over 'religious real estate' became central to the more extreme, fundamentalist versions of competing Israeli and Palestinian nationalisms, thus making compromise all the more difficult.

A final note on the use of the names 'Israel' and 'Palestine' in this book. Whilst Palestine is only one of the names given to the territory known to many as 'the Holy Land', it has been used at different times by both Arabs and Jews. For many centuries before Israel was re-established in 1948, Palestine was the geographical name for the area between the Jordan River and the Mediterranean Sea, even though it was not a single political or administrative unit until the establishment of the British Mandate. Accordingly, the name Palestine will be used in the following two chapters to refer to the land prior to 1948, after which it again becomes appropriate to use the name Israel.

The origins of the Arab-Israel conflict and the contemporary struggle for the land can be traced to the final decades of the 19th century, which are the subject of the following chapter.

# Review and research questions

1. Research the basic tenets of Judaism, Christianity and Islam and the connection that each has to Israel/Palestine.

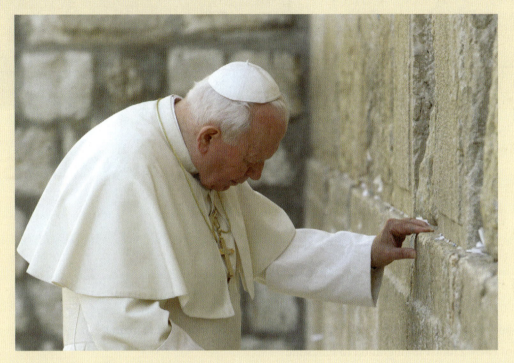

**Figure 2.10 The late Pope, John Paul II at the *Kotel* (the 'Western Wall').** During the last day of his six-day pilgrimage to the Holy Land in March 2000, Pope John Paul II visited the three holy sites in Jerusalem: the *Kotel*, the Church of the Holy Sepulchre, and *al-Haram al-Sharif*. Here he rests his hand on the *Kotel*.

2. In order to ensure the appropriate use of terms, review the following:
   - Judaism, Judaea, Jew, *Yisra'el*, Israel, Israelite and Israeli
   - Christianity, Christian and the Latin Kingdom of Jerusalem
   - Islam and Muslim, Arab, Palestine and Palestinian

3. How did the Jewish people come to be a small minority in Palestine prior to the 20th century?

4. How did Palestine become a predominantly Arab Muslim country prior to the 20th century?

## Discussion question

1. In Chapter 1 it was stressed that history plays a very important role in understanding the Arab-Israeli conflict and in the efforts to resolve it. Both Arabs and Jews are ancient peoples and are associated with the birth of two of the world's major religions. In the light of the material in this chapter, what events in pre-modern history, and which religious beliefs, do you think might inform the narratives of the national groups involved in today's conflict over Israel/Palestine?

# 3 The Origins of the Arab-Israeli Conflict

By the end of this chapter you will be familiar with the:

- concept of nationalism
- origins and aspirations of Jewish nationalism (Zionism) and its different streams
- impact of early Zionist immigration to Palestine
- origins and early aspirations of pan-Arab nationalism
- origins of the Arab-Israeli conflict in Palestine in the late 19th and early 20th centuries.

As the Ottoman Empire declined during the 19th and early 20th centuries, European influence in the Middle East increased. This had a profound impact on politics in the region. Distinct national groups began to assert their identity and to seek political independence. With the outbreak of World War I in 1914, leaders of these national groups aligned themselves to one or other of the European powers in the hope that this would further their own quest for statehood. But in the aftermath of the war, the nationalist aspirations of some groups remained unfulfilled, fuelling conflicts that remain unresolved to this day. One of these was the Arab-Israeli conflict, although it was particular in a significant way: of the two modern nationalisms which clashed over Palestine, Arab and Jewish, the latter first emerged in Europe, not in the Middle East.

In the final decades of the 19th century, a revived sense of nationhood inspired immigration of Jews from Europe to Palestine. Its specific aim was to re-establish the sovereignty of the Jewish people there after some 1750 years of what Jews called the *galut* (exile). The majority Arab population did not share, and were unwilling to accommodate, the historical perspectives and aims of the Jewish immigrants. Conflict developed soon after large-scale Jewish immigration to Palestine commenced. The purpose of this chapter is to examine the origins and early aspirations of Zionism, the parallel rise of the pan-Arab nationalist movement, and the early conflict between the Arab and Jewish populations of Palestine before World War I.

| Timeline | Event |
|---|---|
| 1858, 1867 | Ottoman land reforms passed. |
| 1862 | Rabbi Zvi Hirsch Kalisher writes 'Seeking Zion'.<br>Moses Hess writes *Rome and Jerusalem: The Last National Question*. |
| 1875 | The Beirut Secret Society is established. |
| 1877 | The Damascus Congress is convened. |
| 1881 | Pogroms against Jews in Russia. |
| 1882 | BILU and *Hibbat Zion* are founded. First Aliyah begins. |
| 1896 | Theodore Herzl writes *The State of the Jews*. |
| 1897 | Herzl convenes the First Zionist Congress in Basel, Switzerland. World Zionist Organisation is formed. |
| 1901 | Jewish National Fund is established. |
| 1903 | Sixth Zionist Congress rejects Britain's 'Uganda Plan'. |
| 1904 to 1914 | Second *Aliyah*. |
| 1905 | Naguib Azoury writes *Le Reveil de la Nation Arabe*.<br>The League of the Arab Fatherland is established. |
| 1908 | The Young Turks Revolution.<br>Arab newspapers are established in Palestine, including *Al-Karmal* in Haifa. |
| 1909 | The first Jewish self-defence organisation, 'The Watchmen', is established. |
| 1909 | Tel Aviv is founded. |
| 1911 | The first Palestinian Arab political party, the Patriotic Ottoman Party, is founded.<br>The Arab newspaper, *Filastin*, is established. |
| 1914 | Raghib al-Nashashibi is elected the Jerusalem representative to the Ottoman Parliament. |

## Concept: Nationalism

The term nationalism is used in two related ways, first, to identify an ideology and second, to describe a sentiment. As an ideology, nationalism is the claim that people belonging to a 'nation' have a right to inhabit a particular territory with a state of their own. From this perspective, nationalism is a basis for drawing territorial boundaries between people.

The origins of this ideology may be found in the works of 18th and 19th century Romantic philosophers who asserted that a legitimate state is based on a 'people' rather than a dynasty, God, or imperial domination.

As a sentiment, nationalism has always meant different things to different people in different contexts. As is the case with the term 'nation', scholars continue to debate its meaning. Some examples of different definitions are:

- Ernest Renan (1882): 'nations are the product of the subjective collective memory of communities rather than the result of objective facts'.

- Arnold Toynbee (1915): nationalism 'like all great forces in life is nothing material or mechanical, but a subjective psychological feeling in a living people.'

- Benedict Anderson (1983): 'Communities are to be distinguished, not by their falsity/genuineness but by the style in which they are imagined.'

- Ernest Gellner (1983): 'Nationalism is primarily a political principle, which holds that the political and the national unit should be congruent.'

Nationalism became a powerful force in the 19th and 20th centuries. This period was marked by the struggle for nationhood and the establishment of independent nation-states all over the world.

# The origins and aspirations of Zionism

By the middle of the 19th century, there were about 10 000 Jews in Palestine, mostly (8000) in Jerusalem. A smaller number lived in the other towns that had religious significance for Jews, namely, Hebron, Tiberias and Safed (Tz'fat). A smaller number lived in the coastal towns of Acre and Jaffa. By the end of the 1880s, the number of Jews in Palestine had increased to about 25 000, representing about 4 per cent of the population. From 1889 onwards, Jews were the majority in Jerusalem. By the beginning of the 20th century, the Jewish population had risen to roughly 50 000, largely as a result of immigration from the Tsarist (Russian) Empire. By 1947, the Jewish population was an estimated 600 000, about one-third of the total population of Palestine.

Why, after their exile by the Romans some 1750 years earlier, did Jews begin to return to Palestine in significantly increased numbers? The short answer is that in the late 19th century there arose a new nationalist movement among the Jewish people living in Eastern and Western Europe. This movement is known as 'Zionism'.

## Ideas and events that impacted on Jews in 19th century Europe

It was noted in Chapter 2 that in Jewish literature throughout the ages, *Zion* is used as another name for Jerusalem, and sometimes as a synonym for the entire land of the ancient Kingdom of Israel. The word 'Zionism' was coined in the latter years of the 19th century to refer specifically to the Jewish nationalist movement that developed at that time. As with most nationalist movements, Zionism focused on identity and territory, and on the right to self-determination through the realisation of sovereignty. What distinguished Jewish nationalism from other nationalisms was that the majority of Jews did not then live in the territory in which they intended to realise their nationalist objectives. For this reason, the recognition of the Jews' historical connection to the land constituted the central justification and motivation for their return. There was no other land with which the Jewish people as a whole identified.

The return of the Jewish people to their ancient homeland was an aspiration that had been expressed in Jewish literature, both religious and secular, since ancient times. However, for centuries following their exile by the Romans, the number of Jews living in Palestine remained relatively small. There were several reasons for this.

### Key concept: Zionism

The central pillars of Zionism are:

- Jews are a distinct people, a national group from ancient times, not merely a religious community.
- Like all other peoples, they have the right to self-determination.
- The Jewish people can only exercise this right meaningfully in their own state, which they have had for much of their history.
- Historically, the state of the Jewish people has only ever been located in their ancient homeland, *Eretz Yisrael* (Israel).

Firstly, until the mid-19th century, the Jewish belief in the 'restoration of Zion' – the return of the Jews to the Holy Land as a sovereign nation – was based upon the expectation of the coming of the *Moshiach* (Messiah). The Jews were to wait, passively, for divine intervention, and not engage actively in this process.

Secondly, before the end of the 19th century Jews were deprived of political and civil rights, a consequence of their minority status whether they lived within Christendom or the realm of Islam. In most parts of the Christian and Muslim worlds, Jews were permitted to engage only in certain trades and suffered many forms of persecution and discrimination. They were subjected to a number of restrictions on their livelihood and on where and how they could live and travel. Many were required to wear a distinctive 'Jew Badge' or other forms of clothing to distinguish them from the rest of the population. This was in part driven by anti-Jewish sentiment, referred to in modern times as anti-Semitism, which had been institutionalised over many centuries, both by the Church in Europe and throughout the Muslim world by *Sharia* (Islamic law).

Figure 3.1 An illustration from an English medieval manuscript, the *Chronicles of Offa*, shows Jews wearing the 'Jew Badge'. In England, the badge worn by Jews depicted two stone tablets inscribed with the Ten Commandments.

These factors prevented the Jews from being able to positively change their political, economic or social conditions. Paradoxically, they also reinforced identity by setting the Jewish people apart from all others, helping to preserve their strong national sentiment throughout centuries of their dispersion. Until the rise of Zionism, this sentiment was sustained by, and expressed through, the beliefs and practices of Judaism.

However, by the beginning of the 19th century, a number of important forces were developing in Western Europe that led to the stirrings of secular national sentiment among many groups, including Jews. The Enlightenment and liberalism inspired the American Revolution in 1776 and the French Revolution in 1789, and the drive for emancipation of many disadvantaged groups, the Jews among them.

By the mid-19th century, these concepts began to be expressed in isolated Jewish writings in which the case was made that Jews should take active responsibility for their return to Zion. This marked a watershed in Jewish history, the point at which European ideas of secular nationalism combined with the centuries-old religious belief that Jews would one day return to their homeland. In the synthesis of these ideas, Zionism was born.

## Key concept: Anti-Semitism

Anti-Semitism is the name given to religious and racist prejudice against Jews. This centuries-old prejudice predates both Christianity and Islam, but was given new forms by both religions. Christian dogma justified the persecution of Jews by teaching that the Jews as a people were responsible for the death of Jesus. Muslim clerics relied on the anti-Jewish teachings in the Koran and other Muslim holy books. They accuse the Jews of attempting to destroy Islam in the days of Muhammad.

For many centuries Jews were forced to live separately in their own communities and this made them perfect scapegoats when governments and religious authorities sought others to blame for society's problems.

In the 19th century, in Western and Central Europe, traditional, religious-based anti-Semitism mutated into racist ideas about the inferiority of the Jews. In 1865, the German writer Eugen Duhring, called for the extermination of the Jews. The Nazis attempted to achieve this during World War II, resulting in the genocide of six million Jews, including the murder of over a million Jewish children.

The actual term anti-Semitism was coined in 1879 by a German anti-Semite, Wilhelm Marr. He did not like the old term, *Judenhass* (hatred of Jews), because it was a sentiment too closely identified with Christianity and he considered Christianity to be a 'Jewish invention'.

A common feature of both religious and racial anti-Semitism is the delusional claim that the Jews as a people control, or are attempting to control, the whole world. This is the theme of the notorious *Protocols of the Learned Elders of Zion*, written in the 1890s by Pytor Ivanovich Rachovsky, a Russian secret police agent. Rachovsky's purpose in writing the text was to discredit popular opposition to the Tsarist government by falsely associating it with the Jews. The entire book is a bogus record of a meeting supposedly held by Jewish leaders planning to control other nations. The fictitious nature of the *Protocols* was proved in several court cases during the 20th century but it remains a favourite tool of anti-Semites to this day.

The European Enlightenment is commonly dated from the middle of the 18th century when the French rationalist philosophers began to advocate the values of rationalism and religious tolerance, and political and economic theories that would dramatically change the face of European society.

Rationalism is the belief that the world can be understood and explained through human reason. After the 17th century this was reflected in the new respect for natural science and the use of scientific method to analyse and describe changes to individual, social, political, and economic life.

### Liberalism

Liberalism developed as a political ideology in the early 19th century. It attacked any form of absolute power and any underlying claim to an unlimited right to rule, whether made by the Church (or any religious authority) or a monarch (or any government). Liberalism asserts the existence in society of a 'private sphere' in which individuals have the right to make their own decisions as they see fit.

### Emancipation

Emancipation refers to the granting of equal legal and civil rights to minority groups previously discriminated against on the basis of religion, gender or ethnicity.

The Jews were emancipated first by the French Government in 1791 and later, throughout the 19th century, in other Western European countries. However, they continued to suffer unofficial religious, social and economic discrimination. Jews were not emancipated in Eastern Europe until the 20th century.

## Western Europe

The first writings that mark the transition from *passive* to *active* Zionism were those of Rabbis Yehuda Alkalai and Zvi Hirsch Kalisher. In 1843, Alkalai published a pamphlet entitled 'The Third Redemption', arguing that Jewish national freedom would come through redemption – the ingathering of the 'scattered of Israel into the Holy Land' – but that this required the Jews' own efforts. He proposed the creation of Jewish agricultural settlements in Palestine, supported by a national fund responsible for the purchase of land. In 1862, Kalischer published his pamphlet entitled, 'Seeking Zion', urging the Jewish people to play a role in their own return to Zion, by working the land with their own hands, and with the political support of international governments.

Also in 1862 *Rome and Jerusalem* was published, an early Zionist text written by the Jewish socialist Moses Hess. The theme of Hess' book was that Jews 'are not [simply] a religious group, but a separate nation', and as such, they have the same right to determine their collective future as any other nation. Hess proposed that Jews follow the example of the Italians who had been inspired by the memory of ancient Rome in establishing their own state in 1861. Hess advocated the establishment of a Jewish state in their ancient homeland, Palestine, and argued that it should be socialist in nature. Hess thereby hoped to resolve one of the basic questions raised by the Jewish encounter with modernity: how to reconcile the particularity of Jewish nationhood with the universality of Jewish values. His ideas strongly influenced many early Zionist leaders including David Ben-Gurion, who later became Israel's first Prime Minister.

# Early Zionist activity

From the 1850s to the outbreak of World War I, there were three distinct geographical arenas of Zionist activity: Western Europe, Eastern Europe and, after 1881, Palestine. The forces at play in these arenas were often very different which helps to explain the different Zionist activities and the responses to them.

Figure 3.2 Moses Hess (1812-1875).

For many years, the writings of early Zionists like Hess were largely ignored by Western European Jews. Most believed that after centuries of persecution, the freedom now offered to them through emancipation and the ability to assimilate into the wider community was all they needed.

## Concept: Socialism

Socialism is an ideology based on a belief in community, cooperation, equality and common (usually state) ownership of the means of production, distribution and exchange. It developed from the early 19th century onwards as a political creed in response to the emergence of industrial capitalism.

## Eastern Europe

The situation for Jews in Eastern Europe was dramatically different from the West. Firstly, they had not been emancipated. Indeed, there had been no change in their lowly status under Tsarist rule for centuries. Secondly, there were many more Jews living in Eastern Europe. They were largely restricted to the densely populated area called the 'Pale of Settlement', a region overlapping parts of modern-day Russia, Ukraine, Poland, and Lithuania.

Figure 3.3 The Pale of Settlement. The Pale of Settlement was created by a decree of Tsar Nicholas I in April 1835. Jews were forced to live in the Pale until 1917 when the Bolshevik revolution removed it from the statute books. According to the census of 1897, there were 4 899 300 Jews living in the Pale, approximately 11.6 per cent of the total population of the region. However, in the urban areas the Jewish presence was much higher such that in some towns they constituted the majority of the population.

At the end of the 19th century, the conditions of Jews living in Eastern Europe deteriorated sharply. In 1881, violent attacks were carried out against Jews in Russia, triggered by the assassination of Tsar Alexander II. These attacks, known as 'pogroms', were officially supported by the government as a way of diverting attention from its own mistakes by pandering to popular anti-Semitic sentiment. Over a few months, thousands of Jews were massacred and many more left homeless.

## Concepts: Colonies, colonisation and colonialism

Colonialism involves the settlement of foreign territory by a state or imperial power, with part of its own population, to enable that state to extend its power and control over that territory and its inhabitants. The relationship between the 'mother country' and the colony is usually exploitative. Until the end of the 19th century, colonialism was so common among the European powers that it generated little opposition. However, with the rise of liberalism, nationalism and the ideas of self-determination and sovereignty, colonialism and the practices associated with it became discredited. Since the period of 'decolonisation' following World War II, colonialism has had a negative connotation that it did not have earlier.

The use of the word 'colonisation' in the WZO program and Herzl's belief that a Jewish revival in the Holy Land would bring European enlightenment to a backward part of the world have been the focus of criticism in the Arab narrative. So, too, have the establishment of Jewish cities, towns and farms in Palestine prior to 1948, and settlements in the Gaza Strip and West Bank after 1967, which have been characterised as acts of Israeli colonialism.

In contrast, the Israeli narrative argues that Jewish immigration to Palestine prior to 1948 represented a drive by the Jewish people to achieve their own state, not to extend the power of any other state. For the Jews, the land to be 'colonised' *was* the 'mother country'. They also point to the prior history of the Jewish people in the land to which they immigrated, in contrast to the complete absence of a prior connection between the colonial powers and the lands they colonised. (For example, Britain had no pre-colonial connection to Australia, New Zealand, and America.)

This prior history is also used as the principal justification for those post-1967 Israeli settlements in the West Bank that are intended to be permanent. Many international lawyers reject this latter argument (see Chapter 10 for further discussion of post-1967 settlements).

Herzl was not a religiously-observant Jew. Brought up in an assimilated family, his Jewish identity was based on a cultural affiliation to the Jewish people, not on Judaism. Accordingly, his vision of the Jewish state was based on secular not religious ideas. For Herzl, a state would simply provide a place where Jews could be sovereign over their own affairs and free from anti-Semitism.

In this latter respect, Herzl differed from the majority of Zionists. For them, establishing a Jewish state was not a response to what others thought of the Jews – anti-Semitism – but was based on what Jews thought of themselves – a nation having the same right to self-determination as others. The location could only be Palestine, the ancient 'Land of Israel', the only territory with which the Jewish people as a whole had a historical connection.

This difference between Herzl and the majority of Zionists over the reason for creating a Jewish state became very clear at the sixth Zionist Congress in 1903, when Herzl announced an offer from the British Government for the Jews to build a homeland in East Africa (modern-day Uganda). The idea of building a Jewish national home anywhere but Palestine was rejected by the Congress, a response for which Herzl, according to one delegate, had not been prepared:

> [Herzl] just couldn't digest what had happened here, how it was that such an unfortunate nation, suffering pogroms and denied all rights and privileges, could be offered an entire country and say 'No.' The Russian Zionists [in whose country thousands of Jews had recently been massacred in pogroms] began to explain: 'We don't just want any country! We are Zionists. We want to return to our ancient, ancestral homeland.'[2]

Escape from anti-Semitism was not enough, argued the delegates. The Zionist movement sought to draw on the positive, creative energies of the Jewish people to revive Hebrew as a spoken language, establish new cultural, trade union, health and educational institutions and, in short, build a new society based on freedom and justice.

Following the congress, Herzl recorded that the key to achieving the objectives of the WZO was to gain, by way of a Charter, international recognition of the Jewish right to Palestine. These efforts gave rise to the expression 'political Zionism'.

In the following decades, the WZO became the umbrella organisation for the Zionist movement, incorporating different streams as they developed, including:

- Political Zionism – the branch originally associated with Herzl that focused on gaining support for the movement through international diplomacy.

- Practical Zionism – the branch originally associated with the group *Hovevei Zion* (Lovers of Zion) who believed that *hityashvut* (settling the land), and not merely political activism, was required if Jewish sovereignty was to be restored in Palestine.

- Labour (socialist) Zionism – the branch that sought to build a socialist Jewish state and became the dominant expression of Zionism within Palestine.

- Religious Zionism – the branch originally represented by the *Mizrachi* Party, founded in 1902 by orthodox religious Zionists.

As membership of the WZO grew, offices were established around the world, providing support and financial aid to Jews wanting to immigrate to Palestine. To assist in this purpose, the *Keren Kayemeth Le'Yisrael*, (the Jewish National Fund – JNF), was created in 1901, at the Fifth Zionist Congress. The JNF sought to buy land in Palestine on behalf of the Jewish people. Between 1881 and 1904, the year of Herzl's death, some 25 000 Jews had immigrated to Palestine, primarily from Eastern Europe. However, not all of them stayed. Indeed, many returned to Europe, unable to survive the harsh economic and social realities of Palestine.

# Palestine in the 19th century

Under Ottoman rule, Palestine was never a separate political or administrative unit. It was divided between three administrative regions: the Vilayet (province) of Beirut, the Vilayet of Damascus, and the *Mutasarriflik* (special subdistrict) of Jerusalem. A *vilayet* was ruled

by a *wali* (governor), and was divided into further *sanjaks* (administrative districts), administered by a *kaymakam* (local governor). The Vilayet of Beirut was divided into various sanjaks including those of Nablus, Acre, and Beirut. The Vilayet of Damascus, essentially located east of the Jordan River and the Wadi Araba, was divided into the sanjaks of Hauran, Ma'an, and Damascus. Although the area which included Jerusalem was located within the Vilayet of Damascus, it was administered directly from Istanbul, and thus given the administrative status of the *Mutasarriflik* of Jerusalem.

**Figure 3.7** Ottoman provincial boundaries.

## Social structure

At the social level in Palestine, the population was divided along several lines, including religious differences, as was the entire Ottoman Empire. An individual's identity was determined by membership of a religious community, each with its own internal organisation and hierarchy. The ruling community were the Sunni Muslims. All others had inferior legal and political rights. This included Jews who, along with Christians, had the particular status of *ahl ad-dhimma* ('protected people'). A person belonging to this category is known as a *dhimmi*.

### Concept: *Dhimmi*

In accordance with *Sharia*, the status of the *dhimmi* is distinctly inferior to Muslims and carries unique obligations. *Dhimmis* are required to pay extra taxes including the *kharaj*, a tax on the yield of their land or produce, and the *jizyah*, referred to as a 'poll' tax, levied on all non-Muslim adult males. Other restrictions placed on *dhimmis* included their exclusion from public office, the refusal of a Muslim court to accept their testimony in a case against a Muslim, refusal to approve the construction of new churches and synagogues and prohibition of the public display of non-Muslim religious sounds and symbols. There were also many laws regulating the clothes to be worn by *dhimmis*.

Another component of the social structure of 19th century Palestine was the rural/urban divide. The majority of the population were Arab *fellaheen* (peasants), living in villages and working the land. Many were heavily indebted to landowners among the village and town elites and much of their produce went to landowners as interest payments. For these *fellaheen*, life was barely at a subsistence level, generation after generation. Illiteracy was widespread, both in villages and towns.

Village elites included sheikhs who enjoyed considerable power as tax collectors for the Ottoman authorities. The urban elite consisted of a number of wealthy and powerful Muslim families, the most prominent of whom were the Husseini, Khalidi, Nashashibi, Nusseibeh, Degani, Masri and Shawaa families.

During the late 1850s and 1860s, a series of financial and administrative reforms known as the *Tanzimat* (reform, reorganisation) were introduced throughout the Ottoman Empire. These had a profound impact on relations between the rural and urban populations.

## The *Tanzimat* and events impacting on land ownership in Palestine

The *Tanzimat* reforms were implemented following the defeat of the Arab nationalist Muhammad Ali, *Pasha* (governor) of Egypt, who had extended his rule to Greater Syria from 1831 to 1839. The purpose of the reforms was to promote stability throughout the Empire, increase taxation revenue and reassert Ottoman authority over Anatolia and the Arab lands.

The taxation reforms had a particular impact on Palestine. Under the new system, responsibility for tax collection was taken from the village sheikhs and given to a small number of prominent Muslim families who made up the urban elites. The families who took over tax collection for the *Mutasarriflik* of Jerusalem also sat on the newly formed administrative councils and filled all key religious posts, including the *mufti* (religious leader) of Jerusalem, and the key secular administrative positions.

As a result, four Muslim families came to dominate political and religious life in Palestine: the Husseinis, Nashashibis, Khalidis and Nusseibehs. Their wealth and land holdings were further enhanced by another *Tanzimat* reform, the 'Ottoman Land Code of 1858', which required all agricultural land to be registered in the names of individual owners. The goal of this law was to regularise land ownership throughout the Empire in order to facilitate the collection of land taxes. By establishing clear proof of title to land, the Ottomans could make the titleholders pay taxes, increasing state revenues for increased military expenditure.

The 1858 Ottoman Land Code resulted in a major transformation in the ownership of land in Palestine, as the legal title to extensive areas of land was acquired by a relatively small number of families. Some of the new registered owners were resident in the cities of Damascus, Beirut and other locations in neighbouring

regions and became absentee landlords. The law also significantly changed the traditional practice of land tenure in Palestine. Previously, most of the agricultural land had not been registered in a single name and peasant farmers had the right to live on the land they cultivated and to pass this right – and their debts – on to their heirs.

The *fellaheen* often only discovered that they had ceased to be the legal occupants of their land some decades after the new Land Code was introduced, when the land their families had lived on for generations began to be sold. From 1882 on, land was increasingly sold to Jewish immigrants who were part of the new Zionist immigration to Palestine. The purchase of land by Jews was facilitated by another *Tanzimat* reform law passed in 1867 that granted foreigners the right to own land, on condition that the new owners paid taxes to the Ottoman government.

# Early Zionist immigration to Palestine

Fifteen years before Theodore Herzl convened the First Zionist Congress, thousands of Jews, mostly from Eastern Europe, moved to Palestine with the specific goal of *hityashvut* and building the foundations of a Jewish state. This initial wave of immigration is referred to in Jewish history as the 'First *Aliyah*' (*aliyah* literally means 'to ascend' or 'to go up'). The immigrants had very different intentions from those who had preceded them over the centuries. The latter had immigrated to Palestine primarily for religious reasons, and lived in towns and cities with the established Jewish community, known as the 'old' *Yishuv* (Jewish community living in Palestine). However, the Jews who began to arrive in 1882 as a part of the First Aliyah, did so primarily for political reasons, to live in freedom, and most became farmers.

## The First Aliyah 1882-1903

The First Aliyah occurred between 1882 and 1903 when some 25 000 Jews moved to Palestine. Among them was a group of Russian students from the University of Kharkov who, in the wake of the 1881 pogroms, had formed a pioneering Zionist group called the *BILU*, a Hebrew acronym formed from a Biblical verse, '*Beit Ya'akov Lekhu Ve-nelkha*' ('House of Jacob, Let Us Rise and Go'). Led by Israel Belkind, the *BILU* were committed to the principles of 'practical Zionism', namely, the settlement of Jews on the land in Palestine. They called for Jews to work the land through farming, a profession denied to Jews in Russia because they were forbidden to own land.

When the first *Bilu'im* (members of the *BILU*) arrived in Palestine in 1882, they established the first *moshav* (cooperative farming community) called *Rishon Le-Zion* ('The First to Zion'). Whilst equipped with enormous reserves of energy and enthusiasm, the *Bilu'im* had little experience of farming and they found life very difficult. Within a few months, they faced starvation, and most had to leave the *moshav*. Some went to other parts of Palestine, others returned to Europe. Other *moshavim* established at this time were Petach Tikvah (established in 1878, then abandoned and resettled in 1882), Zichron Ya'akov, and Rosh Pina. Some of the new immigrants also settled in the established towns and cities including Jerusalem.

Another group associated with the First Aliyah was the *Hovevei Zion* organisation, also founded in 1881. Like the *BILU*, its specific aim was to assist Jews to immigrate to and develop agricultural settlements in Palestine. Whilst some of its members moved to Palestine, others remained in Europe and supported the immigrants with their philanthropic work. Among the leaders of *Hovevei Zion* was Rabbi Samuel Mohilever, founder of the religious Zionist organisation, *Mizrachi*. Mohilever was successful in securing financial support from Baron de Rothschild who established the Palestine Jewish Colonisation Association (PICA), which purchased land and established industries in Palestine. It is estimated that Rothschild spent over $50 million dollars to support *Hovevei Zion* and establish agricultural settlements such as Hadera in 1891. He also helped pay for the development of an electrical power station, the first in Palestine.

Following the publication of Herzl's *Der Judenstaat* in 1896 and the establishment of WZO the following year, most of the European branches of *Hovevei Zion* aligned with the new international body. By the end of the First Aliyah in 1903, some of the earlier problems associated

with 'practical Zionism', such as a lack of planning and support, had been addressed by the WZO and the JNF which came to provide much needed infrastructure, training, and financial assistance. As a result, in addition to the 28 Jewish agricultural settlements founded by the First Aliyah, the urban Jewish population had also increased, especially in Jaffa, which 3000 newcomers made their home. During this period, Hebrew was revived as the common language spoken by the new *Yishuv*. The first Hebrew elementary schools were established and a modern Hebrew dictionary began to be compiled.

A new wave of Jewish immigrants entered the country between 1904 and 1914, referred to in the Jewish narrative as the Second Aliyah. They would have a profound impact upon the internal development of the *Yishuv* as it strove to build a Jewish state in Palestine.

## The Second Aliyah 1904-1914

Like the First Aliyah, most of the Jewish immigrants of the Second Aliyah came from Russia. Many were fleeing the Kishinev Pogroms of 1903 and other outbreaks of violence that lasted until 1907. However, the immigrants of the Second Aliyah were of a younger generation, had grown up in different circumstances to the First Aliyah, and were influenced by a different set of concepts and ideas, in particular, socialism and communism. In the early years of the 20th century, socialist and communist organisations had attracted growing support from impoverished Russian workers and peasants.

This new stream of Zionism, imbued with socialism, was called 'Labour Zionism' and came to dominate the politics of the *Yishuv*. Many of the symbols, political ideals, and leading personalities that contributed to the establishment of a self-sufficient Jewish community in Palestine before World War I, were developed during the Second Aliyah. They included David Ben-Gurion, who arrived in Palestine in 1906. Ben-Gurion believed that the fate of Zionist settlement in Palestine depended on the creation of a strong Jewish economy.

### Concept: Labour (Socialist) Zionism

Moses Hess' argument for realising Zionism through the creation of a socialist state in Palestine was revived in the 1890s by Nachman Syrkin and Dov Ber Borochov, the intellectual founders of 'Labour Zionism'. They argued that a Jewish state could only be created as part of the universal class struggle by the efforts of the Jewish working class settling in Palestine and constructing a state through the creation of agricultural collectives in the countryside and a Jewish proletariat in the cities.

Aaron David Gordon, another early Labour Zionist, and a founding member of the *kibbutz* movement, argued that only by physically working on their national land could Jews achieve their national aspirations. Gordon founded the political party, *haPoel haZair* (The Young Worker), dedicated to establishing Jewish communities in Palestine organised according to socialist principles. Two of the key principles of Labour Zionism in Palestine were the 'conquest of labour' and the 'conquest of land'.

Labour Zionism became the dominant stream of Zionism in Palestine from early 1900 onwards. Its ideology left an indelible stamp on the politics and institutions of the *Yishuv* and post-independence Israeli society.

The first Labour Zionist party was *Poalei Zion* (Workers of Zion), which grew quickly between 1906 and 1914. In time it split into Left and Right factions. The Left faction became the *Mapam* party, which more recently joined with other parties to create *Meretz* and *Yachad*. In 1930 the Right faction of *Poale Zion* became the *Mapai* Party, and then *HaAvoda*, the Labor Party in 1968. The *Mapai*/Labor Party dominated *Yishuv* and later Israeli politics until 1977.

In his 1944 essay, 'The Imperatives of the Jewish Revolution', Ben-Gurion argued:

> The diaspora means dependence – material, political, cultural, and intellectual dependence – because we are aliens, a minority, bereft of a homeland, rootless and separated from the soil, from labour, and from basic industry. Our task is to break radically with this dependence and to become masters of our own fate – in a word, to achieve independence. [3]

As a socialist, Ben-Gurion believed that Jewish independence could only be accomplished through the creation of a Hebrew-speaking working class and highly centralised Jewish economic structures. He and his fellow Labour Zionists were therefore dedicated to creating the institutional framework that would be needed for a Jewish workers' state in Palestine.

One of the institutions established by the Labour Zionists was a new form of communal, collective agricultural settlement known as *kevutzah*, the first of which was Degania, established on the Sea of Galilee in 1910. The *kevutzah* was like an enlarged family where everyone worked and made decisions together, and depended upon one another for material and moral support. In time the *kevutzah* developed into the larger collective farm called a *kibbutz*.

The kibbutz farmers developed a system of joint cooperative trading, enabling them to keep the cost of supplies as low as possible. The farmers were assisted by the WZO's Palestine Office, which established and ran agricultural training schools. Students of these institutions founded new agricultural communities. By the outbreak of World War I, there were some 40 agricultural communities, located mainly in the north of Palestine, with an estimated population of 12 000.

In 1909, *kibbutz* members formed the first Jewish self-defence organisation, *HaShomer* (The Watchman), to take responsibility for the security of as many Jewish communities as possible, training workers to provide a self-defence network in addition to working as agricultural labourers.

However, not all of the immigrants of the Second Aliyah sought a new life on the land. Some settled in the traditional Jewish towns of Jerusalem, Hebron, Nablus, Tiberias, Safed, Jaffa and Haifa. Others founded new towns such as Tel Aviv, which was established in 1909. Across Palestine, the Jewish population grew steadily. By 1914, it was approximately 85 to 90 thousand, about 12 per cent of the overall population.

## Increase in Arab and Jewish populations 1882-1914

In the period before 1882, the number of Jews living in Palestine had remained relatively static for many centuries. Between 1882 and 1914, the period that spans the First and Second Aliyot, the Jewish population of Palestine rose significantly from approximately 24 000 to between 85 000 and 90 000.

During this same period, the Arab population of Palestine also rose more rapidly than previously. Based on the 1897 Ottoman figures, the area of Palestine is thought to have had an Arab population numbering about 529 500. By the outbreak of World War I, this figure had risen to between 555 000 and 585 000. This increase was due to two factors:

natural increase, enhanced by improvements in sanitation and health care which accompanied the improved economic conditions, infrastructure, and agricultural techniques introduced to Palestine by Jewish immigrants; and Arab immigration, mainly from Lebanon and northern Syria, attracted by increased work opportunities resulting from the economic stimulus created by Jewish immigration.

|  | 1880 | 1914 |
|---|---|---|
| Arabs | 525 000 | 555 000 to 585 000 |
| Jews | 24 000 | 85 000 to 90 000 |

Arab and Jewish population growth in Palestine, 1880 to 1914.

The increasing number of Jewish immigrants, whose ideas and activities differentiated them from the 'old' Yishuv, did not go unnoticed by the majority Arab population who were concerned about the sale of land to the immigrants, economic competition and religious and cultural differences. It was also evident that the Jewish immigrants' perception of their place in Palestinian society was in direct conflict with the values of traditional Muslim society, and with *Sharia* in particular. Members of the new *Yishuv* refused to be subservient, second-class citizens.

Soon after the First Aliyah began, the Arabs of Palestine began to express opposition to Zionism and conflict developed.

# Early Arab opposition to Zionism

Much of the early conflict between Arabs and Jews was over land sales. Although the Jews bought land legally from Arab owners, their settlement resulted in considerable antagonism by the former Arab tenants and by neighbouring Arab villagers who considered the Jews as unwelcome intruders. Arab religious leaders and notables from the cities also opposed Jewish immigration and complained to the Ottoman authorities about the dangers posed to the local Arabs by the Jews' behaviour and aspirations for political independence.

## Dispossession of the *Fellaheen*

When the JNF was established in 1901 to buy land for Jewish settlement, there was no shortage of Arab landowners ready to sell, particularly among those who were absentee owners, resident in Damascus, Beirut and elsewhere, who had become landowners following the Ottoman Land Code in 1858.

Between 1882 and 1948, between the First Aliyah and the creation of the State of Israel, the JNF purchased just under 6 per cent of the total area of Palestine. Whilst much of this land was uninhabited swampland such as the Jezreel Valley, some of it was rich agricultural land, farmed by the *fellaheen* for many generations. In order to sell the land, the Arab owners often needed to

evict the *fellaheen*. This became a common cause of dispute between *fellaheen* and Jews in the early years of Zionism.

Disputes also broke out as a result of the Jews' unfamiliarity with local grazing customs. In 1892, for example, there was a violent incident between the Jews of Rehovot and the Arab farmers from the village of Zarnuga when the former tried to stop Arab flocks from grazing freely in their fields after the harvest, a traditional practice of the *fellaheen*.

**Figure 3.8** Arab tenant farmers, Esdraelon Valley, 1894.

**Figure 3.9** Jewish farmer c. 1900.

Although there were relatively few cases of extreme violence or long legal disputes during the First Aliyah, the tension between Arab and Jewish farmers was always present. By the outbreak of World War I, relations between Arab and Jewish farmers were characterised by estrangement, suspicion, and animosity on both sides.

## Religious antagonism towards the Jews

Adding to the tensions was the fact that Muslims viewed some of the behaviour of Jewish immigrants as offensive, such as women working side by side with men in the fields, and wearing Western-style clothing which was considered to be provocative. In 1897, Muhammad Tahir al-Husseini, the Mufti of Jerusalem, called for all 'foreign Jews to be terrorised and expelled'. He established an Arab commission to examine the impact of the sale of land to Jews and reported its findings to the Ottoman Government. Muslim antagonism was heightened when the Mufti and other Muslim leaders spread false accusations that Muslim holy sites would come under Jewish control.

## Economic competition in the towns

In the towns, Arab opposition to Jewish immigration was not as immediate as in the rural areas. When it did arise, it was largely a symptom of economic competition, and not only with Muslim notables, but also with wealthy Christian Arabs. Many Christians were merchants, tradesmen and officials and some also owned land. There was a sizeable Christian population in Jerusalem, and also in the port of Haifa where, from the 1850s onwards, Christians were the largest single group, many of them Lebanese traders who had come to take advantage of the growing commerce passing through the port.

Between 1881 and 1891, the Jewish population of Jerusalem almost doubled, from 13 920 to 25 322 while the Arab population of the city remained at 14 000. In Jaffa the Jewish population increased from virtually nil in 1880 to 2500 by 1893, although the Arab population also increased.

In 1891 news reached Jerusalem that still larger numbers of Jews were expected from Russia. In response, and in an effort to curb the sale of land to Jews, a number of Arab notables, both Christian and Muslim, sent a petition to the Ottoman government demanding a halt to Jewish immigration and land purchases. They claimed that the Jews were taking land out of the hands of traditional Arab owners and gradually gaining control of local commerce. This was the first official Arab protest against modern Jewish settlement in Palestine and it spelt out two demands which became the Arabs' position thereafter:

- a halt to Jewish immigration
- cessation of land sales to Jews.

## Opposition recorded in the Arab press

The Arab press became an important means through which the Arabs expressed opposition to Zionism. Following a visit to Palestine in 1895, the Egyptian journalist, Najib al-Haj, wrote in the Egyptian journal *Abu al-Hul*, accusing the Jews of depriving the Palestinian Arabs of their means of living. In 1898, Rashid Rida wrote in his influential Egyptian newspaper, *al-Manar* (The Beacon), of the pending threat of Jewish immigration to the Arabs of Palestine:

> You complacent nonentities … look at what peoples and nations do … Are you content for it to be reported in the newspapers of every country that the penniless of the weakest of peoples [the Jews], whom all governments are expelling, have so much knowledge and understanding of civilisation and its ways that they can take possession of your country, establish colonies in it, and reduce its masters to hired labourers and its rich to poor men?[4]

When a number of Arab newspapers were founded in Palestine after 1908, including *al-Quds* in Jerusalem and *al-Asmai* in Jaffa, the sale of land to Jews was a key focus of protest. One of the most prominent newspapers was the Haifa based *al-Karmal*. In 1910, it published an article by Shukri al-Asali, a Syrian member of the Ottoman Administration, who sought to warn of 'corrupt officials and treacherous Arab landowners' responsible for the sale of land to the Jews.

The following extract provides an insight into how some Arabs perceived Zionism in the period before World War I:

> (The Jews) have striven and are striving to buy most of the villages, lands and estates in our illustrious Empire … They own the Anglo-Palestine Bank which makes loans to them at a rate not exceeding 1 per cent per annum ... They have a blue flag in the middle of which is a 'Star of David', and below that is the Hebrew word meaning 'Zion', because in the Torah, Jerusalem is called the 'Daughter of Zion'. They raise this flag instead of the Ottoman flag at their celebrations and gatherings; and they sing the Zionist anthem ... They teach their children physical training and the use of arms; you see their houses crammed with weapons, among them many Martini rifles. They have a special postal service, special stamps, etc, which proves that they have begun setting up their political aims and establishing their imaginary government. If the Government does not set a limit to this torrential stream, no time will pass before you see that Palestine has become a property of the Zionist Organisation and its associates or of the nation mentioned above [the Jews].[5]

In 1911, another newspaper, *Filastin*, was established in Jaffa. It supported *al-Karmel* in its efforts to arouse the Arab public against the influx of Jews and their efforts to build up their own communities.

## Initial Ottoman response to Arab opposition to Zionism

The Ottoman administration responded to the 1891 Arab petition demanding an end to Jewish immigration and land purchases by passing a series of discriminatory laws. These included an edict curtailing the ability of Jews to purchase land in the *Mutasarriflik* of Jerusalem for the next decade and restricting Jewish immigration to small groups which were only permitted to stay in Palestine for one year. In 1900, a new law was passed stipulating that any Jew staying more than three months in Palestine would be expelled. When a resolution was passed during the 1905 Zionist Congress that called for increased Jewish settlement, the Ottomans suspended all land transfers to Jews in both the *Mutasarriflik* of Jerusalem and throughout the entire Vilayet of Beirut.

Whilst the edicts appeared to address the fears of the Palestinian Arabs, in practice Ottoman governmental instructions were largely ignored by Arab landowners who would not be deterred from selling their land at high prices. The sale of land to Jews continued, as did Zionist immigration. In 1900, the Jewish Colonisation Association established an office in Beirut when it was discovered that it was easier to buy land in the northern area of Palestine, which fell within the Vilayet of Beirut. As attested to by Shukri al-Asali, many of the Arab absentee landowners in Beirut were keen to sell land for inflated prices and bribed Ottoman officials to ignore regulations forbidding such sales.

## The 1908 Young Turks' Revolution and the Committee of Union and Progress

In 1908, a group of Turkish nationalists known as the Young Turks gained de facto control of the central administration of the Ottoman Empire, forcing Sultan Abdul Hamid II to restore the 1876 Ottoman constitution. This provided for the Ottoman provinces to be represented in the imperial parliament by elected delegates. The Empire's non-Turkish subjects viewed this as a positive move towards a greater degree of equality and self-government in the provinces.

However, it soon became clear that the Committee of Union and Progress (CUP), the group formed by the Young Turks that dominated Ottoman politics for the next decade, had very different ideas. They were primarily interested in pursuing a program of 'Turkification' of the empire, which meant intensifying Turkish control over Arab lands not the granting of local autonomy. Turkish was imposed as the language of schools and courts, while Turkish officials took control of the *waqf* (property held by endowment for religious purposes), dismissing local officials. The campaign was bitterly resented by many Arabs, particularly those who had for a number of decades been arguing for Arab independence and the re-establishment of the Arab caliphate.

# The rise of pan-Arab nationalism

The Palestinian historian, Rashid Khalidi, identifies the early expressions of Arab opposition to Zionist immigration and land purchases as evidence of the 'sense of Palestine as a special and sacred space … under threat from without', and as a focus of identity that was central to local Muslim Arab patriotism. These sentiments were a forerunner of the emergence of a distinct Palestinian identity that would become more concrete early in the 20th century. Like expressions of other Arab nationalisms that arose in the Middle East following World War I, the roots of Palestinian nationalism can be found in the pan-Arab nationalist movement that emerged in the 19th century.

The aspirations of pan-Arab nationalism were first expressed through literary societies, focused on the revival of Arab language, literature, and heritage. Their efforts were assisted in the mid-19th century by American and French Christian missionaries in Syria (and what is today Lebanon). The missionaries placed an emphasis on education, and with the introduction of the printing press, significantly expanded the availability of Arab literature. In 1866, the Syrian Protestant College was founded in Beirut (now the American University of Beirut), and became a new focal point for the ideas of Arab nationalism and independence from the Turks.

In the pan-Arab narrative, the late 19th century is known as *al-nahda*, the Arab Renaissance, which featured experiments with modern literary forms, the spread of print journalism, and the first stirrings of secret nationalist organisations. In time, these societies took on a political orientation with the purpose of exposing the despotism of Ottoman Turkish rule and arousing an Arab consciousness in order to achieve greater autonomy or independence.

## Key concept: Pan-Arab nationalism

The core pillar of pan-Arab nationalism is that the Arab people constitute a single nation. In the early history of the movement, pan-Arab nationalists sought independence from the Ottoman Empire, and a united Arab government with *Bilad al-Sham* (Greater Syria) as its centre. As pan-Arab nationalism developed after World War I, competing streams developed which sought to create several independent, though allied, Arab states.

The first Arab literary society was *al-Jam'iyyah al-'Ilmiyyah as-Suriyyah* (the Syrian Scientific Society), formed in 1868. Its main activities involved holding symposia and lectures by its members, concentrating on Arabic language and heritage. The Society's stated purpose was 'to work for all that leads to common benefit … in matters of literature and art' and its membership was open 'to those who are zealous for the real benefits of the fatherland.'

Among the founders of the society were some of the early Arab nationalists, Nassif al-Yazigi and Butrus al-Bustani. Al-Yazigi, a Lebanese Christian intellectual, was an outspoken advocate of pan-Arab nationalism and became one of the leaders of the movement after 1866. Al-Bustani, another Christian Arab, was one of the active leaders in the national movement following the Lebanese civil war of 1860. Al-Bustani was a philologist (a classical linguist) who showed great interest in national education and the establishment of civil and religious liberty. Among his contributions to the revival of Arab literacy and cultural regeneration were an Arab dictionary and a seven volume Arabic encyclopedia. He also published a journal, *al-Jinan*, in which he wrote about the indivisibility of faith and love of the Arab homeland, calling upon his fellow Arabs 'to awake and arise'.

In 1875, the 'Beirut Secret Society' was established by graduates of the American University of Beirut who advocated the study of Arab history, literature, and language as a means of reviving Arab identity. They printed and circulated publications which called for independence of *al-watan al-arabi*, ('the Arab Nation') from the Turks. Other Arab societies were formed with similar objectives, and like the Beirut Secret Society, were forced to work underground to escape arrest by the Ottoman authorities.

In 1877, representatives of the various Arab nationalist societies convened the Damascus Congress at which it was decided to declare the independence of *Bilad al-Sham* (Greater Syria), while recognising the Ottoman Caliphate. The Ottomans rejected the demands and put the leaders under house arrest. This did not deter other Arab leaders from pursuing their bid for Arab independence. In 1881, a number of young Arabs formed the *Jam'iyyat Hafez Haqouq al-Millah al-Arabiyyah* (the Society for Preserving the Rights of the Arab Millah), whose leaders emphasised the need for Christian-Muslim cooperation to achieve Arab independence.

Another important influence on the developing pan-Arab nationalist movement was Abdul Rahim al-Kawakibi. In his 1902 and 1903 publications, al-Kawakibi emphasised the need for Arabs to oppose Turkish despotism and, on the basis of their distinct role in the history of the Muslim world, to regain the Caliphate from the Turks. He called for administrative powers and responsibilities to be given to the Arabs as a step towards eventual independence from the Turks.

A milestone in the history of pan-Arab nationalism came in 1905 when several activists met in Paris and established *La Ligue de la Patrie Arabe*, The League of the Arab Fatherland. Naguib Azoury, a prominent Christian Arab and founding member of the League, outlined its mission to establish a pan-Arab Empire in his 1905 publication, *Le Reveil de la Nation Arabe*:

> The League wants, before everything else, to separate the civil and the religious power, in the interest of Islam and the Arab nation, and to form an Arab Empire stretching from the Tigris and the Euphrates to the Suez Isthmus, and from the Mediterranean to the Arabian Sea ... The mode of government will be a constitutional sultanate based on the freedom of all the religions and the equality of all the citizens before the law.[6]

Azoury's words capture the main sentiment of the pan-Arab nationalist movement before World War I. Its two central goals were:

- to achieve full independence from the Ottoman Turks
- to establish a single Arab political entity across the Middle East.

However, by the time World War I began, the ideas of al-Kawakibi and other secular Arab nationalists had not found widespread support. The concept that all Arab peoples constituted a single Arab nation, in the way that the European and Jewish nationalist movements understood the term, still had not taken root. Arab leaders generally favoured the continuation of the Ottoman Empire although some argued for schemes within the empire for decentralisation of power and Arab equality. As the historian of Arab nationalism, C Ernest Dawn, has pointed out, before World War I, the number of Arab nationalists was limited as most Arabs involved in politics favoured reform or at most autonomy, but not independence.

## Ongoing Palestinian Arab Opposition to Zionism

Following the re-establishment of the Ottoman Parliament by the Young Turks, a small number of Palestinian Arabs turned their attention to gaining provincial representation in Istanbul as a platform to launch a campaign to stop Jewish immigration. In 1911, the first Palestinian Arab political party, *al-Hizb al-Watani al-Uthmani* (the Patriotic Ottoman Party) was founded in Jaffa. Its members called for a struggle against Jewish immigration and settlement.

**Figure 3.10** Raghib al-Nashashibi (1881-1951).

In 1914, on the eve of the provincial elections for the Ottoman Parliament, Raghib al-Nashashibi of the prominent Nashashibi family, declared that 'if I am elected as a representative, I shall devote all my strength, day and night, to doing away with the damage and threat of Zionists and Zionism.' He was successful in his campaign and was elected to the Ottoman Parliament. Similar promises made during the 1914 election campaign suggest that Palestinian candidates for the Ottoman Parliament, if they wanted to be elected, were expected to voice opposition to Zionism. However, the politicisation of anti-Zionism had not yet evolved into a distinctive Palestinian nationalist movement, mainly because:

- The majority of Palestinian Arabs of the late 1890s and early 1900s still regarded themselves, first and foremost, as Muslims, and subjects of the Ottoman (Islamic) Empire.

- Palestinian Arabs were deeply divided between numerous clans and groups of affiliated clans. There were also strong class distinctions between the urban notables and the *fellaheen* (landlords and tenants), and religious divisions between Muslims and Christians.

# Summary

Jewish nationalism – Zionism – emerged in Europe in the latter half of the 19th century. What distinguished Zionism from other nationalisms was that the territorial focus of its aspirations for statehood was not where the majority of Jews lived. Rather, the focus was Palestine, their ancient homeland where the Jews had been a minority among an Arab majority for many centuries.

By the end of the 19th century, the World Zionist Organisation had been established and immigration to Palestine had begun. Between 1880 and 1914, the Jewish population had increased from 24 000 to around 85 000 to 90 000. The national aspirations of the Zionist immigrants inspired hostility in Palestinian Arabs who viewed the Jews' efforts to implement their aspirations as akin to other settler-colonial projects. Early Arab opposition to immigration and the sale of land to Jews was expressed through violent and non-violent means, driven by disputes over farming and land rights, religious attitudes, and economic competition.

In the early years of the 20th century, with a strong clan and religious consciousness, Palestinian Arabs had not yet developed a sense of a national community or an organised nationalist movement, distinct from the pan-Arab nationalist movement of the last decades of the 19th century. This would change in the post-World War I period when Palestine came under British rule. In the course of their struggle against both the British and the Zionists, the Arabs' parochial ties began to give way to a broader, Palestinian identity. Why and how Britain came to enter the political arena of Palestine and its impact on Arab-Jewish relations will be examined in the following chapter.

# Review and research questions

1. Using The Nationalism Project website http://www.nationalismproject.org/what.htm, research the meaning of the following terms relevant to the concept of nationalism: 'primordialists', 'modernists', and 'instrumentalists'. In your view, what is a 'nation' and what is 'nationalism'?

2. For about 1800 years, Jews wrote about and prayed for a return to their historic homeland but did little in practical terms to bring this about. This changed in the late 19th century which saw a significant increase in Jewish immigration to Palestine. How do you account for this? In your answer, consider the terms 'passive' and 'active' Zionism and European events during the 19th century.

3. Considering other nationalist movements in Europe during the 19th century, what was particular about Zionism? Why did Zionists reject all proposals to establish a Jewish national home anywhere other than Palestine?

4. Research the personal background of Theodore Herzl and the times in which he lived. What were the values and attitudes that influenced his actions in relation to the origins of Zionism? What were the major events in which he was involved that impacted upon the early history of Zionism? How would you assess his contribution to this history?

5. What were the key characteristics of the pan-Arab nationalist movement from its origins in the late 19th century up to World War I? Why do you think Christian Arabs played such a central role in this movement?

6. Read again the objectives set out for the World Zionist Organisation at its inception and those from the League of the Arab Fatherland. What are the similarities and differences? Do you think these differences could have been reconciled at the time? If so, how? If not, why not?

7. By the outbreak of World War I, Arab opposition to Zionist immigration was well underway. List the reasons for Arab opposition to Jewish immigration to Palestine between 1880 and 1914. Did the expression of Arab opposition to Jewish immigration change during this period? If so, how?

## Discussion questions

1. How relevant are ideas of 'nationhood' to your understanding of 'identity', 'culture' and 'politics'? How might the factors that contributed to identity in the pre-modern period differ from those today?

2. Discuss the following extract by Israeli historian Yosef Gorny which analyses the nature of the early conflict between the Arabs and Jews in Palestine:

> The protagonists of the conflict in Palestine were an Arab community whose nationality had not yet been defined, but whose historical foothold, as regards to length of residence, was firm, and a Jewish community which in the main was convinced of its national identity, but whose actual status therein was weak and tenuous.[7]

# 4 World War I and the Conflict in Palestine

By the end of this chapter you will be familiar with the:

- British domestic and imperial interest in Palestine before, during and after World War I
- key documents concerning Britain's wartime commitments regarding Palestine including the Sykes-Picot Agreement, McMahon-Hussein correspondence and the Balfour Declaration
- conflicting Arab and Jewish responses to the Balfour Declaration
- origins of Palestinian nationalism
- establishment of the Palestine Mandate and initial Arab and Jewish responses.

By the end of the 19th century, the last of the great Muslim imperial powers, the Ottoman Caliphate, was financially bankrupt and on the verge of political collapse. Corruption and economic decay over preceding centuries had left the Ottoman Empire unable to compete with the newly industrialised imperial powers of Europe – Austria-Hungary, Britain, France, Germany, Italy and Russia. By the mid-19th century, the 'Sick Man' of Europe, as the Ottoman Empire was known, became the focus of attention of European powers vying to fill the power vacuum left by its decline.

When the Ottoman Empire entered World War I on Germany's side, its fate was sealed. Following its defeat, the Ottoman Empire was dissolved and much of its former territory was lost. The Arab lands came within the responsibility of the newly established international body, the League of Nations, which, at the instigation of Britain and France, redrew the map of the Middle East. New borders were drawn creating Palestine (and later Transjordan), Lebanon, Syria and Iraq. The League granted Britain Mandates (legal authority) to administer Palestine, Transjordan and Iraq. France was granted Mandates over Lebanon and Syria.

The Mandate of Palestine specifically incorporated the terms of Britain's wartime promise to the Zionist movement, set out in the 1917 Balfour Declaration. This required Britain to facilitate the establishment of a national home for the Jewish people in the same territory in which the Arab population was also to gain self-rule, a policy which the Arabs rejected outright and viewed as a betrayal of Britain's wartime promises to the Arabs.

| Timeline | Event |
|---|---|
| 1905 | Pogroms in Russia.<br>Aliens Act is passed limiting Jewish immigration to Britain. |
| 1904 to 1914 | Second Aliyah. |
| November 1914 | The Ottomans enter the war on the side of the Germans and the Austrians. |
| July 1915 to March 1916 | The McMahon-Hussein correspondence. |
| May 1916 | The Sykes-Picot Agreement. |
| June 1916 | Arab revolt against the Turks begins. |
| November 1917 | The Balfour Declaration. |
| December 1917 | British and ANZAC forces seize Palestine from the Turks. |
| January 1919 | The Paris Peace Conference.<br>The Faisal-Weizmann Agreement. |
| March 1919 | The First General Syrian Congress in Damascus. |
| July 1919 | Second Syrian General Congress is held in Damascus; Palestine claimed as an integral part of 'Greater Syria'. |
| April 1920 | San Remo Conference allocates Palestine Mandate to Britain; adopts aims of Balfour Declaration.<br>Arab riots in Palestine protest the Palestine Mandate. |
| July 1920 | The British civil administration of Mandatory Palestine is established. Herbert Samuel is appointed first High Commissioner. |
| December 1920 | Jewish defence force, the *Haganah*, is established.<br>Jewish trade union, the *Histadrut*, is established.<br>Third Arab Congress is held in Haifa; Palestine defined as a distinct political entity; Palestinian Arab Executive is established. |
| May 1921 | Arab-Jewish clashes throughout Palestine; Haycroft Commission. |
| June 1922 | Churchill White Paper. |
| July 1922 | The League of Nations ratifies the Mandate of Palestine; Transjordan is established as a separate administrative unit. |

The background to these events forms the focus of this chapter, along with the further development of the Arab-Israel conflict, and the beginnings of a distinct Palestinian Arab nationalism.

# World War I and the end of the Ottoman Empire: British plans for the postwar Middle East

The decline of the Ottoman Empire in the 19th and early 20th centuries resulted in the so-called 'Eastern Question', or 'what to do with the Ottoman Empire', becoming a principal preoccupation of European imperial powers. Russia, Austria, France, and Great Britain each had their own territorial designs on what remained of the Ottoman Empire, seeking to curb the others' claims while promoting their own. Even before oil was discovered in the Middle East, the region was considered important, for both strategic and economic reasons. By 1914, a number of European countries had already established significant interests in the region. From 1870, for example, Britain had gained de facto control of the Suez Canal which was strategically located on the trade route to India, the 'jewel in the crown' of the British Empire.

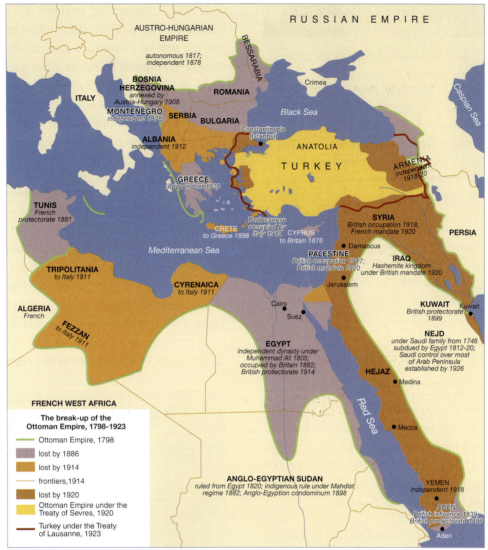

**Figure 4.1** The decline of the Ottoman Empire over the 19th century and the expansion of the European powers into the Middle East.

When World War I began, British imperial forces, which included troops from Australia and New Zealand, were sent to the Middle East to defeat Turkish and German forces, to defend Britain's local interests and expand its influence in the region. The campaign began well when Egypt was declared a British protectorate in December 1914. By the end of 1917, British forces had gained the upper hand on both the Mesopotamian and Mediterranean fronts. Palestine fell to the British on 11 December 1917, followed by Syria in 1918.

During the war Britain entered into several secret agreements with its European allies about how the Ottoman territories would be divided between them.

Britain also entered into an agreement with an Arab leader, Sharif Hussein of Mecca, as well as with the Zionist leadership, to help secure its victory in the war and also to ensure a strengthened position in the postwar period. At the end of the war, Britain was called upon to honour these commitments but not all parties involved were satisfied. Britain's wartime negotiations and agreements relevant to Palestine include:

1. The Sykes-Picot Agreement, May 1916.

2. The McMahon-Hussein correspondence, July 1915 to March 1916.

3. The Balfour Declaration, November 1917.

## The Sykes-Picot Agreement

The official name of the Sykes-Picot Agreement was the Asia Minor Agreement. In the event of an Allied victory, it would divide and allocate Ottoman territory between British and French spheres of influence. It was secretly ratified in May 1916, by the British and French diplomats, Sir Mark Sykes and Charles Georges-Picot, and later approved in-principle by Russia.

The accompanying map and extract from the agreement (over) illustrate that whilst Britain and France would support the establishment of an independent Arab State, or Confederation of States, in areas A and B (to fulfil the promises made by Britain in the McMahon-Hussein correspondence, discussed below), they would establish direct influence in the region in the red and blue zones. Palestine was intended to become an internationalised region, represented by the brown zone on the map (Figure 4.3).

## The McMahon-Hussein correspondence

In February 1914, six months before the outbreak of World War I, Hussein ibn Ali al-Hashimi, the Sharif of Mecca, sent his son, Abdullah, to inform the British representative in Egypt of his opposition to the Ottoman Sultan, and to seek British support to establish an independent Arab Kingdom. Ten months later, following Turkey's entry into the war on Germany's side, the British Government thought it desirable to secure Arab support to defeat the Turks, or at least to limit their assistance to the Turkish war effort. British officials in Cairo were therefore instructed to explore the possibilities of encouraging an armed Arab revolt against the Ottomans with the assistance of Sharif Hussein.

By this time, Faisal, another of Sharif Hussein's sons, had been approached by representatives of secret Arab nationalist societies in Damascus who feared French postwar designs on Arab provinces. They set out a number of conditions for supporting the Sharif as spokesman of the Arabs and his call for an anti-Turk uprising. Their proposition was that they would support Britain against the Turks if the British promised to grant them independence in all of the Arab provinces of the Ottoman Empire and recognise an Arab Caliphate under Hussein's rule.

**Figure 4.2** Britain's General Allenby enters Jerusalem through the Jaffa Gate, 11 December 1917.

## Extracts from the Sykes-Picot Agreement

It is accordingly understood between the French and British Governments [and approved in principle by Russia]:

1. That France and Great Britain are prepared to recognise and protect an independent Arab State or a Confederation of Arab States in the areas (A) and (B) on the annexed map, under the suzerainty of an Arab chief …

2. That in the blue area France, and in the red area Great Britain, shall be allowed to establish such direct or indirect administration or control as they desire and as they think fit to arrange with the Arab State or Confederation of Arab States.

3. That in the brown area there shall be established an international administration, the form of which is to be decided upon after consultation with Russia, and subsequently in consultation with other Allies, and the representatives of the Shereef (sic) of Mecca.

4. That Great Britain be accorded (1) the ports of Haifa and Acre, (2) guarantee of a given supply of water from the Tigris and Euphrates in area (A) for area (B) …

5. That Alexandretta shall be a free port as regards the trade of the British Empire … That Haifa shall be a free port as regards the trade of France, her dominions and protectorates …

7. That Great Britain has the right to build, administer, and be sole owner of a railway connecting Haifa with area (B), and shall have perpetual right to transport troops along such a line at all times …

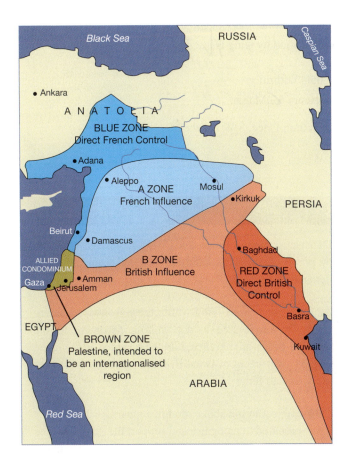

**Figure 4.3** The 1916 Sykes-Picot Agreement.

An exchange of eight letters between Sharif Hussein and Sir Henry McMahon, the British High Commissioner in Egypt, began on 14 July 1915, and continued until March 1916. The letters, known as the McMahon-Hussein correspondence, generally set out what Hussein wanted from Britain in return for organising an Arab revolt against the Ottoman forces in the Middle East. As the extracts from the letters below show, McMahon committed Britain in vague terms to 'recognise and support the independence of the Arabs' (letter of 30 August 1915) in return for their support against the Turks. In their exchange concerning the location of the intended Arab Kingdom under his rule, Hussein argued that all the Arab territories should be included (letters of 14 July and 9 September 1915). However, McMahon identified areas to be 'reserved' for British and French interest. In the end, final boundaries were left unresolved and discussion about the Vilayets of Aleppo and Beirut (northern Palestine, Lebanon and northern Syria) was inconclusive. The intention was to discuss the matter again after the war.

On 10 June 1916, three months after the last exchange of letters, Hussein declared the Arabs' independence from the Turks and so began what became known as the Great Arab Revolt. Three of Hussein's sons took to the field to

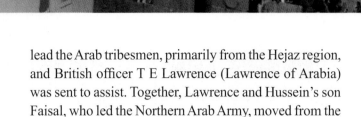

lead the Arab tribesmen, primarily from the Hejaz region, and British officer T E Lawrence (Lawrence of Arabia) was sent to assist. Together, Lawrence and Hussein's son Faisal, who led the Northern Arab Army, moved from the Hejaz and captured Aqaba (today Jordan) in July 1917.

After the war, controversy erupted about whether or not Palestine had been promised to the Arabs in the McMahon-Hussein correspondence. Hussein argued that Arab regions not specifically mentioned in the correspondence, including Palestine, should be included in the Hashemite Kingdom promised by Britain. The British denied Hussein's claim to Palestine and in a 1922 White Paper, declared that Palestine west of the River Jordan was not part of its pledge made to Hussein by McMahon. During a later enquiry into the Arab-Jewish conflict, McMahon gave his interpretation in a letter to the British newspaper, *The Times*:

---

### Independence of the Arabs: 'The McMahon Pledge'

A DEFINITE STATEMENT
TO THE EDITOR OF THE TIMES

Sir. – Many references have been made in the Palestine Royal Commission Report and in the course of the recent debates in both Houses of Parliament to the 'McMahon Pledge,' especially to that portion of the pledge which concerns Palestine and of which one interpretation has been claimed by the Jews and another by the Arabs.

It has been suggested to me that continued silence on the part of the giver of that pledge may itself be misunderstood.

I feel, therefore, called upon to make some statement on the subject, but I will confine myself in doing so to the point now at issue – i.e., whether that portion of Syria now known as Palestine was or was not intended to be included in the territories in which the independence of the Arabs was guaranteed in my pledge.

I feel it my duty to state, and I do so definitely and emphatically, that it was not intended by me in giving this pledge to King Hussein to include Palestine in the area in which Arab independence was promised.

I also had every reason to believe at the time that the fact that Palestine was not included in my pledge was well understood by King Hussein.

Yours faithfully,
A Henry McMahon,

5, Wilton Place, S.W.1, July 22. (1937)

---

### Extracts from the McMahon-Hussein letters

**McMahon to Sharif Hussein, 30 August 1915:**

… We confirm to you … our desire for the independence of Arabia and its inhabitants, together with … an Arab Khalifate when it should be proclaimed ... With regards to the question of limits and boundaries, it would appear to be premature to consume our time in discussing such details in the heat of war, and while, in many portions of them, the Turk is up to now in effective occupation …

**McMahon to Hussein, 24 October 1915**
**(see Figure 4.6):**

… The two districts of Mersina and Alexandretta and portions of Syria lying to the west of the districts of Damascus, Homs, Hama and Aleppo cannot be said to be purely Arab, and should be excluded from the limits demanded …

As for those regions lying within those frontiers wherein Great Britain is free to act without detriment to the interests of her ally, France, I am empowered in the name of the Government of Great Britain to give the following reply to your letter:

1. Subject to the above modifications, Great Britain is prepared to recognise and support the independence of the Arabs in all the regions within the limits demanded by the Sharif of Mecca ...

**Hussein to McMahon, 5 November 1915:**

... In order to facilitate an agreement and to render a service to Islam ... we renounce our insistence on the inclusion of the Vilayets of Mersina and Adana in the Arab Kingdom. But the two Vilayets of Aleppo and Beirut and their sea-coasts are purely Arab vilayets, and there is no difference between a Muslim and a Christian Arab: they are both descendants of one forefather ...

**McMahon to Hussein, 14 December 1915:**

With regard to the Vilayets of Aleppo and Beirut, the Government of Great Britain has fully understood and taken careful note of your observations, but as the interests of our ally, France, are involved in both of them, the question will require careful consideration and a further communication on the subject will be addressed in due course ...

**Hussein to McMahon, 1 January 1916:**

... As regards the northern parts and their coasts, we ... find it our duty that the eminent minister should be sure that, at the first opportunity after this war is finished, we shall ask you (what we avert our eyes from today) for what we now leave to France in Beirut and its coasts.

**Hussein to McMahon, 1 January 1916:**

... We [have] sent one of our sons [Faisal] to Syria to command the operations deemed necessary there. ... He is awaiting the arrival of the forces announced from different places, especially from the people of the country and the surrounding Arab regions ... [Concerning] the amount of £50 000 in gold for the monthly pay of the troops levied, and other things the necessity of which needs no explanation, we beg you to send it with all possible haste.

## Hussein ibn Ali al-Hashimi (1852-1932)

**Figure 4.4** Hussein ibn Ali al-Hashimi (1852-1932).

Hussein ibn Ali al-Hashimi (1852-1932) was head of the *Banu Hashem*, the Hashemite clan of Arabia. The clan is of the Quraysh tribe to which Muhammad belonged. The Hashemites claim descent from the Prophet through Muhammad's daughter Fatima and son-in-law Ali, and their son Hassan. Like all descendants of that line, the Hashemites carry the title 'Sharif', including the title of Sharif of Mecca.

Sharif Hussein Ibn Ali was appointed as Emir of Mecca by the Ottomans in 1908. In 1916, Hussein launched an Arab revolt against the Turks and declared himself 'King of the Hejaz' (the western region of modern-day Saudi Arabia).

In 1924, he and his family were driven out of the Arabian Peninsula by Ibn Saud, the founder of the Kingdom of Saudi Arabia. Hussein died in exile in 1932.

Two other Hashemite monarchies were established by the British: Hussein's son, Faisal, was appointed Emir and later King of Iraq, while another son, Abdullah, was appointed Emir and later King of Transjordan.

**Figure 4.5 The three sons of Hussein ibn Ali al-Hashimi, Sharif of Mecca.** Seated left to right: Faisal I, King of Iraq, Abdullah I, King of Transjordan, and Ali, who was briefly the King of the Hejaz.

**Figure 4.6 The McMahon-Hussein correspondence.**
McMahon argued that the area to the left of the dotted line should be excluded from the proposed limits and boundaries demarcated by Sharif Hussein for an independent Arab Kingdom, while Hussein argued that the pink coloured area was 'purely Arab' and should be part of the 'pure Arab Kingdom'.

McMahon's 1937 statement did not settle the dispute and still today, Arabs claim that Britain promised Palestine to the Hashemites and then reneged on the promise. This was in spite of Britain's attempt in 1922 to placate the Hashemites by partitioning Palestine into two – one area to the east of the Jordan River and the other to its west, appointing Hussein's son, Abdullah, as the Emir of the eastern section named Transjordan (today Jordan).

The Arabs also pointed to the so-called 'Balfour Declaration' as evidence of British duplicity. This was the November 1917 letter from British Foreign Secretary, James Arthur Balfour to a senior Jewish leader, Lord Walter Rothschild, stating that Britain 'viewed with favour the establishment of a Jewish homeland in Palestine'. At the time, the British Government considered the 'Balfour Declaration' essential for both domestic and foreign policy reasons.

# The Balfour Declaration

## Domestic policy issues: The 1905 Aliens Act

Between 1880 and 1914, over 3 million Jews fled pogroms in Russia instigated by the Tsarist government. Whilst a minority of committed Zionists sailed for Palestine, most Jewish refugees went to America, Britain and Western Europe in search of a better life.

In Britian, the Jewish immigrants were met with hostility, and by 1905 public pressure on the government resulted in the introduction of the 'Aliens Act' designed to exclude 'undesirable and destitute immigrants', who might become 'a charge on public funds or detriment to public health'. During the parliamentary debate in May 1905, Prime Minister Arthur Balfour argued that the focus was not on the Jews per se, but on whether or not Britain had a right to decide 'who is to be added to its community from the outside, and under what conditions.' A supporting speaker argued: 'Our desire is not to exclude undesirable aliens because they are Jews but because they are undesirable aliens.'

Whilst the 'Aliens Act' reduced the number of Jews entering Britain (and under its provisions, 1378 Jews were deported over four years), desperate Jews from Eastern Europe continued to enter the country. By 1914, the Jewish population had increased to 300 000 (from 60 000 in 1880) and anti-Semitism continued to gain momentum, as did pressure to prevent further entry of East European Jews.

When a new government was formed in Britain in December 1916, with David Lloyd George as Prime Minister and Arthur Balfour as Foreign Minister, Balfour was asked by the World Zionist Organisation to support Zionism as a way of diverting Jewish immigration elsewhere. The WZO delegation included Herbert

Samuel, a Jewish member of the British Parliament, and Dr Chaim Weizmann, a scientist whose work had contributed significantly to Britain's bomb making capacity during the war. During discussions with the War Cabinet, Weizmann also argued that support for the Zionist movement would help secure victory during the war, and extend British influence in the Middle East in the postwar period. Both the domestic and foreign policy arguments struck a chord with British officials.

## Foreign policy issues: Britain's wartime concerns and postwar interests

Following the February 1917 revolution, the primary aim of Britain (and France) was to keep Russia in the war. A Russian defeat would enable Germany to shift hundreds of thousands of troops to the Western Front in France. The British were also anxious for American troops to join the defence of the Western Front before an expected German onslaught.

Based upon an unfounded view of Jewish influence, some in the British War Office believed that publication of a pro-Zionist declaration would encourage the large American and Russian Jewish populations to urge their governments to support these military objectives. This view was put by Balfour to the War Cabinet in October 1917: 'The vast majority of Jews in Russia and America, as, indeed, all over the world, now appeared to be favourable to Zionism,' Balfour said. 'If we could make a declaration favourable to such an ideal, we should be able to carry on an extremely useful propaganda both in Russia and America.'

The Lloyd George Government also placed a high priority on gaining a British foothold in Palestine in the postwar period, viewed as an ideal base from which Britain could protect its other Middle Eastern interests, including its trade routes through the Suez Canal.

The British believed that a significant Jewish population in Palestine would be more sympathetic to their interests than the Arabs.

## Chaim Weizmann (1874-1952)

Figure 4.7 Chaim Weizmann (1874-1952).

One of 15 children, Chaim Weizmann was born in Motol, near Pinsk, in the Russian Pale of Settlement. After finishing school, Weizmann studied chemistry in Germany and Switzerland where he was awarded his Doctor of Philosophy. In 1901, he was appointed assistant lecturer at the University of Geneva and, in 1904, senior lecturer at the University of Manchester.

At Manchester Weizmann developed a new method for the efficient manufacture of acetone, an important component in bomb making which became significant during World War I.

Weizmann was the President of the WZO from 1920 to 1931 and from 1935 to 1946. He was one of the founders of the Hebrew University of Jerusalem, opened in 1925. In May 1948, Weizmann was elected President of the Provisional Council of the newly established State of Israel and on 16 February 1949, became the first President of the State of Israel.

## Publication of the Balfour Declaration

With its own domestic and foreign policy objectives in mind, the British Government provided support for the Zionist movement. The terms of this support were written in a letter sent from Balfour to Lord Rothschild on 2 November 1917. The letter, which became known as the 'Balfour Declaration' was first approved by the French and American Governments before its publication.

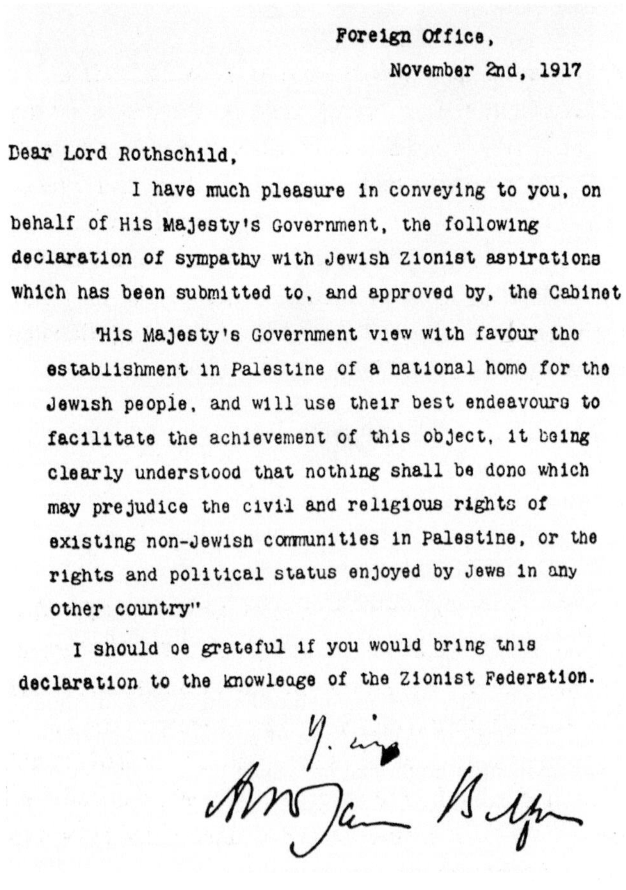

Foreign Office,
November 2nd, 1917

Dear Lord Rothschild,

I have much pleasure in conveying to you, on behalf of His Majesty's Government, the following declaration of sympathy with Jewish Zionist aspirations which has been submitted to, and approved by, the Cabinet

'His Majesty's Government view with favour the establishment in Palestine of a national home for the Jewish people, and will use their best endeavours to facilitate the achievement of this object, it being clearly understood that nothing shall be done which may prejudice the civil and religious rights of existing non-Jewish communities in Palestine, or the rights and political status enjoyed by Jews in any other country"

I should be grateful if you would bring this declaration to the knowledge of the Zionist Federation.

**Figure 4.8** A copy of the original 'Balfour Declaration'.

However, as the copy of the letter above shows, British support for Zionism was vague and ambiguous. Although the Balfour Declaration gave support for 'a Jewish National Home in Palestine', in 1917 there was no existing geographically defined territory of Palestine. The Declaration neither defined this 'national home' as an independent state nor specified its precise location.

## Responses to the Balfour Declaration

The British Government had completely misjudged the Jews' ability to influence the Russian and American governments. On 7 November 1917, the long-expected Bolshevik uprising occurred, and the All-Russian Congress of Soviets convened to elect Vladimir Lenin as President of the First Council of People's Commissars. Lenin, Trotsky, and the other Bolshevik leaders, including some Jews, were opposed to Zionism and all national movements, which they believed were used to mobilise the workers to fight in the interests of their rulers.

It is also unlikely that British support for Zionism would have had much impact on American timing of sending troops to France. America had officially entered the war on the British and French side in February 1917, some nine months before the Balfour Declaration. The speed with which American forces could be mobilised, equipped, trained and dispatched to France largely depended on logistical, rather than political, considerations. Nevertheless, US President Wilson welcomed the Balfour Declaration. A deeply committed Christian, Wilson believed that the return of the Jews to their ancestral homeland was a prelude to the fulfilment of the Christian prophecy concerning the 'Second Coming of Christ'.

The American Government also shared Britain's view of Palestine as an alternative destination for Jews seeking to leave Eastern Europe. Between 1880 and 1914 more than 2 million Jews immigrated to America, which had sought immigrants in order to remedy an acute labour shortage. But by 1914 these labour shortages had come to an end and Jewish immigration was ended and severe restrictions introduced in 1924.

## Conflicting Jewish and Arab responses

When the Balfour Declaration was issued in November 1917, the Jewish population in Palestine numbered about 60 000 while the Arabs numbered about 600 000. The Declaration was regarded as a major achievement by Jews all around the world. Britain's recognition of Jewish rights to a 'national home' was seen as a significant step forward in achieving political independence. Balfour's letter was hailed as the fulfilment of Herzl's strategy of marrying the 'symbolic with the practical'. In Odessa in Russia, for example, 200 000 Jews lined the streets in celebration, while in Covent Garden in London, Lord Rothschild declared that the Balfour Declaration was 'the greatest event that has occurred in Jewish history for the last eighteen hundred years.' Zionism was no longer a distant hope, but an immediate aspiration. In Palestine, David Ben-Gurion, leader of the Labour Zionists, declared:

> Britain has made a magnificent gesture; she has recognised our existence as a nation and has acknowledged our right to the country. But only the Hebrew people can transform this right into a tangible fact; only they, with body and soul, with their strength and capital, must build their National Home and bring about their national redemption.

The Arab response to the Declaration was one of shock and sense of betrayal. The British, the Arabs argued, had promised the Jews land that they believed not only belonged to them, but had been promised to them in the McMahon-Hussein Correspondence as an independent Arab Kingdom. Further, the claim that the Arabs would not be disadvantaged did not address the perceived injustice of the Declaration, as Palestinian academic Dawoud El-Alami explains:

> The British, uncertain of the outcome of the war, had made conflicting undertakings in an attempt to keep all potentially friendly elements on the side of the Allies. It has been argued that the Declaration had a proviso that the interests of the indigenous population should not be prejudiced. This, however, does not lessen the fundamental injustice of such an undertaking.[1]

Arab protests were ignored in the postwar negotiations and the Balfour Declaration was incorporated into Britain's Palestine Mandate and ratified by the League of Nations.

# Postwar events: Palestine becomes a British Mandate

## The 1919 Paris Peace Conference

At the end of the war, the victorious Allied countries met at Versailles near Paris to draw up a peace treaty to formally end the war (fighting had ceased on 11 November 1918). The Paris Peace Conference also redrew the map of Europe, as the prewar Russian, German, Austro-Hungarian and Ottoman empires no longer existed.

At Versailles, it was decided that the Arab lands of the defeated Ottoman Empire would be the responsibility of the newly created League of Nations. A system of 'Mandates' was established and Britain and France were given the power to rule over one or more of these territories. Category 'A' Mandates, which were intended by the League to be granted self-rule within ten years, included the territories of Iraq and Palestine (allocated to Britain), Syria and Lebanon (allocated to France).

## The pan-Arab response: Palestine declared a part of 'Greater Syria' with Faisal ibn Hussein as King

When it became clear at the end of the war that the plan for an independent Arab kingdom under Hashemite rule would not be realised, the pan-Arabists and those who had supported the Arab Revolt were outraged. In response, Sharif Hussein's son Faisal, who had fought in Syria during the revolt, rose to become the leader of the Arab nationalist movement against Allied efforts to divide Arab lands.

In July 1919, Faisal presided over the First General Syrian Congress, which called for an independent Arab Kingdom in Greater Syria (incorporating Syria, Lebanon and Palestine), and rejected French claims in the area. The Congress also rejected the establishment of a Jewish commonwealth in Palestine.

Palestinian delegates were also present, representing the First Palestinian Arab Congress formed in January that year. Their platform declared that, 'We consider Palestine as part of Arab Syria as it has never been separated from it at any time.' Their support for pan-Arab nationalism, which included Palestine as the southern region of Greater Syria, remained consistent until the second half of 1920.

The independence of 'Greater Syria' was declared at the Second Syrian General Congress in Damascus in March 1920, and Faisal was proclaimed King with the support of demonstrations throughout the country. The French reacted by ordering their commander in Beirut to move against Faisal and take Damascus. The French succeeded in this objective by July 1920 when Faisal fled the city. The British arranged for him to leave Syria and installed him as Emir of Iraq, one of Britain's Mandates.

## The Faisal-Weizmann Agreement 1919

In the immediate postwar years, Chaim Weizmann sought to reach some understanding with Arab leaders in an attempt to accommodate both Arab and Jewish national aspirations in Palestine. Weizmann believed that Arab opposition to Zionism was based on a misunderstanding, which fostered Arab fears of Jewish settlement based on economic, not national factors. If this misunderstanding could be overcome, he argued, Arab opposition would decline.

Weizmann put his case to Faisal before the First Syrian Congress. After discussions, they signed the Faisal-Weizmann Agreement on 3 January 1919. It declared 'the closest possible collaboration in the development of the Arab state and Palestine' and measures 'to encourage and facilitate the immigration of Jews into Palestine on a large scale.' Faisal supported the terms of the agreement on condition that the Arabs attain their independence. If that was fulfilled, he said: 'We will be happy to welcome the Jews back home.'

**Figure 4.9** Dr Chaim Weizmann and Emir Faisal.

However, following his expulsion from Syria in July 1920, Faisal dissociated himself from Weizmann, recanted their agreement, and became a vocal opponent of Zionism.

## The King-Crane Commission

At the Paris Peace Conference in 1919, US President Woodrow Wilson expressed concern about secret wartime British and French negotiations about the future of Arab territories that had been part of the Ottoman Empire. He was also committed to the principle of self-determination, set out in his 'Fourteen Points' presented to the conference. In an effort to gauge the views of the Arabs and other peoples of the Middle East, Wilson appointed Henry Churchill King and Charles R Crane to investigate and report back to him.

The report of the King-Crane Commission was completed on 29 August 1919. It recommended that Palestine, Lebanon, and Syria be united within a single state with Faisal as its leader, and argued against the establishment of a separate 'Jewish home' in Palestine, due to the fact that the goals of pan-Arab and Jewish nationalisms were completely incompatible.

It was several years before the Commission's recommendations were published, by which time they represented a significant departure from the final outcome of the postwar negotiations concerning future borders in the Middle East.

Self-determination is a principle that affirms the right of a group that considers itself to have a separate and distinct national identity, to govern itself and to determine the political and legal status of the territory it occupies. It was first applied in international relations by US President Woodrow Wilson in his 'Fourteen Points' following World War I, and underpinned the process of decolonisation after World War II. Self-determination is therefore both a concept and a process.

The right to self-determination has been invoked by ethnic and religious minorities seeking independence from a majority to escape prejudice or persecution.

Despite becoming one of the 'absolutes' of contemporary international thinking, featuring prominently in the UN Charter, the concept of self-determination has never had a clear legal definition and its implications are controversial in international law.

## The 1920 San Remo Conference and the Mandate of Palestine

At the San Remo Conference in April 1920, the Allies endorsed the decision of the Paris Peace Conference to establish a system of Mandates to administer territories that were previously part of the Ottoman Empire. The region of 'Greater Syria' was divided into three separate Mandates: Syria and Lebanon under France; and Palestine under Britain. The Palestine Mandate incorporated Britain's commitments from the Balfour Declaration.

The Mandate was ratified by the League of Nations in July 1922 and officially came into force on 20 September 1923. By then, the territory of the Palestine Mandate was divided into two separate administrative units: the area east of the Jordan River became known as Transjordan and was excluded from the territory in which the 'Jewish National Home' was to be established (see Figures 4.12 and 4.13 on page 61).

The Mandate's reaffirmation of the Balfour Declaration further enraged Arab nationalists who had campaigned against Zionism and Palestine's separation from Greater Syria. The Arabs of Palestine feared that Jewish immigration would increase under the Mandate. This fear was immediately realised. During the period of the Third Aliyah (1919 to 1923), about 35 000 Jewish immigrants arrived in Palestine and this trend continued until 1939.

| | |
|---|---|
| British Mandates | French Mandates |

**Figure 4.10** Former Ottoman lands established as British and French Mandates at the 1920 San Remo Conference.

The Council of the League of Nations:

… confirming the said Mandate, defines its terms as follows:

### Article 1

The Mandatory shall have full powers of legislation and of administration, save as they may be limited by the terms of this Mandate.

### Article 2

The Mandatory shall be responsible for placing the country under such political, administrative and economic conditions as will secure the establishment of the Jewish national home … and the development of self-governing institutions, and also for safeguarding the civil and religious rights of all the inhabitants of Palestine, irrespective of race and religion.

### Article 3

The Mandatory shall, so far as circumstances permit, encourage local autonomy.

### Article 4

An appropriate Jewish agency shall be recognised as a public body for the purpose of advising and cooperating with the Administration of Palestine in such economic, social and other matters as may affect the establishment of the Jewish national home and the interests of the Jewish population in Palestine …

### Article 6

The Administration of Palestine, while ensuring that the rights and position of other sections of the population are not prejudiced, shall facilitate Jewish immigration under suitable conditions and shall encourage, in cooperation with the Jewish agency referred to in Article 4, close settlement by Jews on the land, including State lands and wastelands not required for public purposes. …

(Confirmed by the Council of the League of Nations on 24 July 1922)

## Initial Palestinian Arab response to the Palestine Mandate: the April 1920 riots

Arab protests against the San Remo Conference went unheeded. In April 1920, violence erupted in Palestine. During the annual *al-Nabi Musa* (Prophet Moses) festival, Muslim leaders stirred up the crowd with false accusations that the Jews were planning to destroy Muslim holy sites in Jerusalem. Jerusalem's Mayor called on the Muslim pilgrims to 'spill Jewish blood for Palestine', while a prominent newspaper editor declared, 'If we don't use force against the Zionists and against the Jews, we will never be rid of them'. The crowd chanted in response: *'Nashrab dam al-Yahud'* (We will drink the blood of the Jews). Following the speeches, Arabs entered the Jewish Quarter in Jerusalem where they attacked Jews and ransacked their property. The riots lasted for four days and about 300 Jews from the Old City were evacuated. Seven Jews and four Arabs were killed and hundreds wounded.

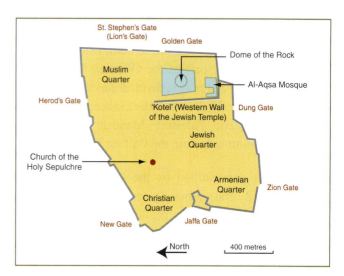

Figure 4.11 **The Old City of Jerusalem is divided into four 'quarters': Jewish, Christian, Muslim and Armenian.** It contains the holy sites of Judaism, Christianity and Islam. See also Figure 2.7.

**Figure 4.12** Borders of the British Mandate of Palestine 1920-1922.

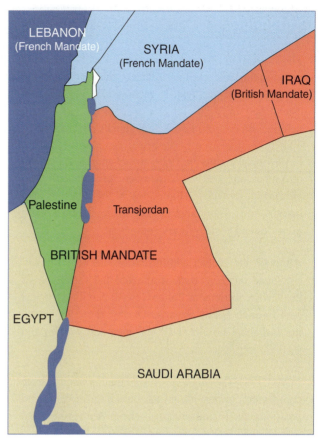

**Figure 4.13** Borders of the British Mandate of Palestine (1922-1948) and Transjordan (1922-1946).

## The Jews establish an underground defence force: the *Haganah*

At the June 1920 meeting of *Ahdut Ha'avodah* (the Unity of Labor Party), members discussed the April riots and concluded that the British forces in Palestine could not protect the Jewish community. They decided to establish their own security force, the *Haganah*, to serve as the *Yishuv*'s underground military organisation, under direction of the Jewish civil authorities.

## Britain appoints the first High Commissioner to Palestine

British military rule in Palestine continued until 1920 when Herbert Samuel was appointed High Commissioner to head the Mandate's civil administration. Samuel was Jewish, had been a member of Lloyd George's government, and had played a key role in the 1917 Balfour Declaration.

Soon after his arrival, Samuel passed a Land Transfer Ordinance to enable land sales to Jews, and an Immigration Ordinance which allowed unrestricted Jewish immigration. The Arabs denounced Samuel's initiatives, but their protests went unheeded. Both Ordinances enhanced the Jews' ability to develop their communal infrastructure in the following decades.

## Haganah

The *Haganah* ('Defence') was initially a loose organisation of civilians under the influence of the *Histadrut*, the Jewish trade union organisation established in 1920. Its role was to defend Jewish neighbourhoods and farms from attacks by Arabs.

Following the riots in 1929, the *Haganah* expanded, encompassing nearly all members of *kibbutzim* and *moshavim*, as well as thousands in the cities. It also bought arms from abroad and made its own hand grenades and basic military equipment.

Although the British administration did not officially recognise the *Haganah*, it allowed the formation of the Jewish Settlement Police, Jewish Auxiliary Forces and Special Night Squads. During the 1936 riots, the *Haganah* mobilised 10 000 men and women and 40 000 reservists.

In May 1941, the *Haganah* created the *Palmach* ('strike companies') to provide military training for command positions, and to find and attack armed Arab groups that had attacked Jews.

The *Haganah* was integrated into the Israeli Defence Forces after Israel's establishment in May 1948.

# A distinctive Palestinian Arab nationalism begins to emerge

Until the collapse of the Ottoman Empire in 1918, the Palestinian urban notables had been mostly loyal to Istanbul. Those who had joined the pan-Arab nationalist movement had supported the formation of an Arab Kingdom, encompassing 'Greater Syria' (including Palestine) based on the principle of *al-qawmiyya al-'Arabiyya* (the Arab nation). The end of the Ottoman Empire and Faisal's departure from Damascus in July 1920 led both groups to focus primarily on local politics.

After July 1920, a sense of Palestinian *wataniyya* (separate territorial nationality) emerged, linked to specific political goals for an independent Palestine. In his book, *The Origins of Palestinian Nationalism*, Muhammad Muslih summarises this development:

> … the fragmentation of the Arab nationalist groups in Faysal's Arab government in Damascus between 1918 and 1920 was a major factor which significantly contributed to the split of the Arab nationalist movement along provincial lines in 1920. This fragmentation tipped the scale in favour of the older generation of Palestinian urban notables, who first subscribed to Ottomanism, then to local Palestinian autonomy at the end of the war. Although Palestinian nationalism was encouraged by the threat of Zionism, it was ushered into its own independent existence mainly as a result of the chaos and disarray of the larger Arab nationalist movement.[2]

In December 1920, the Third Arab Congress was held in Haifa, attended by delegates from all over Palestine who confirmed their continuing support for the idea of 'Greater Syria'. However, it was clear that a new strategy was required as one delegate, Musa Qassem al-Husseini, stated: 'Now, after the recent events in Damascus, we have to effect a complete change in our plans here. Southern Syria no longer exists. We must defend Palestine.'

The delegates agreed, and a new platform was drawn up, which became the basis of emerging Palestinian Arab nationalism. Its central principles were:

1. The territory of Palestine, as defined by the League of Nations Mandate, is a distinct political entity.

2. Jewish political and moral rights in Palestine are totally rejected.

3. The unity of Palestinian Arabs supersedes other loyalties such as religion, region or clan.

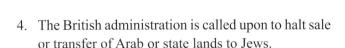

4. The British administration is called upon to halt sale or transfer of Arab or state lands to Jews.

5. Palestine is to be closed to further Jewish immigration.

6. The British administration is called upon to recognise the Palestinian Arab Executive Committee (the 'Arab Executive') as the legitimate representative of the population.

The Arab Executive, elected at the meeting, was chaired by Musa Qassem al-Husseini and became the official voice of the Palestinian movement until the Arab Higher Committee was formed in 1936. Whilst the British recognised it as the representative body of the Palestinian Arabs, it would be nearly two decades before they agreed to the Executive's demands to halt the sale of land to Jews and limit Jewish immigration.

### Key concept: Palestinian nationalism

The central pillar of Palestinian Arab nationalism is that the Arab population originating in the area of the Palestine Mandate is distinct from other Arab groups, and has a right to its own state in that territory.

The development of Palestinian nationalism was evident in the establishment of associations, clubs, and new periodicals relevant to Palestinian Arabs. Debates on how to struggle against the British and the Jews became commonplace, with some arguing for the need to maintain good working relations with the Mandatory power while others claimed that the British were the Arabs' enemy and that violence was required to expel both the British and the Jews. The advocates of violence carried the day, their arguments culminating in the 1921 riots.

Figure 4.14 (Top left) Musa Qassem al-Husseini (1853-1934), President of the Arab Executive from 1920 to 1928. His son, (top right) Abd al-Qader al-Husseini (1907-1948), was a commander of the Palestinian forces during the 1948 War; and his grandson, (above) Faisal al-Husseini (1940-2001), was an executive member of the PLO and Minister for Jerusalem Affairs under the Palestinian Authority.

## The 1921 riots and the June 1922 Churchill White Paper

In May 1921 a scuffle between two rival Jewish socialist groups in Jaffa prompted neighbouring Arabs to attack Jewish shops and homes, supported by the Arab police. The Jews fought back and the violence spread to Petah Tikva, Kfar Saba, Rehovot, Tiberias and other Jewish communities north of Jaffa. The fighting lasted for a week during which 48 Arabs and 47 Jews were killed, with over 200 wounded. Arabs again attacked Jerusalem's Jewish Quarter in November and 5 Jews and 3 Arabs were killed in the fighting.

In response, High Commissioner Samuel established a Commission of Inquiry headed by Lord Haycroft, Britain's Chief Justice. Haycroft found the Arabs responsible for the violence, but concluded that:

> The fundamental cause of the Jaffa riots and the subsequent acts of violence was a feeling among the Arabs of discontent with, and hostility to, the Jews, due to political and economic causes, and connected with Jewish immigration, and with their conception of Zionist policy as derived from Jewish exponents.

In particular, Haycroft found the eviction of *fellaheen* from their traditional lands magnified Arab fears of dispossession, whether or not lands had been legally purchased by the Jews.

Following the Haycroft Commission's report, Britain published the Churchill White Paper in June 1922 (Sir Winston Churchill was British Colonial Secretary), which attempted to reassure the Arabs that it was not Britain's intention to impose a Jewish majority in Palestine. It announced that Jewish immigration would be permitted only if it did not 'exceed whatever may be the economic capacity of the country at the time to absorb new arrivals'.

The Arabs rejected the White Paper on the grounds that it did not provide for the complete end to Jewish immigration. Tensions between the two communities continued to mount during the 1920s and exploded again in 1929.

## Summary

The Jews celebrated Britain's commitment to create a Jewish homeland in Palestine as stated in the 1917 Balfour Declaration, but the Arabs viewed it as a betrayal and an injustice. At the 1920 San Remo Conference, the League of Nations determined the formal borders of the territory of Palestine, and appointed Britain as the Mandatory authority.

Britain's obligations under the Mandate included recognising 'the historical connection of the Jewish people with Palestine' as the basis for 'reconstituting their national home in that country.' It did not recognise the same political rights for the Arabs. The British were merely required to act 'without detriment to any of the civil and religious rights of the Arab population'. This meant that whilst the Palestine Mandate addressed the British commitment to support a Jewish national home in Palestine, it did not recognise the political claims of the Arabs to the same land, a factor which further enraged the Arabs. The outcome was the emergence of the Palestinian nationalist movement, a process explained by the Palestinian nationalist, Khalil al-Sakakini, in 1925:

> A nation which has long been in the depths of sleep only awakes if it is rudely shaken by events, and only arises little by little … This was the situation in Palestine, which for many centuries had been in the deepest sleep, until it was shaken by the great war, shocked by the Zionist movement, and violated by the illegal policy [of the British], and it awoke, little by little.[3]

The establishment of the Palestine Mandate deepened the rift between Arabs and Jews which had begun before the war. The majority of the Arab leadership refused to accept a Mandate whose function, they believed, was to establish a Jewish 'homeland' in an Arab territory. Conflict between Arabs, Jews and the British intensified throughout the Mandate which ended in 1948. The events of this period and the factors contributing to escalating conflict will be examined in the following chapter.

# Review and research questions

1. Read the extracts from the McMahon-Hussein letters. Then answer the following questions:

   (a) What was the purpose of the letters?

   (b) What did McMahon offer Hussein on behalf of the British Government?

   (c) What did Hussein have to offer in return?

   (d) Do you think the intentions and expectations on both sides were the same?

   (e) How clear and precise were the commitments made? Give reasons for your answers.

   (f) How do the promises made by McMahon to Hussein compare with the Sykes-Picot Agreement?

2. Read the Balfour Declaration and answer the following questions:

   (a) What was the promise made by Britain to Lord Rothschild?

   (b) What conditions were attached?

   (c) What is the difference between 'civil and religious rights' and 'political' and 'national rights'?

   (d) How does Balfour's commitment compare to the Sykes-Picot Agreement and the McMahon-Hussein correspondence?

3. What were the Jewish responses to the Balfour Declaration?

4. What were the Arab responses to the Balfour Declaration?

5. Research the background of Chaim Weizmann and the times in which he lived. What were his values and attitudes that influenced him towards Zionism? What major events was he involved in that impacted upon the history of Zionism and the State of Israel? How would you assess his contribution?

6. Immediately after World War I, Arabs from Palestine involved in the pan-Arab nationalist movement hoped to create an independent Arab Kingdom in Greater Syria, incorporating Palestine. Why do you think a separate Palestinian Arab nationalist movement emerged following Faisal's departure from Damascus in 1920?

7. What was the Palestinian Arab response to the establishment of the Palestine Mandate? How would you account for this response?

## Discussion question

1. Consider the following statement made by historian James Gelvin. Do you agree with it? In your discussion, also review the origins of Zionism.

> Palestinian nationalism emerged during the interwar period in response to Zionist immigration and settlement. The fact that Palestinian nationalism developed later than Zionism and indeed in response to it does not in any way diminish the legitimacy of Palestinian nationalism or make it less valid than Zionism. All nationalisms arise in opposition to some 'other'. Why else would there be the need to specify who you are? And all nationalisms are defined by what they oppose.[4]

# 5 Palestine under British Mandatory Rule 1922 to 1947

By the end of this chapter you will be familiar with the:

* development of the conflict during the period of the British Mandate
* impact of the Holocaust on the conflict in Palestine
* Arab and Jewish responses to the question of Jewish statehood in Palestine following World War II
* concept of terrorism
* implications of United Nations General Assembly Resolution 181 to partition Palestine.

From the commencement of its Mandate, Britain had to govern two peoples with irreconcilable nationalist aspirations in the same land. The Arab and Jewish communities in Palestine had different views about virtually every aspect of religious, economic, social and political life. It took until April 1947 for the British Government to admit failure and hand the 'Palestine Question' to the international community.

The conflict in Palestine during Britain's Mandatory rule falls into three phases: from the Mandate's ratification in 1922 until publication of the British White Paper in 1939, marking a significant change in British policy towards Jewish aspirations in Palestine; World War II including the Holocaust, which impacted significantly on Jewish efforts to establish a state in Palestine; and from 1945 to 29 November 1947, when the UN General Assembly passed Resolution 181 to partition Palestine. These events provide the framework of analysis for this chapter.

## British Mandatory rule 1922 to 1939

The first 17 years of the Mandate saw significant changes in both Arab and Jewish communities. As both grew in number, they invested their energies in developing strategies and institutions which they believed would help realise their aspirations for statehood.

## Population growth during the Mandate period

In 1900, Palestine's population was just over half a million. By 1948, it was 1.8 million. The transformation was not merely in its size but also in its composition. In 1900, 80 per cent of the population were Muslim Arabs; about 10 per cent Christian Arabs; and another 10 per cent Jewish.

| Timeline | Event |
|---|---|
| 1919 to 1923 | Third *Aliyah*. |
| April 1921 | Hajj Amin al-Husseini is appointed Grand Mufti of Jerusalem. |
| January 1922 | Husseini is appointed President of the *Majlis* (Supreme Muslim Council). |
| 1922 to 1923 | British efforts to create legislative councils fail. |
| 1924 to 1931 | Fourth *Aliyah*. |
| March 1925 | Palestinian Arab Workers Society is formed. |
| 1929 | The Jewish Agency is established. |
| August 1929 | Violent demonstrations and riots. |
| December 1930 | *Mapai* Party is founded; led by David Ben-Gurion. |
| October 1930 | Passfield White Paper. |
| August 1932 | *Hizb al-Istiqlal* (Palestinian Independence Party) established. |
| 1932 to 1939 | Fifth *Aliyah*. |
| January 1933 | Hitler comes to power in Germany. |
| 1935 | Palestinian Arab political parties are formed. |
| 1936 | The Arab Higher Committee is formed, replacing Arab Executive. |
| 1936 to 1939 | The Arab Revolt. |
| July 1937 | Peel Commission recommends Palestine be partitioned. |
| February to March 1939 | St James Conference in London. |
| May 1939 | MacDonald White Paper establishes new British policy in Palestine. |
| 1939 to 1945 | World War II and the Holocaust. |
| May 1942 | Zionist leaders meet at the Biltmore Hotel in New York and call for a Jewish State in Palestine. |
| March 1945 | The League of Arab States is formed. |
| April 1946 | Anglo-American Committee of Enquiry is published; US President Truman calls for the admission of 100 000 Jewish refugees to Palestine. |
| July 1946 | Irgun carries out terrorist bombing of King David Hotel. |
| April 1947 | Britain hands the 'Palestine Question' to the United Nations. |
| 29 November 1947 | The UN General Assembly passes Resolution 181 to partition Palestine. |
| 30 November 1947 | The Arab Higher Committee rejects UN Resolution 181 and announces it will use force to prevent its implementation. |

By 1948, Palestine's population was two-thirds Arab (about 8 per cent Christian) and one-third Jewish (Arabs about 1 200 000 and Jews about 600 000).

During the Mandate, Britain conducted two censuses, in 1922 and 1931.

In 1922, Palestine's population was 752 048:

- 589 177 Muslims (78%);
- 83 790 Jews (11%);
- 71 464 Christians (10%); and
- 7617 (1%) belonging to other groups (mainly Bedouin).

In 1931, it had grown to 1 036 339:

- 761 922 Muslims (74%);
- 175 138 Jews (17%);
- 89 134 Christians (9%); and
- 10 145 (1%) others.

There were no further censuses during the Mandate, but births, deaths and migration statistics were kept.

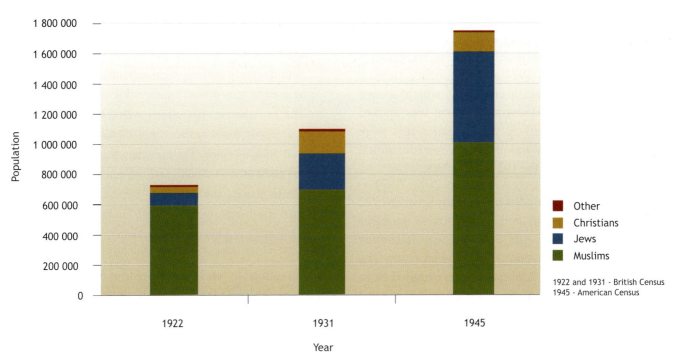

**Figure 5.1** Population of Palestine.

In 1945, the Anglo-American survey showed that the population of Palestine had grown to 1 764 520:

- 1 061 270 Muslims (60%);
- 553 600 Jews (31%);
- 135 550 Christians (8%); and
- 14 100 (1%) others.

As Figure 5.1 shows, Jewish immigration to Palestine increased steadily after the Mandate commenced and then rapidly during the early 1930s, when Nazi persecution of Jews began in Germany after Hitler took power in 1933. Jewish immigrants between 1924 and 1939 were mainly from Germany and Central Europe. Many were highly educated and some were internationally-renowned scientists, mathematicians, writers and musicians. Others brought business skills and modern industrial management experience. This impacted significantly on the *Yishuv's* economy and on Palestine as a whole: between 1932 and 1940, total production of goods and services by the Jewish sector nearly tripled in value and demand for labour (Jewish and Arab) grew proportionally.

Jewish immigration was the *Yishuv* leadership's highest priority. There were three periods of Jewish immigration before World War II. The **Third Aliyah**, from **1919 to 1923**, brought about **35 000 immigrants**: 53% from Russia, 36% from Poland and the rest from Lithuania, Rumania and other Eastern European countries. Many joined the ranks of the Labour Zionist movement, settling in or establishing new *kibbutzim* and *moshavim* and strengthening Jewish agriculture. Others settled in towns, providing labour for the construction of housing and roads and to start industry.

The **Fourth Aliyah**, from mid **1924 to 1931**, brought **88 000 immigrants**. Many were shopkeepers and artisans from Poland who settled in towns, particularly Tel Aviv. They invested in factories, small hotels, restaurants and shops. There was also significant rural development in the Coastal Plain with citrus orchards and other rural industries founded in new Jewish villages.

The **Fifth Aliyah**, from **1932 to 1939** was numerically the most significant with some **215 000** Jews arriving in Palestine. Between 1933 and 1936 alone, over 164 000 Jews arrived, mostly from Germany. Most settled in the cities and towns and their skills and experience raised business standards and improved

urban facilities. Many German and Austrian immigrants were medical practitioners or distinguished academics, who joined the Technion (Israel Institute of Technology) established in Haifa in 1924 and Jerusalem's Hebrew University, the first Jewish university, which opened in 1925. The nearby Hadassah Hospital was opened in 1939. Musicians, artists, writers and actors were also among the arrivals and many new Jewish cultural organisations began in the 1920s and 1930s.

The Arab population also grew significantly between 1922 and 1939, although not as dramatically. Arab immigrants were attracted by new job opportunities and higher wages available in Palestine's expanding economy. The largest increases in the Arab population occurred close to Jewish population centres. British reports show that most Arabs immigrating to Palestine came from Egypt, Syria and Transjordan. The Palestinian Arab population had fallen significantly during the 18th and 19th centuries and so some of the Arab immigrants might have included returnees from neighbouring countries. Another factor was the unusually high birthrate in the Muslim Arab community which had benefited from improved health services introduced by the Jewish immigrants and the British authorities.

## Institution building within Palestine

As noted previously, the League of Nations Mandate gave international recognition to the Jewish people's national identity and their right to build their 'National Home' in Palestine. However, it did not recognise the Palestinian Arabs as a distinct national group or contemplate the development of an Arab polity. British obligations towards the Arab population were simply 'to safeguard the *civil* and *religious* rights of all the inhabitants of Palestine' (Balfour Declaration), not their *national* or *political* rights. As one British official noted, Britain faced the problem of 'how A should restore the property of B to C without deprivation of B.'

Although the Palestine Mandate was not formally ratified by the League of Nations until 1922, Britain's civil administration began in June 1920, when the first High Commissioner, Herbert Samuel, began his five-year term. Historian Charles Smith summarised Samuel's difficulties as follows:

He hoped to gain Arab participation in mandate affairs and to guard their civil and economic rights while simultaneously refusing them any authority that could be used to stop Jewish immigration and purchase of land in Palestine. His efforts were 'subtly designed to reconcile Arabs to the … pro-Zionist policy' of the civil administration. On the other hand, Samuel felt that Great Britain should establish conditions in which Zionist activity could flourish, but that he should not intervene directly on their behalf. His tactics ultimately led to recriminations from both sides.[1]

In an effort to seek reconciliation with the Arabs, Samuel pardoned the leaders of the 1920 riots, among them Hajj Amin al-Husseini, a member of the prominent al-Husseini family. In 1921, Samuel appointed Hajj Amin as the Grand Mufti of Jerusalem, even though a rival candidate from the Nashashibi family had won the election held for the post. The al-Husseini clan was particularly anti-British and Samuel hoped that by appointing Hajj Amin to the position of Mufti, he would help maintain calm among the Palestinian Arab Muslims. It was a significant miscalculation.

Hajj Amin, an ardent Palestinian nationalist, used his appointment as Mufti to foster Arab opposition against the British. In July 1921, he headed an Arab delegation to London which petitioned for abandonment of the Balfour Declaration and establishment of an Arab national government in Palestine. Whilst the British rejected these demands, they offered to establish a representative council that would reflect the make-up of Palestine's population, therefore having an Arab majority. The Arab delegation rejected the offer because they felt it would have left intact the basic terms of the Mandate.

## Failed efforts to establish joint Arab-Jewish representative bodies

Despite the failure of the London talks, Samuel attempted to establish a joint Arab-Jewish consultative body to advise him on matters of concern to their respective communities. Representation would be determined by

## Muhammad Amin al-Husseini (1893-1974)

**Figure 5.2** Muhammad Amin al-Husseini (1893-1974).

Muhammad Amin al-Husseini was born either in 1893 or 1895 in Jerusalem. He studied religious law at al-Azhar University in Cairo, and at the Istanbul School of Administration. In 1913 he went to Mecca on a pilgrimage, earning the honorary title of 'Hajj'.

During World War I he joined the Turkish army but returned to Jerusalem in 1917. In 1920 he was involved in anti-Jewish and anti-British riots and was sentenced in absentia to ten years imprisonment. He was later pardoned and then appointed by Sir Herbert Samuel as Grand Mufti of Jerusalem, making him de facto leader of the Palestinian Arab community. In 1922, he was appointed President of the first Supreme Muslim Council, a position he held until 1936 when he became head of the newly formed Arab Higher Committee.

In 1937, he fled to Lebanon following his involvement in the Arab revolt and then Italy and Germany, where the Nazis put him in charge of its Arab Office in Berlin. The Mufti made pro-Nazi radio broadcasts to the Middle East, supervised Nazi espionage in the Arab world and helped organise Muslim military units in the German army, including the 'Free Arabia' unit that was to 'liberate Palestine from the Jews'. He wrote in a memorandum during the war that he wanted 'a solution of the Jewish problem in Palestine and the Arab countries, according to the same methods by which the problem was solved in Nazi Germany'. He established a Muslim SS Division in Yugoslavia, which committed many atrocities and after the war was indicted for war crimes by the Allied powers.

Following Nazi Germany's defeat, Hajj Amin fled to Egypt and headed the Palestinian National Leadership. His tireless efforts were rewarded in 1948 when he was appointed President of the National Assembly (All-Palestine government), set up in Gaza by the Arab Higher Committee Congress on 1 October 1948.

When the West Bank fell under Jordanian military occupation in 1949, Hajj Amin was not permitted to return to Jerusalem and went into exile in Lebanon. He died in Beirut in July 1974.

the numerical size of each community in the overall population, guaranteeing an Arab majority. The Arab Executive (formed in Haifa in December 1920) rejected the proposal and boycotted the elections fearing that participation in any Mandate-sanctioned institution would signify their acquiescence in the Mandate and in the Balfour Declaration which they demanded should be renounced. They insisted that Jewish immigration be halted and that Palestinian Arabs be offered self-determination. The Arabs calculated that in time, their policy of non-cooperation would force Britain to accept their demands.

Samuel then proposed establishing an Arab Agency, modelled on the Jewish Agency (discussed below), to administer the social affairs of the Arabs, and to be consulted in regard to immigration. This, too, was rejected. Arabs and Jews were thus left to create and develop their own independent institutions.

# Institution building within the Arab community

In March 1922, Hajj Amin al-Husseini became President of the newly created Supreme Muslim Council, which was the highest body in charge of Muslim affairs in Palestine and provided Muslim Arabs with a degree of self-rule. It controlled the revenues of the public *awqaf* (Ministry of Islamic endowments or trusts), which the Ottomans had previously controlled. Other Council duties included control over Muslim religious, cultural, educational, and judicial institutions. In his positions as both Grand Mufti and President of the Supreme Muslim Council, Hajj Amin exercised wide powers over religious funds, which he used to control a vast network of financially dependent supporters. Before long, he was the most politically powerful Arab in Palestine.

## Internal rivalries among the Arab political elites

Inevitable tensions arose from the concentration of so much power in the hands of a small number of elites. Rivalries broke out between the dominant Arab families of Jerusalem, in particular between the Husseinis and Nashashibis, as well as elites from other towns, such as Hebron and Haifa, who resented the monopoly exercised by the British-supported Jerusalem-based notables. The schism became so deep that the Husseinis (led by Hajj Amin) and the Nashashibis (led by Raghib al-Nashashibi, elected Mayor of Jerusalem in 1927), held rival Islamic Congresses in December 1931, one at the *Rawdat al-Ma'aref* school and the other at the King David Hotel, both in Jerusalem. The two families frequently used anti-Zionist slogans to attack each other, spreading false rumours of collaboration with the Jews in their takeover of Palestine.

In addition to rivalries within the Supreme Muslim Council, other organisations operated outside its authority and sometimes in overt opposition to Hajj Amin. After the new High Commissioner, Lord Plumer, arrived in 1925, the Nashashibis campaigned in favour of Herbert Samuel's 1921 proposal, previously rejected by Hajj Amin. Later, the Arab Executive also supported the idea.

When the third High Commissioner, Sir John Chancellor, announced in January 1929 that he would consider the Arab Executive's proposal, some members of the Nashashibis and Husseinis worked together on the initiative. However, Hajj Amin boycotted the talks, which were then ended when riots began later in that same year.

In 1936, the Arab Higher Committee replaced the Arab Executive, and this, too, came under Hajj Amin's leadership. The Committee achieved a measure of unity among the various Palestinian groups pursuing their national objectives, although this unity was short-lived. By 1939, endemic rivalry between the Arab elites, and the absence of unified policies to develop their community meant that the Palestinians had not established sustainable national institutions to prepare for self-rule and independence. The Arab leadership had also refused to work with the British to administer the Mandate. As a result, unlike Arabs in neighbouring countries, the Palestinian Arab leadership did not gain experience in governance before the Mandate ended.

## Arab political parties and other organisations

In addition to the organisations controlled by the major Palestinian families, several grassroots societies and political parties emerged. In April 1923, the first women's economic society, *An-Nahda*, was set up to develop self-sustaining projects for the Arab community. In June 1924, a journalist's congress was held in Haifa, which included a call for the formation of an Arab journalists' trade union. In March 1925, a more broadly based Arab union movement, the Palestinian Arab Workers Society (PAWS), was established in Haifa.

The first half of the 1930s saw a number of political parties formed with specific nationalist objectives. In 1932, *Hizb al-Istiqlal* (the Independence Party) was formed to express dissatisfaction with the ineffectiveness of Palestinian politics dominated by the elite families. It was the first Palestinian political party based primarily on a nationalist platform. However, the Istiqlal Party's call for non-cooperation with the British failed to gain support, as many of the elites were on the British payroll, including the Mufti.

In response to grassroots organisation, the leading clans formed their own parties, including the National Reform Party of Dr Hussein Fakhri al-Khalidi; the Arab Party, linked to the Husseinis; and the National Defence Party, headed by Naguib al-Nashashibi.

## Izz al-Din al-Qassam

By 1935, many unaffiliated Palestinian Arabs concluded that political and diplomatic efforts were ineffective in achieving national objectives and only anti-British armed rebellion could yield results. In November 1935, Izz al-Din al-Qasssam (a Muslim cleric), and a group of his supporters were killed by British troops near Jenin when they attempted to spark armed revolt. Al-Qassam's death was portrayed as martyrdom, and huge crowds followed his body to his grave near Haifa. His memory remains in the Palestinian nationalist narrative. In 1988, when the Islamic Resistance Movement (Hamas) was formed during the first Palestinian intifada, they named their military wing the Izz al-Din al-Qassam Brigades.

# Institution building within the Jewish community

Between 1919 and 1948, the *Yishuv* established the institutions necessary for the eventual formation of a sovereign state, including a democratically elected *Knesset* (parliament) with its own Executive, health services, education system, and defence force. In 1920, the *Histadrut* trade union organisation was established, partly to facilitate an autonomous Jewish economy within Palestine. The *Yishuv's* success in labour programs can be judged by the fact that by the end of the Mandate period, Jews made up the majority of industrial workers, paying over half of Palestine's taxes. The *Histadrut* also provided social services and security, helped with absorbing new Jewish immigrants, and taught them the Hebrew language.

## Governance and political parties

In August 1929, the WZO established the Jewish Agency in order to provide effective representation to Britain and to the world Jewish community. The role of the *Knesset*, on the other hand, was to administer internal *Yishuv* matters, such as religious, educational, and welfare services. It consisted of democratically-elected representatives of the various Jewish trade unions and political parties, including:

- The *Mapai* **Party**, a socialist party led by David Ben-Gurion, later the Labor Party.
- The **Revisionists**, a strongly nationalist party led by Ze'ev Jabotinsky and later by Menachem Begin.
- The *Mizrachi* **Party**, a religious Zionist party.
- The **General Zionists**, a free enterprise party whose members included Chaim Weizmann.

*Knesset* members elected an executive body called the *Va'ad Leumi* (National Executive) to implement *Knesset* policies and decisions. The Jews' success in creating a coherent and effective political structure was largely due to David Ben-Gurion's leadership, whose *Mapai* Party dominated Jewish politics from the 1930s.

## Militia groups

In addition to the *Mapai*-controlled *Haganah*, the main opposition party, the Revisionists, created a militia called the *Irgun Tzvai Leumi* (the National Military Organisation, acronyms *Etzel*, *IZL*). A third militia formed in the 1940s was *Lohamei Herut Yisrael* (Fighters for the Freedom of Israel, acronym *Lehi*) also known as the Stern Gang, whose members had left Irgun to pursue a more violent strategy against both Britain and the Arabs. On rare occasions rivalry between these groups spilled over into armed conflict.

# The 1929 riots

For seven years after the 1920-21 riots, there was relative calm in Palestine. But ongoing tensions between the political and national aims of Arabs and Jews led to violence in 1929 following a long-running dispute concerning the *Kotel* (the Western Wall of Jerusalem's Temple Mount).

Trouble began in September 1928, on the eve of the Jewish holy day, *Yom Kippur*, when Jews set up a movable screen at the place where they prayed at the *Kotel*. Its purpose was to separate men from women during prayers, according to orthodox Jewish tradition. The placement of fixtures at

## David Ben-Gurion (1886-1973)

**Figure 5.3** David Ben-Gurion (1886-1973).

David Ben-Gurion (David Gruen) was born on 16 October 1886 in Plonsk, Russia (later Poland). His father was a member of the *Hovevei Zion*. At 17, Ben-Gurion joined *Poalei Zion* and in 1906, moved to Palestine, becoming a farmer and activist in the Labour movement.

In 1921, he became General Secretary of the *Histadrut*; in 1930 he formed the *Mapai* Party; and in 1935 became chairman of the Executive Committee of the Jewish Agency for Palestine. In 1939, when Britain ordered limited Jewish immigration to Palestine, Ben-Gurion led the Jewish opposition.

At a May 1942 meeting of Zionist leaders in New York, Ben-Gurion argued strongly for the establishment of a Jewish state, not simply a Jewish national home, in Palestine. He proclaimed Israel's independence in Tel Aviv on 14 May 1948. He was both Prime Minister and Defence Minister in the first government.

Ben-Gurion continued as Prime Minister for 15 years (except for 1953-1955), during which Israel fought two wars (1948 and 1956). After he lost the leadership of his party, he remained in the Knesset until 1970. He died on his Negev kibbutz, Sde Boker, on 1 December 1973. His memory is still revered in Israel and many consider him to be the 'Father of the Nation'.

religious sites was prohibited under the Mandate's law and although it was not a permanent fixture, the Arabs voiced their opposition to the authorities. During the prayer service, British police removed the screen. The British accepted the Arabs' argument that the screen had upset the status quo between Jewish and Muslim worshippers.

Following the incident, the Mufti launched a fierce campaign warning that the Zionists threatened the Holy Places of both Muslim and Christian Arabs. Jews responded with counter-demonstrations, claiming their right to worship at the *Kotel* according to their faith. Things came to a head in August 1929, when a young Jewish boy kicked a football into a neighbouring Arab home. A brawl followed and the boy was stabbed to death. After his funeral, Jabotinsky's Revisionist party organised a demonstration at the Western Wall.

A week later, the Mufti declared that Jews wanted to take control of Jerusalem and incited Muslims to violence. Attacks on Jews in Jerusalem began on 23 August 1929, and quickly spread throughout Palestine including Tel Aviv and Haifa. In response, the Jewish leadership deployed forces from the *Haganah*, but not in Hebron where Arabs massacred 66 Jews, wounding many others.

## The 1930 Passfield White Paper

The British sent a Commission of Inquiry to investigate the cause of the riots and to recommend ways to avoid future violence. The commission's head, Sir Walter Shaw, presented his report in March 1930, identifying the immediate cause of the violence as the Jewish demonstrations at the Western Wall. However, he found

that there were deeper causes of Arab anger springing from their general fears arising from the Mandate. He noted that Jewish immigration and land purchases had aroused Arab fears of Jewish domination; and that Arabs objected to Arab labour being excluded from land purchased by the Jewish National Fund. He argued that if these policies were continued it would create a landless Arab class.

The report recommended establishing a scientific enquiry into land cultivation and settlement policies to remedy this situation. Britain sent Sir John Hope Simpson, an agrarian expert, to Palestine to conduct the investigation. He noted that the country had 6.5 million dunams (0.7 million hectares) of arable land, one million of which were already in Jewish ownership, and that the remaining 5.5 million dunams were insufficient to provide the Arabs (30 per cent being landless) with a decent livelihood. He therefore concluded that there was no more room for Jewish agricultural settlements and advocated restrictions on further Jewish immigration and measures to protect tenant farmers from eviction when the land they tilled was sold.

Following the Hope Simpson report, Britain commissioned Lord Passfield to prepare another White Paper on future policies for the Mandate. The 1930 Passfield White Paper recommended that the Palestinian Arabs should have economic parity with the Jews, and that the Jewish area of Palestine should not be permitted to develop unless the Arab area did too. The policy required suspension of Jewish immigration if it prevented Arabs from obtaining employment, or even if Jewish employment harmed the Arabs in any way. It also urged restriction of land sales to Jews.

Jewish leaders denounced the White Paper and lobbied Britain to amend the proposed policy. As a result, British Prime Minister, James Ramsay MacDonald, wrote to Chaim Weizmann on 13 February 1931, and provided a more favourable interpretation of the White Paper for the Zionists. Referred to as the 'Black Letter' by the Arabs, it gave assurances that Jewish immigration and land settlement would continue. This further undermined Arab trust in Britain and strengthened their opposition to the Mandate.

Tensions between Arabs and Jews were further exacerbated by the influx of Jews to Palestine, escaping from Nazi Germany after 1933.

# The Arab Higher Committee and the Arab Revolt 1936 to 1939

A third phase of violence in Palestine began in April 1936, following the murder of two Jews by a group of Arabs, and the revenge murder of two Arabs by Jews two days later. Anti-Jewish and anti-British demonstrations followed in Jaffa, Nablus and elsewhere. The High Commissioner ordered a 24-hour curfew in Jaffa and Tel Aviv.

Following these events, and in an effort to unite against the British and work to halt Jewish immigration, the Arab political elites and political parties met and formed the Arab Higher Committee. The Mufti became leader of the Committee which called the Arabs to join a general strike by not paying taxes and to boycott municipal governments until three demands were met:

- cessation of Jewish immigration
- an end to land sales to the Jews
- the establishment of an Arab national government.

Large numbers of the Arabs supported the strike, but it soon became clear that it was causing them great economic hardship, with little effect on the Jews or the British. In mid October, the strike was called off, and Britain removed Hajj Amin as President of the Muslim Supreme Council and outlawed the Arab Higher Committee. In October 1937 Britain ordered al-Husseini's deportation, and he fled to Lebanon, where he reconstituted the Arab Higher Committee and remained de facto leader of the Palestinian nationalist movement.

In the meantime, the 'Arab Revolt' (as the general strike had become known) was reignited. From early 1937 until 1939, sporadic outbreaks of violence eventually resulted in Britain losing control of large areas of Palestine. Tens of thousands of troops and aircraft squadrons carried out a campaign of repression before finally restoring order.

By the end of the revolt, around 5000 Arabs had been killed, 10 000 wounded, and about 5700 imprisoned. The Palestinian Arab economy was also severely damaged, with businesses greatly weakened, especially citrus exports, quarrying, transportation, and industry. As a result of the Arab strikes many Arab port workers in Jaffa lost their jobs while the Jewish port at Tel Aviv flourished.

The revolt was also politically disastrous and by 1939, the Palestinian leadership had been disbanded. Britain had exiled many Arab leaders in 1937, while others had fled. Many never returned, including Hajj Amin al-Husseini. With so many Palestinian Arab leaders outside the country, a vacuum emerged just when leadership was most needed. The void was partly filled by Arabs from neighbouring areas, especially Emir Abdullah of Transjordan. This was an important development in the history of the conflict, which became evident during the First Arab-Israeli War in 1948.

## The Peel Commission and the first recommendation for partition

Britain established another Commission of Inquiry in November 1936, this time headed by Lord Peel. His July 1937 report found that the Arabs' desire for national independence and their fears concerning a Jewish National Home in Palestine were the underlying causes of the disturbances. The Peel Report concluded that Arab and Jewish interests could not be reconciled, and suggested that Palestine be partitioned between the two peoples. Professor Reginald Coupland, a member of Peel's Commission, described the conflict in a way that still captures its essence today:

> An irrepressible conflict has arisen [between Arabs and Jews] within the narrow confines of one small country. There is no common ground between them. They differ in religion and language. Their cultural and social life, their ways of thought and conduct, are as incompatible as their national aspirations. Arabs and Jews could possibly learn to live and work together in Palestine if they would make a genuine effort to reconcile their national ideals and build up in time a joint or dual nationality. But this they cannot do. National assimilation between Arabs and Jews is ruled out. The national home cannot cease to be national. In these circumstances to maintain that [a single Arab-Jewish] Palestinian nationality has any meaning is a mischievous pretence. Neither Arab nor Jew has any sense of service to a single state. Peace and order and good government can only be maintained in a unitary Palestine for any length of time by a rigorous system of suppression. The answer to the question which of them will in the end govern all of Palestine surely must be neither. But while neither race can justly rule all Palestine we see no reason why each should not rule part of it. There is little value in maintaining the political unity of Palestine at the cost of perpetual hatred, strife and bloodshed.[2]

The Peel Report argued that the Jewish National Home had passed the experimental stage and that although the Arabs had prospered since 1920, the anti-Jewish mood had not declined as a result. For the first time, an official government report concluded that the promises made to Jews and Arabs were irreconcilable and that the Mandate was effectively unworkable. The Peel Report recommended that Jewish immigration should be limited to 12 000 per year; that sale of land by Arabs to Jews should be restricted; and that an Arab Agency should be created based on the Jewish model.

The Report's recommendations were considered to be only 'stopgap' measures. It concluded that the Mandate should be terminated and Palestine partitioned into independent Arab and Jewish states. According to the report, the Jewish state should consist of the Galilee, the Yezreel Valley and the Coastal Plain to a point midway between Gaza and Jaffa, about 20 per cent of

Palestine's total area. The remainder should be united with Transjordan to form a single Arab state, with the exception of a small corridor of land linking Jerusalem and Bethlehem to the Mediterranean Sea which Britain would retain as a Mandatory zone.

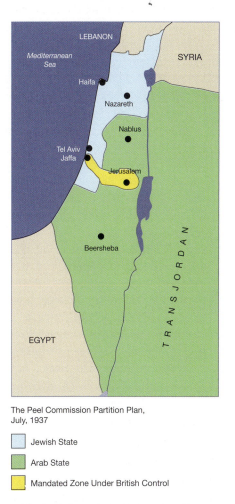

The Peel Commission Partition Plan,
July, 1937

Jewish State

Arab State

Mandated Zone Under British Control

**Figure 5.4** The Peel Commission's Partition Plan.

The exiled leadership of the Arab Higher Committee immediately rejected the partition plan. Only the National Defence Party of Raghib al-Nashashibi was willing to accept the principle of territorial partition as long as Arabs retained sufficient land and could merge with Transjordan. However, when the Peel Commission's proposed partition map was released, the National Defence Party also rejected the proposal because it allocated the olive and grain-growing areas of the Galilee, the orange groves on the Mediterranean coast, and the urban port cities of Haifa and Acre to the Jews.

The Jewish leadership accepted the plan with qualifications. Britain at first adopted the proposal, but reversed this because of the growing menace of Nazi Germany and the strategic need to secure support in the Arab world. In November 1938, Britain scrapped the Peel Report recommendations arguing that 'the political, administrative and financial difficulties involved in the proposal to create independent Arab and Jewish states inside Palestine are so great that this solution of the problem is impracticable'.

# British Mandatory rule 1939 to 1945

These were increasingly difficult times for Britain. By late 1938, it faced the prospect of war with Germany, and therefore had to consider the Middle East's strategic importance as a military base, and the need to retain control over its oil. As a result, momentum grew for support for Arab demands, abandonment of the partition proposed and an end to British support for a Jewish National Home in Palestine. In January 1939, Britain's Committee of Imperial Defence reported:

> We feel it necessary to point out … the strong feeling which exists in all Arab states in connection with British policy in Palestine. … We assume that, immediately on the outbreak of war, the necessary measures would be taken … in order to bring about a complete appeasement of Arab opinion in Palestine and in neighbouring countries … if we fail thus to retain Arab goodwill at the outset of a war, no other measures which we can recommend will serve to influence the Arab States in favour of this country.

## The St James Conference, London February-March 1939

Fearing a negative impact from the unresolved conflict in Palestine, Britain decided to investigate ways to solve the 'Palestine Question'. To that end, Britain called a conference at St James' Palace in London in February-March 1939. Arab and Jewish delegates attended,

although the Arabs refused to sit at the same table as the Jews. During separate discussions with British officials, the Arabs reiterated their rejection of the Mandate and demanded prohibition of Jewish immigration and land purchases. The Jews, on the other hand, reminded the British of their legal commitments under the Mandate, pointing to increasing Nazi persecution of German Jews, and pressing for an increase in Jewish immigration quotas and the establishment of a Jewish defence force under British command.

It was clear to Britain that at best only one side's demands could be satisfied. Needing to secure Arab support on the eve of a new war with Germany, Britain sided with the Arabs, setting out its new policy in a May 1939 White Paper, drafted by Colonial Secretary, Ramsay MacDonald. This new policy was to relinquish the Mandate and establish a unitary (single) state in Palestine, effectively ending support for a Jewish National Home.

## The 1939 MacDonald White Paper: British policy reversed

The stated purpose of the 1939 White Paper was to 'clarify' some points that Britain thought had caused confusion in the past. Firstly, it stated that it 'is not part of [Britain's] policy that Palestine should become a Jewish state', as distinct from a 'national home'. Secondly, 'the whole of Palestine, west of the Jordan, was excluded from Sir Henry McMahon's pledge and we, therefore, cannot agree that the McMahon correspondence forms a just basis for the claim that Palestine should be converted into an Arab state.' Thirdly, the Mandate was not intended to be permanent. Its purpose was to prepare the peoples of Palestine for self-government, to be shared between Arab and Jewish communities who would, supposedly, coexist peacefully. The White Paper went on to make specific proposals, which were:

- no partition of Palestine into separate Jewish and Arab states, but the creation of a unitary independent State of Palestine within ten years
- further restrictions on Jewish immigration with a limit of 75 000 over five years, after which no Jews would be allowed to immigrate without the agreement of Palestine's Arabs.

### Extract from the 1939 White Paper

1. Jewish immigration during the next five years will be at a rate which, if economic absorptive capacity permits, will bring the Jewish population up to approximately one-third of the total population. Taking into account the expected national increase of the Arab and Jewish populations, and the number of illegal Jewish immigrants now in the country, this would allow of the admission, as from the beginning of April this year, of some 75 000 immigrants over the next five years. These immigrants would, subject to the criterion of economic absorptive capacity, be admitted as follows:

   (a) For each of the next five years a quota of 10 000 Jewish immigrants will be allowed, on the understanding that a shortage in any one year may be added to the quotas for subsequent years, within the five-year period, if economic absorptive capacity permits.

   (b) In addition, as a contribution towards the solution of the Jewish refugee problem, 25 000 refugees will be admitted as soon as the High Commissioner is satisfied that adequate provision for their maintenance is ensured, special consideration being given to refugee children and dependents.

2. The existing machinery for ascertaining economic absorptive capacity will be retained, and the High Commissioner will have the ultimate responsibility for deciding the limits of economic capacity. Before each periodic decision is taken, Jewish and Arab representatives will be consulted.

3. After the period of five years, no further Jewish immigration will be permitted unless the Arabs of Palestine are prepared to acquiesce in it.

4. His Majesty's Government is determined to check illegal immigration, and further preventative measures are being adopted. The numbers of any Jewish illegal immigrants who, despite these measures, may succeed in coming into the country and cannot be deported will be deducted from the yearly quotas.

The MacDonald White Paper thus marked the end of Britain's Palestine policy established in the 1917 Balfour Declaration. The Government claimed that a Jewish National Home in Palestine had now been achieved and so it had no further obligations in this regard.

## The Arab response to the 1939 White Paper

Much to Britain's frustration, the Arab Higher Committee rejected the White Paper and demanded that Palestine immediately be declared an Arab state; that Jewish immigration cease immediately; and that the status of every Jewish immigrant since 1918 be reviewed.

In response, Britain established new Land Transfer Regulations in February 1940, banning Jewish land purchases in two-thirds of the territory and restricting them in the remainder of the country.

## The Jewish response to the 1939 White Paper

The Zionist leadership totally rejected the White Paper, which failed to offer even autonomy to the Jews who it intended would become a minority in the proposed unitary Arab state. Further, the White Paper came at a critical time in Jewish history. After Hitler assumed power in 1933, Nazi persecution of German Jewry became progressively worse. In January 1939, Hitler had openly threatened 'the extermination of the Jewish race in Europe' in the event of war.

On 1 September 1939, Hitler's troops invaded Poland, and ignored Britain and France's ultimatum to withdraw immediately.

On 3 September, Britain declared war on Germany, and the Jewish Agency issued the following statement:

His Majesty's Government has today declared war against the Germany of Hitler. At this fateful moment, the Jewish community has a threefold concern: the protection of the Jewish homeland, the welfare of the Jewish people, the victory of the British Empire. The White Paper of May, 1939, was a grave blow to us. As heretofore, we shall defend to the utmost of our ability the right of the Jewish people in its National Home. Our opposition to the White Paper was, however, never directed against Great Britain or the British Empire.

The war which has now been forced upon Great Britain by Nazi Germany is our war, and all the assistance that we shall be able to and permitted to give to the British Army and the British People we shall render wholeheartedly.

## The Final Solution: The Nazis' attempt to eradicate Europe's Jews

Hitler's wartime plan to exterminate the Jews of Europe was the culmination of years of anti-Jewish measures which are summarised as follows:

| | |
|---|---|
| 1933 | Violence against Jewish-owned shops; Jews dismissed from the public service; burning of Jewish books; government hate campaigns against Jews. |
| September/ November 1935 | Nuremberg Laws passed depriving Jews of citizenship and legalising anti-Jewish measures. |
| 9/10 November 1938 | Officially organised anti-Jewish violence on *Kristallnacht* (The Night of Broken Glass), when Nazi storm-troopers destroyed synagogues and mobs vandalised Jewish property. Many Jewish men (although not charged with any offence) were imprisoned. |

| 1939-1940 | Creation of ghettos to isolate Jews living under Nazi occupation, the most notorious being the Warsaw Ghetto in Poland. The Nazis hoped that most Jews would die from starvation and disease created by the squalid conditions. |
| --- | --- |
| June 1941 | Mass shootings of Jews following the Nazi invasion of the USSR. Jews were rounded up with the assistance of collaborators, forced to dig their own graves, stripped of their clothing and possessions and shot. This procedure was so distressing for many of the executioners that the Nazis sought a more 'efficient' approach. |
| December 1941- January 1942 | German officials met at Wannsee and devised the 'Final Solution', the mass killing of the Jews by gassing. To achieve this, five *vernichtungslageren* ('finishing-off' camps) were established in Poland, where gas chambers were built. |
| 1943 | In April 1943, the Warsaw Ghetto rose in revolt. With few weapons the Jews held out for nearly four weeks, but the Nazis killed most of them and razed the Ghetto. |

**Figure 5.5** Bodies piled on a cart in the Warsaw Ghetto, 1941.

From 1942 to 1945

Jews were transported by train from all over Europe to be killed in the death camps.

In addition to the five death camps, dozens of concentration and labour camps were established in which Jews were worked to death or died from the appalling conditions.

The largest of the Nazi camps was Auschwitz-Birkenau in southern Poland. From 1942, Birkenau operated four gas chambers and crematoria. Most of those not gassed and cremated upon arrival died from cruel mistreatment, disease and starvation.

It is estimated that 1.5 to 2 million people died in Auschwitz, including over 300 000 prisoners of war. The victims were mostly Jews, but also priests, Romani Gypsies, homosexuals, Poles and Soviet POWs. The majority were murdered in the gas chambers but many were shot, starved, beaten or died from medical experiments involving surgery without anaesthetics.

**Figure 5.7** Jewish women forced to undress, prior to their execution by the Nazi Einsatzgruppen, Schkeden, Latvia 1941.

Six million Jews died during the Nazi Holocaust, including over one million children. As a result of this genocide, the world Jewish population was reduced by one-third, from 18 million in 1939 to 12 million in 1945. In Europe, few Jews survived.

Greece: 2000 survived out of 65 000 to 72 000.

Czechoslovakia: 4000 survived out of 281 000.

Austria: 5000 survived out of 70 000.

Hungary, including Transylvania: 200 000 survived out of 650 000.

Poland: 250 000 survived out of 3.1 million with a further 1.5 million Jews killed in Soviet-controlled areas.

**Figure 5.6 The selection.** Upon arrival by train at the Auschwitz-Birkenau death camp in Poland, Jews were 'selected' either to work in a forced labour camp or to be sent to the gas chambers.

**Figure 5.8** Nazi *Einsatzgruppen* shooting into a group of naked Jewish women, Mizocz, Poland.

## Arab responses to the war

During the 1930s, Nazi Germany had shipped arms to the Palestinian Arabs while Nazi agents were sent to forge alliances with Palestinian leaders to urge them to reject all proposals for partition of the country between the Arab and Jewish populations. One Nazi official wrote in 1937 that 'Palestine under Arab rule would ... become one of the few countries where we could count on a strong sympathy for the new Germany.' The Nazis were particularly confident that they could count on the loyalty of the Palestinian nationalist leader Hajj Amin al-Husseini. The Mufti's links to Nazi Germany help to explain his continuing opposition to Britain, even after the publication of the 1939 White Paper which conceded almost everything the Arab leadership had demanded.

During the war, Hajj Amin lobbied Germany and pro-Nazi governments to stop Jewish immigration to Palestine, and privately urged that they be sent to Nazi death camps in Poland. An example of his representations is presented below.

Other Arab leaders also sided actively with the Nazis to remove British influence and eradicate the Jewish presence in Palestine. In contrast, about 8000 Palestinian Arabs joined the British military forces to fight against Germany and its allies.

## Jewish responses to the war

When war broke out in 1939, the Jews in Palestine were in a difficult position. The 1939 White Paper had inflamed them against Britain, but Nazi Germany was the common enemy. Despite British and Jewish cooperation in the war effort, tensions were heightened in December 1941 when a ship called the *Struma* arrived in Istanbul carrying 769 Romanian Jewish refugees. Britain refused them entry visas to Palestine, and the Turks forced the ship back out to sea where it sank, killing all passengers.

In May 1942, Zionist leaders met at the Biltmore Hotel in New York and determined official policy until the end of the Mandate.

**Letter to the Minister of Foreign Affairs for Hungary**
**From Hajj Amin al-Husseini**
Rome
June 28, 1943

His Excellency
The Minister of Foreign Affairs for Hungary

Your Excellency,

You no doubt know of the struggle between the Arabs and the Jews of Palestine, what it has been and what it is, a long and bloody fight, brought about by the desire of the Jews to create a national home, a Jewish State in the Near East, with the help and protection of England and the United States. In fact, behind it lies the hope which the Jews have never relinquished, namely, the domination of the whole world through this important, strategic centre, Palestine. In effect, their program has, among other purposes, always aimed at the encouragement of Jewish emigration to Palestine and the other countries of the Near East. However, the war, as well as the understanding which the members of the Three-Power Pact have of the responsibility of the Jews for its outbreak and finally their evil intentions towards these countries which protected them until now – all these are reasons for placing them under such vigilant control as will definitely stop their emigration to Palestine or elsewhere ...

This is the reason why I ask your Excellency to permit me to draw your attention to the necessity of preventing the Jews from leaving your country for Palestine; and if there are reasons which make their removal necessary, it would be indispensable and infinitely preferable to send them to other countries where they would find themselves under active control, for example, in Poland, in order thereby to protect oneself from their menace and avoid the consequent damage.

Their resolutions became known as the 'Biltmore Program' and included:

- founding of a Jewish state in Palestine to fulfil the Balfour Declaration and the Mandate
- integration of the Jewish state into the structure of the world community of democratic states
- total rejection of the 1939 White Paper.

By publicly advocating Jewish statehood in the face of the 1939 White Paper, the Zionists were now in open conflict not only with the Arabs, but also with Britain. Ben-Gurion declared that, 'We must assist the British in the war as if there were no White Paper, and we must resist the White Paper as if there were no war'.

Until 1945, the *Yishuv's* policy mixed support for Britain's war effort (18 000 Jews from Palestine enlisted in the British forces) with resistance to Britain's Palestine policies. The *Haganah* collected arms and the Irgun (under Menachem Begin's command), declared a war of liberation against the British, which came into full effect at the war's end.

**Figure 5.9** Hajj Amin al-Husseini visits Hitler in Berlin.

# British Mandatory rule 1945 to November 1947

When the British Labour Party came to power in July 1945, its policy was to continue with the principles of the 1939 White Paper. The new Foreign Secretary,

Ernest Bevin, refused to lift restrictions on Jewish immigration, even for Jews in displaced persons' (DP) camps in Europe who he declared should return to their prewar homes.

However, most Jews could not return to their prewar homes which were often occupied by non-Jews. Furthermore, family and community support networks had been destroyed and in some places (e.g. Kielce in Poland) attempts by Jewish survivors to reclaim their homes led to their deaths at the hands of anti-Jewish mobs. Most Jews felt that Europe as a whole was deeply implicated in the Nazis' genocidal racism and that it was no longer a fit place for Jews to live. Instead, many wanted to go to Palestine.

**Figure 5.10** Jewish DPs at the Zeilsheim displaced persons' camp hold a rally for immigration to Palestine.

## Anglo-American Committee of Inquiry

Under American pressure, Britain agreed to establish an Anglo-American Committee of Inquiry to consider the situation of Jewish Holocaust survivors in Europe, as well as mounting violence in Palestine. The committee reported on 22 April 1946, noting that most Jewish DPs wanted to immigrate to Palestine, and recommended the immediate admission of 100 000 Jewish refugees and that future immigration be facilitated in accordance with the Mandate, 'pending early reference to the United Nations'. But the report also recommended that other countries should take Jewish refugees, as Palestine could not accommodate all European Jews.

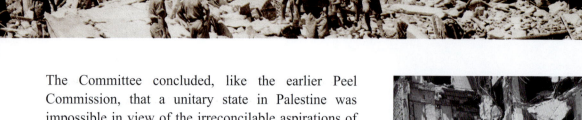

The Committee concluded, like the earlier Peel Commission, that a unitary state in Palestine was impossible in view of the irreconcilable aspirations of Arabs and Jews and the limited chances of cooperation. It recommended a United Nations Trusteeship over Palestine to pave the way for a binational (federated) state, although the Committee did not explain how Arabs and Jews could successfully function in a federated structure.

Both the Arabs and Britain rejected the Anglo-American committee's recommendations. Foreign Minister Bevin promoted instead the 1939 White Paper idea of a unitary state 'in which Arabs and Jews would live and work together as equals', but he was faced with a dilemma. Arab cooperation was vital to Britain's dominance in the Middle East, an objective that had been paramount since the opening of the Suez Canal in the late 19th century. However, Britain was struggling to rebuild from the devastation of the war, and realised that American economic and military support was essential to its status as a world power. Bevin thus needed a solution to the Jewish DP problem that would satisfy the Americans but minimise the Arabs' antagonism.

## Mounting violence

Meanwhile, both Arabs and Jews attempted to undermine British authority in Palestine to hasten its departure. Violence between Arabs and Jews and attacks on British property thus intensified. On 22 July 1946, the *Irgun* blew up British offices in the King David Hotel in Jerusalem, killing over 80 people and injuring another 70, mostly British army officers. The bombing polarised British public opinion, increasing opposition to the loss of life in Palestine and the burden of the Mandate. It was increasingly clear that Britain had lost control, and the public wanted to terminate responsibility for Palestine.

**Figure 5.11** British troops dig through rubble of the King David Hotel, Jerusalem, 22 July 1946.

## The United States favours partition

On 4 October 1946, President Truman declared his support for partition of Palestine and separate Arab and Jewish states. 'Partition' now became the central focus of what to do about the 'Palestine Question'. Britain still argued against a two-state solution, but sections of the US administration lobbied hard for it. As Britain's Ambassador in Washington, Lord Inverchapel, put it, 'the breeze blowing in the direction of partition developed into a whirlwind' and 'could be felt in all major discussions'. America and Britain were now seriously out of step over Palestine, and the British Opposition, led by Winston Churchill, argued that Britain should hand responsibilities for the Mandate to the newly established United Nations.

By the end of 1946, Britain's Palestine policy had become untenable. The conflict had disintegrated into outbreaks of terrorism carried out by Arabs and Jews, and Britain's High Commissioner, Sir Alan Cunningham, was instructed to organise the evacuation of British women and children.

Although there is no universally-agreed definition of 'terrorism', it is widely understood to mean the threat or use of violence against civilians in order to create extreme fear to achieve political objectives. It is the means used to achieve the objectives that make terrorism a crime internationally, not the objectives themselves.

There are 12 international treaties that the UN lists as 'Conventions on Terrorism'. Each aims to combat a specific terrorist crime such as hijacking aircraft, taking hostages or exploding bombs in public places.

In addition, the UN Sixth (Legal) Committee has established a Working Group whose task is to draft a general treaty against all forms of terrorism. This has not been completed because of arguments about what 'terrorism' means. Some states, for example the 56 countries of the Organisation of the Islamic Conference (OIC) argue that intentional killing of unarmed people is justified in certain circumstances, for example if it is part of a struggle for national independence. This view is reflected in the saying that 'one man's terrorist is another man's freedom fighter'.

However, in recent years international support for this view has declined significantly. In January 2003, the UN Security Council adopted Resolution 1456, which included the following statement:

> [A]ny acts of terrorism are criminal and unjustifiable, regardless of their motivations, whenever and by whomsoever committed and are to be unequivocally condemned, especially when they indiscriminately target or injure civilians.

## The 'Palestine Question' is handed to the United Nations

At the end of January 1947, Britain held a conference in London to hear from Palestinian Arabs, other Arab delegations, and representatives of the Jewish Agency as to how each group proposed to resolve the conflict. The government put forward its own plan (the 'Bevin Plan'), which proposed a trusteeship to prepare the country for independence over five years. This plan provided that each community would retain a degree of autonomy, but would be associated with a central government. Both Arabs and Jews rejected the proposal.

On 18 February, Bevin finally announced that Britain would ask the UN to 'recommend a settlement' to the Palestine problem. On 2 April 1947, Britain requested that the Palestine Question be placed on the agenda of the next regular session of the General Assembly, and for a special committee to be formed to investigate the issue.

# United Nations Resolution 181

## The process

In April 1947, a special session of the UN General Assembly was held to debate the Palestine Question. In May, a Special Committee on Palestine (UNSCOP) was established, consisting of 11 member states, including Australia, Canada, Czechoslovakia, Guatemala and Yugoslavia. Between May and August, UNSCOP members visited the Middle East, hearing submissions from Britain and the Jewish Agency. The Arab Higher Committee boycotted UNSCOP stating that to do otherwise would be an act of 'collaboration' and that the natural rights of the Palestinian Arabs 'are self-evident and cannot continue to be subject to investigation but deserve to be recognised on the basis of principles of the United Nations Charter.' However, UNSCOP members did meet with representatives of the Arab governments of Egypt, Iraq, Lebanon, Saudi Arabia and Syria as well as with King Abdullah of Jordan. A smaller group of UNSCOP representatives also visited the Jewish DP camps in Europe.

On 31 August, after exhaustive debate, the majority of UNSCOP members voted in favour of a proposal that the Mandate should end and that Palestine should be partitioned into separate Arab and Jewish states. The basic premise underlying this proposal was that two peoples, with their own distinct and intense nationalisms, were in conflict over Palestine; both nationalisms possessed validity but were totally irreconcilable. The Arab League responded to

UNSCOP's majority vote in favour of partition by issuing a communiqué setting out its opposition to partition and, in violation of international law, its preparedness to use force to oppose it.

A second UNSCOP report was also prepared which proposed a unitary state in Palestine. Whilst this report reflected all of the Arab demands (and none of the Jewish demands), and was supported by the Palestinian leadership and the Arab states, it received the support of only a minority of the members of UNSCOP.

In September 1947, the General Assembly established an ad hoc committee on Palestine, chaired by Australia's Minister of External Affairs, Dr Herbert Vere Evatt. Its purpose was to consider the UNSCOP reports and to make a recommendation to the General Assembly for the settlement of the Palestine conflict. The majority report recommending partition was accepted and referred to the General Assembly for approval.

## The General Assembly vote 29 November 1947

On 29 November 1947, the crucial vote took place in the UN General Assembly where a two-thirds majority was needed for the partition plan to be passed. Backed by both the Soviet Union and the US, the partition plan was formally adopted in UN Resolution 181. The vote was 33 in favour, 13 against and 10 abstentions. In the alphabetically-ordered rollcall, Australia was the third country to vote, and the first to vote 'yes' for partition.

## UN Resolution 181: The partition plan

UN Resolution 181 stipulated that Palestine was to be partitioned into two separate states, one Arab and one Jewish, with economic union between the two. The resolution also provided for UN control of the holy

**Figure 5.12** Jews celebrating in the streets of Tel Aviv on the evening of 29 November 1947.

places, including Jerusalem and Bethlehem. Further, a five-nation Palestine Commission was set up to effect the transfer of power from the Mandatory authority to the two new Arab and Jewish states to be established.

The partition plan delineated 9978 square kilometres for a Jewish state within Palestine, more than half of it consisting of the sparsely-populated Negev Desert in the south. Approximately 6437 square kilometres was allocated to the Arab state, with Jerusalem to be under international control. The line of partition was based largely on population distribution.

**Figure 5.13** Partition of Palestine in accordance with UN Resolution 181.

## Arab responses to UN Resolution 181

The Palestinian and wider Arab leadership immediately rejected the UN General Assembly resolution to partition Palestine. For them, Resolution 181 wrongly legitimised the Jewish claim to a state in part of Palestine,

and unfairly awarded a larger area of land to the Jewish minority. The Palestinian Arabs had asserted at the UN, as they had consistently done since the beginning of the Palestine Mandate, that Palestine was Arab territory inhabited by an Arab majority where the British had promised them independence after World War I. They argued that the Jewish community were intruders who had bought up the best Arab lands and had established settlements there. Now, following World War II and the Holocaust, the Arabs were being asked to 'atone for the sins' of the Nazis and of the other European peoples who wanted to get rid of the Jews. Ibn Saud, King of Saudi Arabia, summarised this view when he argued to US President Roosevelt that, 'Amends should be made by the criminal, not the innocent bystander. What injury have Arabs done to the Jews of Europe? It is the Christian Germans who stole their homes and lives'.

When news of the UN's decision reached Palestine, the Arab Higher Committee, meeting in Jerusalem on 30 November 1947, rejected outright any solution other than an Arab state covering the whole of Palestine. They viewed the UN partition plan as an illegal and illegitimate attempt to divide Palestine. They passed a resolution which rejected partition and called for a general strike, warning the UN that 'not a single Jew would be allowed to migrate to Palestine ... [and that] the Arabs will fight to the last man to defend their country, to defend its integrity and to preserve it as an Arab country'. The Palestinian Arabs' view was that the vote by the UN to partition Palestine was the culmination of a series of illegal acts, which constituted a denial of the rights of the Arab majority.

Further, the Palestinian leaders and the leaders of the Arab states announced their intention to use force to resist the implementation of Resolution 181. They stated that Israel's declaration of independence would be viewed by the Arab world as a *casus belli* (cause of war), an act of aggression that endangered Arab interests. The threat of Arab military intervention was made most explicitly by Azzam Pasha, Secretary-General of the Arab League, who openly defied the UN by declaring that 'the partition line shall be nothing but a line of fire and blood.' This decision to resort to force was to have catastrophic consequences for the Arab population of Palestine.

## Jewish responses to UN Resolution 181

As for the Jews, UN Resolution 181 was greeted everywhere with jubilation and rejoicing. Although the 'partition resolution' (as it became known) fell short of the Zionists' aspirations for a state comprising the whole of Palestine with Jerusalem as its capital, it did provide international legitimacy for the creation of a Jewish state. Celebrations were soon tempered, though, by the realisation that the Arabs meant what they said about resorting to war. Within hours after the General Assembly's adoption of Resolution 181, Arab forces ambushed a bus carrying Jewish passengers from Petah Tikvah to Lod, killing five people on board.

In their deliberations over Resolution 181, not all of the *Yishuv's* leadership were prepared to accept the proposed partition lines as they did not provide for a contiguous land mass, but three separate 'cantons'. However, Ben-Gurion successfully lobbied all of the national Zionist institutions to agree to the plan, arguing that the creation of a Jewish state in even part of Palestine would provide the opportunity to open the state's borders to millions of *olim* (Jewish immigrants). It was also Ben-Gurion's assessment that in view of the Arabs' rejection of the partition proposal and their ensuing declaration of war, it was impossible to predict at that time what the future borders of the Jewish State would be.

## Summary

Under the Mandate, the British were faced with the task of governing a population of Arabs and Jews, two peoples described by the 1937 Peel Commission as having 'no common ground between them', differing 'in religion and language … cultural and social life' and having 'ways of thought and conduct' that 'are as incompatible as their national aspirations.' Further, the Arab majority rejected outright the establishment of the Mandate, viewing it as illegal, with responsibilities that ran completely counter to the national aspirations of the Palestinian Arabs. The conflict between the Arabs and Jews continued to intensify, as did the Arabs' opposition to the Mandatory authorities.

The British Government's attempt to placate the Arabs on the eve of World War II, by restricting Jewish immigration and promising to support a unitary state in Palestine in the postwar period, was unsuccessful. Britain's reversal of policy regarding the Yishuv, as outlined in the 1939 White Paper, resulted in the Jews carrying out attacks against the Mandatory Administration after 1945. By 1947, the British Government concluded that the continuation of the Mandate was untenable, and turned the 'Palestine Question' over to the newly established United Nations.

At the end of November 1947, after months of in-depth investigations, deliberation and debate, the United Nations General Assembly voted, in Resolution 181, to partition Palestine into two separate states: one Arab and one Jewish. The day after the vote, the Arab League announced that its members would use force to ensure that the partition plan was not implemented.

In the months that followed UN Resolution 181, intercommunal violence between Arabs and Jews in Palestine escalated to the point of civil war. When Britain's High Commission sailed out of Haifa port on 15 May 1948, the Palestine Mandate was formally ended. That day, the armies of five Arab states invaded Palestine, opening the First Arab-Israeli War. As it turned out, the declaration of war by the Arab leadership in 1947, in opposition to the UN and in violation of its Charter, ultimately proved disastrous for the Arabs of Palestine. The reasons for this will be examined in the following chapter.

# Review and research questions

1. At the commencement of British rule over the Mandate of Palestine what were the objectives of the Arabs of Palestine, the Jews of Palestine, and the British Government respectively? In your answer be sure to use the documents provided in the text above, including the 1922 Churchill White Paper.

2. What forces and ideas were significant in Palestine during the first half of the 20th century? Assess their significance in contributing to continuity and change during this period.

3. Compare and contrast the development of Jewish and Arab political and religious institutions in Palestine during the Mandate period. Assess their significance in contributing to Arab and Jewish aspirations for statehood.

4. When and why did Arab leaders from outside Palestine become more involved in the conflict?

5. Summarise the findings of and responses to the 1937 Peel Commission:

    (a) What did it identify as the cause of the conflict between the Arabs and Jews of Palestine?

    (b) Why did it recommend the partition of Palestine into separate Jewish and Arab states?

    (c) What were the Arab, Jewish and British responses to the Peel Commission's Report?

6. Review Britain's Palestine policy as set out in the 1939 White Paper:

    (a) Assess this policy in relation to the League of Nations document that established the terms of the Palestine Mandate. What motivated Britain's change of policy?

    (b) What were the similarities and differences between the 1922 Palestine Mandate and the 1939 British White Paper?

    (c) What were the Arab and Jewish responses to the 1939 White Paper? What were the reasons for their responses?

7. Compare and contrast the Arab and Jewish responses to the idea of establishing a Jewish homeland in Palestine during the post-World War II period.

8. On 29 November 1947 the United Nations General Assembly passed Resolution 181. Summarise the processes by which the United Nations considered the Palestine issue between April and November 1947. From other resources, assess the role that the US and the USSR played in the creation of Israel.

9. Research the personal background of Hajj Amin al-Husseini, the Grand Mufti of Jerusalem, and the times in which he lived. What were the values and attitudes that influenced his actions in opposition to Zionism and the Palestine Mandate? What were the major events in which he was involved that impacted upon the development of Palestinian nationalism? How would you assess his contribution to the Palestinian cause?

## Discussion questions

1.  Historians have interpreted the reasons for the establishment of the State of Israel in 1948 in different ways. Some argue that the Holocaust was the most important cause. Others disagree with this and argue instead that the success of Zionism in establishing the infrastructure for statehood before the Holocaust were central to Israel's foundation. This latter group argues that a Jewish state would have been created in any event and that the Holocaust merely accelerated its establishment. Which argument would you favour and why?

2.  'There is no common ground between [Arabs and Jews]. They differ in religion and language. Their cultural and social life, their ways of thought and conduct, are as incompatible as their national aspirations … The answer to the question which of them in the end will govern all of Palestine surely must be neither. But while neither race can justly rule all of Palestine we see no reason why each should not rule part of it.' Do you agree or disagree that these statements of the Peel Commission accurately summarised the political situation in Palestine in 1937? In the light of these statements, if you had been given the responsibility by the United Nations to propose a solution to the conflict in Palestine in November 1947, what would you have proposed? Provide reasons for your answers.

# Part 2

## The Arab-Israeli Conflict 1947-1999

'No two historians ever agree on what happened, and the damn thing is they both think they're telling the truth.'

US President Harry S Truman

# 6   The First Arab-Israeli War 1947 to 1949

By the end of this chapter you will be familiar with the:

- civil war in Palestine in the final months of the British Mandate
- significance of the First Arab-Israeli War (1947-1949)
- plight of the Palestinian refugees
- historiography of the 1948 War
- immediate consequences of the war.

The final months of the Palestine Mandate (December 1947 to May 1948) saw law and order break down as Arabs and Jews prepared for the end of the British Mandate and the war that the Arab League had promised. In the face of escalating violence, hundreds of thousands of Palestinian Arabs fled, anticipating their return upon the defeat of the Jews by the Arab armies.

On 14 May 1948, David Ben-Gurion declared the establishment of the State of Israel. The next day, the British High Commissioner sailed from Haifa, and five Arab armies invaded what had been Mandatory Palestine. In contrast to their rhetoric, the Arab rulers did not fully support the Palestinians. Instead, Egypt and Transjordan pursued their own territorial ambitions. By the time armistices were signed in early 1949, the area of Palestine under Arab control had shrunk to only 22 per cent of Mandatory Palestine, with no territory under Palestinian control. Egypt held the Gaza Strip while Palestine's central hills were occupied by Transjordan and renamed the West Bank, which was annexed to what now became the Hashemite Kingdom of Jordan.

The 1947-49 War, called *Milchemet Ha'Atzma'ut* ('The War of Independence') by Israelis, and *al-Nakba* ('The Catastrophe') by Palestinians, had a profound effect on the lives of both peoples. It completely changed the dynamics at the local level of the Arab-Israeli conflict, as the Palestinians were left stateless and destitute, many as refugees. It also marked the start of regional conflict between Israel and its Arab neighbours. These events and their consequences provide the focus of this chapter.

| Timeline | Event |
|---|---|
| 17 November 1947 | King Abdullah of Transjordan meets with Golda Meir regarding the partition of Palestine. |
| 6 February 1948 | Meeting between Tawfiq Pasha, Lieutenant General Glubb and Ernest Bevin regarding partition of Palestine. |
| 14 May 1948 | The Palestine Mandate is terminated. |
| 14 May 1948 | Israel declares independence. |
| 15 May 1948 | Five Arab armies invade the former Mandatory territory of Palestine. The First Arab-Israeli War begins. |
| 11 June 1948 | UN brokers a cease-fire. Truce lasts until 7 July 1948. |
| 22 June 1948 | The 'Altalena Incident'. |
| 17 July 1948 | UN brokers a second cease-fire. Truce lasts until 15 October 1948. |
| 22 July 1948 | Israel and Transjordan sign an agreement establishing a no-man's-land at the Jerusalem front. |
| 1 October 1948 | The Palestinian National Council (PNC) declares Palestinian independence and the establishment of an Arab government of Palestine. |
| 1 October 1948 | 'Palestinian Congress' in Amman declares Palestine and Transjordan to be a single entity. |
| 11 December 1948 | UN General Assembly passes Resolution 194 . |
| January 1949 | The First Arab-Israeli War ends. First elections for Israel's Knesset. David Ben-Gurion elected Prime Minister and Chaim Weizmann President. |
| January to July 1949 | Armistice agreements signed by Israel with Egypt, Lebanon, Jordan, and Syria. |
| January 1949 | Egyptian administration of the Gaza Strip begins. |
| May 1949 | Israel becomes a member of the United Nations. |
| 11 December 1949 | Israel declares Jerusalem its capital. |
| April 1950 | Transjordan occupies and annexes the West Bank. |

# The final phase of the Palestine Mandate: The 'unofficial war' begins

Intercommunal violence between Arabs and Jews escalated as the end of the British Mandate approached. Historians refer to the period between 30 November 1947 and 15 May 1948 as the 'unofficial war', or 'civil war'. From 30 November 1947 to the beginning of April 1948, the Arabs dominated the fighting and the *Haganah* was on the defensive, as it was poorly armed compared to the Arabs. In April, the tide turned when the Haganah was reorganised and received its first arms shipment. As battles for the towns and roads raged, an attack from one side drew retaliation from the other and atrocities were committed by both sides. These included ambushing civilians, shooting prisoners, car bombs and massacres.

# Arab political goals and military strategy

The Palestinians rejected UN Resolution 181, declared they would defeat the Jews in battle and aimed to establish an Arab state in Palestine. Lacking political cohesion and military strength, they required support from Arab states. In January 1948, the Arab League established a 'Technical Military Committee' responsible for organising a volunteer force in neighbouring Syria and Jordan. The Arab Liberation Army (ALA) was formed under the command of Fawzi al-Qawukji, and consisted of between 3000 and 5000 relatively well armed troops, who were supported by local Palestinian volunteers.

**Figure 6.1** Arab Liberation Army troops guard entrance to Jerusalem railway station against *Haganah* forces, 7 May 1948.

Among those who entered Palestine was 'Abd al-Qadir al-Husseini, one of the Palestinian leaders exiled by Britain during the 1936-1939 Revolt. Returning after a ten-year exile, he led the militia group operating in the Ramallah-Jerusalem area until he was killed in April 1948.

During the months of the civil war, before the Mandate formally ended, the Arabs maintained an advantage in both armaments and men (the Arabs' forces were between 15 000 and 30 000 while the *Yishuv*'s forces were between 15 000 and 25 000). However, their campaign was weakened due to insufficient coordination between the ALA forces, Abd al-Qadir al-Husseini and other local Palestinian militias. The organisational weaknesses of the Arabs were exposed in April 1948 when the *Haganah* came under central command and received arms from abroad enabling it to carry out more sustained attacks. The lack of centralised Arab leadership became a major handicap once formal war began in May 1948 and contributed to the devastating defeat of the Palestinian Arabs.

Further, contrary to their public statements, not all neighbouring Arab states were committed to the Palestinian goal of expelling the Jews and establishing an independent Arab state in all of Mandatory Palestine. King Abdullah of Transjordan, for example, openly sought to expand his territory at the expense of the Palestinians, a policy he had pursued for several years. His efforts caused heightened tensions in the Arab League and contributed to political and military disunity.

## King Abdullah's plan to annex the West Bank

King Abdullah had long desired to expand his kingdom over *Bilad al-Sham* (Greater Syria). Following World War II, he concluded that if he was to achieve this, at least in Palestine, he would have to work with the *Yishuv* leadership. He sought direct discussions with the Jewish Agency and proposed 'a Palestine-Jordanian unity under Arab domination with certain safeguards for Jewish interests regarding immigration and land acquisition'.

Ben-Gurion rejected Abdullah's offer, but many Zionists preferred a friendlier Hashemite regime on their eastern border to one led by the pro-Nazi Hajj Amin al-Husseini, who was expected to return from exile when a Palestinian state was established. As early as August 1946, two meetings were held between King Abdullah and the Jewish Agency. No agreement was reached, but the stage was set for a later understanding about the future partition of Palestine.

Following publication of UNSCOP's majority report on 1 September 1947 recommending partition, Abdullah maintained public opposition, but sent a message to the Jewish leadership declaring he was ready to sign an agreement to partition Palestine that would include a small Jewish State and annexation of the rest by Transjordan. For Ben-Gurion, the proposal had merit because in the event of a war, the Arab Legion (Jordan's army), trained and equipped by Britain, was the most serious threat to Jewish security. Accordingly, Ben-Gurion pursued secret negotiations with the King.

The key secret meeting was held on 17 November 1947, between King Abdullah and Golda Meir, Head of the Political Department of the Jewish Agency (later Israel's Prime Minister). Abdullah offered a quasi-independent Jewish 'republic' within the Hashemite monarchy, that would include Transjordan and Mandatory Palestine. Meir rejected the offer. Abdullah then reverted to his proposal that Jordan would accept the Jewish state and would annex only the 'Arab part of Palestine'.

According to Golda Meir's account of the meeting, Abdullah went on to state that he 'would not join in any Arab attack on us. He would always remain our friend, he said, and like us, he wanted peace more than anything else. After all, we had a common foe, the Mufti of Jerusalem, Hajj Amin al-Husseini'. Abdullah said his forces would not cooperate with other Arab forces against the Jews. Meir agreed to support Abdullah's annexation plan in return for his absolute commitment not to attack the future Jewish state. They agreed to meet again after the UN General Assembly vote on 29 November 1947.

In further meetings in December 1947, Abdullah reiterated his support for the partition of Palestine between Transjordan and a Jewish state, such that the area allocated to the Palestinians bordering the Jordan River would go to the King.

By the end of 1947, a broad but imprecise understanding had been reached between Abdullah and the *Yishuv* leadership. In short, their interest in partition was mutual and both opposed a Mufti-led Palestinian state. But beyond this broad understanding, or 'non-aggression pact', no details were ever agreed, nor was anything written down. Despite this, Yaacov Shimoni, a senior Jewish Agency official who had been involved in the negotiations with Abdullah, recorded that the understanding was:

> … clear in its general spirit. We would agree to the conquest of the Arab part of Palestine by Abdullah. We would not stand in his way. We would not help him, would not seize it and hand it over to him. He would have to take it by his own means and stratagems but we would not disturb him. He, for his part, would not prevent us from establishing the State of Israel, from dividing the country, taking our share and establishing a state in it.[1]

A major and unresolved point of disagreement was who would get Jerusalem. In the end, they would fight it out during the 1948-9 War. In the battle for East Jerusalem and the Old City, the Jordanians were victorious.

## British support for the 'alternative' partition plan

To realise his plan to annex 'Arab Palestine', Abdullah needed British permission, as they armed, trained and paid for his army, the Arab Legion. For this purpose, he sent his Prime Minister, Tawfiq Pasha, and the Commander of the Arab Legion, Lieutenant General John Glubb (a British officer) to London seeking support from British Foreign Minister, Ernest Bevin.

The secret meeting took place on 6 February 1948. Tawfiq Pasha told Bevin that the Jews had prepared for independence, establishing their own government, police force and army, but the Palestinian Arabs had made no preparations, had no army, and no means of creating one. King Abdullah believed there were only two possible outcomes once the Mandate was terminated: either the Jews would seize all of Palestine up to the River Jordan; or the Mufti would return and make himself ruler of Arab Palestine. Neither alternative suited British interests in the Middle East, Tawfiq Pasha suggested, nor would they suit Abdullah's territorial ambitions. At the end of the Mandate, therefore, Abdullah would send the Arab Legion across the Jordan River to occupy that part of Palestine that was to go to the Arabs under UN Resolution 181 (other than Gaza).

After hearing the details, Bevin agreed to Abdullah's plan. It would prevent establishment of a hostile independent Arab state led by Hajj Amin, and maintain part of Palestine as a British strategic asset through Abdullah. He was also in favour of Abdullah seizing the Negev Desert, which the UN had allocated to the Jewish state. This would give the British direct access to the Sinai Peninsula and the Suez Canal. But Bevin was to learn that Abdullah was less interested in occupying the arid, sparsely-populated Negev.

From February 1948, therefore, two partition plans existed for Palestine: a two-state solution sanctioned by the international community in UN Resolution 181; and another secret plan for only one new state (Israel) with Transjordan annexing the area allocated to the Palestinians that was contiguous to the Jordan River. The latter plan was only a loose unwritten understanding between Abdullah and the Zionist leadership sanctioned by Britain. When word of it leaked to the other Arab capitals just before the Mandate was to end, tensions flared and rivalries dominated negotiations during the Arabs' invasion plans.

## The response of the other Arab states

Since its inception in 1945, the Arab League (the highest pan-Arab policy body) was divided between a Hashemite bloc consisting of Transjordan and Iraq, and an anti-Hashemite bloc led by Egypt and Saudi Arabia. The Palestine issue was the first major test of the Arab League but dynastic rivalries spilled over into their efforts to find a united approach. King Farouk of Egypt and King Abdul Aziz of Saudi Arabia considered Abdullah's ambitions regarding 'Greater Syria' to be a threat to their own plans to dominate the region. Syria and Lebanon considered Abdullah's intentions a threat

---

### Historiography case study 1: Israeli revisionist historians assess the competing partition plans for Palestine

Around the time of Israel's 40th anniversary (1988), several books were published challenging the official history which had depicted Israel as a besieged and fledgling state, invaded by a united Arab enemy that had conspired with Britain to strangle Israel at birth.

A new generation of Israeli historians shifted away from this traditional history to what they considered a more 'objective' historiography. 'New historiography', writes Ronald Zweig, 'is fuelled as often by the shifting perspectives of succeeding generations of historians looking at old issues with new insights as it is driven by the sudden availability of new archival material.'[2]

Israel has the same '30-year rule' as other democratic countries for the declassification of foreign-policy documents. Documents concerned with the birth of Israel and the First Arab-Israeli War began to be released from the late 1970s. The revisionist historians focused on 1948, because the documents became available, and because, according to Benny Morris, 'that was the central, natal, revolutionary event in Israeli history'.

The first revisionist works were Tom Segev's, *1949: The First Israelis* (1986), Simha Flapan's, *The Birth of Israel: Myths and Realities* (1987), and Benny Morris', *The Birth of the Palestinian Refugee Problem, 1947-1949* (1987). While the official Israeli version of the 1948 War portrayed Israel as the underdog, struggling for independence against massive odds, these works suggested the story was more ambiguous. Segev argued, for example, that Israel must 'bear part of the responsibility for the tragedy of the Palestinian refugees' and that after the war Israel did not pursue 'every chance to make peace with its Arab neighbours'.[3]

In 1988, two further works were published documenting Israel's involvement with King Abdullah of Jordan and Britain in negotiating an alternative partition plan for Palestine that directly conflicted with UN Resolution 181. These were Ilan Pappé's, *Britain and the Arab-Israeli Conflict, 1948-51*, and Avi Shlaim's, *Collusion Across the Jordan: King Abdullah, the Zionist Movement, and the Partition of Palestine*. Pappé and Shlaim debunked the myth (held by both Arabs and Israelis) that the Arab world stood united with the Palestinians against Israel in the 1948 War.

Avi Shlaim focused on the 'Jewish-Transjordanian understanding' between Abdullah and the Zionists, and 'the clandestine diplomacy that led to the partition of Palestine' between Jordan and Israel which 'left the Palestine Arabs without a homeland'. Shlaim argued that Britain acquiesced in Abdullah's invasion of Palestine in May 1948, which aimed to conquer territory for Transjordan at the expense of the Arab inhabitants of Palestine, not to assist them to drive the Jews into the sea as previous historians had claimed.

The conclusions of Israeli revisionist historians concerning the Hashemite-Zionist accord and Britain's role have come under scrutiny by other Israeli historians. Efraim Karsh's work, *Fabricating Israeli History: The 'New Historians'* (1997), examines Shlaim and Pappé's sources to try and disprove the claim that there was 'collusion across the Jordan' or that Britain gave tacit support to such an agreement.

Whilst both revisionist historians and some of their critics agree that before May 1948, Abdullah made a deal with the Zionists to take some of Palestine's territory west of the Jordan River, there is no consensus about whether it was a firm agreement or a loose understanding, which Abdullah abandoned as the fighting progressed. Either way, Abdullah's efforts to expand his kingdom at the expense of the Palestinian Arabs profoundly affected the result of the First Arab-Israeli War.

to their sovereignty, as his public statements over the years had made clear his intention to incorporate them into 'Greater Syria', under his rule. When full-scale war began on 15 May 1948, Syria sent troops into Palestine more to prevent Abdullah's forces from marching on Damascus after taking Jerusalem than to help the Palestinians.

When the Mandate ended, therefore, the Arab League armies had no coordinated plan and the war began without a unified strategy to 'liberate Palestine', while requests from the Palestinians to the Arab League for money and arms had been ignored. As Palestinian historian Yezid Sayigh records:

> Reluctance to commit major resources to the conflict and mutual distrust provoked constant disputes over diplomacy and strategy, leading to incessant behind-the-scenes manoeuvring, half-hearted and poorly conceived military intervention, and, ultimately, defeat on the battlefield. [4]

# The *Yishuv's* political goals and military strategy

Regardless of their negotiations with Abdullah, the *Yishuv's* strategy for war took into consideration the need to fight, simultaneously, on several fronts. As events unfolded, they also ensured a Jewish majority in the territory that would become the State of Israel.

## *Tochnit Dalet* (Plan D)

Until April 1948, the *Haganah* lacked the weapons to do more than defend against Arab operations to control the roads and isolate Jewish towns, neighbourhoods and farms. The dynamics of the conflict changed significantly in April when the *Haganah* received arms from Czechoslovakia and restructured into a regular army. As a result, the *Haganah* took the initiative from the Arab forces and implemented *Tochnit Dalet* (Plan D), which had been drawn up by operations chief, Yigal Yadin.

The plan was to defeat the Palestinian militias and foreign Arab irregulars within the territory allocated by the UN for Jewish statehood before the Mandate expired and to prepare for invasion by regular Arab armies. If the plan was not successfully implemented, Yadin argued, the Arabs would win. The *Haganah's* key objectives were to control strategic points vacated by Britain, regain control of roads, main towns and lines of communication, and secure the Jewish state's borders. Arab villages on main roads and those used as bases for Arab fighters would have to be evacuated so they could not be used to attack the *Haganah* from the rear once the Arab invasion began. Permission was given to commanders to empty and/or raze such hostile villages.

Israeli and Palestinian historians have debated whether Plan D was essentially defensive or offensive. Some Israelis argue that it was purely *defensive*, citing the following extract from Yadin's plan:

> Generally, the aim of this plan is not an operation of occupation outside the borders of the Hebrew state. However, concerning enemy bases lying directly close to the borders which may be used as springboards for infiltration into the territory of the state, these must be temporarily occupied and searched for hostiles according to the above guidelines, and they must then be incorporated into our defensive system until operations cease.
>
> Bases located in enemy territory which are intended to be temporarily occupied and controlled will be listed among the operational targets for the various brigades.

Palestinians and some revisionist Israeli historians argue that Plan D was *offensive*, using the following extract, which concerned action to be taken towards hostile Arab population centres:

Mounting operations against enemy population centres located inside or near our defensive system in order to prevent them from being used as bases by an active armed force. These operations can be divided into the following categories:

- Destruction of villages (setting fire to, blowing up, and planting mines in the debris), especially those population centres which are difficult to control continuously.

- Mounting search and control operations according to the following guidelines: encirclement of the village and conducting a search inside it. In the event of resistance, the armed force must be destroyed and the population must be expelled outside the borders of the state.

It would appear from the extracts above that Plan D incorporated both defensive and offensive elements. The plan to secure the area intended by the UN for the Jewish state was defensive. However, the plan to subdue areas outside that territory was offensive.

The arguments are relevant to competing Arab and Israeli narratives concerning the 1948 War: did the Jews have a prewar plan to expel Arabs from areas that would become the State of Israel? Revisionist Israeli historian, Benny Morris, concluded in *The Birth of the Palestinian Refugee Problem Revisited* that Plan D was not 'a political blueprint for the expulsion of Palestine's Arabs'. Rather, it was 'governed by military considerations and geared to achieving military ends' necessitated by the Arab League decision to use force to oppose the partition of Palestine. This meant that, 'given the nature of war and the admixture of populations, securing the interior of the Jewish State and its borders in practice meant the depopulation and destruction of the villages that hosted the hostile militias and irregulars.'[5]

As Britain withdrew from Palestine throughout April and May, Plan D was implemented. Both sides suffered many casualties, and both sides committed atrocities. Two of the more infamous incidents were the massacre of Arab villagers at Deir Yassin, and the burning alive of a convoy of Jewish doctors, nurses, teachers and students on their way to a Jerusalem hospital and university.

## The Deir Yassin and the Hadassah convoy massacres

On 9 April 1948, members of the Irgun and Stern Gang attacked the Arab village of Deir Yassin, located on the road between Jerusalem and Tel Aviv. After a fierce battle, the Jewish fighters carried out brutal acts of revenge for their losses, killing Arab fighters who had surrendered and some civilians. Arab and Jewish eye witnesses reported that 20-25 villagers were shot in a nearby quarry. Soon after the attack, Jewish doctors, *Haganah* officers, and a representative of the Red Cross reported 'bullet-riddled, sometimes charred bodies of the men, women and children.' The *Yishuv* leadership strongly condemned the atrocity.

Heated debate continues between Israelis and Palestinians about the events leading to, during and following the attack at Deir Yassin. The number killed has been disputed, but most sources estimate around 250 dead, based on reports given by participants, observers and journalists immediately afterwards. One Arab survivor claimed the head of the National Committee in Jerusalem, Dr Hussein Fakhri El-Khalidi, instructed him to make false claims 'that the Jews slaughtered people, committed atrocities, raped and stole gold.' The Arab leadership magnified the number killed 'so that the Arab armies would finally make a move and come to liberate Palestine from the Jews.' Those responsible for the atrocities (Irgun and Stern Gang members) also misrepresented the number to provoke terror and frighten Arabs into fleeing.

Recent Israeli and Palestinian research indicates that the number of Arabs massacred at Deir Yassin was exaggerated at the time; the more accurate figure is 107 killed, most of whom died during the battle. Researchers from the Palestinian Bir Zeit University have concluded that the number killed did not exceed 120. But whatever the number, the nature of the atrocity is not diminished, nor its short and long-term effects. The massacre is cited as a symbol of terror and repression in the Palestinian historical narrative. At the time, news of the massacre resulted in many Arab civilians fleeing because they feared the same fate.

'Deir Yassin!' became a rally cry for Arab fighters and those who sought revenge. Four days after reports from Deir Yassin were published, Arabs in the Jerusalem area ambushed a Jewish convoy carrying 70 doctors, nurses, teachers and students to Jerusalem's Hadassah Hospital and Hebrew University. Of the 112 Jewish passengers, 78 were massacred, with many burned alive in the trucks.

## The first wave of Palestinian refugees

News of the massacre at Deir Yassin spread rapidly among Palestinian Arabs, facilitated by exaggerated coverage in the Arab media. As Bregman and el-Tahri record in *The Fifty Years War*, the intention was to 'alert the Arab countries to what was happening' but the broadcasts had the effect of triggering the first wave of Palestinian refugees. Hazen Nusseibah from the Palestine Broadcasting Corporation recalled that:

> We transmitted Dr Hussein Fakhri El Khalidi's statement mentioning rape and this and that. It had a devastating impact on everyone in Palestine, and the exodus began … It was the biggest blunder that could have happened.[6]

When the UN considered the 'Palestine Question' in November 1947, the Arab population was about 1 200 000, but in the following six months, some 300 000 Arabs fled their homes in the areas allocated to the Jewish state. By January 1949, more than 700 000 Palestinians had become refugees.

**Figure 6.2** Arab villagers evacuate their homes, 18 April 1948.

# The State of Israel is proclaimed and the First Arab-Israeli War begins

The Palestine Mandate was terminated at midnight on 14 May 1948. At 4.00 pm, the leader of the *Yishuv*, David Ben-Gurion, read out Israel's Declaration of Independence, proclaiming a new state within the boundaries defined by UN Resolution 181.

That evening, Egyptian aircraft bombed Tel Aviv and on 15 May 1948, five Arab armies (Egypt, Transjordan, Syria, Lebanon and Iraq) invaded while Saudi Arabia and Yemen each sent small contingents. Small groups of Palestinian Arab fighters also took part.

The 'unofficial' phase of the war was over. The Arab states' invasion marked the beginning of the First Arab-Israeli War. The Arab League set out the reasons for their intervention and the League's Secretary General, Azzam Pasha, announced that 'This will be a war of extermination and a momentous massacre [of the Jews], which will be spoken of like the Mongolian massacres and the Crusades'. The UN condemned the Arab states' invasion as a violation of its Charter and an illegal use of force.

## Early Arab victories

In the initial weeks of the war, the Arab armies gained the upper hand as Israel faced a war with regular armies on all its borders. In the centre of the country, Iraqi forces tried to cut the new state in two, penetrating to within ten kilometres of the Mediterranean coast. Egyptian forces reached the outskirts of Tel Aviv and Jerusalem and occupied all of the Negev, while Jordan occupied the Old City of Jerusalem. Jordan sent a preliminary force on 4 May to attack the Jewish community at Kfar Etzion, on the southern route to Jerusalem, which was repulsed, returning on 13 May with a heavily armed and larger force, which defeated the Jews. The survivors surrendered and were massacred by their Arab captors.

**Figure 6.3** David Ben-Gurion reading the proclamation of Israel's establishment, 14 May 1948.

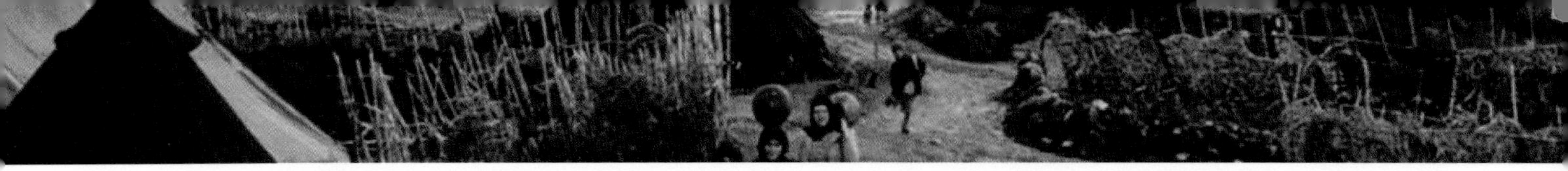

## Extract from the declaration of the independence of Israel, 14 May 1948

The Land of Israel was the birthplace of the Jewish people. Here their spiritual, religious and national identity was formed. Here they achieved independence and created a culture of national and universal significance. Here they wrote and gave the Bible to the world.

Exiled from the Land of Israel, the Jewish people remained faithful to it in all the countries of their dispersion, never ceasing to pray and hope for their return and the restoration of their national freedom.

... Jews strove throughout the centuries to go back to the land of their fathers and regain their statehood. In recent decades they returned in their masses. They reclaimed the wilderness, revived their language, built cities and villages, and established a vigorous and ever-growing community, with its own economic and cultural life. They sought peace yet were prepared to defend themselves ...

It is the natural right of the Jewish people to lead, as do all other nations, an independent existence in its sovereign state.

We hereby proclaim the establishment of the Jewish State in Palestine, to be called *Medinat Israel* (the State of Israel) ...

... we yet call upon the Arab inhabitants of the State of Israel to preserve the ways of peace and play their part in the development of the state, on the basis of full and equal citizenship and due representation in all its bodies and institutions – provisional and permanent.

We extend our hand in peace and neighbourliness to all the neighbouring states and their peoples ...

## The flag of Israel

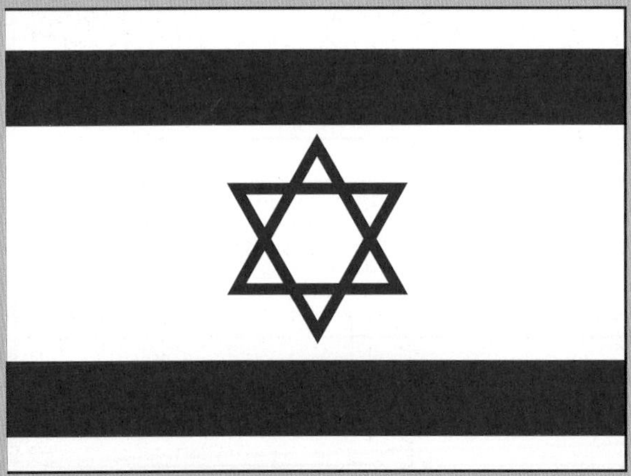

Figure 6.4 The flag of Israel.

The flag of Israel was adopted on 28 October 1948. It is white with a blue six-pointed linear star, known as the *Magen David* (Shield of David), with two horizontal blue bands top and bottom, representing a *tallit*, the traditional Jewish prayer shawl.

Fierce fighting between Jordan's Arab Legion and Israel's Defence Forces (IDF) at the strategic location on the hill of Latrun (west of Jerusalem) again saw the defeat of the Jews. The Arab Legion also occupied *kibbutzim* to the south of Jerusalem in the area that Abdullah wished to annex.

Meanwhile, the Syrian army attacked the Jordan Valley in the north, and Lebanon sent a small force into northern Galilee.

By late May, between 25 000 and 30 000 regular and irregular Arab troops were operating in Palestine, but this was well short of the number required to defeat the IDF. After June, the Arab armies never exceeded the total number of Jewish forces. When the Arab invasion began, the IDF had about 15 000 troops in the field and another 30 000 engaged in local defence; by July 1948 the IDF's total forces had risen to some 65 000 and by December reached their peak at more than 94 000.

## Ruling parties and Prime Ministers of Israel, 1948 to 2005

At its founding, the State of Israel adopted a democratic parliamentary system, with a Prime Minister heading the government (Knesset) which has 120 seats, and a largely ceremonial President as head of State. Under the law, the President asks the leader of the party that has won the most number of seats in the Knesset to form the government, who then becomes Prime Minister after a government is successfully formed with the support of at least 61 members in the Knesset.

Elections were held for the first Knesset in January 1949. David Ben-Gurion became Prime Minister when his *Mapai* Party won the largest number of seats. Chaim Weizmann became the first President.

Since these first elections, no one party has won enough seats on its own to form a government, so every government has been a coalition of parties. On two occasions (1984 and 1988) the two major parties, Labor and Likud, combined to form a 'unity government'.

In 1992, the law concerning the formation of a government was amended to provide for direct election of the Prime Minister, separate from the Knesset election. Three elections were held under this system: 1996, 1999, and 2001, when the law was amended again, reverting to the original system.

There have been 16 Knessets elected between 1949 and 2005, and 11 Prime Ministers, 4 of whom have served more than one term.

| Knesset | Years | Prime Minister and party |
|---------|-------|--------------------------|
| 1st | 1949-1951 | David Ben-Gurion (*Mapai*) |
| 2nd | 1951-1955 | David Ben-Gurion (1951-1953) and Moshe Sharett (1953-1955) (*Mapai*) |
| 3rd | 1955-1959 | David Ben-Gurion (*Mapai*) |
| 4th | 1959-1961 | David Ben-Gurion (*Mapai*) |
| 5th | 1961-1965 | David Ben-Gurion (1961-1963) and Levi Eshkol (1963-1965) (*Mapai*) |
| 6th | 1965-1969 | Levi Eshkol (*Mapai*/Labor) |
| 7th | 1969-1973 | Golda Meir (Labor) |
| 8th | 1973-1977 | Golda Meir (1973-1974) and Yitzhak Rabin (1974 to 1977) (Labor) |
| 9th | 1977-1981 | Menachem Begin (Likud) |
| 10th | 1981-1984 | Menachem Begin (1981-1983) and Yitzhak Shamir (1983-1984) (Likud) |
| 11th | 1984-1988 (1st unity government) | Shimon Peres (1984-1986) (Labor) and Yitzhak Shamir (1986-1988) (Likud) |
| 12th | 1988-1992 | Yitzhak Shamir (Likud) |
| 13th | 1992-1996 | Yitzhak Rabin (1992-1995) and Shimon Peres (1995-1996) (Labor) |
| 14th | 1996-1999 | Benjamin (Bibi) Nentanyahu (Likud) |
| 15th | 1999-2001 | Ehud Barak (Labor) |
| 16th | 2001-2006 | Ariel Sharon (Likud from 2001 to 2005; Kadima from 2005 to January 2006) and Acting Prime Minister Ehud Olmert (January-March 2006) |

## The June 1948 cease-fire

The UN brokered a month-long cease-fire on 11 June 1948, but all parties simply used the time to regroup and rearm. Britain's departure also ended its arms embargo, enabling the Israelis to buy arms freely and to mobilise their population more effectively. During the following months, until the end of the war in January 1949, the Arab advantage in heavy weaponry gradually decreased though they maintained a greater number of fighter aircraft and tanks.

1. Palestine was part of the former Ottoman Empire subject to its laws and represented in its parliament. The overwhelming majority of the population of Palestine were Arabs. There was in it a small minority of Jews ...

2. The Arabs have always asked for their freedom and independence. On the outbreak of the First World War, and when the Allies declared that they were fighting for the liberation of peoples, the Arabs joined them and fought on their side with a view to realising their national aspirations and obtaining their independence ...

4. When the war came to an end England did not keep her promise ...

5. England administered Palestine in a manner which enabled the Jews to flood it with immigrants and helped them to settle the country. England did not pay regard to the interests or rights of the Arab inhabitants, the lawful owners of the country ...

9. When the General Assembly of the United Nations issued, on 29 November 1947, its recommendation concerning the solution of the Palestine problem, ... the Arab states drew attention to the injustice implied in this solution ... [and also] declared the Arabs' rejection of [that solution].

The Governments of the Arab states declare the following:

First: That the rule of Palestine should revert to its inhabitants ...

Second: Security and order in Palestine have become disrupted. The Zionist aggression resulted in the exodus of more than a quarter of a million of its Arab inhabitants from their homes and in their taking refuge in the neighbouring Arab countries.

The events which have taken place in Palestine have unmasked the aggressive intentions and the imperialistic designs of the Zionists, including the atrocities committed by them against the peace-loving Arab inhabitants, especially in Deir Yasin, Tiberias and others ...

Sixth: ... in order to fill the gap brought about in the governmental machinery in Palestine as a result of the termination of the Mandate and the non-establishment of a lawful successor authority, the Governments of the Arab states have found themselves compelled to intervene in Palestine solely in order to help its inhabitants restore peace and security and the rule of justice and law to their country, and in order to prevent bloodshed.

Eighth: The Arab states most emphatically declare that [their] intervention in Palestine was due only to these considerations and objectives, and that they aim at nothing more than to put an end to the prevailing conditions in [Palestine] ...

## Renewed fighting between Israel and the Arabs

The 11 June cease-fire expired on 7 July. In the next round of fighting, the IDF halted any further Arab advances and took control of the western Galilee which was in the territory allocated to Palestinian Arabs by Resolution 181. During fighting in the north, more Palestinians fled, some having been expelled by advancing Israeli troops. However, sizeable Arab populations of about 150 000 stayed in the towns of Nazareth and Acre and became Israeli citizens at the end of the war.

## Another truce and renewed fighting

A second truce began on 17 July and lasted until 15 October. When the fighting resumed, the IDF expelled the Egyptians from the Negev and secured a corridor linking the coastal plain with West Jerusalem by taking the towns of Lydda (Lod) and Ramle from the Arab Legion and Palestinian irregular forces. During this period, Jewish forces expelled 60 000 Arab villagers and sent them to Jordanian-held territory.

However, the IDF failed to gain control of East Jerusalem, including the 'Old City', which was secured by Abdullah's forces. The Jordanians also successfully occupied the central areas of Arab Palestine (the 'West Bank') and expelled all Jews from these areas.

- ☐ Held by Israel on eve of Arab invasion
- ☐ Arab-controlled areas on eve of Arab invasion

**Figure 6.5** Arab states' invasion of Palestine, May 1948.

# The competition for Arab Palestine: King Abdullah versus Hajj Amin al-Husseini and the All-Palestine Government

King Abdullah's aim of seizing the area contiguous with the Jordan River caused intense inter-Arab conflict, climaxing in September 1948. To thwart Abdullah's plan to annex Palestinian territory, other members of the Arab League, led by Egypt, established the *Umum Filastin*, the 'All-Palestine Government' (APG) in Gaza.

On 22 September, the APG declared that the Palestinians were entitled to self-determination and that 'all of Palestine – within the borders extant at the termination of the British Mandate – was to be an independent state'. The Arab League also hoped this declaration would placate Arab opinion that was critical of Arab governments for not doing enough to defeat the Jews and assist the Palestinians in establishing their own state.

Abdullah opposed the creation of the APG, arguing that it was 'against the wishes of the Arabs of Palestine', the majority of whom now lived within territory under his control. He threatened to conclude a separate agreement with Israel if the other Arab states continued to support the APG, causing the League to withdraw support for the APG.

## Hajj Amin declares Palestinian independence

Meanwhile, Hajj Amin al-Husseini, who had been in Cairo seeking Arab League assistance against the Jews, arrived in Gaza at the end of September and established the Palestinian National Council (PNC) to function as the executive arm of the APG. The PNC convened on 1 October 1948 and elected Hajj Amin President of both the APG and PNC. After a three-day session, the APG declared independence and the establishment of an Arab government of Palestine.

## The *Altalena* incident

On 1 June 1948, Menachem Begin signed an agreement with Prime Minister Ben-Gurion to disband the Irgun and transfer to the IDF where they would form separate battalions, but fall under central command. Irgun units in Jerusalem (not then a part of Israel) remained independent.

During the UN-brokered truce, the ship *Altalena*, arrived from Europe at a beach north of Tel Aviv, with Irgun units and arms. A dispute arose over allocation of the arms between Ben-Gurion and the Irgun's leader, Menachem Begin. Begin wanted most of arms to go to Irgun battalions within the IDF and independent units in Jerusalem. Ben-Gurion refused, arguing that this would create 'an army within an army'.

When the ship anchored, Irgun troops took control and IDF troops in turn surrounded the area and fire was exchanged before the Irgun surrendered. Begin then ordered the ship to sail south to Tel Aviv to evade the IDF. On 22 June, Ben-Gurion ordered an attack on the ship and the *Altalena* was sunk and most of the arms lost, with 18 killed, mostly Irgun members.

After the shelling of the *Altalena*, Ben-Gurion ordered the arrest of over 200 Irgun fighters, but most were released soon after, with the exception of five commanders detained for more than two months. The so-called 'Altalena Incident' was important in the early months of Israel's history, ending competition between independent Jewish militias and the new state's central authority.

**Figure 6.6** The *Altalena* on fire, 22 June 1948.

## Abdullah's response: Palestine and Transjordan declared a single entity

Delegates to the PNC meeting were limited to those who could come from in and around Gaza because the Jordanian and Iraqi armies refused to admit Palestinian delegates residing in areas under their control. Abdullah further challenged the PNC in Gaza by organising a 'Palestinian Congress' in Amman on 1 October, the same day that the PNC met in Gaza. Mayors, tribal leaders and Palestinian notables attended and adopted their own resolutions, in opposition to Hajj Amin's APG and his election in Gaza as its President. They declared that establishing the APG in Gaza was contrary to the Palestinians' wishes and interests; that Transjordan and Palestine were a single territorial entity; and that a Palestinian government could only be formed after the liberation of all of Palestine.

Abdullah's Palestinian Congress met again on 18 October in Ramallah in the West Bank, under the auspices of the 'Hashemite Propaganda Association'. Local Palestinian notables proclaimed that Abdullah would be entrusted with solving the Palestine problem, 'by war or by peace', and called on Palestinian youth to join the Jordanian army.

The third and most important gathering was held in Jericho (in the West Bank) on 1 December 1948. Chaired by Sheikh Muhammad al-Ja'abari (Hebron's Mayor), the Jericho Conference was attended by hundreds of delegates, representing all sectors of Palestinian society, including religious leaders, Jordanian military governors and many Arab journalists. King Abdullah instructed his military governors to ensure that 'all the Palestinian representatives invited did attend'. The delegates elected al-Ja'abari as president. He railed against the APG establishment in Gaza and called on Abdullah to annex Palestine to Transjordan, as a 'first step towards the unification of the Arab states'. The meeting declared Abdullah 'King of Palestine'.

## The end of the war and the 1949 armistice agreements

By January 1949, Israel had gained control of 78 per cent of the previous Mandatory territory of Palestine. The remaining 22 per cent was under Egyptian and Transjordanian control when the UN-sponsored cease-fire went into effect on 7 January 1949, ending the First Arab-Israeli War.

### The 1949 armistice lines

Between February and July 1949, armistice agreements were signed by Israel with Egypt, Lebanon, Syria, and Transjordan. Iraq and Saudi Arabia refused to sign an agreement.

The armistice lines were not international borders, but were intended 'to delimit the line beyond which the armed forces of the respective parties shall not move'. The 'line' could only be altered by mutual agreement and each side undertook not to plan, threaten or commit violent attacks against the other or to allow attacks to be launched from its territory.

By the time the First Arab-Israeli War ended and armistice agreements were signed, the British-sponsored, Israeli-Jordanian partition 'plan' had largely been realised, not UN Resolution 181. Conflict was set to continue.

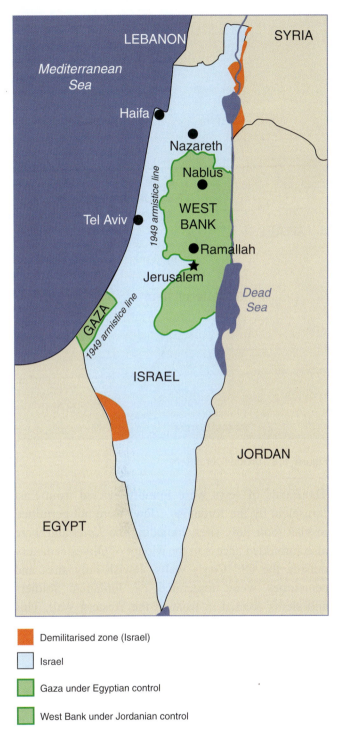

**Figure 6.7** The 1949 armistice lines delineating Israel, the West Bank and Gaza Strip.

Legend:
- Demilitarised zone (Israel)
- Israel
- Gaza under Egyptian control
- West Bank under Jordanian control

# Consequences of the First Arab-Israeli War

Despite the armistice agreements, the Arab states remained in an official state of war with Israel. The Jewish state's very existence in the heartland of the Arab-Muslim world remained a constant source of anger across the entire region. More locally, King Abdullah's annexation of the West Bank and his efforts to thwart the establishment of an independent Palestinian state, fuelled antagonism among pan-Arab and Palestinian nationalists alike.

## Arab nationalism and the 1948 defeat

When war officially began on 15 May, it appeared that one of the objectives of pan-Arab nationalism had been achieved: political unity of the Arab states, affirmed by the invasion of Palestine by five Arab armies. Arab rulers promised to destroy Israel and assist the Palestinians to establish a single state throughout Mandatory Palestine. However, the Arab League's rhetoric of unity did not match the reality of disarray and disunity of its interstate politics. As Adeed Dawisha argues in *Arab Nationalism in the Twentieth Century*, 'the ostensible show of Arab unity hid deep divisions that had little to do with ideological commitment and everything to do with personal ambitions and rivalries', which he summarised as follows:

> King 'Abdullah coveted the incorporation of Palestine into his domain, and preferably the creation of a Hashemite Greater Syria. The Syrians, eyeing 'Abdullah's enormous irredentist appetite 'feared Jordan more than Israel.' The Iraqis had no objection to a Hashemite takeover so long as they became the senior partners; the Egyptians on the other hand were not about to allow the Hashemites to claim the spoils of war; nor would Ibn Sa'ud, whose Saudi Arabia was created only after defeating the Hashemites [in the kingdom of the Hejaz].[7]

The Arab armies' failure to liberate Palestine and the Israeli army's ability to defend its state and even expand its territory, dealt a substantial blow to the pan-Arab nationalist movement. Widespread resentment was felt towards the Arab monarchs, who were seen as a major obstacle to pan-Arab unity. In time, some would be overthrown.

## A Jewish state in the Arab Middle East

At the end of the war, Israel's Arab population numbered about 150 000, and its Jewish population about 600 000, the latter doubling within two years. Many Jews arrived from Europe, primarily survivors of the Holocaust, and from Arab countries. After 1948 more than 700 000 Jews were expelled from Arab countries which had stripped their homes, businesses, jobs and belongings. Most settled in Israel.

The large number of Holocaust survivors gave the new state a strong unity of purpose and determination to survive. The insecurity felt by Israel's majority Jewish population was reinforced by the knowledge that many of their Arab enemies had collaborated with Nazi Germany during World War II. Most Israelis saw parallels between the Nazis' genocidal policies and the Arab governments' genocidal rhetoric concerning Israel. Israel's leaders believed that if they were not perceived to be strong, Israel would fall to Arab aggression, resulting in a 'second Holocaust'. Within Israel's narrative, much of its foreign policy from 1948 until today is explained by this.

## Jerusalem: A divided city

Before the war, neither the Jews nor King Abdullah agreed to the internationalisation of Jerusalem recommended by the UN. On 22 July 1948, Israel and Jordan agreed to establish a no-man's-land on the Jerusalem front. Four days later, Israel announced that it would regard the New City (West Jerusalem) as Israeli territory, and on 11 December 1949, the *Knesset* declared Jerusalem the capital of Israel. The Old City (East Jerusalem) remained under Jordanian control, except for Mount Scopus (the site of the Hebrew University and Hadassah Hospital), which was demilitarised and divided into Israeli and Jordanian sectors.

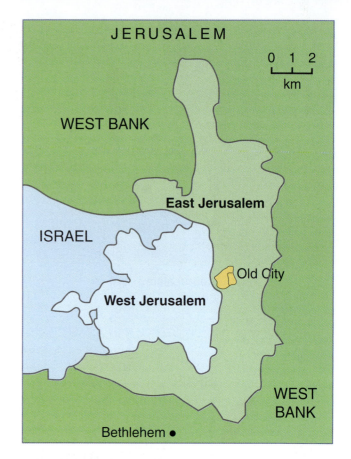

**Figure 6.8** Divided Jerusalem.

Thousands of Jews were forcibly evicted from East Jerusalem by the Jordanians. Jews were not permitted to visit their holy sites, including the *Kotel* and were also forbidden access to the Mount of Olives cemetery outside the Old City's walls. Jewish holy sites and cemeteries were desecrated by Jordanian soldiers and slums erected in front of the Western Wall. This situation prevailed until the 1967 Arab-Israeli War.

## No State of Palestine

The January 1949 cease-fire saw over 700 000 Palestinians become refugees (60 per cent of the population) and ten major Palestinian towns and 418 villages fall into Israel's hands. No independent Palestinian state emerged from the ashes of war. The Egyptians held the Gaza Strip, and kept it under military occupation while the Jordanians occupied and annexed the West Bank. In 1950, King Abdullah held elections for the Jordanian Parliament, allowing candidates from both sides of the Jordan River to stand for office.

At the heart of much of the literature on the Palestinians' failure to establish their state in 1948 (as intended by the UN) is what might be described as 'a blame game': each side blaming the other for *al-Nakba*, 'the Catastrophe'. The traditional Zionist version places responsibility on the Arab side, while traditional Arab accounts lay the blame for the war and the Palestinians' subsequent plight at the door of the Jews and the British.

As with most significant events in history, 'black and white' explanations ignore the complexity of all the factors. This is argued by Arab revisionist historians who base their research on British and Israeli government, and Palestinian media archives. For Issa Khalaf and Rashid Khalidi, blame for *al-Nakba* does not rest solely with the *Yishuv* and Britain. In *Politics in Palestine: Arab Factionalism and Social Disintegration 1939-1948*, Khalaf argues that if 'there is one characteristic feature of Palestinian politics and society during the mandate, it is the pervasiveness of factionalism [which] continued to hold sway until 1948. This factionalism is a manifestation of traditional, largely agrarian societies dominated by vertical cleavages, identities and divisions. In Palestinian society, the central cleavages were based on family, kinship, and clan.' This 'led to the undoing of Palestinian society in 1947-48', and must be considered in the analysis of 'what went wrong' in 1948.[8]

Amal Jamal also argues in *The Palestinian Nationalist Movement*, that 'the inability of the Palestinian nationalist movement to achieve its goals' in the pre-1948 period, can be attributed to 'the divisions among the various political elites that formed during years of the British mandate in Palestine. Many scholars of Palestinian nationalism point out that the competition between supporters of Haj Amin al-Husayni and Raghib al-Nashashibi paralysed the national movement and prevented coordinated mobilisation against the Zionist movement in the 1920s and 1930s.'[9]

In his article, 'The Palestinians and 1948: The Underlying Causes of Failure', Rashid Khalidi locates the root causes of *al-Nakba* in the Mandate period, some time before the outbreak of war in May 1948:

'Between early spring and late fall of 1948, Arab Palestine was radically transformed. At the beginning of that year, Arabs constituted over two-thirds of the population of the country, and were a majority in 15 of the country's 16 subdistricts. Beyond this, Arabs owned nearly 90 per cent of Palestine's privately owned land. In a few months of heavy fighting in the early spring of 1948, the military forces of a well-organised Jewish population of just over 600 000 people routed those of an Arab majority more than twice its size. ... At the end of the fighting, Jordan took over the areas of Palestine controlled by its army west of the Jordan River, while the Egyptian Army administered the strip it retained around Gaza, adjacent to its borders. In the wake of this catastrophe ... the Palestinians found themselves living under a variety of alien regimes, were dispossessed of the vast bulk of their property, and had lost control over most aspects of their lives.

How and why did this momentous transformation happen? Most conventional accounts of the 1948 War tend to focus on events after 15 May 1948, the date when the State of Israel was founded, and the [Arab] armies intervened unsuccessfully in Palestine in the wake of the stunning collapse of the Palestinians. In fact, however, the decisive blows to the cohesion of Palestinian society were struck even before 15 May, during the early spring of 1948. Furthermore, ... the underlying causes of this collapse, and of the larger Palestinian political failure, lay even further in the past, and were related to the constraints on and the structural weaknesses of Palestinian political institutions, factionalism among the notable stratum which dominated Palestinian society and politics, and grave shortcomings in leadership.[10]

When the new Parliament convened, Abdullah was declared ruler on both sides of the river. The name Palestine was abandoned and the territories west of the Jordan were named the 'West Bank of the Jordanian Hashemite Kingdom'.

Abdullah ignored the Arab League's pressure to abandon his annexation of the West Bank. Later, the League adopted an Iraqi-Lebanese proposal that Jordan be considered the 'trustee of Palestine' and this prevailed until the 1967 War when Israel captured and occupied the West Bank and Gaza Strip.

For the Palestinians, *al-Nakba* marked the birth of the Palestinian refugee problem.

# The Palestinian refugees

By the end of the war, only 150 000 of approximately 850 000 Palestinian inhabitants remained in the areas incorporated into Israel. The rest had either fled or were forced out by Israelis during the course of the fighting. Most became refugees in neighbouring countries: Jordan and the West Bank (38%); Egypt and the Gaza Strip (26%), Lebanon (14%) and Syria (10%). This constituted the core of the Palestinian *ghurba* (diaspora). Israel refused to allow their return, to offer reparations for their belongings, or to accept any responsibility for their plight. Some, together with their children, grandchildren and great-grandchildren, continue to live in refugee camps today.

## The historical debate

The cause of the Palestinians' flight is subject to controversy and debate, not only between Israelis and Palestinians, but also between so-called traditional and revisionist historians on each side. The debate centres around the question of ultimate responsibility. The Arab position has been that Ben-Gurion instructed the IDF to follow 'Plan D' and drive the Arabs out of their towns and villages to reduce the number of Arabs who would remain in Israel after the war. The Israeli position (until relatively recently) has been that the Palestinians were not forced to leave their homes but did so at their leaders' urging.

The traditional accounts of both sides have been undermined by revisionist Israeli historians using extensive Israeli archival research. They have concluded there was no single cause for the Palestinian flight. Unprovoked attacks on some Arab villages by Jewish forces (for example Deir Yassin) were among the reasons. In other cases, the Palestinians left at the urging of their leaders, who promised they would return and share the spoils after the Jews had been defeated. But most fled to avoid being caught up in the fighting.

In his works, *The Birth of the Palestinian Refugee Problem 1947-1949* and *The Birth of the Palestinian Refugee Problem Revisited*, the Israeli historian Benny Morris argues that both Israelis and Palestinians are responsible for the refugee problem: 'For what [the primary source] documents reveal is that there were both far more expulsions and atrocities by Israeli troops [than previously believed] and, at the same time, far more orders and advice to various communities by Arab officials and officers to quit their villages or to at least send away their women, old folk and children, substantially fuelling the exodus'. Morris emphasises that this occurred in the context of war:

> In general, it cannot be stressed too strongly… that the [events of] the Palestinian exodus occurred in wartime and were a product, direct and indirect, of that war, a war that the Palestinians started. The threat of battle and the battle itself were the immediate backdrop to the various components of the exodus.[11]

The argument that the Palestinians' motive for fleeing was so that they would not be caught up in the fighting is supported by the writings of Khalil al-Sakakini, a prominent Palestinian nationalist, who lived in the Katamon district of Jerusalem which saw fierce fighting between the Arab and Israeli forces.

Al-Sakakini's April 1948 diary vividly describes the events that led him to leave the city:

> The battle over Katamon grew ever more fierce. 'The whistle of the bullets and the thunder of the shells do not stop day or night; we heard nothing like this in the past world wars.' … Every time he entered his home he expected it to explode, and on the streets he stayed close to the walls, afraid that a stray bullet might find him. … 'In this situation it is no wonder the residents are thinking of moving to another area or another city,' Sakakini wrote, listing the names of neighbours who had already gone. On April 7 Sakakini found a bullet on his balcony. It had hit the right doorjamb, leaving a faint mark, he noted, adding that had anyone been sitting on the balcony at the time, he would have been killed. …
>
> On April 13, Sakakini felt like he was on the battlefield. 'Night comes and we cannot close our eyes. We say that if we live to see the day, we will leave this neighbourhood, Katamon, for another, or leave this country completely.' A week later he and his two daughters left, taking only their clothes. They thought they would be coming back.[12]

Another reason for the Palestinian exodus was their unwillingness to live as citizens in Israel and be considered 'traitors' by other Arabs.

Whatever the rights and wrongs of all involved, the uprooting of more than 700 000 Palestinian refugees during the 1947-1948 War, constituted what Yezid Sayigh has described as 'a collective trauma of immense, devastating proportions'.

## UN General Assembly Resolution 194

On 11 December 1948, the UN General Assembly passed Resolution 194. Article 11 has become the basis of the Palestinians' claim of a 'right of return' to their former homes in Israel:

> Article 11. The refugees wishing to return to their homes and live at peace with their neighbours should be permitted to do so at the earliest practicable date, and compensation should be paid for the property of those choosing not to return and for loss of or damage to property which, under principles of international law or in equity, should be made good by the governments or authorities responsible.

However, the resolution's main purpose was to establish the Palestine Conciliation Commission to:

> … facilitate the repatriation, resettlement and economic and social rehabilitation of the refugees and the payment of compensation, and to maintain close relations with the Director of the United Nations Relief for Palestine Refugees and, through him, with the appropriate organs and agencies of the United Nations.

Israel voted against Resolution 194. So did every Arab state, because the 'right of return' was conditional on returnees' preparedness to 'live at peace' with their Israeli neighbour. Except for a small number of refugees who were reunited with families that had remained in Israel, the rest did not return. Nor were they compensated. With the exception of Jordan, which gave the refugees citizenship, the Arab host countries refused to absorb the refugees, insisting they remain in camps to 'keep the refugee issue alive'. Some refugees did not want to be resettled in neighbouring countries as they believed this would prevent them from returning home. This has remained the situation ever since.

## Refugees and politics

The refugees of the 1947-1949 and 1967 wars constitute a humanitarian tragedy of monumental proportions, which remains unresolved because it is intimately linked to the politics of the Arab-Israeli conflict, and the solution relies on resolution of the wider conflict. This is evident in the positions taken by each side towards the refugee problem.

**The Arab view**

- The Arabs claim that Israel was fully responsible for a policy of 'ethnic cleansing' which drove the Palestinians out of their towns and villages, committing many atrocities in the process.

- The Arab states and the Palestinian leadership demand unlimited, unconditional 'right of return' for the refugees to their former homes in Israel, consistent with their interpretation of Resolution 194.

**Figure 6.9** Palestinian refugee camp: Nahr el-Bared, Lebanon, 1955.

From 1949, the basic needs of Palestinian refugees have been provided by the UN Relief and Works Agency for Palestine (UNRWA). Some 800 000 refugees were registered with UNRWA in 1949. Today the number is over 3 million as, uniquely, their descendants are also deemed to be refugees.

With the exception of Jordan, the Arab states have prohibited assimilation of the Palestinian refugees, leaving them and their descendants in their original camps. This ambivalence towards the Palestinian refugees added to their sense of alienation and humiliation at being a stateless people.

The Palestinian academic Edward Said summarised the predicament of the refugees living in Arab states for over 50 years in *The War for Palestine*:

It is still the case, … that the 40 000 to 50 000 Palestinian refugees resident in Egypt must report to a local police station every month; vocational, educational, and social opportunities for them are curtailed, and the general sense of not belonging adheres to them despite their Arab nationality and language.

In Lebanon the situation is dire still. Almost 400 000 Palestinian refugees have had to endure not only the massacres of Sabra, Shatila, Tel el Zaatar, Dbaye, and elsewhere, but have remained confined in hideous quarantine for almost two generations. They have no

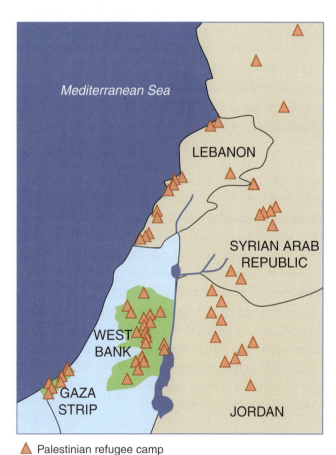

▲ Palestinian refugee camp

**Figure 6.10** Palestinian refugee camps.

legal right to work in at least 60 occupations, they are not adequately covered by medical insurance, they cannot travel and return, and they are objects of suspicion and dislike. In part … they have inherited the mantle of opprobrium draped around them by the PLO's presence (and since 1982 its unlamented absence) there, and thus they remain in the eyes of many ordinary Lebanese a sort of house enemy to be warded off and/or punished from time to time.

A similar situation in kind, if not in degree, exists in Syria.

As for Jordan, though it was (to its credit) the only country where Palestinians were given naturalised status, a visible fault line exists between the disadvantaged majority of that very large community and the Jordanian establishment …

It is also worth asking why it is that a destiny of confinement and isolation has been imposed on a people who quite naturally flocked to neighbouring countries when driven out of theirs, countries which everyone thought would welcome and sustain them. More or less the opposite took place: no welcome was given them (except Jordan) – another unpleasant consequence of the original dispossession of 1948.[13]

**The Israeli view**

- Israel denies a 'right of return' for Palestinians, arguing that the refugee problem resulted from an illegally declared and instigated war by the Arabs, who should therefore take responsibility for Palestinians in their countries.
- Israel also argues that the war effected a 'population transfer' similar to those that have occurred after other ethnically-based conflicts. After 1948, hundreds of thousands of Jews were forced out of Arab countries and came to Israel where they were absorbed. Israel maintains that the Arab states should do the same for the Palestinians.

- Finally, Israel argues that only those Palestinians who fled in 1948 are genuine refugees. Those who were born later in other countries are properly nationals of those countries. One cannot be a 'refugee' from a country in which one has never even lived.

A further obstacle to the return of Palestinians to their former homes in Israel is that most of their homes no longer exist, having been replaced by office blocks, shopping malls and apartments. Many Arab villages were demolished and replaced by new Israeli towns and cities.

# The Jewish refugees

Persecution of Jews in Arab countries began soon after UN Resolution 181 of November 1947. In Iraq, Jewish shops, homes and synagogues were burned and looted; hundreds of Jews were murdered, thousands were imprisoned, or their movement restricted, and many were deprived of citizenship. In 1948, Iraq passed a law making support for Zionism punishable by death, and in 1949, declared it would 'force an exchange of population under UN supervision and the transfer of 100 000 Jews beyond Iraq in exchange for the Arab refugees who had already left the territory in Israeli hands.' Laws passed in 1950 and 1951 deprived Jews of Iraqi nationality and ownership of property without compensation. The synagogue where Jews were required to register for expulsion was bombed by an Iraqi army officer in January 1951, killing all present.

With the start of the First Arab-Israeli War, more Jews were forced out of Arab countries: 250 000 from Morocco and a further 130 000 from Iraq. Jews from Yemen were evacuated to Israel between 1948 and 1951, as was almost the entire community of Libya. Altogether, from 1948 to the mid 1970s, 856 000 Jews left Algeria, Egypt, Iraq, Lebanon, Libya, Morocco, Syria, Tunisia and Yemen. Some 600 000 went to Israel, while another 200 000 emigrated to France, England, the Americas and Australia. Today, only about 5000 Jews remain in Arab lands, most in Morocco.

As the decades have passed, Israel has consistently argued that resolution of the Palestinian refugee problem, including compensation, must also involve compensation for Jewish refugees from Arab states as part of any comprehensive peace.

# Summary

A civil war erupted in Palestine following the UN vote on partition. It escalated into full-scale war on 15 May 1948, when the Mandate had ended and Israel's independence had been declared. The conflicting Arab and Israeli narratives – each subsequently challenged by revisionist historians – are most evident in their accounts of the events of this war. The differences begin with the very names given to it. For Israelis, 'the War of Independence' represents the fulfilment of their nationalist aspirations in roughly 78 per cent of the area of Mandatory Palestine. For Palestinians, 'the Catastrophe' represents destruction of their community, now without a land and with some 60 per cent of their people living as refugees.

In the words of Palestinian historian Yezid Sayigh, the '1947-1948 war marked the end of a lengthy chapter in the conflict between Arab and Jew for possession of Palestine.' The subsequent armistice agreements simply marked the beginning of a new chapter in a new region-wide conflict. When asked by an Israeli delegate at the Egyptian-Israeli armistice talks why peace could not be made then and there, Mahmoud Riad, later Egypt's Foreign Minister and Secretary-General of the Arab League replied:

No, we cannot accept you. An armistice, that is one thing, but to make peace with you would mean that we have to accept that you are here to stay. We are not ready. The [political] situation in our country and in the Arab world will not permit it. We cannot yet live in peace with you.

The destiny of the Palestinian refugees lay with the Arab states. Palestinian nationalism only developed into an influential force in the 1960s, as will be examined from Chapter 9 onwards. In the following three decades, full-scale war erupted between Israel and its Arab neighbours in 1956, 1967 and 1973. The 1956 and 1967 wars are examined in the following chapter.

# Review and research questions

1.  Compare and contrast the Arab and Jewish responses to UN Resolution 181 in the period leading up to termination of the Palestine Mandate. How would you account for these responses? Were alternative responses available? Refer to the above extracts from Israel's Declaration of Independence on 14 May, and the Arab League's declaration on 15 May.

2.  Assess the economic, political, religious, social and technological features of the Arab and Jewish communities in Palestine in the lead-up to and during the First Arab-Israeli War. To what extent did they contribute to the outcomes of the war?

3.  What were the causes of the Palestinian exodus during the 1947-1949 War?

4.  Many accounts depict the First Arab-Israeli War as a two-cornered contest: Arabs versus Israelis. Would you agree or disagree with this version of events? Why?

5.  What were the outcomes and consequences of *Milchemet Ha'Atzma'ut* ('The War of Independence') for the Israelis?

6.  What were the outcomes and consequences *al-Nakba* ('The Catastrophe') for the Palestinians?

7.  Research the personal background of David Ben-Gurion, and the times in which he lived. What were the values and attitudes that influenced his actions in relation to Zionism? What were the major events that impacted upon the creation of the State of Israel and its conflict with the Arabs while he was a Zionist leader and then Prime Minister? Assess his contribution to this history.

8.  What effect have the works of Arab and Israeli revisionist historians had on the study of the Arab-Israeli conflict, in particular, the First Arab-Israeli War?

## Discussion questions

1.  Assess the extent to which you think the 1947-1949 War may be identified as the origin of the Arab-Israeli conflict.

2.  Israelis call the 1947-1949 War *Milchemet Ha'Atzma'ut* ('The War of Independence') while the Palestinians call it *al-Nakba*, ('The Catastrophe'). Why were these names chosen? What do they convey about the perceptions held by the two peoples?

Egypt's President Gamal Abdel Nasser was a key player in Middle East politics from the mid 1950s until his death in 1970. His political ideology, which combined revolutionary, pan-Arab nationalism with socialism, was known as the 'Nasserite Movement', or 'Nasserism'. Its aims included secularising and modernising the Arab world, ridding the region of European influence and any other non-Arab presence or entity including Israel. The movement also identified conservative Arab monarchs as 'puppets of the West' and called for their overthrow.

Nasserites called for a pan-Arab revolution, declaring Arab natonalism the 'primary ideological and emotional identification of every Arab' even taking precedence over state sovereignty. Any Arab state thus prepared to serve the Arab nation had 'not only the right, but the duty, to intrude into the affairs of other countries that were not conducting themselves in accordance with Arab nationalist principles.' Throughout the 1950s and 1960s, Nasserism competed with other versions of pan-Arabism such as Ba'athism in Syria and Iraq.

Nasser became President of Egypt in 1954, two years after the Egyptian monarchy was overthrown by a group of army officers called the 'Free Officers'. As a pan-Arabist, Nasser rejected all non-Arab influences in Egypt and the wider Middle East. He sought the expulsion of British and French military personnel from the region and continually called for Israel's destruction. He promoted Egypt as the power that would free Palestine, 'liquidate the Zionist existence there', and 'push the Jews into the sea'.

## The Arab economic, aviation and maritime boycott of Israel

Arab governments acted on their anti-Zionist rhetoric through boycotts of Israel. As early as December 1945, an economic boycott of *Yishuv* products was set in place by the Arab League: 'Jewish products and manufactured goods shall be considered undesirable to the Arab countries. [All Arab] institutions, organisations, merchants, commission agents and individuals [are] to refuse to deal in, distribute, or consume Jewish products

or manufactured goods.' After 1948, the boycott developed at three levels:

- The **primary boycott** prohibited Arab states from direct trade with Israel.
- The **secondary boycott** was directed against companies anywhere in the world that did business with Israel.
- The **tertiary boycott** blacklisted firms trading with companies that did business with Israel.

An aviation boycott prohibited civilian aircraft which flew to or from Israel from flying over or landing in an Arab state. Egypt also initiated a maritime boycott by prohibiting ships carrying cargo to or from Israel from using the Suez Canal. Despite UN Security Council Resolution 95 (1 September 1951) condemning the Egyptian blockade, it remained in place.

## Israel's response: Military power versus diplomacy

Egypt's maritime blockade hindered Israel's trade and economic growth. Within the Israeli government, the so-called 'hardliners' (led by Prime Minister Ben-Gurion and supported by Chief of Staff Moshe Dayan) argued that Israel could only survive, be respected, and make peace with its neighbours by demonstrating the extent of its military power. The so-called 'moderates' (led by Foreign Minister, later Prime Minister Moshe Sharett) argued that Israel's security would only come from peace with the Arabs, achieved through diplomacy and negotiations. Israel pursued both policies in the early years of Nasser's presidency. For a short time, the 'moderates' sponsored secret Egyptian-Israeli negotiations code-named 'Operation Alpha', but these efforts were eventually undermined by the actions of Israel's hardliners in what became known as the 'Lavon Affair'.

## The Lavon Affair

When Britain and Egypt reached an agreement in early 1954 on the withdrawal of British troops from the Suez Canal Zone, Israel viewed this as a threat to its security because it feared that without the 'moderating presence' of British troops, Egypt would attack it. In an effort to

# Gamal Abdel Nasser (1918-1970)

Figure 7.1 Gamal Abdel Nasser (1918-1970).

Gamal Abdel Nasser was born in 1918 in Alexandria, Egypt. After finishing school, he joined the army. He commanded an Egyptian battalion in the 1948 Arab-Israeli War, which was captured and besieged by Israel until the January 1949 armistice. In 1951, he was promoted to Colonel and became a lecturer at the Egyptian military academy.

During his army years, Nasser became a leading member of a secret revolutionary group called the 'Free Officers' who conspired to depose King Farouk and oust the British from Egypt. On 22 July 1952, their successful coup established a new one-party government. Nasser became President in October 1954. In that year the Islamist group *al-Ikhwan al-Muslimoon* (the Muslim Brotherhood) failed in an attempt to assassinate him, resulting in Nasser outlawing the group.

Once in power, Nasser began a program of agrarian reforms, the nationalisation of banks and major businesses, and the building of a dam at Aswan to supply Egypt with water for irrigation and electricity. In 1956, Nasser nationalised the Suez Canal Company (owned mainly by Britain and France) to pay for the construction of the dam. The 1956 Suez War followed, resulting in enhanced prestige for Nasser.

Nasser sought to establish Egyptian hegemony in the Arab world, believing that Egypt, under his leadership, would unite the Arabs and free them from Western imperialism. In 1958 he appeared to have succeeded when Egypt and Syria formed the United Arab Republic (UAR) with Nasser as President. However, the union dissolved in 1961 amid much acrimony between the two states as they vied for leadership of the Arab world with competing versions of pan-Arab socialism. At times Nasser used force to pursue his pan-Arab aspirations, as was the case with Egypt's military intervention in Yemen in 1962.

Even after Egypt's disastrous defeat by Israel in the 1967 War, Nasser remained popular, continuing as President until his death from a heart attack on 28 September 1970.

reverse Britain's decision, Israel's military intelligence initiated 'Operation Suzannah'. Its aim was to carry out terrorist bombings in Egypt to create an atmosphere in which Britain would decide to maintain troops there to protect its citizens. The operation was planned and executed without the knowledge of Moshe Sharett, the new Prime Minister.

Egyptian Jews were recruited to carry out the attacks in places frequented by Westerners. A post office in Alexandria was firebombed on 2 July, and on 14 July, the US Information Agency libraries in Alexandria and Cairo and a British-owned theatre were bombed. When the plans backfired, Jewish suspects were arrested and put on trial. Two were hanged in public and others imprisoned.

The Israeli Government claimed no prior knowledge of the plan and Sharett ordered an enquiry into the events, which became known as the 'Lavon Affair', (named after the Defence Minister Pinhas Lavon). But when Israel took no action against the Egyptian Government, whose actions had outraged the Israeli public, Sharett was depicted as a weak leader and the public called on Ben-Gurion to return to power. He did so in January 1955, also replacing Lavon as Defence Minister.

Whilst the Lavon Affair had a destabilising effect on Israeli politics for some years, it also resulted in heightened tensions with Egypt.

## Border raids, counter-raids

Throughout the early 1950s, raids and counter-raids across the Gaza-Israel and West Bank-Israel borders were common. In both Gaza and the West Bank, Palestinian *fedayeen* (guerillas) set up training bases in the refugee camps, from which they launched terrorist raids into Israel. Israel retaliated, or at times acted pre-emptively, hoping to deter Arab states from sponsoring the raids.

In 1951, the IDF set up a 'special force', Unit 101, to carry out retaliatory raids against Palestinians and neighbouring Arab states in an effort to bolster Israeli morale and to deter further *fedayeen* attacks. In October 1953, following a brutal murder of an Israeli woman and child by *fedayeen*, Unit 101, led by Ariel Sharon, carried out a reprisal raid against the West Bank village of Qibya. More than 60 Palestinians died, many of them women and children. The raid was widely criticised inside and outside Israel.

By 1956, more than 400 *fedayeen* raids had caused the deaths or wounding of over a thousand Israeli civilians. Counter-raids resulted in equally high Arab casualties. In February 1955, the IDF attacked Egypt's military headquarters in Gaza resulting in the deaths of 38 Egyptians and Palestinians.

# Underlying dynamics of the conflict 1949-1956: The international context

## The Cold War — Superpower rivalry in the Middle East

The Middle East became an important arena in Cold War politics from the late 1940s onwards. The location of various air and naval facilities in and around the Mediterranean, the Red Sea, and the Indian Ocean, and the region's wealth of key natural resources, particularly oil, heightened its strategic importance.

The two Cold War superpowers, America and the Soviet Union, sought to expand their influence by adopting 'client' states in the region. Arab states that were more revolutionary in their domestic and foreign policies aligned themselves with the Soviet Union. These included Syria, Iraq after 1958, and Egypt, although Nasser publicly maintained an image of 'non-alignment' (neutrality toward America and the USSR). The Soviets exerted influence over their client states through arms supplies, military training and economic aid. By the late 1960s, Egypt and Syria hosted the largest Soviet military presence outside the communist bloc. The more conservative Arab states were aligned with America. These included Jordan, Iraq until 1958, Saudi Arabia and other Gulf states. While the latter depended on America for security, America relied on their supplies of 'cheap oil'.

After a very brief period of Soviet support for Israel between 1948 and 1951, Stalin condemned Zionism and prohibited Jews from leaving the Soviet Union. He murdered or imprisoned Jewish public figures, and made the study of Hebrew illegal. America kept at 'arms length' from Israel throughout the 1950s and 1960s as part of its policy to build good relations with the Arab states. Prior to 1967, America occasionally urged Israel to cede territory to its Arab neighbours and to allow the return of Palestinian refugees. But after the 1967 War, Israel also became an American client state.

## The Baghdad Pact and the Eisenhower Doctrine

In 1955, the US and Britain sponsored the 'Baghdad Pact', in which Pakistan, Iran and Turkey agreed to form a barrier against the further spread of Soviet influence in the Middle East. In 1957, America announced the Eisenhower Doctrine (named after US President Dwight Eisenhower), offering military and economic assistance 'to any nation or group of nations involved in the battle against communist infiltration or aggression'. America gave military, economic and diplomatic support to any Arab government that appeared anticommunist or that might help safeguard US interests in the Middle East.

The Eisenhower administration rejected Israel's efforts to join the alliance, and NATO did likewise.

# The convergence of regional and international politics

Nasser's pan-Arab nationalism and his call to rid the region of European imperialism aroused support among Arabs but caused concern in Western capitals. Tensions climaxed when Egypt significantly increased its military capability following an arms deal brokered by the Soviet Union.

## The 1955 Egyptian-Czech arms deal

Following Israel's attack on Egypt's Gaza headquarters in February 1955, Nasser asked France, Britain and the US to increase Egypt's military hardware. They turned Nasser down because the three powers had maintained an arms embargo on the region since May 1950 in an effort to prevent an arms race between Israel and the Arabs.

Nasser then turned to the Soviets who were eager to assist him. They facilitated the 'Egyptian-Czech Arms Deal' in September 1955. A large delivery of armaments from Czechoslovakia followed, including jet fighters and bombers, tanks, heavy artillery, warships and submarines.

This dramatic increase in Egypt's military capability was viewed by Israel as a significant shift in the balance of power between the two states. Ben-Gurion, still Israel's Defence Minister, considered taking pre-emptive action before Egypt grew strong enough to make good on Nasser's oft-repeated threat to destroy Israel. He argued that Egypt's blockade of the Straits of Tiran (the entrance to the Gulf of Aqaba) and its sponsorship of Palestinian attacks launched from Gaza justified military action. The opportunity to act came a year later when Nasser nationalised the Suez Canal Company and its largest shareholders, Britain and France, sought Israel's help to topple the Egyptian President.

# The 1956 Suez War

## The Aswan Dam and the nationalisation of the Suez Canal Company

Nasser's program for Egypt's economic development included the construction of a dam above Aswan (near the Sudanese border) to harness the waters of the Nile River to provide much-needed electricity and irrigation. America and Britain had agreed to finance the project, but when Egypt purchased arms from Czechoslovakia in contravention of their arms embargo, and then recognised Communist China, America, Britain and the World Bank cancelled their funding commitment on 19 July 1956.

In response, Nasser nationalised the Suez Canal Company on 23 July. The company owned and ran the Canal, and Nasser intended to use the canal tolls to finance the Aswan construction. Britain and France, the main shareholders of the company, were outraged and after international diplomacy failed, they conspired to resolve the dispute by force, in clear violation of international law.

## British, French and Israeli plans: The 'Sèvres Protocol'

Between 22 and 24 October 1956, representatives of Britain, France and Israel met for a series of secret meetings in Sèvres (near Paris), France, in order to plan a military response to Nasser. It was decided that Israeli forces would invade the Sinai Peninsula on the evening of 29 October and head for the Canal Zone. Britain and France would announce an ultimatum to the combatants on the following day, demanding a withdrawal of Israeli and Egyptian troops from the Canal Zone, and Egypt's agreement to permit a 'temporary' stationing of British and French troops in 'key positions' along the Canal. Anticipating Egyptian refusal, British and French forces would occupy the Canal Zone on 31 October. The plan was recorded in the 'Sèvres Protocol', signed on 24 October 1956.

## The birth of Israel's nuclear program

At the final tripartite meeting, Israel's Shimon Peres, under instructions from Ben-Gurion, obtained a commitment from France, with British acquiescence, to assist in developing a nuclear facility at Dimona in southern Israel. In an interview for the Israeli documentary, *The Bomb in the Basement: Israel's Nuclear Option*, Peres recalled the 1956 discussions: 'Of the four countries which at that time had a nuclear capacity – the United States, the Soviet Union, Great Britain and France – only France was willing to help us.' When asked whether Israel requested a nuclear reactor from the French delegate, Peres replied: 'I asked for more than that. I asked for other things, too; the uranium and those things. I went up to Ben-Gurion and said, 'It's settled.' That's how it was.'

For decades Israel has maintained a policy of 'nuclear opacity', never stating publicly whether it has or does not have a nuclear weapons capability. Israel is not party to the Nuclear Non-Proliferation Treaty (NPT). However, it is widely believed that Israel does have nuclear weapons as an ultimate security guarantee against the threat frequently and openly made by the Arab states, and by Iran after 1979, to 'wipe Israel off the map'.

## The invasion of the Suez Canal Zone

The early stages of the war went according to the Sèvres plan. Israel launched its invasion on 29 October, and within six days its troops had occupied the Gaza Strip and had moved across the Sinai to within 70 kilometres of the Suez Canal. In so doing, they had ejected the Egyptians from the Gulf of Aqaba, occupied Sharm el-Sheikh and thus broken the Egyptian naval blockade at the Straits of Tiran, while taking about 6000 Egyptian troops prisoner. With Israeli forces on the east side of the Suez Canal, British and French troops landed at Port Said and demanded a military withdrawal by Egypt and Israel from both sides of the Canal. When Egypt refused, British and French troops moved to occupy the Canal Zone.

However, events in Europe had altered the context of international affairs in a way that Britain and France had not anticipated. Soviet intelligence almost certainly knew the details of the Sèvres Protocol from the outset and made use of this information to implement its own imperialist plan. While the world's attention was focused on the Suez crisis, Soviet troops began invading Hungary on 31 October in an effort to suppress an anticommunist uprising. America was caught completely by surprise by the dual invasions. When the Soviets pointedly declared that the USSR possessed missiles that could reach the capitals of Britain and France, a none too subtle threat to use nuclear weapons against them, Eisenhower pressured Britain, France and Israel to withdraw from the Suez.

# Results of the 1956 Suez War

The Suez War was a disaster for Britain. Its reputation in the Middle East was damaged, leading to the final eclipse of British power in the region in favour of the competing influences of America and the Soviets. While Soviet support increased for Egypt, Syria, and Iraq after 1958, America increased its support for conservative Arab states including Jordan and Saudi Arabia.

For Israel, the 1956 Suez War was very successful. It achieved a significant victory with relatively few casualties; the Gulf of Aqaba was reopened to Israeli shipping; and its border with Egypt was secured with the UNEF stationed in the Sinai. Further, Israel's prospects for long-term survival were enhanced by its acquisition of nuclear technology.

The 1956 Suez War was also a success for Nasser. Despite Egypt's military defeat, his defiance of Britain and France enhanced his reputation as a defender of pan-Arab nationalism. But as Nasser's prestige grew among the general population, so, too, did his conflict with other Arab leaders.

## The Arab Cold War and the conflict with Israel

The late 1950s and 1960s have been described by some as the period of the 'Arab Cold War', reflecting the intensity of inter-Arab tensions and rivalries as conservative and revolutionary regimes competed for local hegemony. In their efforts to embarrass and belittle each other, Arab leaders used anti-Zionist rhetoric to prove their own leadership credentials.

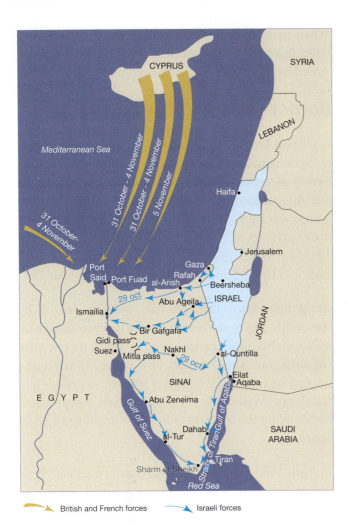

**Figure 7.2**    Israeli, British and French Invasion of Egypt, October 1956.

Britain and France acquiesced and withdrew their forces on 6 November. Israel refused to withdraw unconditionally, determined to achieve peace on its Egyptian border and safeguards for its shipping in the Gulf of Aqaba. The UN accommodated these demands by stationing a United Nations Emergency Force (UNEF) in the Gaza Strip to monitor the border and prevent *fedayeen* raids into Israel, and at Sharm el-Sheikh to prevent any attempt by Egypt to reimpose its maritime blockade. Israel withdrew its forces from Gaza and Sinai in March 1957.

Malcolm Kerr describes the impact that the mix of anti-Israel rhetoric and inter-Arab state rivalries had on the politics of the region:

> It was not hard to imagine, early in May 1967, that the mounting tension in the Arab world would lead to some sort of violent outbreak. The conflict to which all signs seemed to point, however, was between Arab revolutionaries and conservatives. The old quarrel with Israel seemed irrelevant: the Arabs were preoccupied not with her but with one another. Even when the Israelis first appeared on the scene in the weeks before the June war, they were merely there as a football for the Arabs, kicked into the field by the discontented Syrians, then back again by Nasser. But of course the Israelis took a rather different view of themselves. It became the case of the football kicking the players.[1]

The causes of the Third Arab-Israeli War of June 1967 thus lie as much in Arab nationalist rivalries as in direct Arab-Israeli hostilities.

# The 1967 War

By the early 1960s, friction between the Arab States and Israel was exacerbated by a continuing arms race, Palestinian *fedayeen* raids into Israel from Jordan and Syria and Israeli counter-raids, and disputes over the water supply to Israel's Lake Kinneret (Sea of Galilee).

## Water disputes and the formation of the United Arab Command

In early 1963, Israel announced that it would build a National Water Carrier, a pipeline to carry water from the Jordan River to other parts of Israel. The Arabs accused Israel of planning to take more than its allocated share of water. At its 1964 Cairo summit, the Arab League voted to divert the river's headwaters in Syria and Lebanon, depriving Israel of two-thirds of its water supply. Anticipating Israeli resistance to the diversion plan, the League established a joint military force, the United Arab Command (UAC). The UAC consisted of Egyptian, Jordanian, Lebanese and Syrian forces, headed by Lieutenant General Ali Amer of Egypt.

When Syria commenced work on the diversion plan, Israel launched air and artillery attacks, resulting in the Arab League abandoning its plan.

## Border raids and counter-raids

In the mid 1960s, Palestinian *fedayeen* groups sponsored by Syria increased their attacks against Israeli civilians. Syria's intention was that the raids would bolster its pan-Arab leadership credentials. One of the *fedayeen* groups was Fatah, founded by Yasser Arafat in 1958, and dedicated to revolution and the destruction of Israel. From 1965, the Syrian government assisted Fatah to carry out raids into Israel from bases in Lebanon and Jordan.

Amid heightened Israeli-Syrian tensions caused by these raids, Egypt and Syria signed a defence agreement in November 1966, under which an attack on one state would be considered an attack on the other. Thus if Syria, through its support for *fedayeen* terrorist incursions into Israel, provoked an Israeli counterattack, Egypt would be bound by the treaty to commence hostilities against Israel.

In April 1967, border conflict between Israel and Syria did indeed intensify. To counter Syrian-sponsored *fedayeen* raids, Israel cultivated land in the demilitarised zone between the two states. The Syrians responded by firing artillery rounds from positions on the Golan Heights on to farms and villages within Israel. The Israelis in turn attacked the Syrian artillery installations. When Syria's air force challenged Israeli fighter planes, six Syrian planes were shot down.

Humiliated by their defeat, the Syrians condemned Nasser for failing to honour the terms of the Egyptian-Syrian treaty, and challenged his leadership of the pan-Arab movement. The Saudis and Jordanians also criticised Nasser for being 'soft' on Israel.

## Rapid escalation of tensions: The events of May and early June

Undeterred by Israel's actions, Syria continued to sponsor what became daily Palestinian raids and attacks on Israeli citizens. On 11 May, Israel's Prime Minister Levi Eshkol warned that if Syria continued its border provocations, Israel 'may have to respond on a much larger scale than on 7 April.' In Arab capitals, this announcement was interpreted as a warning of a major Israeli campaign against Syria.

Tensions were further heightened on 13 May when the Soviets falsely informed Egypt that Israel had massed 10 to 13 brigades – a minimum of 30 000 troops and 2000 vehicles – on its Syrian border in preparation for an attack. Representatives of the United Nations Truce Supervision Organisation (UNTSO), who visited the Israeli-Syrian border, confirmed that the Soviet 'information' was false.

Nasser was also told directly from other sources, including Syria, that the Soviet reports of an Israeli troop build-up were false. At Nasser's request, Egyptian General Muhammad Fawzi visited Damascus and was shown Syrian aerial photographs of the border area taken on 12 and 13 May showing no Israeli troop presence. Fawzi then flew over the border and reported to Nasser on 14 May that 'there is nothing there'. His report was corroborated by Egypt's Chief of Military Intelligence, Lieutenant General Muhammad Ahmad Sadiq, who told Nasser 'there are no [Israeli] force concentrations'.

There has been much speculation as to why the Soviets fed Egypt with false reports of an Israeli troop build-up. One theory is that the Soviets were genuinely concerned about another possible Israeli attack on their client state, Syria. By precipitating a crisis, the Soviets hoped to force Egypt to fulfil its obligations under the Egyptian-Syrian Defence Agreement and align itself more closely with the USSR. Another theory is that by 1967, Israel was on the threshold of building its first nuclear weapon. The Soviets, with the tacit support of America and other nuclear powers, may have hoped, again by precipitating a crisis leading to a mobilisation of Egyptian troops in the Sinai, to pressure Israel to abandon its plans for developing a nuclear weapons capability.

Whatever the Soviets' motive, they apparently miscalculated the Egyptian response. Under fire for failing to assist Syria a month earlier, Nasser sought to reinforce his leadership credentials in the Arab world. He announced publicly that the Soviet reports, which he knew to be false, were genuine, and that Egypt was obliged by its 1966 treaty to defend Syria 'in the face of Israeli aggression'.

Significantly, by May 1967, Nasser was convinced that the inflow of Soviet weaponry had allowed Egypt to reach military superiority over Israel. For years Nasser had told his people that when they had the capability to fight Israel and win, Egypt would act. Egypt's military chief, Marshal Abd al-Hakim Amr, had convinced Nasser that the time had come. Nasser thus began a series of belligerent actions against Israel that escalated tensions to the point of war.

**Figure 7.3 A cartoon from the Egyptian newspaper *Ruz al-Yusuf*, published on 5 June 1967.** It depicts the 'Zionist midget' about to be destroyed by the powerful arms of Egypt and Syria.

## Countdown to war

On 14 May 1967, two Egyptian divisions moved into the Sinai Peninsula towards Israel. At first, Israeli intelligence reports assessed the troop build-up as a gesture to enhance Nasser's standing in the Arab world. Israel's military commander, Yitzhak Rabin, later confirmed that he did not believe the initial entry of Egyptian troops into Sinai on 14 May signified an Egyptian intention to attack Israel.

However, the Egyptian build-up in the Sinai escalated rapidly, as did the bellicosity of Nasser's rhetoric against Israel. Altogether, about 100 000 Egyptian troops, organised into five infantry and two armoured divisions, with over 1000 tanks and hundreds of artillery pieces began moving into previously prepared positions in the Sinai Peninsula facing Israel.

On 17 May, Nasser demanded that the UN withdraw its UNEF from Sinai, which had been deployed in the wake of the 1956 Sinai War as a condition of Israel's withdrawal. UNEF had successfully kept the peace along the Egyptian-Israeli border for ten years. To the surprise of many, the UN complied with Nasser's demand, and within two days the UNEF forces withdrew from Sharm el-Sheikh overlooking the Straits of Tiran.

On 22 May, Nasser ordered the Egyptian navy to blockade the Straits, cutting off the Gulf of Aqaba and blockading Eilat, Israel's southern port. This action re-created the circumstances preceding the 1956 War, and constituted an act of aggression under international law. Israel requested international action to reopen the Straits. Failing this, Israel maintained, it had the right under Article 51 of the UN Charter to defend itself by taking military action to break the blockade. No international assistance was forthcoming.

On 23 May, convinced of Israel's political isolation, Nasser declared to his air force officers in the Sinai: 'We are in confrontation with Israel. In contrast to what happened in 1956, when France and Britain were at its side, Israel is not supported by any European power. ...We are face to face with Israel. Henceforward the situation, my gallant soldiers, is in your hands.' The speech was publicly broadcast and listened to in Israel.

On 24 May, Nasser's confidante, Mohamed Heikal, then editor of Egypt's semi-official newspaper *al Ahram*, boasted that Nasser had manoeuvred Israel into a position that made war inevitable. Nasser's belligerency had now taken Egypt past the point of no return along the road to war.

On 26 May, in a speech to the Arab Trade Union Congress, Nasser confirmed that Egypt was ready to fight Israel and explained how he had made this inevitable:

> One day two years ago, I stood up to say that we have no plan [as yet] to liberate Palestine. ... Recently we felt we are strong enough, that if we were to enter a battle with Israel, with God's help, we could triumph. On this basis we decided to take actual steps. ... Once we were fully prepared we could ask UNEF to leave. And this is what actually happened. The same thing happened in regard to Sharm el-Sheikh. ... Taking Sharm el-Sheikh meant confrontation with Israel. Taking such action also meant that we were ready to enter into a general war with Israel. It was not a separate operation. Therefore we had to take this fact into consideration when moving to Sharm el-Sheikh. ... Egypt will, thanks to this war, at long last wipe Israel off the face of the earth. We have waited for this moment for eleven long years.

An Egyptian air attack against Israel, named 'Operation Dawn', was scheduled for 27 May but was called off at the last minute.

By this time, Yitzhak Rabin's earlier view that the Egyptians did not intend war had changed dramatically. Under extreme stress, he suffered a nervous collapse and for 48 hours his duties were performed by Major General Ezer Weizman.

## The Arab Mutual Defence Treaty

Until May 1967, as an expression of the interstate rivalry between Egypt and Jordan, Nasser constantly denounced King Hussein of Jordan as a British puppet, deriding him as 'the Hashemite Harlot' for his pro-Western sympathies. In response, Hussein accused Nasser of megalomania in his ambitions to lead the Arab world. But at the end of May, when war seemed inevitable, Hussein wanted to avoid being accused of not supporting the 'Arab cause' and so suggested an Egyptian-Jordanian Mutual Defence Treaty. Nasser agreed and the treaty was signed in Cairo on 30 May, with Nasser extending a warm public greeting to the

Jordanian monarch. The treaty stipulated that Jordan's forces were to be placed under the command of Egyptian General Abdul Moneim Riad. Iraq also signed the pact, but the Syrians did not, in the light of their existing military pact with Egypt signed a year earlier.

The Arab states now prepared their troops and weaponry. By early June, the forces mobilised against Israel to its south-west, east and north-east included 250 000 troops, over 2000 tanks and approximately 700 aircraft.

## Israel's response

While calling on the international community to pressure Egypt to reverse its blockade of the Straits of Tiran, Israel also called up its reserve (civilian) army. By early June, Israel's economy was grinding to a halt as a large percentage of its working population had been mobilised in preparation for war. When it became clear that the international community was not going to intervene to end the blockade, the War Cabinet decided to use military force, and to strike before the Arab forces were fully mobilised. Moshe Dayan, who had led the IDF to victory against Egypt in 1956, was appointed as Defence Minister.

## The course of the war

Early in the morning of 5 June 1967, as Israel launched air strikes against Egyptian air bases, its ground troops moved west into the Sinai Peninsula and Gaza Strip. Syria, Jordan and Iraq launched air attacks against Israeli cities and Jordanian gunners directed fire at targets on the Israeli side of the Jerusalem border.

By the end of the first day of the war, Israel had destroyed most of the Egyptian and Jordanian air forces and two-thirds of the Syrian air force. After the second day, 416 Arab aircraft had been destroyed, mostly on the ground. Israel had lost 26 planes. Bitter fighting took place between Egyptian and Israeli troops in the Sinai. After the third day of fighting, Egyptian forces were defeated and Israel occupied the entire area up to the Suez Canal.

**Figure 7.4** Egyptian planes destroyed on the runway, 5 June 1967.

There was also fierce fighting between Israeli and Jordanian forces. On the first day of the war, the Jordanian army launched an artillery barrage and small arms fire against Tel Aviv, western Jerusalem and other targets in Israel. By 7 June, Israel's offensive had resulted in the capture of all of East Jerusalem, and most of the West Bank.

**Figure 7.5** Senior Israeli figures enter the Old City of Jerusalem, 7 June 1967: Uzi Narkiss (left), Moshe Dayan (centre), and Yitzhak Rabin (right).

## UN calls for a cease-fire

On 7 June, the UN Security Council called for a cease-fire. Israel and Jordan agreed immediately, while the Egyptians stalled. The Syrians refused to agree and from their well-fortified positions on the Golan Heights, continued shelling Israeli farms and villages in the valley below.

On 9 June, with the Egyptian forces defeated, Israel turned its full attention northward and attacked the Syrian positions. After 20 hours of fighting, the Syrian forces retreated and Israel captured the Golan Heights. On 10 June Syria, too, accepted the cease-fire.

Thus after six days, the fighting was over. Most of the air forces of Egypt, Syria, Jordan, and Iraq had been destroyed, as had most of their tanks and heavy armaments. At least 10000 Arab troops had been killed and thousands more were taken as prisoners of war. Israel had lost approximately 700 soldiers, 26 airplanes and 60 tanks.

By the time a UN-declared cease-fire finally took effect on 11 June, Israel had captured large swathes of Arab territory, including the entire Egyptian Sinai, Syria's Golan Heights, and most significantly, what remained of Arab Palestine: the West Bank, including East Jerusalem, and the Gaza Strip.

# Immediate consequences of the 1967 War

In Israel the war became known as *Milchemet Sheshet ha'Yamim* (the 'Six-Day War'), while Arabs call it *al-Naksah* (the 'Setback'). The Egyptians, Jordanians and Syrians, so bellicose in their prewar rhetoric, were left shocked and humiliated. For the Palestinians hope turned to despair as those living in the West Bank and Gaza now fell under Israeli military rule. The 1967 War thus marks a major turning point in the history of the Arab-Israeli conflict and in the geopolitics of the entire Middle East. Its consequences have defined the parameters of negotiations to resolve the Arab-Israeli conflict ever since.

## Israel annexes East Jerusalem

On 7 June, the third day of the war, Israeli soldiers under the command of Major General Uzi Narkiss captured the Old City of Jerusalem from the Jordanians. This was profoundly significant for Israelis, and for all Jews. The *Kotel* and Temple Mount, the holiest site in Judaism, were again under the control of the Jewish people after nearly 2000 years. Israeli Chief of Staff, Yitzhak Rabin, recalled that the experience of 'restoring the Western Wall to the Jewish people' was one that would remain with him for the rest of his life, knowing 'that never again would I experience quite the same peak of elation'.

**Figure 7.6** ░░░ Territories captured by Israel In June 1967.

On 28 June 1967, Israel formally annexed East Jerusalem, declaring Jerusalem to be the 'undivided capital of Israel'. East Jerusalem's Arab inhabitants, numbering about 67 000 after the war, became citizens of Israel. Israel's annexation of East Jerusalem was not recognised by any other state.

**Figure 7.7** Israeli soldiers looking up at the *Kotel* (Western Wall) following the capture of the Old City on 7 June 1967.

# The Arab League's 'Three No's of Khartoum'

On 19 June, the Israeli government offered to exchange the Sinai Peninsula and the Golan Heights for permanent peace treaties with Egypt and Syria.

At the September 1967 Arab Summit in Khartoum, Sudan, the Arab states rejected the Israeli proposal in a written response known as the 'Three No's of Khartoum':

> The Arab Heads of State have agreed to unite their political efforts at the international and diplomatic level to eliminate the effects of the [Israeli] aggression and to ensure the withdrawal of the aggressive Israeli forces from the Arab lands which have been occupied since the aggression of 5 June. This will be done within the framework of the main principles by which the Arab states abide, namely **no peace with Israel, no recognition of Israel, no negotiations with it**, and insistence on the rights of the Palestinian people in their own country.

This response was tempered when Egypt and Jordan accepted UN Security Council Resolution 242 two months later.

## Israel's 'Allon Plan'

Israel's response to the Arab League's Khartoum declaration was the so-called 'Allon Plan', named after its author, Yigal Allon. The plan established the Labor Party's attitude and policies towards Gaza and the West Bank until the Oslo peace process of 1993.

The Allon Plan sought a compromise between two competing priorities that confronted the Israeli government following the war: how to avoid ruling over the large number of Palestinians in the occupied territories; and how to maintain a buffer zone along the Jordan River valley in the West Bank to protect Israel from an attack from the east. Under the plan, Israel would annex a strip about 13 kilometres wide along the western bank of the Jordan River, and Palestinians living in the remaining territory would be given autonomy.

In the meantime, a 'Military Government' was established within the Ministry of Defence, responsible for health, finance, education, infrastructure, religious affairs, communications, transport and utilities in the Palestinian territories. Existing legal systems in Gaza and the West

Bank were maintained, including very harsh security ordinances left over from the British Mandate.

While Israel came to rule over more than 750 000 Palestinians in 1967, some 300 000 Palestinians moved from the West Bank to Jordan. For many, this was the second uprooting in two decades, having fled their original homes in 1948.

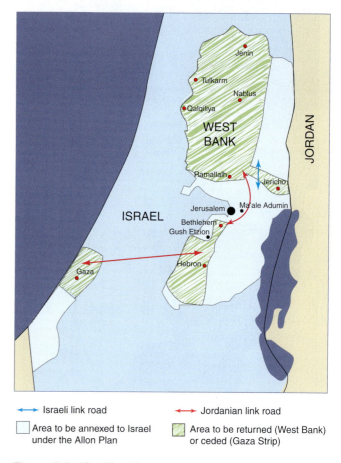

Israeli link road — Jordanian link road

Area to be annexed to Israel under the Allon Plan — Area to be returned (West Bank) or ceded (Gaza Strip)

**Figure 7.8** The Allon Plan.

## The international response: UN Security Council Resolution 242

In contrast to what happened after the 1956 War, Israel did not come under international pressure to withdraw its troops from the areas it occupied as a result of the 1967 War. The Arabs and the Soviets proposed several motions at the UN blaming Israel for the war and requiring it to withdraw from 'all the territories' it had captured. However, each motion was defeated or withdrawn for lack of support.

## UN Security Council Resolution 242, 22 November 1967

The Security Council,

*Expressing* its continuing concern with the grave situation in the Middle East,

*Emphasising* the inadmissibility of the acquisition of territory by war and the need to work for a just and lasting peace in which every State in the area can live in security,

*Emphasising* further that all Member States in their acceptance of the Charter of the United Nations have undertaken a commitment to act in accordance with Article 2 of the Charter,

*Affirms* that the fulfilment of Charter principles requires the establishment of a just and lasting peace in the Middle East which should include the application of both the following principles:

Withdrawal of Israeli armed forces from territories occupied in the recent conflict;

Termination of all claims or states of belligerency and respect for and acknowledgement of the sovereignty, territorial integrity and political independence of every State in the area and their right to live in peace within secure and recognised boundaries free from threats or acts of force;

*Affirms* further the necessity

For guaranteeing freedom of navigation through international waterways in the area;

For achieving a just settlement of the refugee problem;

For guaranteeing the territorial inviolability and political independence of every State in the area, through measures including the establishment of demilitarised zones;

*Requests* the Secretary-General to designate a Special Representative to proceed to the Middle East to establish and maintain contacts with the States concerned in order to promote agreement and assist efforts to achieve a peaceful and accepted settlement in accordance with the provisions and principles in this resolution;

*Requests* the Secretary-General to report to the Security Council on the progress of the efforts of the Special Representative as soon as possible.

On 22 November 1967, the Security Council passed Resolution 242. Instead of apportioning blame to one side, the resolution affirmed two interdependent principles for resolving the conflict between Israel and the Arab states:

1. withdrawal of Israeli forces from 'territories' occupied in the 1967 War; and

2. termination of the Arab states' belligerency towards Israel and respect for and acknowledgement of the sovereignty of 'every State in the area and their right to live in peace within secure and recognised boundaries free from threats or acts of force'.

These principles established what is referred to as the 'land for peace' formula.

Whilst Israel, Egypt and Jordan accepted Resolution 242, Syria and the Palestinian leadership did not. The Palestinians rejected Resolution 242 because it did not acknowledge their right to self-determination or to return to their homeland; it called only for 'a just settlement of the refugee problem'.

However, Israel and the Arab states, including Egypt and Jordan, had very different interpretations of both the English and French versions of Resolution 242. The Arabs required Israel's unconditional withdrawal from *all* the territories occupied during the war, and for this to occur before any peace negotiations could begin.

Israel, on the other hand, supported by Lord Caradon, the British diplomat chiefly responsible for drafting the resolution, argued that demands to withdraw to the prewar lines had been defeated in the General Assembly

# Summary

Britain's failed efforts in the 1956 Suez War marked the 'final nail in the coffin' of its power and prestige in the Middle East, paralleled by a meteoric rise in the popularity of Egypt's President Nasser. He was viewed across the region as the only Arab leader to have successfully stood up to European imperialism.

However, Arab gains in 1956 were far outweighed by the losses of *al-Naksah* in 1967. In six days, Israel conquered Arab areas more than three times the size of its territory. Palestinians were again on the move, adding to the number of refugees living in camps in Jordan. Those who remained in Gaza and the West Bank came under Israeli military rule. Arab intellectuals and artists voiced harsh criticisms of their regimes and in the vacuum left by the failure of pan-Arabism, groups with a religious agenda grew significantly stronger.

The humiliation felt by the Arabs in the wake of the 'Six-Day War' was in stark contrast to the euphoria felt by Israelis. Having passed through a period of great danger, Israelis' prewar anxiety was replaced by confidence, and in time, by a dangerous sense of invincibility. The 'liberation' of Jerusalem was a particular cause for celebration not only in Israel but across the entire Jewish world.

Another war would erupt between Israel and Egypt and Syria before changes in the dynamics of the conflict would occur, resulting in the pursuit of peace through negotiations rather than bloodshed. The causes, course and consequences of this fourth Arab-Israeli War in 1973 and the Egyptian-Israeli Peace Treaty that followed are examined in the following chapter.

# Review and research questions

1. What were the causes of the 1956 Suez War?

2. Following the 1956 Suez War, Nasser was immensely popular among many Arabs from Morocco in the west to Iraq in the east. What political and social factors account for this? How did this impact on Nasser's relations with other Arab leaders?

3. Successive Israeli governments have been committed to maintaining a strong military capability. What political and social factors account for this?

4. Why did a political crisis between Egypt and Israel develop in May 1967? Why did the crisis result in war?

5. Re-read UN Resolution 242. What did the resolution call for? Assess the differences between Arab and Israeli interpretations of its 'land for peace' formula.

6. What were the main outcomes of the 1967 War? Which factors contributed to further conflict and which factors might have laid the foundations for later peace negotiations?

7. Did the outcomes of the 1967 War strengthen or weaken extremist sentiments among Arabs and Israelis? Give your reasons.

8. During the period from 1949 to 1970, what were the objectives of the Soviet Union and the United States concerning Arab-Israeli relations? Which of the two superpowers was more successful in achieving its objectives? Why?

9. Research the personal background of Gamal Abdel Nasser, and the times in which he lived. What were the values and attitudes that influenced his actions in relation to pan-Arabism? What major events was he involved in that impacted upon the Arab-Israeli conflict? How would you assess his contribution to this history?

## Discussion questions

1. What are the similarities and differences between the causes and outcomes of the 1948 and 1967 wars?

2. What alternative policies could the Arab states have followed in relation to Israel during the period between 1950 and 1970? What alternative policies could Israel have followed in relation to the Arab states?

# 8 From Hot War to Cold Peace 1973 to 1979

By the end of this chapter you will be familiar with the:

- causes, course and consequences of the 1973 Arab-Israeli War
- Egyptian-Israeli peace process including the 1978 Camp David Accords and the 1979 Egyptian-Israeli Peace Treaty
- biography of Golda Meir
- role and objectives of the superpowers in relation to these events
- attitude and policies of the Israeli Likud Party towards the occupied territories and the political rise of the settler movement.

Gamal Abdel Nasser died on 28 September 1970. His successor, Vice President Muhammad Anwar Sadat, sought from the commencement of his presidency to recover the Sinai Peninsula lost to Israel in the 1967 War. After various diplomatic efforts failed, Sadat attempted to recover it by force. The new president of Syria, Hafez al-Assad, became an ally in this cause as Assad sought the return of the Golan Heights, lost by Syria in that same war. Sadat and Assad secretly planned and orchestrated a surprise military assault against Israel on 6 October 1973. Although the Israelis succeeded in winning the war militarily, Arabs saw it as a major political success. The war also brought to a head US-Soviet rivalry in the region, while the Arab oil-producing states used the so-called 'oil weapon' for the first time to bring international political pressure upon Israel. Following the war, new possibilities for peace negotiations emerged, especially between Egypt and Israel, who signed a peace treaty in 1979, marking a watershed in the conflict at the regional level.

The period also witnessed a significant change in Israeli internal politics. In 1977 Labor domination of Israeli politics ended, and the Likud Party formed a government for the first time. Committed to the ideology of *Eretz Yisra'el Ha'Shlema* (the 'Greater Land of Israel'), Likud provided government support for the settler movement. This would have a significant, long-term impact on the conflict between Israelis and Palestinians at the local level.

The causes, course and consequences of the 1973 War, including the first Arab-Israeli peace treaty, form the focus of this chapter.

| Timeline | Event |
|---|---|
| February 1969 | Golda Meir becomes Prime Minister of Israel. |
| October 1970 | Anwar Sadat becomes President of Egypt. |
| February 1971 | Sadat makes overture for peace with Israel. |
| March 1971 | Hafez al-Assad becomes President of Syria. |
| July 1972 | Sadat orders Soviet military personnel to leave Egypt. |
| 6 October 1973 | The 1973 War begins. |
| 22 October 1973 | UN Resolution 338 calls for a cease-fire and the implementation of UN Resolution 242. |
| 25 October 1973 | Cease-fire comes into effect. |
| December 1973 | The Geneva Conference. |
| January 1974 | First Sinai Disengagement Agreement. |
| June 1974 | Israeli-Syrian Disengagement Agreement. |
| 4 September 1975 | Second Sinai Disengagement Agreement. |
| May 1977 | Likud wins Israeli elections. |
| November 1977 | Sadat visits Jerusalem. |
| 17 September 1978 | Camp David Accords. |
| December 1978 | Begin and Sadat win the Nobel Peace Prize. |
| January to February 1979 | Islamic Revolution in Iran. |
| 26 March 1979 | Egyptian-Israeli Peace Treaty. |
| 31 March 1979 | Egypt expelled from the Arab League. |
| 1980-1988 | Iran-Iraq War. |
| 6 October 1981 | Sadat is assassinated.  Hosni Mubarak becomes President of Egypt. |
| May 1982 | Israel completes its withdrawal from the Sinai. |
| September 1982 | The 'Fez Plan' is adopted by the Arab League. |

# The October 1973 ('Ramadan' or 'Yom Kippur') War

As the new President of Egypt, Anwar Sadat did not intend to follow Nasser's pursuit of popularity among the Arabs through confrontation with Israel and the West.  Instead, he reconsidered all aspects of Egyptian policy, both domestic and foreign, in an attempt to address the country's significant economic problems.  Egypt had been forced to borrow heavily to finance the development of infrastructure and services.  Its financial burden was compounded by the perennial state of 'neither peace nor war' with Israel which required massive spending on the military.

To solve these difficulties, Sadat introduced *al-Infitah* ('the Opening'), a set of initiatives intended to liberalise the economy and attract Western investment.  However, it soon became clear that sustained economic development would require political stability and peace.  A new 'political-security' policy was thus deemed necessary, which meant a change of policy towards Israel.

In February 1971, Sadat requested UN representative Gunnar Jarring to deliver a formal proposal to Israel, stating that 'Egypt will be ready to enter into a peace agreement with Israel containing all the aforementioned obligations as provided for in Security Council Resolution 242.' Golda Meir, Israel's Prime Minister, sent a brief reply: 'Israel will not withdraw to the pre-5 June 1967 lines.'

Undiscouraged, Sadat requested help from America. To win its support, Sadat expelled all Soviet military personnel from Egypt in July 1972, and significantly downgraded the Egyptian-Soviet alliance. In the greater scheme of Cold War rivalry, this was an important victory for the Americans who decided to reward Egypt by pressuring Israel to negotiate.

However, Sadat's strategy failed due to Egypt and Israel's conflicting interpretations of UN Resolution 242. Sadat required a unilateral, unconditional Israeli withdrawal from the Sinai before indirect peace negotiations began. Meir required direct negotiations, stipulating that any Israeli withdrawal from Sinai would occur only as a part of a comprehensive peace settlement.

## Plans for a 'limited' war: 'Operation Badr'

Sadat had announced that 1971 would be Egypt's 'year of decision' in recovering its lost territory from Israel. When nothing developed for two years, Sadat and his advisers decided they needed a limited war to restore their credibility among Egyptians and to show Israel that its military establishment was not invincible, and that its military strength alone would not bring it peace.

Sadat found Hafez al-Assad, Syria's President since March 1971, a willing ally in secretly planning a war with Israel. Throughout the early months of 1973, they prepared for a surprise attack to be launched simultaneously in the Sinai and the Golan Heights. The plan, called 'Operation Badr', involved unprecedented numbers of Egyptian and Syrian troops. Reverting to a war strategy against Israel, Sadat sought assistance from the Soviets, who supplied both Egypt and Syria with large quantities of sophisticated military equipment.

## The failure of Israel's military intelligence

In March 1973, Israel's armed forces were placed on full alert following intelligence warnings of a large build-up of Egyptian forces on the Suez Canal. However, no attack was launched. When a similar report was made in early October, Israel's leaders, including Prime Minister Meir, mistakenly did not give it credence until a few hours before the Egyptians and Syrians began their invasion.

## The course of the war

On 6 October at 2.00 pm, some 80 000 Egyptian and 40 000 Syrian troops simultaneously attacked Israeli positions along the Suez Canal and on the Golan Heights. It was *Yom Kippur* (the Day of Atonement), the holiest day in the Jewish calendar, on which Jews do not eat or drink for 25 hours and many spend the day in prayer in the synagogue. The month of October also marked Ramadan, a time in the Muslim calendar for daytime fasting and prayer.

When the attack began, Israel's army was underprepared and understrength. As a result, the war began with substantial Arab successes and Israeli losses.

### The Suez front

Egypt launched its operation with a massive artillery barrage across the Suez Canal, disabling the Bar-Lev Line, a chain of Israeli fortifications along the east of the Canal between Kantara and Port Tewfik. Egypt used pontoon-mounted water cannons to slice gaps through the high sandbank on the east side of the Canal, permitting Egypt's armoured vehicles to cross on assault craft. By midnight ten bridges and fifty ferries had carried 80 000 Egyptian troops across the waterway and one kilometre beyond the embankment. Most of Egypt's Second and Third Armies crossed the following day. By 9 October, the Egyptians had penetrated up to ten kilometres east of the Canal. Soviet-supplied antitank missiles and rockets set in place west of the Canal during and after the War of Attrition successfully repulsed initial Israeli counterattacks.

Of the 441 Israelis stationed on the Bar-Lev Line, 126 were killed, and 161 captured. High casualties and shortages of military hardware motivated Golda Meir on 13 October to announce her willingness to accept a cease-fire *in situ*. However, Sadat refused the offer, against his military chief's recommendation, believing that Egypt would defeat the Israelis in the Sinai. This proved to be a major error of judgement.

By 15 October, the battle had turned in Israel's favour after a massive tank battle, described by some as the largest since World War II. On 14 October, Egyptian forces attempted to break out of their narrow zone and push forward into the Sinai Peninsula but were routed by the Israelis, who had now been able to mobilise their reserves and had received much needed arms from the US.

Five days later, Israeli forces counterattacked under the leadership of General Ariel Sharon, commander of the 'Southern Front'. Driving a wedge between Egypt's Second and Third Armies, the IDF crossed to the west of the Canal. The Egyptian Third Army was encircled and its 45 000 officers and men were left isolated on the eastern side of the Canal with their supply lines cut.

## The Syrian front

Syria was also able to overwhelm Israeli forces in the first week of the war, resulting in heavy Israeli casualties on the Golan Heights. Although Jordan did not invade Israel, Jordanian army units were sent to the Syrian front and, under Syrian command, took part in the fighting. Iraqi troops were also sent to support the Syrians.

By 7 October, 90 per cent of Israeli officers on the Golan Heights, and most of their men, were killed or wounded. Syrian forces were only a ten-minute tank journey from the Jordan River and the Sea of Galilee, and had captured the Israeli fortifications on Mount Hermon. The Israelis were able to stop the Syrian advance at Quneitra and Nafakh and on 10 October, the Israelis counterattacked and retook the positions they had lost, subsequently driving the Syrians from the Golan Heights. The IDF then advanced to about 30 kilometres from Damascus, close enough to shell the Syrian capital, thus occupying more Syrian territory than before the war.

**Figure 8.1** An Egyptian soldier following the successful crossing of the Suez Canal.

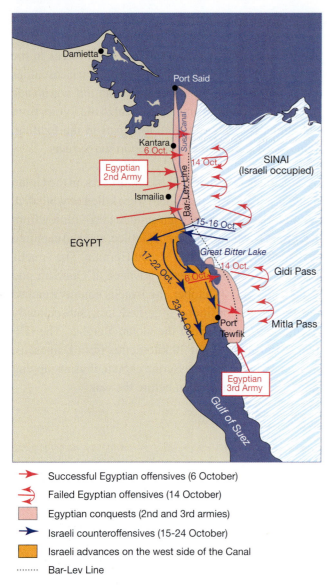

Successful Egyptian offensives (6 October)

Failed Egyptian offensives (14 October)

Egyptian conquests (2nd and 3rd armies)

Israeli counteroffensives (15-24 October)

Israeli advances on the west side of the Canal

Bar-Lev Line

**Figure 8.2** Egyptian attack and Israeli counterattack, October 1973.

# Superpower confrontation

Heavy losses in the opening days of the war caused Israel to appeal to America for help. At first, the Nixon Administration was reluctant to respond as it wanted to avoid harming relations with Arab allies on whom the US had become increasingly dependent for oil. America also wanted to avoid driving Egypt back into the Soviet fold. However, after learning of Soviet airlifts of large amounts of weaponry to Syria as well as Egypt, President Nixon gave the order to fulfil Israel's request.

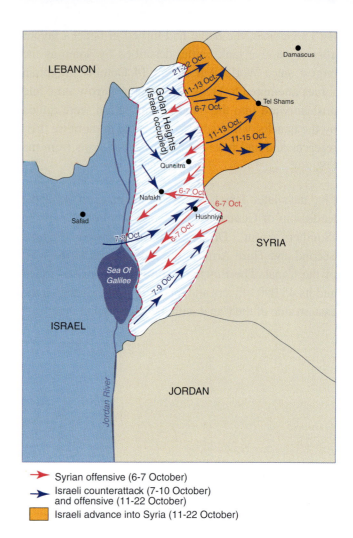

Syrian offensive (6-7 October)

Israeli counterattack (7-10 October) and offensive (11-22 October)

Israeli advance into Syria (11-22 October)

**Figure 8.3** Syrian attack and Israeli counterattack.

On 12 October, six days into the fighting, America airlifted fighter planes, tanks, helicopters, antitank missiles and munitions to Israel. The cost was worth it, Nixon said, 'to maintain a balance of forces and achieve stability in the Middle East', a key principle of US Middle East policy. The resupply came at a critical time for Israel, helping it to repel the Syrian and Egyptian armies and pursue them into their own territories.

Tension between the two superpowers over their respective client states heightened with Israel's encirclement of the Egyptian Third Army. When the Soviets threatened to intervene directly unless Israel lifted its siege, America put some of its forces on high alert, including a nuclear submarine stationed in the Mediterranean off the Egyptian coast. At the same time it pressed Israel to lift the siege.

## UN Security Council 338

During the fighting, the US and the Soviets took the issue to the UN Security Council. On 22 October it passed Resolution 338, calling for a cease-fire and the implementation of Resolution 242 'in all of its parts'. Egypt, Syria and Israel accepted the UN-sponsored cease-fire on 25 October, thus ending the war.

### UN Resolution 338, 22 October 1973

The Security Council:

1. Calls upon all parties to the present fighting to cease all firing and terminate all military activity immediately, no later than 12 hours after the moment of the adoption of this decision, in the positions they now occupy;

2. Calls upon the parties concerned to start immediately after the cease-fire the implementation of Security Council resolution 242 (1967) in all of its parts;

3. Decides that, immediately and concurrently with the cease-fire, negotiations start between the parties concerned under appropriate auspices aimed at establishing a just and durable peace in the Middle East.

**Figure 8.4**   An Israeli armoured brigade makes its way up to the Golan Heights to relieve IDF forces under Syrian fire.

## The oil weapon

In the latter days of the war the ten Arab oil-producing states placed an oil embargo on any country that offered support to Israel. They also threatened to cut overall production by 5 per cent each month until Israel withdrew from *all* territories it had occupied since 1967. Although the latter threat did not eventuate, it resulted in an oil price rise of 380 per cent. In the process, many countries withdrew their previous diplomatic support for Israel, which led the Arabs to believe that the 'oil weapon' had proved its effectiveness.

# The impact and consequences of the 1973 War

## Military costs of the war

The 1973 War exacted a high casualty toll on both sides. In 18 days of fighting, more than 18 000 Arabs and 3000 Israelis were killed. There was also significant loss of military equipment: Egypt and Syria lost 514 aircraft, Israel 102. Syria lost 1150 tanks, Egypt 1100, Iraq 100, and Jordan 50, Israel 340.

## An Israeli military victory but an Arab political victory

In purely military terms, the 1973 War was a victory for Israel. By the time the cease-fire had come into effect, Israeli troops were on the Egyptian side of the Suez Canal, only a hundred kilometres from Cairo, and within Syria they were within artillery range of Damascus.

Despite this, the Arabs regarded the 1973 War as a political victory, drastically altering the post-1967 status quo and balance of power. In their eyes, their armies' initial success had restored their honour, expunging the legend of the invincibility of Israel's armed forces. On the first day, Egypt moved five army divisions across the Canal over some 20 newly-erected bridges, preparations for which had been made in total secrecy, catching the Israelis by surprise. Not since the 1948-49

War had so many IDF soldiers died or been wounded or taken prisoner. Although Israel remained the region's dominant military power, the war established that the Arabs could inflict heavy damage on Israel, albeit at a great cost to their own armed forces.

In his 'victory' speech to the Egyptian Parliament Sadat announced, perhaps optimistically, that, 'Today I declare to our people and to the whole Arab nation that the centuries of backwardness and defeat are past and gone'. Sadat inaugurated an October anniversary for 'the unprecedented victory'.

## Change of mood and government in Israel

Israel's sense of invincibility that followed the 1967 War was shaken deeply in the early days of the 1973 War when an unprepared IDF had suffered significant setbacks. Called *ha mechdal* ('the blunder'), the war undermined the view held by some Israelis that they could hold on indefinitely to the territory occupied in the 1967 War. Significant changes in Israel's domestic politics and national security policies soon followed. Worn out by the public outcry over the government's lack of preparedness for war and by Labor Party infighting, Golda Meir resigned as Prime Minister and was replaced by Yitzhak Rabin. In the May 1977 elections, the Likud bloc won the elections, ending a 50-year period of Labor's political domination in Israel.

# The road to peace

Sadat had calculated correctly that in a period of détente, the two superpowers wished to avoid the outbreak of another destabilising war in the Middle East into which they might be drawn. In the month following the 1973 War, America and the Soviet Union convened a peace conference in Geneva, in an effort to break the deadlock in Arab-Israeli hostilities. Whilst Egypt and Israel attended, Syria did not.

## Muhammad Anwar el-Sadat (1918-1981)

**Figure 8.5** Muhammad Anwar el-Sadat (1918-1981).

Anwar el-Sadat was born in 1918 in Mit Abul Kom, north of Cairo. He was among the first students of a new military school established by the British in 1936. Upon graduating from the academy, Sadat was stationed at an outpost where he met Gamal Abdel Nasser, beginning a long political association. Together they formed the 'Free Officers' group that overthrew the Egyptian monarchy in 1952.

Sadat became a member of Nasser's government and in 1969, became Egypt's Vice President. Upon Nasser's death in September 1970, Sadat became head of the ruling party, the Arab Socialist Union, and the following month was elected Egypt's new President (he was the only candidate).

During his presidency, in an effort to save Egypt from bankruptcy, Sadat reversed a number of Nasser's economic and political policies. He also replaced Egypt's dependence on Soviet aid with support from America.

After unsuccessful diplomatic efforts to regain the Sinai lost to Israel in 1967, Sadat went to war in 1973 in an attempt to force a change in the status quo. Despite Egypt's military defeat, the war created a momentum for peace both in Egypt and in Israel. This was realised in 1979 with the signing of the Egyptian-Israeli Peace Treaty.

For their efforts, Sadat and Israeli Prime Minister Menachem Begin jointly won the Nobel Prize for Peace in December 1978. However, Sadat's new relationship with the West and the peace treaty with Israel were not well received by many Egyptians, including Islamist groups. On 6 October 1981, Sadat was assassinated by members of the Muslim Brotherhood during anniversary celebrations of the 1973 War. Sadat was succeeded by Hosni Mubarak.

---

The conference marked the beginning of a diplomatic initiative driven by US President Richard Nixon and Secretary of State Henry Kissinger. It resulted in a series of military agreements between Egypt and Israel and eventually a peace treaty between the two states.

## The Sinai Disengagement Agreements

Kissinger knew that in order to move Egypt squarely into America's sphere of influence America needed to assist Egypt to recover the Sinai and to achieve economic development. Following the 1973 conference, he began the process of 'shuttle diplomacy', travelling between Jerusalem and Arab capitals, particularly Cairo and Damascus, seeking a set of common denominators that would form the basis of negotiations between the two sides.

Kissinger's first success came in January 1974, when Sadat and Israeli Defence Minister, Moshe Dayan, endorsed the First Sinai Disengagement Agreement, calling for mutual reduction of forces in the Suez Canal Zone and the restoration of the UNEF in the Sinai. Israel withdrew its forces to the east side of the Canal, the Egyptian Third Army was withdrawn to the west side of the Canal, and a UNEF 'buffer zone' was positioned between the two.

On 4 September 1975, Egypt and Israel signed the Second Sinai Disengagement Agreement resulting in a further Israeli withdrawal to the east of the Gidi and Mitla passes in the Sinai. Strict limits were placed on the number of troops and weapons deployed within the buffer zone.

Figure 8.6 Golda Meir (1898-1978).

The life of Golda Meir was inextricably linked to the birth and development of the modern State of Israel. From her work on a kibbutz as a young pioneer during the 1920s until her period of office as Israel's fourth Prime Minister from 1969 to 1974, Golda Meir's adult life was devoted to building up, and then defending, the Jewish state.

Born Goldie Mabovitch on 3 May 1898 in Kiev, Ukraine, Meir's family fled violent anti-Semitism and economic hardship, moving to America in 1906. In Milwaukee, Wisconsin, Meir had a secular education and worked as a teacher after graduation. She married Morris Meyerson in 1917. (In 1956, Golda changed her last name to the Hebrew 'Meir', meaning 'to burn brightly').

Meir's interest in Zionism began as a child, and in her teens, she joined the Zionist group, *Poalei Zion*, a choice reflecting Meir's commitment to both socialism and Jewish nationalism. In 1921 she and her husband moved to Palestine. Like other young Jewish immigrants in the early 20th century, Meir wished to contribute to the Zionist enterprise – the restoration of statehood and dignity to the Jewish people in their historic homeland. Meir's childhood memories of pogroms in Eastern Europe deepened her determination to work for a secure and independent Jewish State.

In Palestine, Meir lived on *Kibbutz Merhavia* and became active in its politics and administration. After three years, she and her husband moved to Tel Aviv where Golda became an official of the *Histadrut*.

In 1928, Meir was elected Secretary of the *Histadrut's* Women's Labour Council and in 1930, she worked with David Ben-Gurion to found the *Mapai* Party. After being elected an international Zionist representative, Meir spent 1932 in America. In 1934, she was elected to the *Histadrut's* Executive Committee and became the head of its Political Department in 1940.

As a central figure in the *Yishuv's* leadership, Meir was appointed in 1946 to head the Jewish Agency's Political Department, replacing Moshe Sharett as the chief Jewish liaison with the British Mandatory Administration. In this role, Meir campaigned against Britain's 1939 White Paper which placed severe restrictions on Jewish immigration to Palestine just before the outbreak of World War II.

In 1947, following the vote by the United Nations General Assembly to partition Palestine (Resolution 181), Ben-Gurion sent Meir to meet secretly with Jordan's King Abdullah who wished to divide the territory allocated to the Palestinians between Jordan and the soon-to-be established State of Israel. Meir consented to Abdullah's plan, requiring the King's commitment not to attack the new Jewish state. This unwritten agreement was critical for Israel's war strategy in 1948, when it was invaded by other Arab states.

When Ben-Gurion proclaimed the State of Israel on 14 May 1948, Meir was a signatory of the formal declaration of independence. During the early months of the ensuing war, she travelled to America to raise funds for much needed armaments and was then sent to Moscow as Israel's first Minister to the Soviet Union.

Figure 8.7 Golda Meir signing Israel's Proclamation of Independence, 14 May 1948.

In 1949, Meir was elected to the first Knesset. Invited by Ben-Gurion to be Deputy Prime Minister, she declined the offer and was instead appointed Labour Minister. She held this position until 1956 when she was appointed Israel's Foreign Minister, which she remained until 1966.

Figure 8.8 Prime Minister David Ben-Gurion and Foreign Minister Golda Meir.

As Foreign Minister, Meir dealt with issues such as the international criticism of Israel's 1956 Suez War and the bringing to trial of the Nazi war criminal, Adolf Eichmann in 1961. On her initiative, Israel also built good relations with many African and Latin American countries.

In 1966, due to health problems, Meir retired for a short period, again declining appointment as Deputy Prime Minister. On her return to work, she became Secretary-General of *Mapai*, Israel's major political party at the time, and then the first Secretary-General of *haAvodah* (the Labor Party) in 1968.

When Prime Minister Levi Eshkol died in 1969, Meir became Israel's fourth Prime Minister, its first, and to-date only woman Prime Minister. Reflecting on her achievement she noted that: 'I have faced difficult problems in the past but nothing like the one I'm faced with now in leading the country.' At the time Meir was almost 71, and she remained in office for almost five years. Israeli Cabinet meetings were often held in the kitchen of her home, rather than the Knesset building, which was the reason her Ministers were sometimes referred to as 'Golda's Kitchen Cabinet'. During her term as Prime Minister, Meir was voted 'the most admired woman' by Americans on three separate occasions, in 1971, 1973 and 1974. In 1973 she was also voted the most admired woman in Britain.

As Prime Minister, Meir dealt with the final stages of the War of Attrition with Egypt (1970), the massacre of Israeli athletes at the Munich Olympic Games in 1972, and the 1973 War. She also had to manage conflicts within her party over Israel's policies towards the occupied Palestinian Territories. Defence Minister Moshe Dayan's faction wanted Israel to maintain permanent control of the territories as a security buffer against further Arab invasions, while the opposing faction, led by Deputy Prime Minister Yigal Allon, favoured returning the Sinai to Egypt and the Golan Heights to Syria as part of a peace settlement, and permitting the West Bank to become an autonomous part of the Kingdom of Jordan. Although Meir generally sided with Dayan, she retained the support of 'moderates'.

Meir's attitudes to the Arabs in general, and the Palestinians in particular, have been described by some as 'self-righteous and simplistic'. On becoming Prime Minister, she adopted two principles that would remain the mainstay of her position on Arab-Israeli relations until her retirement. The first was that, for security reasons, Israel could not and would not return to the pre-1967 borders. The second was that Israel would not withdraw from any Arab territories occupied during the war without direct negotiations and peace treaties with the Arab states.

Meir rejected Arab demands that Israel first withdraw from territory captured by it in 1967 before peace negotiations could begin.

Meir's stance was criticised by her opponents for 'intransigence', particularly for her rejection of Sadat's peace overtures before the 1973 War. Her supporters, on the other hand, argued that the peace deal eventually entered into between Israel and Egypt after the war was far better for Israel than the deal offered by Sadat before the war.

After the 1973 War, the Knesset established the Agranant Commission of Enquiry (named after its Chair), which concluded in 1974 that the government and the IDF leadership had erred seriously in assessing Arab intentions in the period before the war. Although Labor won the December 1973 elections under her leadership, Meir resigned in 1974, handing the Prime Ministership to Yitzhak Rabin.

Golda Meir died in Jerusalem on 8 December 1978. She was buried on Mount Herzl at the National Cemetery in Jerusalem. She had two children, a boy and a girl.

During his time as Prime Minister, David Ben-Gurion once said of Meir that she was 'the only man in the Cabinet'. She was described by her friends as tough yet warm, strong yet simple, an 'idealist without illusions.' She was described by her opponents as intransigent, overbearing, dominant, and intolerant of opposition. She was a formidable woman in every respect, referred to by many as 'the Iron Lady', years before that description was applied to British Prime Minister Margaret Thatcher.

## Golda Meir quotes

Reflecting on her identity as a Jew, Meir wrote in her memoir, *A Life*, that '[I]t is not only a matter, I believe, of religious observance and practice. To me, being Jewish means and has always meant being proud to be part of a people that has maintained its distinct identity for more than 2000 years, with all the pain and torment that has been inflicted upon it.'

And on being Israeli: 'Above all, this country is our own. Nobody has to get up in the morning and worry what his neighbours think of him. Being a Jew is no problem here.' And 'Let me tell you something that we Israelis have against Moses. He took us 40 years through the desert in order to bring us to the one spot in the Middle East that has no oil!'

When questioned about how it felt to be Israel's first woman Foreign Minister, she replied: 'I don't know. I was never a man minister'. She also would say: 'Whether women are better than men I cannot say – but I can say they are certainly no worse.' However, 'To be successful, a woman has to be much better at her job than a man.'

Regarding her view on the conflict with the Arab states, Meir stated, 'We have always said that in our war with the Arabs we had a secret weapon – no alternative'. Also, 'We don't thrive on military acts. We do them because we have to, and thank God we are efficient.' And, 'We will have peace with the Arabs when they love their children more than they hate us'.

As Prime Minister, Meir made the oft-quoted remark: 'How can we return the occupied territories? There is nobody to return them to'. Equally controversially, she stated: 'There was no such thing as Palestinians, they never existed. Before 1948, we were the Palestinians … Formerly the Palestinians considered themselves 'southern Syrians'.

And in regard to the return of Palestinian refugees to their homes in Israel, Meir said: 'Any one who speaks in favour of bringing the Arab refugees back must also say how he expects to take the responsibility for it, if he is interested in the State of Israel. It is better that things are stated clearly and plainly: We shall not let this happen.'

American technicians established an electronic early warning station to monitor military movements on either side of the disengagement line. Egypt also regained the Abu Rudeis oilfields that Israel had explored and developed after 1967. In return, Egypt pledged not to threaten or use force against Israel, and to open the Suez Canal for the first time to non-military cargoes to and from Israel.

Both sides promised to resolve the conflict by peaceful means, using diplomatic negotiations to reach a 'final and just peace settlement'. This was a significant breakthrough in the long road from war to peace between Israel and the Arab States.

## The Israeli-Syrian Disengagement Agreement

Following the First Sinai Disengagement Agreement, Kissinger pursued his shuttle diplomacy between Damascus and Jerusalem, producing the Israeli-Syrian 'Agreement on Disengagement' that was signed on 31 May 1974. Under the terms of the agreement, Israel withdrew from all the territory it had captured in the October 1973 War as well as from a small area it had captured in the 1967 War, including the town of Quneitra. Syrian civilians who had fled during the hostilities were able to return to areas vacated by Israel. A UN Disengagement Observer Force (UNDOF) was stationed in 'limited-force zones' on either side of a central buffer zone.

However, unlike the Egyptian-Israeli agreements, there was no mutual commitment to continue negotiations in order to reach an end to the conflict between Israel and Syria. Since 1974, Israel has continued to occupy the Golan Heights.

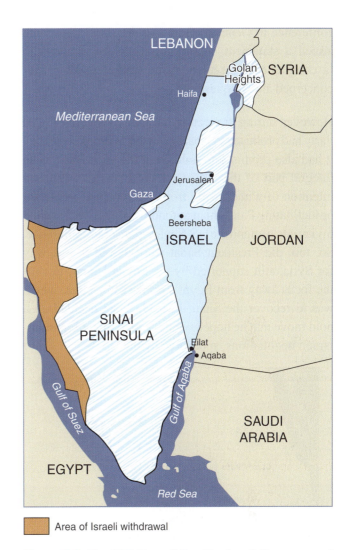

☐ Area of Israeli withdrawal

**Figure 8.9** The 1975 (Second) Egyptian-Israeli Disengagement Agreement.

# The Egyptian-Israeli peace process

## A change in government in Israel corresponds to Soviet and US commitment to an Arab-Israeli peace process

In 1977, the long period of Labor Zionist rule in Israel ended and the Likud Bloc was elected to power under the leadership of Menachem Begin. Soon after, new US President Jimmy Carter and Soviet leader Leonid Brezhnev advocated a jointly sponsored peace conference in Geneva. On 1 October 1977, they both issued a statement committing their governments to 'a comprehensive settlement incorporating all parties concerned and all questions'.

However, during its election campaign, while the Likud Party had promised to 'spare no effort to promote peace', it had also promised to hold on to the West Bank as an integral part of the 'Greater Land of Israel'. With no intention of withdrawing from the occupied territories or facilitating Palestinian autonomy, Begin declined the invitation to attend the US-Soviet sponsored conference. So, too, did President Sadat who viewed it as a way for Syria, still supported by the Soviet Union, to shift the focus away from Egypt's primary objective, which was to recover the Sinai. Instead, Sadat decided on a bold move that he hoped would lead to direct Egyptian-Israeli negotiations, sponsored by the US.

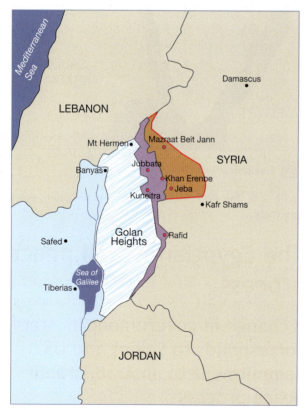

— Previous forward line of Israeli Defence Forces (from 1973 War)

Under Israeli control after Six-Day War

UN patrolled demilitarised zone

Towns returned to Syria

Area of Israeli withdrawal

**Figure 8.10** The 1974 Israeli-Syrian Disengagement Agreement.

## Sadat's visit to Jerusalem November 1977

On 9 November 1977, in a speech to the Egyptian parliament, Sadat announced his readiness to go to Israel to discuss peace. This was a dramatic reversal of decades of policy by Arab states not to recognise or deal directly with Israel. In response, Begin invited Sadat to address the Knesset in Jerusalem. Sadat accepted.

Sadat made his historic journey to Jerusalem on 20 November 1977, stating in his address to the Knesset: 'In the past, we rejected you … But, I tell you today, and declare to the whole world, that we accept to live with you in a durable and just peace.' In return, Sadat required Israel to withdraw to its pre-1967 borders, and allow the Palestinians to establish a state in Gaza and the West Bank. Whilst the Israeli government rejected Sadat's call for the creation of a Palestinian state, Begin offered to return the Sinai to Egypt on condition that it would be demilitarised and that Egypt would sign a peace treaty with Israel.

## The Camp David Accords September 1978

US President Carter, who had strongly supported the convening of an international conference at Geneva, was forced by the momentum of Sadat's visit to Israel to abandon the idea and instead to sponsor bilateral negotiations between Egypt and Israel. In July 1978, Carter invited Begin and Sadat to meet with him at Camp David, the Presidential retreat in Maryland.

The meetings took place in September and lasted for two weeks. On 17 September, Begin and Sadat signed two sets of agreements which became known as the Camp David Accords. The first Accord outlined an agreement for peace between Israel and Egypt; the second Accord was for peace with Jordan and the Palestinians. The details of the Camp David Accords may be summarised as follows:

### Accord One: Egypt and Israel

Egypt and Israel agreed to sign a peace treaty within three months. Israel would be required to return the Sinai Peninsula to Egypt in stages, dismantling Israeli settlements. In return, Egypt would formally recognise Israel and enter into normal diplomatic, cultural, commercial and tourist relations; guarantee Israeli shipping rights in the Suez Canal and the Gulf of Aqaba; and sell oil to Israel from the Sinai oil fields. Further, Egypt would lend its support to America's call to Jordan, Syria and Lebanon to sign peace treaties with Israel.

### Accord Two: Israel, Jordan and the Palestinians

Provision was made for a five-year transitional period when Palestinians living in the West Bank and Gaza would be granted full autonomy and Israel's military and civilian administration would progressively be withdrawn. The accord specified:

1. An elected 'self-governing authority' to be established with powers defined by Israel, Egypt, and Jordan, to replace the existing Israeli administration in these areas;

2. A five-year period marked by the staged withdrawal or redeployment of Israeli troops;

3. Negotiations in the third year between Israel, Jordan, Egypt, and the Palestinian-elected representatives on the 'final status of the West Bank and Gaza'.

4. At the end of the five years, the final status agreement would lead to a formal peace treaty between Israel and Jordan.

The accords were accompanied by letters addressed to President Carter from Begin and Sadat. Begin's letter promised that the removal of settlers from Sinai would be put to a vote in the Knesset; the letter from Sadat stated that the peace treaty between Egypt and Israel was dependent on the withdrawal of Israeli settlers from Sinai. The day after the accords were signed, they were ratified in Israel by the Knesset.

Following the signing of the Accords, Carter remained personally involved and worked hard to get the two sides to sign a formal peace treaty, promising increased American aid to both countries.

## The Egyptian-Israeli peace treaty March 1979

Six months later, after delays caused by last minute disagreements, Egypt and Israel signed the 'Treaty of Peace between Egypt and Israel' on 26 March 1979.

Egypt and Israel exchanged ambassadors and established commercial, trade, and cultural ties. As agreed, Israel withdrew its forces and settlers from the Sinai, returning it formally to Egypt in May 1982. Both states received large sums of American economic and military aid.

## What of Accord Two?

In the end, only the first Camp David Accord was implemented. Sadat protested the lack of progress on the Palestinian accord but he was unwilling to halt the bilateral Egyptian-Israeli peace process for fear that this would leave the Sinai permanently in Israeli hands.

Whilst not implemented, the Second Camp David Accord established a legal framework for Palestinian self-determination in the West Bank and Gaza Strip. Whether Begin had any intention of pursuing the plan is highly doubtful in view of his party's ideological commitment to Israel's retention of the West Bank. However, Begin was never put to the test as the Palestine Liberation Organisation (PLO), the internationally recognised representative of the Palestinians at this time, rejected the plan outright. Not until 1993 did Israel and the PLO sign a 'Declaration of Principles' based upon the framework for Palestinian self-determination set out in the 1978 Camp David Accords.

In the meantime, while the Begin government dismantled settlements in the Sinai, it pursued a policy of settlement expansion in the occupied territories.

Figure 8.11   Egyptian President Anwar Sadat arrives at Ben-Gurion Airport, 21 November 1977.

## Extract from a 1991 interview with US President Jimmy Carter concerning his involvement in the Camp David Accords

Interviewer [from The Academy of Achievement]: One of your greatest accomplishments was Camp David and peace between Israel and Egypt. It has become the model for peace between Israel and its Arab neighbours. What were the conditions that made Camp David possible?

Carter: … We had two bold and courageous political leaders then, particularly, Anwar Sadat, combined with a very receptive leader in Menachem Begin, who was willing to make decisions that were very difficult for him [in regard to] his own constituency in Israel. And I had done my homework. I had met with the Israeli leaders and the Egyptian leaders and the Jordanian and Lebanese and Syrian leaders – so we were able to provide some means by which these two bold and courageous political leaders could come together. They were incompatible. We were at

Camp David 13 days. They never saw each other the last 10 days. Every time they got in the same room, we went backwards instead of forward. So Begin and Sadat stayed separate. And I would go to one and then go to the other one, back and forth.

And eventually, we came out with the Camp David Accord, which people forget is called 'a framework for peace'. It's a set of principles on which peace can be predicated in the future, and that framework is still absolutely applicable to any negotiations in the Middle East now. The people who rejected it then – the Jordanians, the Palestinians and the Syrians – are now willing to negotiate on the basis of Camp David. We used the Camp David principles six months later to conclude the peace treaty between Israel and Egypt.[1]

**Figure 8.12** Egyptian President Anwar Sadat, US President Jimmy Carter, and Israeli Prime Minister Menachem Begin sign the Camp David Accords in the East Room of the White House, 17 September 1978.

# Likud policy concerning the occupied territories

Begin's 1977 election campaign had committed his Likud party to the principle of *shlemut hamoledet* ('the integrity of the homeland'). The principle, also a central tenet of the settler movement, claims the West Bank (Judaea and Samaria) as an integral part of the territory that should constitute the State of Israel. Likud's platform entitled, 'The Right of the Jewish People to the Land of Israel' stated:

(a) The right of the Jewish people to the Land of Israel is eternal and indisputable and is linked with the right to security and peace; therefore, Judaea and Samaria will not be handed to any foreign administration; between the sea and Jordan there will only be Israeli sovereignty.

(b) A plan which relinquishes parts of Western *Eretz Yisra'el*, undermines our right to the country, unavoidably leads to the establishment of a 'Palestinian State,' jeopardises the security of the Jewish population, endangers the existence of the State of Israel, and frustrates any prospect of peace.

The policy was to become action through a settlement program:

Settlement, both urban and rural, in all parts of the Land of Israel is the focal point of the Zionist effort to redeem the country, to maintain vital security areas and serves as a reservoir of strength and inspiration for the renewal of the pioneering spirit. The Likud Government will call the younger generation in Israel and the diaspora to settle and help every group and individual in the task of inhabiting and cultivating the wasteland, while taking care not to dispossess anyone.

Once in government, Begin appointed former Major-General Ariel Sharon as Minister of Agriculture and Chairman of the Ministerial Committee for Settlements, a position he held until 1981. Sharon was a strong supporter of expanding settlements in the occupied territories and, despite being responsible for dismantling the Jewish settlements in the Sinai in 1982 as part of Israel's peace treaty with Egypt, became patron of the settler movement. He supported the group's efforts to settle in areas adjacent to large Arab centres of population, providing land that had been acquired (at times confiscated) by the military administration which governed the Palestinian territories. By the end of his tenure, Sharon had overseen a doubling in the number of Jewish settlements in the West Bank and Gaza Strip.

Support for the establishment of Israeli settlements close to densely populated Arab areas was one example of the differences between the settlement policies of Labor and Likud governments. The historian Avi Shlaim explains further:

> The fundamental difference between the foreign policy of the Labor Alignment and that of the Likud was that the former was pragmatic whereas the latter was ideological. Labor's policy in regard to the occupied territories was governed primarily by security considerations, whereas the Likud's was governed chiefly by ideological considerations. To say this is not to suggest that Labor was indifferent to nationalist ideology or that the Likud was indifferent to security but simply to point out their different priorities.[2]

## The Israeli settler movement

When Zionism emerged as a political movement in the 1880s, it was primarily a secular nationalist movement. However, after Israel's capture of the West Bank in 1967, religious Zionism came to play a more important role in Israeli politics. This entailed the rise of the settler movement.

Central to the settler movement's ideology is the call to Jews to resettle *Eretz Yisra'el*, the Biblical 'Land of Israel' in order to bring on the 'Messianic Age', the coming of the Messiah as prophesied in the Hebrew Bible. The heart of this land consists of the areas known as Judaea and Samaria, much of which is located in the modern day West Bank.

The settlement movement found allies in the Israeli political system, forming a strategic alliance with the Likud Party after the 1977 elections. With government funding, the settlers embarked on a building program in the West Bank in areas adjacent to densely populated Palestinian cities, and expanded suburban housing communities adjacent to Israeli cities near the pre-1967 border. The Yesha Council (Yesha is an acronym for Judea, Samaria, and Gaza) was established to function as the settlements' local council.

Since 1967, Israeli settlers have had a variety of reasons for choosing to live in the occupied territories. Yesha members did so out of religious and/or political idealism, while others were motivated by the lower price of the real estate and tax incentives provided by the government.

The major settlement blocs in the West Bank are the towns of Modi'in Illit, Ariel and Ma'ale Adumin, located to the north-west, north and east of Jerusalem, and Beitar Illit to the south of Jerusalem. Each has a population in the tens of thousands, with stable infrastructure and other features of permanence. Smaller settlement blocs in east and south-east of Jerusalem, such as Gush Etzion, have been built on the ruins of Jewish communities from the pre-1948 period. Further from Jerusalem, located on hilltops across the West Bank, are so-called 'frontier villages' and 'residential outposts', the latter consisting of campervans and even tents.

Though religiously and ideologically-motivated settlers are a minority, they represent the dominant voice within the settler population.

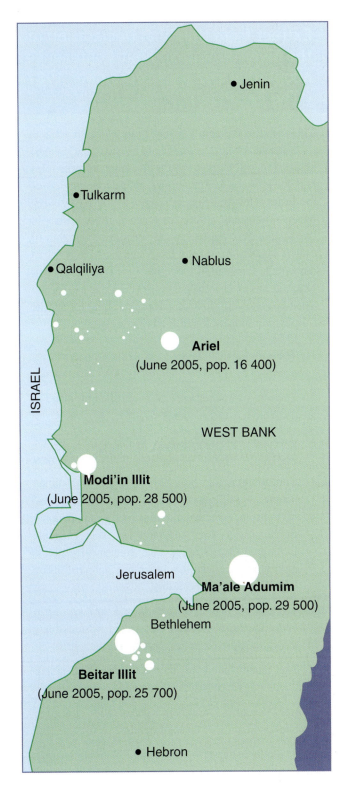

Jenin

Tulkarm

Qalqiliya

Nablus

**Ariel**
(June 2005, pop. 16 400)

ISRAEL

WEST BANK

**Modi'in Illit**
(June 2005, pop. 28 500)

Jerusalem

**Ma'ale Adumim**
(June 2005, pop. 29 500)

Bethlehem

**Beitar Illit**
(June 2005, pop. 25 700)

Hebron

**Figure 8.13** Large Israeli settlement blocs in the West Bank.

# The Arab response to the Egyptian-Israeli peace treaty

## Egypt expelled from the Arab League

By signing the peace treaty and extending diplomatic recognition to Israel, Sadat violated an Arab taboo that had been maintained for more than three decades, encapsulated in the 1967 Khartoum policy of 'no peace, no negotiations, no recognition'. The Egyptian President was denounced throughout the Arab world and on 31 March 1979, the Arab League condemned Egypt's unilateral actions in making peace with Israel. With the exception of Sudan and Oman, its members voted to expel Egypt from the organisation and other Arab bodies.

However, only a short time later, other Arab states started to shift away from the Arab League's official policy towards Israel. The most notable among these was Saudi Arabia, which, along with other Persian Gulf states, came to face what appeared to be a more pressing danger to stability in the region, that of revolutionary Iran.

## The 1981 Fahd Plan

In 1979, a revolution in Iran brought to power a radical Islamist regime that was seen as a threat by neighbouring Arab governments. This perception was magnified when a dispute between Iran and Iraq over the *Shatt al-Arab* waterway erupted into full-scale war in 1980. In August 1981, in an attempt to bring stability to other parts of the region, Crown Prince (later King) Fahd of Saudi Arabia published an eight-point plan to resolve the Arab-Israeli conflict and to establish an independent Palestinian state.

The Prince's plan called for: Israel to withdraw from *all* lands occupied in the 1967 War; all Jewish settlements built in the occupied territories to be dismantled; Palestinian refugees to be allowed to return to their former homes in Israel; and for the creation of an independent Palestinian state, with East Jerusalem as its capital. Importantly, the plan also stated that *all* states in the region had the right to live in peace. Although it did not mention Israel by name it was understood that Israel was included among the 'states' to which the plan referred.

Before the Fahd Plan was formally tabled in November 1981 at the Arab League Summit in Fez, Morocco, it was debated and discussed in Arab capitals across the region. The Plan was contentious because it implied Arab recognition of Israel, and seemed to endorse a 'two state solution' of the Israeli-Palestinian conflict. This limited the Palestinians' independence to the West Bank and Gaza Strip, not the entire territory of Mandatory Palestine, as the Palestine Liberation Organisation demanded.

## The 1982 Fez Plan

At the September 1982 Arab League Summit in Fez, Fahd's proposal was adopted with emendations and became the Arab League's official peace plan, known as the 'Fez Plan'. A copy was sent to the UN Security Council entitled, 'Final Declaration of the Twelfth Arab Summit Conference, adopted at Fez on 9 September 1982'.

Although the Fez Plan did not lead to negotiations with Israel, its publication marked an important shift in the position of some of the Arab states, in particular the Persian Gulf states whose priorities had changed significantly with the 1979 Islamist Revolution in Iran and the subsequent outbreak of war between Iran and Iraq. For the first time, the Arab states voted as a group to pursue a process of peace with Israel while at the same time seeking justice for the Palestinians. For this reason, both the 1981 Fahd Plan and the 1982 Fez Plan were a significant departure from the 'Three No's' policy of 1967, while Saudi Arabia showed that it was prepared to take the initiative, although within the context of pan-Arab agreement.

---

### Extract from the Final Declaration of the Twelfth Arab Summit Conference, adopted at Fez on 9 September 1982 ('The Fez Plan')

Convinced of the ability of the Arab nation to achieve its legitimate objectives and to put an end to the [Israeli] aggression, on the basis of the fundamental principles laid down by the Arab Summit Conferences, in view of the desire of the Arab States to continue to strive by every means for the achievement of peace based on justice in the Middle East region, taking account of the plan of … His Majesty King Fahd Ibn Abdul Aziz for peace in the Middle East and in the light of the discussions and observations of Their Majesties, Their Excellencies and Their Highnesses, the Kings, Presidents and Emirs, the Conference adopted the following principles:

1. The withdrawal of Israel from all the Arab territories occupied by it in 1967, including Arab Jerusalem;

2. The removal of settlements established by Israel in the Arab territories after 1967;

3. Guarantees of freedom of worship and performance of religious rites for all religions in the Holy Places;

4. Confirmation of the right of the Palestinian people to self-determination and to the exercise of their inalienable and imprescriptible national rights, under the leadership of the Palestine Liberation Organisation, their sole and legitimate representative, and the indemnification of those who do not desire to return;

5. The placing of the West Bank and the Gaza Strip under the supervision of the United Nations for a transitional period not exceeding a few months;

6. The establishment of an independent Palestinian State with Jerusalem as its capital;

7. UN Security Council guarantees for the implementation of these principles;

8. The establishment by the United Nations Security Council of guarantees of peace between all states of the region, including the independent Palestinian State;

9. The guaranteeing by the Security Council of the implementation of these principles.

## The assassination of Anwar Sadat

Sadat's pursuit of a bilateral peace process with Israel was opposed by a number of groups within Egypt, among them the Nasserites and the Muslim Brotherhood. At an anniversary celebration of the 1973 War on 6 October 1981, four members of the Brotherhood fired guns at the group where Sadat was seated and assassinated him.

Sadat's successor was his Vice-President, Hosni Mubarak who, despite Sadat's violent end, reaffirmed Egypt's commitment to the 1979 treaty with Israel. However, Mubarak placed severe restrictions on the development of normal relations in the economic, political and cultural spheres, creating what is often referred to as a 'cold peace' between the two states.

But regardless of the absence of a 'warm peace', a further important outcome of the 1979 treaty was that without Egypt, the Arab world lacked the military strength to fight another conventional war with Israel.

# Summary

Full-scale war between Israel and its Arab neighbours erupted again in October 1973. A particular feature of this war was the limited objectives of Egypt and Syria, whose principal aim was to regain the territory lost to Israel in the 1967 War. Neither state achieved its objective by the war's end.

In 1977, in an effort to break the deadlock in Egyptian-Israeli relations, Sadat boldly travelled to Israel and proclaimed in the Knesset that he was willing to negotiate an end to the conflict on the basis of a 'land for peace' formula. The initiative resulted in American-brokered talks in 1978 resulting in the Camp David Accords, and the first Arab-Israeli peace treaty in 1979. Diplomatic relations were established between the two states and by 1982 Israel had completed its withdrawal from the Sinai.

The experience of war and peace provided lessons for both sides. When Anwar Sadat was asked by an Israeli diplomat why he had agreed to sign the 1979 treaty, Sadat answered: 'Because you had my land. I tried every way to recover it without the hazard of making peace: I tried UN action, four-power, three-power, two-power pressure. I tried war, armistice, international condemnation. I reached the answer that only by peace could I recover my land.' Mustafa Khalil, the Secretary-General of Egypt's ruling party, provided a similar reason as to why he and others gave their support for Sadat's peace initiative: 'We knew that we have no chance of winning a war, and we knew that you [Israelis] have the atomic bomb … Egypt has no military solution, and [so] we [had to] seek another solution.'

The 1973 War had also taught Israelis that their military supremacy could no longer be viewed as the sole guarantor of the state's security as it had not deterred the Arabs from planning and executing a coordinated military attack. With the Israeli-Egyptian peace treaty, it became apparent to some in Israel, particularly those on the political left, that 'things had changed in the Middle East' and that diplomatic and political opportunities for peacemaking had at last arisen which could provide Israel with a firmer and less costly foundation for its long-term security.

Thus by 1979, two competing policies had emerged within Israel concerning the occupied territories: the Right was committed to maintaining Gaza and the West Bank and supported building settlements as a way of achieving this long-term objective; those on the Left saw the need to relinquish most settlements and to accommodate Palestinian national aspirations in Gaza and the West Bank, as provided for in the second Camp David Accord.

For all parties, the 1978 Camp David negotiations and the 1979 Peace Treaty highlighted the role that the US was willing and able to play for leaders wanting to find a way to conduct negotiations with the 'other side'. In return, America could provide an environment for bilateral, secret discussion and, as an incentive to reach a positive outcome, economic, military and political rewards to each side.

A further lesson was that two nationalistic peoples could reach a political accommodation if they each made painful concessions. The 'cost in the present' was seen to be necessary in order to bring 'peace in the future'.

# Review and research questions

1.  Why did another Arab-Israeli war erupt in October 1973?

2.  How did the objectives of the two superpowers, America and the Soviet Union, influence Arab-Israeli relations immediately before and during the 1973 War?

3.  Compare and contrast the impact of the 1967 and 1973 wars on relations between Israel and the Arab states.

4.  Outline the Egyptian-Israeli peace process between 1974 and 1979. How important was the role played by America? What were the motivations of the key players?

5.  Review the efforts at peacemaking between Israel and the Arab states from 1949 to 1979. What factors changed during those 30 years that led to peace between Egypt and Israel in 1979?

6.  In the light of the Arab League's condemnation of Egypt in 1979, account for the Arab League's adoption of the 1982 Fez Plan.

7.  Compare and contrast the attitudes and policies of the Israeli Labor and Likud parties towards the occupied Palestinian territories and the building of settlements there.

8.  Research the personal background of Golda Meir and consider the historical context in which she lived. Examine her rise to prominence in Israeli politics; her leadership role in the *Histadrut* and Labor Party; and her actions as Foreign Minister and Prime Minister. What were the major events in which she was involved that impacted upon the Arab-Israeli conflict? In the context of your assessment of Meir's contribution to both the history of Israel and the Arab-Israeli conflict, do you consider her to have been a 'trailblazing stateswoman', an 'inflexible adversary', or both? Give reasons for your answers.

## Discussion question

1.  How would you assess the significance of the Egyptian-Israeli Peace Treaty in the history of the Arab-Israeli conflict? Give your reasons.

# 9 The PLO, the Arab States and Israel 1967 to 1987

By the end of this chapter you will be familiar with the:

- formation of the Palestine Liberation Organisation in 1964
- re-emergence of the Palestinian nationalist movement under Yasser Arafat's leadership; its aims, methods and effectiveness to 1987
- Jordanian and Lebanese civil wars
- Israel's 1982 invasion of Lebanon and its significance for Israelis and Palestinians.

Whilst the 1979 Egyptian-Israeli Peace Treaty ended the conflict between Israel and its largest Arab neighbour, the Palestinians' claim for land, statehood and the 'right of return' of their refugees remained unresolved. Palestinian independence had been the catchcry of pan-Arab nationalism since the 1950s, but the Arab states' defeat in the 1967 War and Israel's occupation of Gaza and the West Bank, had provided a sober lesson for the Palestinians, namely, that liberation of Palestine would not be achieved while Arab political disunity prevailed.

In the following years, the Palestinian national movement re-emerged under Yasser Arafat's leadership as his Fatah group aimed to destroy Israel through 'armed struggle'. In turn, the PLO became a formidable force within Jordan, and then Lebanon, threatening stability in both countries.

By the mid 1970s, Arafat's efforts to raise international awareness of the Palestinians' struggle for self-determination through diplomacy and international terrorism had paid dividends. The PLO was recognised by the Arab League as the 'sole legitimate representative of the Palestinian people' and given 'observer status' at the United Nations. PLO attacks on Israel from Lebanon drew Israel into the Lebanese civil war in 1978 and again in 1982, the second time involving full-scale invasion.

These events and their consequences for the Arab-Israeli conflict in regional and international affairs form the focus of this chapter.

| Timeline | Event |
|---|---|
| 1958 | First Fatah cell is founded. |
| January 1964 | Arab League votes to establish the Palestine Liberation Organisation (PLO). |
| May 1964 | PLO formally established by Ahmad Shuqeiri in East Jerusalem. |
| 1965 | Fatah begins guerilla raids inside Israel. |
| December 1967 | George Habash forms the Popular Front for the Liberation of Palestine. |
| 1968 | Popular Front for the Liberation of Palestine – General Command is founded by Ahmad Jibril. |
| February 1968 | Syria establishes *al-Saiqa*. |
| March 1968 | IDF-PLO Battle at Karameh in Jordan. |
| February 1969 | Popular Democratic Front for the Liberation of Palestine is founded by Nayif Hawatmeh. Fatah assumes control of the PLO and Yasser Arafat becomes Chairman. |
| November 1969 | The 'Cairo Agreement' is signed between Lebanon and the PLO. |
| September 1970 | Civil War in Jordan. |
| November 1970 | Hafez al-Assad takes power in Syria; becomes President in March 1971. |
| 1970 | The Black September Organisation formed. |
| July 1971 | PLO is expelled from Jordan. |
| September 1972 | Black September massacres Israeli athletes at Munich Olympic games. |
| June 1974 | The PLO adopts the 'Strategy of Stages' for the liberation of Palestine. |
| October 1974 | Arab League summit in Rabat, Morocco declares the PLO the 'sole legitimate representative of the Palestinian people.' |
| November 1974 | Arafat addresses the UN General Assembly; PLO given 'observer status' at UN. |
| November 1975 | UN General Assembly characterises Zionism as 'racism'. |
| April 1975 | Civil War begins in Lebanon. |
| January 1976 | Syrian troops enter Lebanon. |
| March 1978 | Israel invades southern Lebanon in 'Operation Litani'. |
| 6 June 1982 | Israel invades Lebanon in 'Operation Peace for Galilee'. |
| August 1982 | PLO is expelled from Lebanon; Israel and Lebanon agree to a cease-fire. |
| September 1982 | Christian militia massacre Palestinians in Sabra and Shatila refugee camps. |
| 17 May 1983 | Peace negotiations between Israelis and Lebanese officials. |
| 1984 to 1988 | First 'unity government' in Israel. |
| February 1985 | The 'Amman Accords' negotiated between King Hussein and Yasser Arafat regarding future talks with Israel. |
| June 1985 | IDF troops are withdrawn to a 'security zone' in southern Lebanon. |
| April 1987 | King Hussein and Shimon Peres sign the 'London Agreement'. |

# The revival of Palestinian nationalism

Throughout the Mandate period, the Palestinians lacked a united leadership and the infrastructure to mobilise the population into political or military action. The events of the 1948 War left them demoralised and in a state of shock and despair, such that their main priority became basic survival, not national liberation.

The Arab countries encouraged Palestinians in the refugee camps to hope for return to their homes, once Israel was destroyed and Palestine liberated. For many years, Palestinians believed the promises of Arab leaders, in particular, Egypt's President Gamal Abdel Nasser, who was seen as the champion of Palestinian rights. 'Arab unity', Nasser promised, would bring 'salvation to the Arab world and liberation to Palestine'.

However, some younger Palestinians believed that the Arab states were not doing enough in their efforts to destroy Israel, and that the Palestinians should contribute more to the armed struggle.

## The founding of Fatah: Its aims and methods

Throughout the 1950s, a number of autonomous, clandestine (secret) Palestinian nationalist groups were established, most importantly *Harakat al-Tahrir al-Watani al-Filastini* ('The Palestinian National Liberation Movement'), better known by its reverse acronym, *Fatah* ('conquest' in Arabic).

Established in Kuwait in 1958, Fatah's founders included Khalil al-Wazir (Abu Jihad) and Yasser Arafat (Abu Ammar) with Salah Khalaf (Abu Iyad) joining a year later. From the outset, Fatah aimed to wage a relentless war on the 'colonialist, Zionist occupation state and society' to regain the lost Palestinian homeland; and to pursue this struggle independently of the Arab states. As the Palestinian historian Yezid Sayigh puts it: 'In short, Fatah sought to destroy Israel as an economic, political, and military entity and restore Palestine as it still existed in the minds of mostly Palestinians, the homeland that was before 1948.'

**Figure 9.1** Fatah logo.

Fatah members believed 'revolutionary violence' and armed struggle were required to 'break through the resignation of the refugees', and destroy Israel. Their strategy had three components: to create a climate of insecurity in Israel through *fedayeen* attacks against civilians; to heighten tensions between Israel and neighbouring Arab states where the *fedayeen* were based; and, ultimately, to draw Arab states into full-scale war with Israel and bring about its destruction.

Fatah established a military wing, *al-Assifa* ('The Storm'), to harass the 'Zionist State' with attacks and sabotage. Arms were bought on the black market and were stored in the refugee camps in Lebanon, Syria, Gaza and the West Bank, which also served as secret guerilla training bases.

## The founding of the Palestine Liberation Organisation

At the 1964 Arab League summit in Cairo, in addition to discussion concerning Israel's decision to build a National Water Carrier, there was also debate about how to rein in the independent *fedayeen* groups whose raids into Israel were heightening tension with Egypt, Jordan and Syria. It was decided to establish an organisation to 'organise the Palestinian people to enable them to carry out their role in liberating their homeland and determining their destiny'. It would have a small army, the Palestinian Liberation Army (PLA), headed by an Egyptian under unified Arab command. It would not be a 'Palestinian government in exile', but simply a vehicle for Palestinians to voice their aspirations. The organisation would be financed by the Arab states and to a lesser extent by the Palestinians themselves.

Under instructions from the Arab League, its Palestinian representative, Ahmed al-Shuqeiri, organised the first Palestinian National Council (PNC) meeting in East Jerusalem. It was attended by 350 delegates who formally established *Munazzamat al-Tahrir al-Filastiniyyah* ('The Palestine Liberation Organisation' – PLO). Membership of the PLO included various Palestinian groups, headed by an Executive Committee (PLO-EC).

**Figure 9.2** Palestinian flag.

The Palestinian flag was adopted at the 1948 conference in Gaza and endorsed by the PNC in Jerusalem in 1964. The flag has three equal horizontal stripes (black, white and green from top to bottom) overlaid by a red triangle on the left side. Each colour represents a period in Muslim history: red represents the Muslim rulers of Andalusia (Spain); black the Prophet Muhammad; white the Umayyad Dynasty; and green the Fatimid Dynasty.

## The 1964 Palestine National Covenant (the PLO Charter)

The PNC's first task was to draw up the Palestine National Covenant (Charter), which set out the PLO's political program. Article 12 provided: 'Arab unity and the liberation of Palestine are two complementary goals; each prepares for the attainment of the other. Arab unity leads to the liberation of Palestine, and the liberation of Palestine leads to Arab unity.' In order to clarify the extent of the intended PLO role in 'Palestinian affairs', Articles 24 and 26 declared:

**Article 24:** This Organisation does not exercise any regional sovereignty over the West Bank in the Hashemite Kingdom of Jordan, on the Gaza Strip or the Himmah Area. Its activities will be on the national popular level in the liberational, organisational, political and financial fields …

**Article 26:** The Liberation Organisation cooperates with all Arab governments each according to its ability, and does not interfere in the internal affairs of any state.

The PLO received formal Arab recognition during a September 1964 summit. Dependent upon the Arab states for funding and operational capability, the PLO could not operate independently of the Arab League generally, and Nasser in particular. The PLA was armed, trained and commanded by Egyptian officers. In Gaza, this provided the Egyptians with the ability to prevent *fedayeen* raids into Israel.

Fatah refused to join the PLO and turned to Syria for arms and logistical support as a counterweight to Egyptian control, a role Syria was eager to play, as it enhanced its prestige among Arabs at Nasser's expense.

To assert its counterclaim for leadership of Palestinian nationalism, on 3 January 1965, Fatah's military wing, *al-Assifa* launched its first operation from Jordan into Israel aimed at sabotaging Israel's National Water Carrier. The mission was thwarted by Israel, but the first Fatah casualty was shot by a Jordanian soldier while crossing the West Bank border.

## The impact of the 1967 War on Palestinian nationalism and the PLO: A change in aims and methods

The defeat of the Arab armies in the 1967 War resulted in Israel's occupation of large tracts of Arab territory. Subsequently Egypt and Jordan accepted UN Resolution 242, which was an implicit recognition by two front-line Arab states that 'Israel is here to stay'. These developments undermined the Arab states' claim to be the champions of the Palestinian cause.

The 1967 War also brought into question the standing of the recently formed PLO. Its PLA forces had prepared for war under Egyptian command and Shuqeiri had promised that 'we will advance [from Gaza] to Jerusalem as the capital of our independent state'. But instead of victory, the Palestinians living in East Jerusalem, the West Bank and Gaza came under Israeli control and within six months, Israel began building settlements in the West Bank.

These events marked a turning point in Palestinian history and the Arab-Israeli conflict. As hope was replaced by despair, Palestinian nationalism was reignited. From the ashes of defeat, the Palestinian national resistance movement arose, its leadership taken up by Fatah which soon controlled the PLO. Fatah and its leader, Yasser Arafat, rose to prominence after the Battle of Karameh in Jordan.

## The Battle of Karameh

In the wake of the 1967 War, Fatah and other Palestinian guerilla groups with bases in Jordan's refugee camps, stepped up attacks on Israeli civilian and military targets. Israel responded with limited retaliatory raids on the camps, hoping the Jordanian Government would rein in the guerillas. As the majority of Jordan's population is Palestinian (a further 300 000 had fled from the West Bank into Jordan during the 1967 War), King Hussein turned a 'blind eye' to the raids to avoid open confrontation with the Palestinian nationalist movement.

In March 1968, Israel launched a more extensive raid on the Karameh refugee camp, which was Fatah's major training and supply headquarters. Israeli troops inflicted defeat upon the Fatah base and many Palestinian fighters were killed. However, a number of Israeli soldiers were also killed and some tanks and armoured vehicles destroyed by Jordanian artillery, which joined in to assist the Palestinians. After the Israelis withdrew, their disabled vehicles were paraded by the PLO through the streets of Amman, causing celebration among Palestinians everywhere.

Although Fatah had lost the Battle of Karameh, its fighters claimed victory for having held out, even if briefly, against the 'invincible' IDF. As Rashid Khaladi points out, this theme 'found a ready response in an Arab world still reeling from the unexpected defeat of June 1967.' The battle 'was a case of a failure against overwhelming odds brilliantly narrated as heroic triumph.'[1]

Instead of crushing the organisation, as Israel hoped, the attack on Karameh served to reinforce the Palestinians' renewed nationalist spirit. Within 48 hours, 5000 new recruits applied to join Fatah.

## The new 1968 Covenant

As Egypt became bogged down in a war of attrition with Israel, Fatah took control of the PLO. At its 1968 National Congress, the organisation changed its Charter to reflect Fatah's strategies and new guerilla groups that now joined the PLO. The 1968 Charter retained the sections of the 1964 version affirming the Palestinians' national identity and their 'integral part of the Arab nation', but the strategy to 'liquidate the Zionist presence in Palestine' would now be 'Palestinian armed revolution'.

The doctrine of armed struggle enshrined in the Palestinian 1968 national covenant led to the domination of guerilla groups in the nationalist movement and its key institutions. In turn, guerilla leaders used violence against any Israeli target, civilian or military, inside or outside of Israel. The central role of violence in the PLO's strategy and in its leadership's mindset was exemplified in a 1967 Fatah publication:

Our correct understanding of the reality of Zionist occupation confirms to us that regaining the occupied homeland cannot happen except through armed violence as the sole, inevitable, unavoidable, indispensable means in the battle of liberation. The process of liberation is not only to eliminate a colonial base but, more importantly, to eradicate a society. Armed violence must take many forms besides destroying the military forces of the Zionist occupation state, that is, to direct itself towards destroying the existential basis of Zionist society in all its industrial, agricultural, and financial aspects. Armed violence must aim to destroy all the military, political, economic, financial, and intellectual institutions of the Zionist occupation state until it is impossible for a new Zionist society to arise [again]. Military defeat [of Israel] is not the only aim of the Palestinian liberation war, but also elimination of the Zionist character of the occupied homeland, both human and social.

## Resolutions of the Palestine National Council, 1-17 July 1968

**Article 1:** Palestine is the homeland of the Arab Palestinian people; it is an indivisible part of the Arab homeland, and the Palestinian people are an integral part of the Arab nation.

**Article 2:** Palestine, with the boundaries it had during the British Mandate, is an indivisible territorial unit.

**Article 3:** The Palestinian Arab people possess the legal right to their homeland and have the right to determine their destiny after achieving the liberation of their country in accordance with their wishes and entirely of their own accord and will …

**Article 9:** Armed struggle is the only way to liberate Palestine. Thus it is the overall strategy, not merely a tactical phase. The Palestinian Arab people assert their absolute determination and firm resolution to continue their armed struggle and to work for an armed popular revolution for the liberation of their country and their return to it. They also assert their right to normal life in Palestine and to exercise their right to self-determination and sovereignty over it …

**Article 15:** The liberation of Palestine is a national obligation for the Arabs. It is their duty to repel the Zionist and imperialist invasion of the greater Arab homeland and to liquidate the Zionist presence in Palestine. The full responsibility for this belongs to the peoples and governments of the Arab nation and to the Palestinian people first and foremost. For this reason, the task of the Arab nation is to enlist all the military, human, moral and material resources at its command to play an effective part, along with the Palestinian people, in the liberation of Palestine. Moreover, it is the task of the Arab nation, particularly at the present stage of the Palestinian armed revolution, to offer the Palestinian people all possible aid, material and manpower support, and to place at their disposal all the means and opportunities that will enable them to continue to perform their role as the vanguard of their armed revolution until the liberation of their homeland is achieved.

**Article 19:** The partition of Palestine in 1947, and the establishment of the state of Israel are entirely illegal, regardless of the passage of time, because they were contrary to the will of the Palestinian people and its natural right in their homeland, and were inconsistent with the principles embodied in the Charter of the United Nations, particularly the right to self-determination.

**Article 21:** The Arab Palestinian people, expressing themselves by the armed Palestinian revolution, reject all solutions which are substitutes for the total liberation of Palestine and reject all proposals aiming at the liquidation of the Palestinian problem, or its internationalisation ...

**Article 23:** The demand of security and peace, as well as the demand of right and justice, require all states to consider Zionism an illegitimate movement, to outlaw its existence, and to ban its operations, in order that friendly relations among peoples may be preserved, and the loyalty of citizens to their respective homelands safeguarded.

**Article 24:** The Palestinian people believe in the principles of justice, freedom, sovereignty, self-determination, human dignity, and in the right of all peoples to exercise them …

**Article 26:** The Palestine Liberation Organisation, representative of the Palestinian revolutionary forces, is responsible for the Palestinian Arab people's movement in its struggle – to retrieve its homeland, liberate and return to it and exercise the right to self-determination in it – in all military, political, and financial fields and also for whatever may be required by the Palestine case on the inter-Arab and international levels.

**Article 27:** The Palestine Liberation Organisation shall cooperate with all Arab states, each according to its potentialities; and will adopt a neutral policy among them in the light of the requirements of the war of liberation; and on this basis it shall not interfere in the internal affairs of any Arab state …

## New Palestinian guerilla groups join the PLO

At the Fifth Palestine National Congress in 1969, Yasser Arafat was elected PLO chairman, a position he held until his death in November 2004. Some Arab states, including Iraq and Syria, sponsored the formation of new Palestinian guerilla groups in opposition to Fatah to curb Arafat's growing influence.

Among the Palestinian guerilla groups formed were:

- *al-Jabhah al-Dimuqratiyya li-Tahrir Filastin* ('The Popular Democratic Front for the Liberation of Palestine – PDFLP). A Marxist group founded in December 1969 with Syrian support, and headed by Na'if Hawatmeh, it changed its name in 1974 to 'The Democratic Front for the Liberation of Palestine – DFLP).

- *al-Sa'iqa or as-Sa'iqa* ('Vanguard for the Popular Liberation War'). Established in 1968 by Syria and operating out of Damascus under Syrian control.

- *Jabhat al-Tahrir al-Arabiyya* ('The Arab Liberation Front' – ALF). Founded in 1969 by Iraq to rival Syria's, al-Saiqa. Until 2003, the ALF was based in Baghdad under Iraq's command.

Other key groups that were formed between July 1967 and 1969 and joined the PLO included:

- *al-Jabhah al-Sha'abiyya li-Tahrir Filastin* ('The Popular Front for the Liberation of Palestine' – PFLP). Founded in 1967 by Dr George Habash with a 'Marxist-Leninist' platform that looked to Soviet socialism as the model for the future Palestinian state.

- *al-Jabhah al-Sha'abiyya li-Tahrir Filastin – al-Qiyada al-'Amma* ('The Popular Front for the Liberation of Palestine-General Command' – PFLP-GC). Formed in late 1968 after Ahmad Jibril, a former Syrian Army officer, split from the PFLP. Its headquarters remain in Damascus.

- *Ailul al-Aswad* ('Black September Organisation' – BSO). Formed in 1971 following the civil war in Jordan, Black September was headed by Salah Khalaf (Abu Iyad, a founding member of Fatah) and functioned as an unofficial wing of Fatah. The BSO was also supported by the PFLP. Abu Iyad and Mohammed Daoud Oudeh (Abu Daoud) planned the operation in which 11 Israeli athletes were kidnapped and murdered at the 1972 Munich Olympic Games.

- *Jabhat al-Tahrir al-Filastiniyya* ('The Palestine Liberation Front' – PLF). Formed in 1977 after a split in the PFLP-GC, which had supported Lebanese Maronite Christians against the Fatah-led PLO forces. (In the early years of the Lebanese civil war, the Christian Lebanese and Syrian forces in Lebanon were aligned against the PLO.)

By 1970, there were at least 15 separate Palestinian guerilla groups of varying numbers, mostly financed and armed by one or more Arab government, including some of the Gulf states. Some of these groups' leaders trained in the Soviet Union, which also supplied arms and money. Most groups were members of the PLO, which functioned as a broad umbrella organisation for Palestinian nationalism. However, ideological disputes and the competing demands of their Arab benefactors led at times to bloody conflict between the groups, as was seen during the Lebanese civil war. On occasions, the actions of one faction had far-reaching ramifications for the entire PLO, as occurred in Jordan in September 1970.

## Civil war in Jordan

The increasing military capability of the *fedayeen* in Jordan and the PLO's popularity among the kingdom's Palestinian population was a growing concern for King Hussein. So, too, was Arafat's attempt to establish a 'state within a state' in the Palestinian camps, which directly challenged the King's authority. Some PLO factions called openly for the King's overthrow and the replacement of his kingdom with a Palestinian state east of the Jordan River, as a first step towards creating a state on both sides of the river. One PFLP slogan was: 'The road to Jerusalem begins in Amman'. There were also attempts by PLO groups to assassinate King Hussein.

**Figure 9.3** Logo for the Popular Front for the Liberation of Palestine (PFLP).

**Figure 9.4** Yasser Arafat (second from left) with Fatah members, Jordan 1969.

Tension between the Jordanian army and PLO militias escalated into a pitched battle for control of the kingdom in September 1970. During what became known as 'Black September', Syrian forces invaded Jordan to help the PLO overthrow King Hussein to help it gain control over the Hashemite kingdom. In response, Hussein sought assistance from Israel and the US.

## Black September

On 6 September 1970, PFLP terrorists hijacked two planes which they landed in Jordan. Six days later they hijacked another plane also landing it in Jordan, while another PFLP team hijacked a Pan American plane, flew it to Cairo and blew it up.

The Jordanian authorities were severely embarrassed as three of the four planes remained on Jordanian territory. Unless the safety of these aircraft and passengers could be secured, the Jordanians faced the prospect of indefinite suspension of all international flights to and from their country. Some members of the government wanted a negotiated settlement, while others, supported by senior army officers, advocated a harsh crackdown on the hijackers.

Arafat was asked to intervene, but he refused to do so. When the hijackers blew up the three remaining planes, King Hussein secretly contacted Israel and asked for military support if the ensuing battle with the PLO did not go in his favour. He knew that the last thing Israel wanted was a PLO-run state on the east of the Jordan River. Israel agreed and placed its forces on alert.

On 15 September 1970, Hussein declared martial law, and fighting between the Jordanian army and the PLO began the following day with an artillery barrage against the PLO stronghold of Zarqa, followed by similar attacks on PLO bases in several areas of Amman. The Jordanian army also shelled refugee camps such as al-Wahdat, which had raised a flag for the 'Republic of Palestine'.

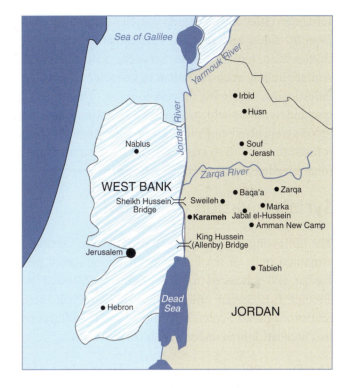

**Figure 9.5** Palestinian refugee camps in Jordan.

**Figure 9.6** Hijacked aircraft blown up by PFLP, 1970.

Jordanian tanks and armoured vehicles entered Amman from all sides, and attacked Palestinian headquarters. Battles also took place in Sweileh, Salt and Irbid. Arafat publicly accused Jordan of genocide against the Palestinians, urging his fighters to resist. He turned to Iraq and Syria for help, as their own Palestinian guerilla groups were also being attacked by the Jordanians. Iraq refused to come to Arafat's aid, but a Syrian armoured force invaded Jordan on 18 September.

## Syria's invasion of Jordan

The following day, Syrian Army units accompanied armoured units of the Palestine Liberation Army into Jordan and advanced towards Amman, followed by another two Syrian armoured brigades, which were reinforced on 20 September. Altogether, 15 000 troops had invaded Jordan under Syrian command.

The Syrian-PLO forces were met by the Jordanian 40th armoured brigade, which initially suffered heavy losses. Sensing victory, Arafat declared northern Jordan a 'liberated Palestinian area'. As the battle raged, 5000 Jordanians defected to the PLO. King Hussein's defeat appeared imminent.

The Arab League called an extraordinary meeting of Heads of State to discuss the crisis. Israel prepared its jet fighters to come to Hussein's aid. The US, concerned to protect one of its client states against the Soviet-sponsored Syrian army, announced that, as a precautionary measure, it would strengthen the Sixth Fleet in the eastern Mediterranean. At Hussein's request, Israeli fighters flew into Jordanian air space to prevent the Syrian air force from supporting its ground forces.

Meanwhile, the street fighting in Amman was bloody and ruthless. No prisoners were taken by either side. Civilians were killed and women raped. The besieged refugee camps where PLO fighters had taken refuge ran out of food and water.

After initial setbacks, the Jordanians slowly gained the upper hand. The Syrian air force was intimidated by the Israeli warplanes over Jordan, and decided against sending planes to provide air cover for Syrian ground forces. As this would leave the invading force exposed to air attack, Syria withdrew its invasion force from Jordan.

## Cease-fire brokered

At an emergency meeting in Cairo on 22 September 1970, the Arab League brokered an agreement between King Hussein and PLO leaders Salah Khalaf and Farouk Qaddoumi, who had been taken prisoner by the Jordanians. But Arafat rejected the agreement and renewed calls for the King's overthrow. The civil war continued.

Over the next few days, Nasser led negotiations to end the fighting. Arafat and Hussein came to Cairo on 27 September and after considerable acrimony agreed to a cease-fire. Nasser died the following day.

By the time the fighting stopped, Jordanian and Palestinian losses were extensive. The PLO suffered most, putting its losses at 30 000 dead and wounded.

Upon his return from Cairo, King Hussein formed a new government and appointed an anti-PLO hardliner, Wasfi Tel, as Prime Minister. Late in 1970, Tel contacted Hafez al-Assad, who had just become Syrian President in a military coup, and the new President of Egypt, Anwar Sadat, who both agreed not to provide further assistance to Arafat. Indeed, from 1970 on, Assad consistently backed Arafat's rivals in order to destabilise and weaken Fatah's control, a policy pursued most effectively in Lebanon. In doing so, Assad wanted to place the Palestinian national movement under Syrian control.

## The PLO is expelled from Jordan

King Hussein was not content with the cease-fire struck with Arafat and did not trust Syria's commitment that it would not provide support for the PLO in Jordan. He wanted Arafat and the PLO command out of Jordan, as Hussein believed he would always be under threat if they remained. He planned another military campaign against the PLO and again turned to Israel for back-up. Israel agreed. With this assurance, in July 1971, the king ordered the expulsion of the PLO leadership from Jordan.

Using tanks, aircraft and heavy artillery, the Jordanian army moved against PLO bases throughout the country. Arafat again accused Jordan of genocide, but Iraq and Syria responded by closing their borders to the fleeing PLO fighters.

The fighting lasted two weeks during which 3000 PLO gunmen were killed. After several unsuccessful attempts to negotiate a cease-fire, Arafat escaped into Syria with 2000 men, where Assad demanded that the Palestinian resistance come under Syrian control. Arafat refused and moved to Lebanon, facilitated by a November 1969 agreement between Lebanon and the PLO. Known as the 'Cairo Agreement' (as it had been negotiated by Nasser in Cairo), it allowed special privileges for the PLO in Lebanon, to recruit, arm, train, and employ fighters against Israel, while Lebanon protected their bases and supply lines.

However, once the PLO established its headquarters in Lebanon, it was drawn into the quagmire of Lebanese politics. The PLO's attempt to once again establish a 'state within a state' was one of the factors that led to Lebanon's civil war in 1975.

The PLO launched actions against Israel from its bases in southern Lebanon, which directly impacted upon the Arab-Israeli conflict. Lebanon had not participated in the 1967 and 1973 wars. After 1973, this relative calm was ended by the PLO's incursions into Israel and Israel's retaliatory raids into southern Lebanon. In 1978 Israel launched 'Operation Litani' in Lebanon to wipe out PLO bases and in 1982, Israel again invaded, this time in an effort to expel the PLO from the entire country. The trigger was PLO terrorist attacks against Israelis, at home and abroad.

**Figure 9.7** From left to right: Libyan leader Muammar Qaddafi, PLO Chairman Yasser Arafat, Egyptian President Gamal Abdel Nasser, and King Hussein of Jordan, meet at the Nile Hilton in Cairo to end the civil war between Jordan and the PLO, 27 September 1970.

**Figure 9.8** Hussein bin Talal (1935-1999).

Hussein bin Talal was born in Amman, Jordan, on 14 November 1935. Hussein became Jordan's third king when his grandfather, Abdullah I, was assassinated in 1951 and his father, Talal, succumbed to mental illness. Hussein was crowned king in May 1953. He was sixteen years of age.

Hussein ruled Jordan (the majority of whose population is Palestinian) during a turbulent time. He survived a number of assassination attempts as well as the September 1970 civil war during which the PLO, backed by Syria, attempted to overthrow him and create a Palestinian state. In 1990-91, he maintained a 'pro-Iraq neutrality' in regard to Iraq's invasion of Kuwait, a policy which isolated him regionally and internationally.

Except for the last five years of his reign, Jordan was in an 'official state of war' with Israel. However, relations between Hussein and Israel were relatively amicable. In 1970, Israel came to Hussein's assistance against the PLO and Syria, and in October 1973, the king warned Golda Meir of the Egyptian-Syrian invasion. In 1994, the two countries signed a peace treaty.

Hussein was married four times and had eleven children. He died of cancer on 7 February 1999 and was succeeded by his eldest son, Abdullah.

## Terrorism as a PLO tactic

Arafat knew from the events of 1970-71 in Jordan that the Arab states would not risk full-scale military confrontation with Israel on behalf of the Palestinians. They would only risk war to regain territory lost in the 1967 War, the aim of Egypt and Syria in the 1973 War. Yet Arafat also knew that the PLO would never be powerful enough to defeat Israel on its own. So once the PLO was re-established in Lebanon, Arafat sought to provoke Israel into war there, which he hoped would ignite another full-scale war with the Arab states. In order to achieve this broader strategy, Arafat's tactic was to carry out terrorist attacks on Israeli citizens, both inside Israel and abroad.

The PLO sought to justify its terrorism by characterising it as 'the weapon of the oppressed'. The PFLP used terrorism, explained George Habash, because 'we believe that to kill a Jew far away from the battlefield has more effect than killing a hundred of them in a battle: it attracts more attention.' The PFLP, PFLP-GC and DFLP targeted Israeli children and schools for the same purpose, as they did in Kiryat Shmona and Ma'alot in 1974.

The PLO also sought to justify its terrorism because of the suffering that Israel inflicted upon Arab civilians when the IDF retaliated against *fedayeen* attacks. Fatah, for example, claimed it used bombs against Israeli civilians 'to convince the Israeli authorities that we are capable of carrying out actions similar to those carried out by Israel against Arab civilians.' Attacking Israeli civilians would also 'weaken the Israeli economy, trigger a flight of capital, and deter tourism, but above all prevent Jewish immigration and encourage reverse emigration ... prevent the bond between immigrants and the land ... [and] make the Zionists feel that life in Israel is impossible.'

More than 160 Israeli civilians were killed in PLO terrorist attacks in the 1970s.

**1970**

- PFLP-GC hijacked and blew up a Swiss airliner: 47 killed.
- PFLP-GC attacked an Israeli school bus: 12 killed.
- PFLP hijacked TWA, Swissair and BOAC aircraft to Jordan. Planes are blown up and spark civil war in Jordan.

**1972**

- PFLP and the Japanese 'Red Army' shot passengers, including nuns, at Lod airport in Israel: 26 killed.
- Black September blew up a West German electrical installation and a Dutch gas plant.
- Black September murdered 11 Israeli athletes at the 1972 Olympic Games, Munich, Germany.

**1973**

- Black September attacked passenger terminals at Athens airport, Greece: 3 killed.
- PLO members bombed a Pan Am office at Fiumicino Airport, Rome: 32 killed. Hostages were then taken on a hijacked plane to Athens, Greece, and then to Kuwait: 1 killed.

**1974**

- PFLP-GC attacked an Israeli apartment block in Kiryat Shmona: 18 killed, including 8 children.
- PFLP attacked an Israeli school in Ma'alot: 21 killed.
- DFLP attacked another school and school bus in Ma'alot: 20 children killed.
- Fatah attacked Israelis at Nahariya: 3 killed.

**1976**

- PFLP attacked a bus carrying Israeli airline crew in London, England: 1 killed.
- Fatah attacked an Israeli bus: 26 killed.
- German Baader-Meinhof group and PFLP hijacked an Air France airliner and flew to Entebbe, Uganda: 3 killed.
- PFLP and Japanese Red Army attacked a passenger terminal at Istanbul, Turkey: 4 killed.

(These figures only include civilians, not terrorists or military personnel killed in rescue operations.)

## Israel's response

Israel responded to PLO attacks by using its secret service, Mossad, to track down and kill the terrorists. Following the 1972 Munich massacre of 11 Israeli athletes by Black September, Israel sent hit squads to assassinate three of the terrorists. Whilst two were assassinated, Mohammed Daoud Oudeh, the mastermind, after being jailed in France, was released in 1977. The French Government had brought pressure to bear to release Daoud to avoid terrorist reprisals against its citizens and to avoid jeopardising its commercial interests in the Arab world.

Figure 9.9 Black September terrorist, Munich Olympic Games 1972.

Israel also responded to terrorist attacks outside Israel by sending its own forces to rescue Jewish hostages. In 1976, Israeli commandos rescued dozens of Jewish hostages from PLO terrorists who had hijacked a plane and taken it to Uganda. Israel also responded with direct assaults on PLO bases in southern Lebanon, including air strikes and occasional ground operations, such as 'Operation Litani' in 1978, a prelude to the 1982 full-scale invasion.

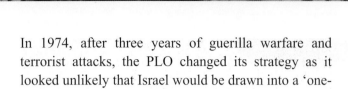

In 1974, after three years of guerilla warfare and terrorist attacks, the PLO changed its strategy as it looked unlikely that Israel would be drawn into a 'one-off' war.

# A shift in PLO strategy

## The 1974 'Strategy of Stages'

In June 1974, the PLO National Council met in Cairo and debated a new, more limited strategy to achieve Israel's destruction. A ten-point plan was adopted, known as the 'Strategy of Stages' or the 'Phases Plan', the aim of which was to destroy Israel in phases. The first phase was to establish a small Palestinian state anywhere that came under PLO rule, even resulting from negotiations with Israel. From this base, the second phase was to conquer all remaining parts of Palestine. PLO Executive member, Salah Khalaf explained it as follows: 'At first a small state, and with the help of Allah, it will be made large, and expand to the east, west, north and south. I am interested in the liberation of Palestine, step by step.'

### Extracts from the PLO's 1974 Phases Plan

**Article 2:** The PLO will struggle by all means, especially the armed struggle, to liberate Palestine and establish an independent and fighting national authority on any part of Palestinian land to be liberated …

**Article 4:** Any liberation that is achieved constitutes a step to continue the PLO strategy of the establishment of the Palestinian democratic state stipulated in previous resolutions …

**Article 8:** After its establishment, the Palestinian national authority will struggle for the unity of the confrontation states in order to complete the liberation of all Palestinian soil.

# Arab League recognition of the PLO: The Rabat Declaration

The PLO's use of terrorism, especially the hijacking of international airliners, brought the Palestinian cause to international attention. Capitalising on growing sympathy for the Palestinians' struggle for self-determination, the Arab League's October 1974 summit in Rabat, Morocco, formally recognised 'the right of the Palestinian people to establish an independent national authority under the command of the Palestine Liberation Organisation, the sole legitimate representative of the Palestinian people, in any Palestinian territory that is liberated.' The 'Rabat Declaration' marked an important turning point in the growing legitimacy of the Palestinian nationalist movement within Arab state politics.

The League's recognition of the PLO coincided with a foiled Fatah attempt to assassinate King Hussein. Although he survived, he had lost a battle with Arafat over who should speak for the Palestinians.

## International recognition of the PLO: Arafat's first UN appearance

With Arab League help, Arafat addressed the UN General Assembly on 13 November 1974. For his speech, Arafat carried an olive branch (a symbol of peace), and his (empty) gun holster. He told the UN, 'Today I have come bearing an olive branch and a freedom fighter's gun. Do not let the olive branch fall from my hand.'

Arafat condemned 'the Zionist project' and defended the Palestinians' armed struggle as legitimate resistance to occupation. He called on Jews to turn away from Zionism and join the Palestinians in establishing a democratic state in place of Israel, in which Jews and Palestinians could live 'in peace and without discrimination.' 'Only then' explained Arafat, 'will our Jerusalem resume its historic role as a peaceful shrine for all religions.'

Arafat's speech was another important milestone in the Palestinian nationalist movement's history. Following the Rabat Declaration, the Palestinian cause received international recognition and legitimacy. Arafat's speech led to the UN General Assembly granting the PLO official UN observer status.

A further diplomatic success came in November 1975 when the General Assembly invited the PLO to participate in debates concerning the Arab-Israel conflict, during which Resolution 3379 was passed, characterising Jewish nationalism (Zionism) 'as a form of racism and racial discrimination'. The resolution was passed by 72 to 35 with 32 abstentions. In the UN's history, no other nationalist movement had been singled out in this way. This set an annual pattern in which the General Assembly passes resolutions condemning Israel for its policies concerning the Palestinians. Resolution 3379 was rescinded in 1990, and although the UN has also passed numerous resolutions condemning terrorism, none has specifically condemned the PLO.

The PLO achieved another victory in 1975 when the US State Department acknowledged that 'the legitimate interests of the Palestinian Arabs must be taken into account in the negotiating of an Arab-Israeli peace.' However, when Israel protested that the PLO's Charter still called for Israel's destruction through armed force, US President Gerald Ford wrote to Israeli Prime Minister Yitzchak Rabin stating that the US would not deal with the PLO if it failed to recognise Israel's right to exist and refused to accept Security Council Resolution 242. It would be some years before the PLO satisfied these conditions.

In the meantime, the PLO became embroiled in internal Lebanese politics when it shifted its headquarters from Jordan to the refugee camps outside Beirut, significantly affecting Lebanon's internal stability.

# The PLO in Lebanon

The arrival of PLO forces in Lebanon in 1971 further destabilised an already fragile political system which, since independence, was based on power-sharing between the various religious communities (known as 'confessionalism'). The most powerful group in Lebanon were the Christian Maronites who viewed the PLO's military forces as a threat to their pre-eminent position.

The PLO established bases in the refugee camps just outside Beirut where its militias operated outside Lebanese government control. In response, Maronites established their own militias, most importantly the Phalange. Between

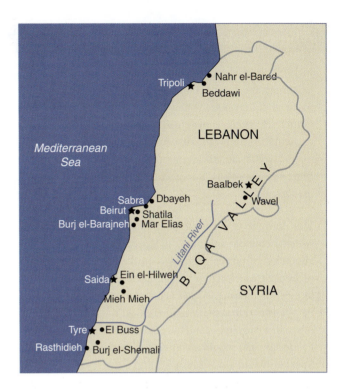

**Figure 9.10** Palestinian refugee camps in Lebanon.

1971 and 1975, numerous bloody battles between the PLO and the Phalange resulted in many civilian deaths and a deep-seated hatred between the two groups.

Syria, too, responded to the PLO's arrival in Lebanon, as Arafat presented a challenge to President Assad's own ambition to control that country. Assad also wanted to avoid confrontation with Israel if it invaded Lebanon to halt PLO attacks launched from its bases in the country's south. To undermine Arafat's Fatah forces, Assad mobilised two rival Palestinian groups in 1975, the Palestine Liberation Army (PLA) and al-Sa'iqa. Assad wanted these groups to control the Palestinian nationalist movement and gain military and political control over Lebanese territory. The Syrian Army provided nearly all of al-Sa'iqa's equipment, while 50 per cent of its troops and 75 per cent of its officers were Syrian. Both groups took their orders directly from Syria's Defence Minister.

## The civil war in Lebanon

By April 1975, Lebanon was highly unstable, following another round of gun battles between the Phalange and the PLO. On 13 April 1975, Palestinian gunmen

## The complex politics of Lebanon

In 1920, the League of Nations granted France a mandate to govern the former Ottoman territories of modern-day Syria and Lebanon. When Lebanon's Constitution was written in 1926, it was different in that it provided a particular formula for parliamentary representation of the major 'confessional' (religious) groups, principally, the Maronite Christians, Sunni Muslims, Shi'ite Muslims and the Druze.

This system of 'confessional' politics was maintained when Lebanon achieved independence in 1943. The allocation of power was based on the respective numbers of Lebanese belonging to the different groups according to the 1932 census. What became known as the 'National Pact' ensured that the Maronites would have the majority of seats in parliament and the position of President, that the Prime Minister would always be a Sunni, and parliament's Speaker would always be a Shi'ite.

However, between 1943 and 1975, the demographic balance in Lebanon gradually changed in favour of the Sunni and Shi'ite Muslim communities and they began to agitate for a revision of the National Pact to reflect changing demographics. This occasionally erupted into violence, most notably in the brief civil war of 1958.

By the mid 1970s, although no census was conducted, Muslims had become the majority. Tensions mounted as Muslims and Druze demanded more representation in the government and armed forces, which remained under Maronite control.

The arrival of PLO headquarters and fighters impacted significantly on this precarious balance of power between the various confessional groups. By the early 1970s, there were between 300 000 and 400 000 Palestinians in Lebanon, including 80 000 refugees. More than 90 per cent were Sunni Muslims, who sided with their brethren against the Maronites.

Another factor complicating Lebanese politics was Syria's pursuit of the Ba'ath Party's policy concerning 'Greater Syria', which held that Lebanon (and Jordan and Palestine) was an integral part of Syria, wrongfully separated by the League of Nations following World War I. Under President Hafez al-Assad, Syria pursued a policy to integrate Lebanon, politically, economically and militarily, into Syria. Assad viewed the PLO's arrival as a challenge to his own ambitions.

In April 1975, fighting between Maronites and the PLO triggered a bloody 15-year civil war, during which most Christians fought the 'National Movement', an alliance including leftist-oriented Muslims backed by Arafat's PLO faction. When the war ended in 1990, Lebanon had become a Syrian puppet state.

opened fire at a congregation outside a Maronite church in a Christian suburb of Beirut. This was followed by a Phalange ambush of a Palestinian bus which killed 26 people. That night, mortar shells were fired by PLO forces on Christian areas and the next day, the DFLP carried out hit-and-run raids against the Maronite dominated Lebanese Army resulting in Phalange retaliations. By 15 April, a full-scale artillery battle marked the beginning of a civil war that was to last for 15 years.

In January 1976, Syrian troops entered Lebanon to support the Christians and prevent a PLO victory. By December 1976, Syria had almost 30 000 troops in Lebanon under the guise of the 'Arab Deterrent Force', nominally under Arab League authority. The following year, Syria shifted its support to the Muslim and left-wing opponents of the Maronites.

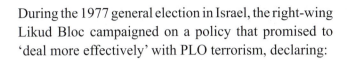

During the 1977 general election in Israel, the right-wing Likud Bloc campaigned on a policy that promised to 'deal more effectively' with PLO terrorism, declaring:

> The PLO is no national liberation organisation but an organisation of assassins, which the Arab countries use as a political and military tool, while also serving the interests of Soviet imperialism, to stir up the area. Its aim is to liquidate the State of Israel, set up an Arab country instead and make the Land of Israel part of the Arab world. The Likud government will strive to eliminate these murderous organisations in order to prevent them from carrying out their bloody deeds.

In view of Fatah's stated aim to 'eliminate the Zionist character' of the land 'both human and social', and to bring about the 'reverse emigration' of Jews from Israel, many in Israel viewed the PLO as being dedicated to the ethnic cleansing or genocide of the country's Jews and so supported Likud's policy.

An alliance was also formed between the Christian forces in Lebanon and the new Likud Government against their common enemy, the PLO.

# Israel's invasions of Lebanon

The PLO's war against the Phalange did not stop it from continuing its guerilla raids from southern Lebanon into northern Israel or its terrorist campaign against Jewish and Israeli targets around the world. By 1978, pressure was mounting on Likud to take tougher action against the PLO, as it had promised.

## Israel's 1978 invasion of Lebanon: 'Operation Litani'

In March 1978, PLO terrorists entered Israel from Lebanon and attacked the Tel Aviv-Haifa road, killing 37 civilians. Israel responded by launching 'Operation Litani', a major military offensive, in which Israel occupied southern Lebanon up to the Litani River. In June, Prime Minister Begin, under intense American pressure, ordered Israeli forces to withdraw. A UN Interim Force in Lebanon (UNIFIL) was deployed in southern Lebanon to prevent further PLO incursions into Israel, but this was ineffective and continuing PLO incursions embarrassed Begin's Government.

## Palestinians' responses to Likud policies

For Palestinians in the West Bank and Gaza, withdrawal of Israeli troops from Lebanon in the face of continuing PLO raids was viewed as a great success. This increased support for the PLO came at a time when Palestinians in the occupied territories were greatly angered by the surge in settlement construction after Likud had won government. The Palestinians knew that building settlements, particularly in the West Bank, was Begin's attempt to lay the foundations for permanent retention of the territory. Through various economic initiatives, Likud linked the West Bank and Gaza more closely to Israel, especially the West Bank. For example, the government had applied Israeli law to Jews residing in the settlements and developed a transport and communications network just for Israelis.

In response, and encouraged by the PLO's raids from southern Lebanon, many young Palestinians turned to violence to resist Israel's occupation. Grassroots Palestinian committees emerged, affiliated with the various PLO factions.

The Begin Government was frustrated by its failure to crush the tide of PLO-instigated Palestinian unrest within the occupied territories, and contemplated a major military operation to expel the PLO's bases from southern Lebanon. This was put on the backburner when US President Carter invited Begin and Sadat to Camp David to negotiate peace between Egypt and Israel.

## The PLO's response to the Camp David Accords and the Egyptian-Israeli Peace Treaty

Sadat had declared in 1977 that he would not reach peace with Israel unless it allowed for a Palestinian state in the West Bank and Gaza, but in the end, he gave priority to Egypt's needs and signed a peace treaty with Israel providing for Palestinian autonomy but not statehood.

The PLO denounced both the 1978 Camp David Accords and the 1979 Egyptian-Israeli Peace Treaty. This attitude was supported by most local Palestinian leaders in the occupied territories who refused to negotiate with Israel until it recognised the PLO as the sole legitimate representative of the Palestinians. They likewise supported PLO attacks on northern Israeli farms and villages, which continued unabated, especially in the Galilee, as did attacks against Israeli settlers in Gaza and the West Bank.

In 1981, after the Likud Bloc won a second election victory, Begin moved against the PLO. Ariel Sharon was appointed Defence Minister and planned a major invasion of Lebanon. To expel the PLO's bases, Sharon knew that Israeli forces would need to penetrate as far north as Beirut. Sharon turned to the Lebanese Phalange for assistance, the latter more than willing to help rid Lebanon of the PLO. The invasion was called Operation 'Shalom Ha'Galil' (Operation 'Peace for Galilee').

## Israel's 1982 invasion of Lebanon: 'Operation Peace for Galilee'

The immediate pretext for the invasion of Lebanon was the PLO's attempted assassination of Israel's Ambassador to Britain on 3 June 1982. The following day, Israel's air force bombed a sports stadium in Beirut, believed to be a PLO ammunition depot. The PLO responded by shelling Israeli towns in the Galilee.

On 6 June, Israeli ground forces crossed into Lebanon, declaring that the operation would free northern Israel from PLO rocket attacks by creating a 40 kilometre security zone in southern Lebanon. However, Sharon's aims were more extensive: to expel completely the PLO from Lebanon; to assist Israel's Christian allies to take control of the country; and to then sign a peace treaty with a Maronite-dominated government.

## The PLO is expelled from Lebanon

Within a month, Israeli troops reached Beirut where heavy fighting occurred for another month. Israel agreed to stop bombing the city only after the PLO was completely evacuated from Lebanon. An estimated 5000 PLO fighters left Beirut by sea for Tunis in North

Africa. Arafat fled to Syria but maintained a command base in the Biqa Valley in the east of Lebanon and in Tripoli in the north of the country. Both areas were occupied and controlled by Syria.

In June 1983, Assad expelled Arafat from Syria and instigated a rebellion against him by members of the anti-Arafat factions within Fatah and the PLO that had remained in Lebanon. By December that year, with the support of the Syrian army, these Palestinian fighters had defeated Arafat's remaining forces and expelled them from the country. The latter were evacuated from Tripoli and taken to Tunisia (although some travelled to Yemen and Algeria).

## The massacre of Palestinians at the Sabra and Shatila camps

On 14 September, Maronite Lebanese President, Bashir Gemayel, was killed by a bomb at his Beirut headquarters. The Syrians were blamed and fighting resumed between pro-Phalange forces and PLO remnants. The following day, the Israeli army occupied West Beirut and surrounded Palestinian refugee camps which they believed hid the remaining PLO fighters.

Christian Phalange forces under Eli Hobeika entered the Sabra and Shatila camps, which the IDF had sealed off. Once inside, the Phalange massacred more than 700 people, including women and children (some accounts put the figure as high as 2000). The Phalange forces claimed they were avenging Gemayel's murder and the massacres of Maronite civilians by the PLO during the civil war.

## The Kahan Commission of Enquiry

In Israel, news of the Sabra and Shatila massacres appalled Israelis. On 25 September alone, an estimated 400 000 Israelis (10 per cent of Israel's population) protested in Tel Aviv. Begin denied IDF responsibility but bowed to the demands of mass demonstrations throughout the country for a full enquiry.

The government established the Kahan Commission to investigate the massacres. It concluded that the killings had been carried out by Christian forces, but some Israeli political and military leaders, including Sharon, bore indirect responsibility because the IDF did not take measures to protect the Palestinians from the Phalange, knowing its hatred of Palestinians. As a result, a number of IDF officers resigned, and Sharon was demoted to a junior Cabinet position.

## A brief peace treaty between Israel and Lebanon

On 28 December 1982, talks began between Israeli and Christian Lebanese officials to broker a peace treaty. On 17 May 1983, an agreement was signed, based upon three principles:

1. Israeli withdrawal from Lebanon.
2. Ending the state of war between the two countries.
3. Creation of a 'security zone' in southern Lebanon to prevent the PLO's return.

However, some groups within the Lebanese government refused to ratify the treaty, bowing to Syrian pressure to cancel the agreement, which the government did on 5 March 1984. At the time, Syria had 30 000 troops in Lebanon.

Regardless of the failure to secure a long-term peace treaty with Lebanon, a new Israeli government moved to reduce its troop numbers there. The 1984 Israeli elections resulted in the formation of a 'national unity' government of the Labor and Likud parties. Labor leader, Shimon Peres became Prime Minister until 1986, when Likud leader, Yitzhak Shamir assumed the post. With broad domestic support, Peres redeployed Israeli troops in Lebanon to the south and established a 10 to 15 kilometre security zone along Israel's border.

Israel maintained its troops in southern Lebanon until May 2000, where they cooperated with the mainly Christian South Lebanon Army (SLA).

**Figure 9.11** Massacre of Palestinians in the Sabra and Shatila camps by Lebanese Phalange.

# Impact of the 1982 invasion of Lebanon on Israelis and Palestinians

Israel's invasion of Lebanon and the expulsion of the PLO had long-term ramifications for both Israelis and Palestinians. In Israel, it caused unprecedented divisions in public opinion and brought about the end of Begin's leadership. Many Israelis supported the government's initial objective of expelling the PLO bases in southern Lebanon, but opposed extending military operations to Beirut. Some Israeli soldiers even refused to fight in Lebanon. The war also reinvigorated Israeli peace groups such as *Shalom Achshav* ('Peace Now') and triggered new protest groups against government policies, especially in the occupied territories. Anti-war demonstrations lasted until Israel redeployed its troops to southern Lebanon in 1985.

The 1982 War was the first fought by the IDF without a domestic political consensus. Unlike the 1948, 1956, 1967 and 1973 wars, Israelis did not view 'Operation Peace for Galilee' as a defensive war essential to their survival. Opposition to the invasion was vindicated because Israel failed to impose a military solution on the intractable Palestinian problem and to force political change in Lebanon. Furthermore, Israel was widely criticised internationally for the invasion.

Another long-term outcome of the 1982 War was the creation of the Iranian-backed *Hizballah* ('Party of God') in response to Israel's occupation of southern Lebanon. Hizballah attacked northern Israeli towns and villages and waged an endless war against the IDF and the SLA within the 'security zone'. Consequently, Israel's confrontation with the PLO in Lebanon was replaced by ongoing fighting with Hizballah.

For the PLO, 12000 fighters had to leave Beirut for other Arab countries and PLO headquarters moved to Tunis, marking the end of the PLO's ability to operate as a 'state within a state' in an Arab country neighbouring Israel. As the years passed, the PLO's status declined as it grew demoralised and fragmented and was treated poorly by the Arab League. In its hour of need, it turned to its old adversary, Jordan's King Hussein.

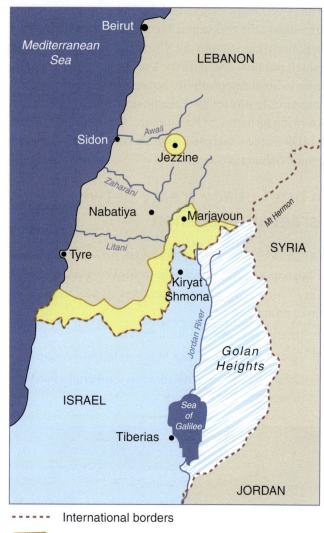

- - - - - International borders

▭ Security zone

◯ Security enclave

**Figure 9.12** Israel's 'security zone' in southern Lebanon.

## 'Unity Governments' in Israel

In September 1983, Menachem Begin resigned as Prime Minister and Likud leader, and was succeeded by Foreign Minister, Yitzhak Shamir. The 1984 Israeli elections provided no clear winner as neither Labor nor Likud gained enough support from smaller parties to form a coalition. After several weeks of difficult negotiations, they agreed on Israel's first government of 'national unity', which provided for the rotation of the office of Prime Minister and the combined office of Deputy Prime Minister and Foreign Minister midway through the government's 50-month term. During the first 25 months, Labor's Shimon Peres was Prime Minister, while Likud's Yitzhak Shamir was Deputy Prime Minister and Foreign Minister. Peres and Shamir switched places in October 1986.

The November 1988 election produced a similar result. Likud gained one more seat than Labor but could not form a coalition with religious and right-wing parties. Likud and Labor formed a second national unity government in January 1989 without providing for rotation. Yitzhak Shamir became Prime Minister, and Shimon Peres Deputy Prime Minister and Finance Minister.

This government fell in March 1990 in a vote of no confidence caused by disagreement over US Secretary of State Baker's 1989 initiative for Palestinian elections in the occupied territories. Labor leader Peres could not attract sufficient support among the religious parties to form government. Yitzhak Shamir then formed a Likud-led coalition government, including members from religious and right-wing parties. Shamir took office in June 1990, and held power for two years.

## The PLO's Jordanian option: the Amman Accords

In the wake of the PLO's defeat in Lebanon, the PLO leadership adopted a strategy advocated by Khalil al-Wazir, the so-called *Khiyar al-Urduni* (the 'Jordanian Option'). Al-Wazir argued (as he had since the PLO first became embroiled in Lebanon's quagmire) that the PLO's future lay in re-establishing itself in the occupied territories. This could only be done, he explained, via Jordan. This would require the PLO to improve its relationship with King Hussein, which had been very poor since Black September, 1970.

There was considerable PLO opposition to *rapprochement* with Hussein, but regardless, the Jordanian Option was developed to achieve the following objectives:

1. To enable the PLO to practise a degree of control over Jordan's operations in the West Bank, in particular, any negotiations King Hussein might hold with Israel.

2. To re-create a significant presence in Jordan based among its majority Palestinian population to assist in initiating activism against Israel in the occupied territories.

3. To ensure the national movement's dominance over the growing Islamist influence among Palestinians.

By early 1985, Arafat and Hussein reached a temporary, if somewhat uneasy, alliance. Hussein saw good relations with the PLO as a positive move to strengthen his legitimacy in the eyes of his Palestinian subjects. Despite the Arab League's 1974 Rabat Declaration, Hussein had not relinquished his ambition to represent the Palestinians, ever mindful that most Jordanians are of Palestinian origin. In January 1984, for example, Hussein reconvened Jordan's parliament for the first time since 1974, and appointed seven new members from the West Bank.

In February 1985, Arafat and Hussein signed the 'Amman Accords' (or the 'Hussein-Arafat Agreement'), pledging PLO and Jordanian cooperation and coordination of a joint peace initiative. Hussein's plan for peace with Israel was based on autonomy for West Bank Palestinians under Jordanian sovereignty. Arafat agreed to an eventual confederation with Jordan, but demanded an independent Palestinian state in the West Bank.

In February 1986, discussions became deadlocked over the PLO's refusal to recognise Israel and its ambiguity regarding terrorism, resulting in an end to Jordanian-PLO negotiations. In March, Hussein ordered the closure of the PLO's offices in Amman, and in a bold attempt to establish his influence in the West Bank, declared that he would now be responsible for the economic welfare of West Bank Palestinians, as a part of Jordan's new five-year Development Plan.

Hussein also increased the number of Palestinian seats (to about half) in an enlarged National Assembly. He wanted to create a Jordanian-Palestinian-Israeli administration and make the West Bank independent of the PLO so he could reach a settlement with Israel in which Jordan would regain at least partial sovereignty over the area.

## Israel and Jordan pursue peace: The 1987 'London Agreement'

In an effort to achieve his objectives, Hussein approached Israeli Foreign Minister Shimon Peres, with whom he had long maintained good relations. In April 1987, after secret negotiations held in Britain, they signed the 'London Agreement', the basic principles of which were a UN-sponsored conference involving all parties to the conflict, the purpose of which would be to conclude a comprehensive peace. It was intended that the Palestinians would be part of a Jordanian-Palestinian delegation.

The 'London Agreement' was endorsed by US President Ronald Reagan whose preferred model for resolving the conflict was a 'Jordanian solution', requiring Israel to cede large parts of the West Bank to Jordanian sovereignty and Palestinian autonomy. However, Likud Prime Minister, Yitzhak Shamir, agreed to meet only with Jordan and resisted US pressure for a comprehensive peace conference. The disagreement between Shamir and Peres highlighted differences between Labor and Likud concerning an Israeli-Palestinian agreement. Although both Labor and Likud refused to negotiate with the PLO while its Charter called for Israel's destruction, Labor was willing to accept Palestinian negotiators who had only indirect relationships with the PLO. Labor also favoured Palestinian autonomy in the West Bank, under Jordanian sovereignty, to which Likud was opposed.

The 'London Agreement' was thus abandoned. It proved to be Israel's last attempt to have Jordan as its principal negotiating partner in resolving the Palestinian issue.

The dynamics of the Arab-Israeli conflict changed dramatically in December 1987 with the outbreak of the first Palestinian *intifada* (uprising), which caught everyone by surprise, including the Israelis, King Hussein, Arafat and the PLO. It marked the point in this history when the conflict's primary focus returned to where it had begun, in the land of Israel/Palestine.

## Summary

With Israel's victory over the Arab states in 1967, four forces competed for legitimate representation of the Palestinians: the PLO; Jordan; Syria; and less well-defined local forces in the occupied territories. Between 1969 and 1982, the PLO appeared to have the upper hand, with its status accepted by the Arab League in the Rabat Declaration in 1974, and by the UN General Assembly granting the PLO Observer Status in 1975.

However, the PLO was dealt a severe blow by Israel's invasion of Lebanon in 1982 and its expulsion to distant Tunis. After years of promises by the PLO and the Arab states, the Palestinians were still no closer to gaining self-determination and liberation of any part of Palestine.

Israel, too, suffered from the Lebanon war, which provoked widespread domestic opposition. For the first time in Israel's history, some of its soldiers refused to fight. Mass demonstrations followed the Christian Phalange massacre of Palestinians in the Sabra and Shatila refugee camps and Ariel Sharon was found 'indirectly responsible' for not stopping the massacre, and was demoted to a junior government position.

Despite the Lebanese setbacks, the Likud government continued its policy of settlement expansion in the occupied territories. This fed into a broader sense of helplessness among the Palestinians, and led in December 1987 to the first intifada. The major focus of the Arab-Israeli conflict thus returned to the local level. A second major war in the Persian Gulf in 1990-91 highlighted the regional conflict for only a short period before it returned to local dynamics.

An examination of the first Palestinian uprising and the impact of the 1990-91 Gulf War on the Arab-Israeli conflict will be examined in the following chapter.

# Review and research questions

1. Why was the Palestine Liberation Organisation established in 1964? Who were the key people and countries involved?

2. What impact did the 1967 War have on the Palestinian nationalist movement?

3. Read the extracts from the original 1964 PLO Charter and the revised 1968 version which you can find at http://www.palestine-un.org/plo/pna_two.html. Identify the differences in the aims and methods of the two documents and account for these differences.

4. What were the causes of the civil war in Jordan in 1970? What impact did it have on the PLO?

5. What were the causes of the civil war in Lebanon? What impact did it have on the PLO?

6. Assess the effectiveness of the PLO in pursuing its goals between 1969 and 1982.

7. Research the policies of the Likud-led government in relation to the occupied territories during the late 1970s and the 1980s. How did these policies differ from those of the previous Labor governments?

8. What were the reasons for Israel's invasions of Lebanon in 1978 and 1982? How effective were these operations in realising Israel's objectives?

9. What was the impact of 'Operation Peace for Galilee' on Israeli society? How did it affect the Palestinians?

10. Research the personal background of King Hussein of Jordan, and the key events in Jordan during his rule. What were his values and attitudes influencing his relations with the Palestinians, the PLO and Israel? What were the major events in which he was involved that impacted upon the Arab-Israeli conflict? How would you assess his contribution to this history?

## Discussion question

1. 'The role of domestic Arab and Israeli politics in shaping the conflict needs to be considered from 1948 onwards. In the Arab world this was compounded by the instability of many Arab regimes, and in Israel, by the importance of coalition forming.' Discuss this statement in reference to the period of the conflict from 1967 to 1987.

# 10 The First Palestinian Intifada and the Madrid Peace Process 1987 to 1992

By the end of this chapter you will be familiar with the:

- first Palestinian *intifada*, 1987-1993
- Israeli Government proposals for peace with the Palestinians
- PLO's proposals for peace with Israel
- 1990-91 Gulf War and its impact on the Arab-Israeli conflict
- Madrid Peace Process.

From 1949 to 1967, the Arab-Israeli conflict was played out in border disputes and wars between Israel and the Arab states. From 1969 until 1982, the Palestinian nationalist movement re-emerged under the PLO's leadership, although its battles were fought primarily in Jordan and then Lebanon. On 9 December 1987, following mounting tension between Palestinians and Israeli settlers in the occupied territories, Palestinian youths, disillusioned with the PLO leadership, initiated a grassroots uprising known by the Arabic word *intifada*. The focus of the Arab-Israeli conflict thus returned to the scene of its inception a century earlier.

The first Palestinian intifada spread rapidly throughout the occupied territories, marked by civil disobedience, general strikes, boycotts of Israeli products, graffiti and barricades. Demonstrators throwing rocks against heavily-armed Israeli troops captured international attention. By the time it ended in 1993, more than 1300 Israelis and Palestinians had died and Palestinian Islamist groups had emerged to challenge the PLO's power and prestige.

Over the following five years, important events took place that impacted on the conflict at both the local and regional levels, planting the seeds for the Arab-Israeli peace process of the 1990s. These included Israel's proposal for Palestinian autonomy in the occupied territories, the PLO's statement of acceptance of a 'two state solution' to the conflict, and a second war in the Persian Gulf from 1990-91.

| Timeline | Event |
|---|---|
| December 1987 | The first Palestinian *intifada* begins. |
| 1988 to 1990 | Second 'unity government' in Israel. |
| February 1988 | The Islamic Resistance Movement (Hamas) is founded. |
| June 1988 | The PLO announces at the Arab League Meeting in Algiers its readiness for a 'two-state solution' to resolve the conflict. |
| July 1988 | King Hussein relinquishes Jordan's claim to sovereignty over the West Bank. |
| November 1988 | The PNC proclaims the establishment of a Palestinian state with Jerusalem as its capital. |
| December 1988 | The USA begins formal talks with the PLO for the first time. |
| May 1989 | The Knesset approves the 'Shamir Plan' for Palestinian autonomy in the occupied territories. |
| March 1990 | Labor resigns from the 'unity government'. |
| June 1990 | Yitzhak Shamir forms new Likud-led government; repudiates May 1989 autonomy plan for Palestinians. |
| August 1990 to February 1991 | The Second Gulf War. |
| March 1991 | Syria, Egypt, and the states of the Gulf Cooperation Council sign the 'Declaration of Damascus' which includes a proposal for an international conference to resolve the Arab-Israeli conflict. |
| October to November 1991 | The Madrid Conference. |
| December 1991 | The Union of Soviet Socialist Republics (USSR) is dissolved. |
| 1991 to 1993 | Arab-Israeli bilateral negotiations are held in Washington. |
| January 1992 | Arab-Israeli multilateral negotiations begin in Moscow. |

These events, and their consequences for the Arab-Israeli and Israeli-Palestinian conflicts are the focus of this chapter.

# Factors leading to the first Palestinian intifada

For Palestinians, the first intifada expressed their anger and frustration after 20 years of Israeli occupation of the Gaza Strip and West Bank, and previous 18 years of Egyptian and Jordanian occupation. After endless vows by the Arab states and the PLO to destroy Israel and liberate Palestine, the status quo seemed unchangeable. Bypassing their discredited leaders, the Palestinians started the intifada as a popular mobilisation that drew on organisations and institutions that had developed under occupation. The PLO officials in Tunis were taken completely by surprise, but quickly claimed leadership of the uprising.

Long-term factors leading to the first Palestinian intifada are as follows.

## Israeli settlements

During the 1970s and 1980s, the number of Israeli settlements in the occupied territories increased significantly, particularly in the West Bank. While on average 770 Israelis per annum settled in the West Bank and Gaza between 1967 and 1977, this number increased to an average of 5960 per annum between 1978 and 1987.

In Gaza, Jewish settlements were built either in the north, close to the border, or along the coast. By 1987, about 2400 settlers lived alongside 750 000 Palestinians. The Israeli settlements were heavily fortified and isolated from Palestinian population centres. Water restrictions were imposed on Palestinians to benefit the settlers' agriculture. This caused a severe decline in the Gazans' citrus industry, with settlers using seven times more water per capita than Palestinians.

## Intifada

The Arabic word *intifada* literally means to 'shake off'. When used in the context of the attempt to shake off an unwanted government, the English equivalent is 'uprising'. The word 'intifada' is best known from two Palestinian uprisings against Israel. The first intifada started in 1987 and ended, officially, in 1993 with the Oslo Accords. It was also called the 'war of the stones' in reference to Palestinian youths throwing rocks and stones at Israeli soldiers.

The second Palestinian intifada began in October 2000, lasting until 2005. It is also called the al-Aqsa Intifada as it officially began on *al-Haram al-Sharif* (the location of the al-Aqsa Mosque) following the visit there of Likud leader Ariel Sharon on 30 September 2000.

Another important though less well known intifada was the 1991 Shi'ite uprising in Iraq. After the 1990-91 Gulf War, Iraqi Shi'ites rose against the regime of Saddam Hussein, hoping to use his defeat for their liberation from years of oppression. The Iraqi army crushed the intifada, killing at least 300 000 Shi'ites, burying many in mass graves.

| | | | | |
|---|---|---|---|---|
| 1 | Elei Sinai | | 12 | Gan Or |
| 2 | Dugit | | 13 | Pe'at Sadeh |
| 3 | Nissanit | | 14 | Bedola'h |
| 4 | Netzarim | | 15 | Atzmona |
| 5 | Kfar Darom | | 16 | Morag |
| 6 | Netzer Hazani | | 17 | Rafiah Yam |
| 7 | Katif | | 18 | Kerem Atzmona |
| 8 | Ganei Tal | | 19 | Shirat Ha Yam |
| 9 | Kfar Yam | | 20 | Slav |
| 10 | Neveh Dekalim | | 21 | Tel Katifa |
| 11 | Gadid | | | |

**Figure 10.1**  Israeli settlements in the Gaza Strip.

Settlement activity in the West Bank was far more extensive under successive Likud governments. In 1977, when Likud first came to power in Israel, approximately 4400 Israeli settlers lived in the West Bank and about 1 000 000 Palestinians (including those in East Jerusalem). Within ten years, the Israeli settler population in the West Bank had increased to 54 500, living among 1 200 000 Palestinians.

As the number of settlements grew, Palestinians feared that Israel might one day permanently annex part, if not all, of the territories. The UN General Assembly passed resolutions condemning the settlements, characterising them as illegal under international law. However, Israeli construction continued.

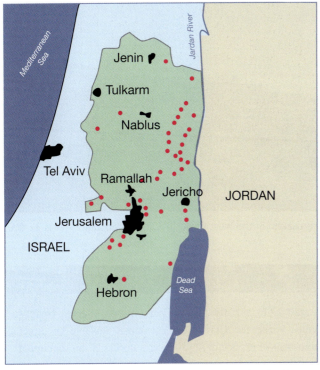

**Figure 10.2** ● Israeli settlements built in the West Bank, 1967-1977.

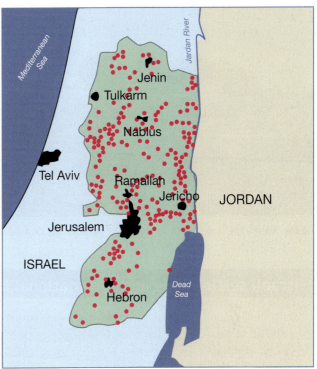

**Figure 10.3** ● Israeli settlements in the West Bank by April 1987.

| West Bank populations | | |
|---|---|---|
| Timeline | Jewish | Palestinian Arabs and others (includes East Jerusalem) |
| 1948-1967 | 0 | 831 000 |
| 1977 | 5000 | 1 000 000 |
| 1987 | 55 000 | 1 200 000 |
| 2000 | 190 000 | 1 850 000 |

# Grassroots leadership

Following the expulsion of the PLO from Lebanon, support for its 'leadership in exile' declined in the occupied territories. The vacuum was filled by younger Palestinians who had grown up under Israeli occupation, questioning their parents' attitude of *sumud* ('fortitude' or 'endurance') and rejecting their submission to daily humiliations.

From the mid 1980s, demonstrations by Palestinians against the occupation began to increase, marking an important turning point in the Israeli-Palestinian conflict. Previously, the majority of attacks on Israelis, both within Israel and in the occupied territories, had come from PLO gunmen sent from outside. Now most of the violence in the territories was initiated from within, which led to more frequent Israeli retaliations. Yitzhak Rabin, Defence Minister in the Unity Government, implemented an 'iron fist' policy to crush the disturbances. Tensions mounted, particularly in Gaza, where the pattern of 'protest and repression' intensified during 1987.

The First Palestinian Intifada

**Figure 10.4** The Israeli settlement of Ma'ale Adumim located east of Jerusalem in the West Bank. In 2005, its population was 32 000.

## Israeli settlements and international law

Undoubtedly one of the most contentious issues in the Israeli-Palestinian conflict has been Israel's policy since 1967 of permitting Jewish settlements in the occupied territories.

Resolutions by the UN General Assembly (for example Resolution ES-10/6 of 9 February 1999) and by the Security Council (for example Resolution 453 of 20 July 1979) have condemned the settlements, but these resolutions of themselves are not legally binding. In their non-binding advisory opinion concerning Israel's separation barrier in 2004, the majority of judges of the International Court of Justice (ICJ) expressed the view that Israeli settlements in the occupied territories are a violation of the Fourth Geneva Convention relative to the Protection of Civilian Persons in Time of War (12 August 1949).

The final paragraph of Article 49 of the Fourth Geneva Convention reads: 'The Occupying Power shall not deport or transfer parts of its own civilian population into the territory it occupies.' Israel has argued that the Convention does not apply to the West Bank and Gaza Strip because these areas have never been part of the territory of any state that is a party to the Convention. Also, in Israel's view, while the Convention prohibits forcible or direct transfers of an occupying power's civilians into occupied territory, it does not prohibit measures that merely permit or finance such transfers, as these are not compulsory.

However, most international lawyers (including the majority of judges of the ICJ) believe that the rules of the Fourth Geneva Convention have universal application, and also prohibit 'indirect' transfers of an occupying power's civilians into occupied territory, a view shared by a majority of UN member states. Article 8(2)(b)(viii) of the Statute of the International Criminal Court (ICC) that was established in 2002, expressly prohibits 'indirect' transfers, unlike the original Fourth Geneva Convention. Israel is a party to the Geneva Conventions, but not the ICC Statute and is therefore not legally bound by the latter.

Nevertheless, Israel withdrew all of its settlers and military forces from Gaza in September 2005, dismantling all the settlements there. Four settlements in the West Bank were also dismantled.

## Economic and social conditions

Whilst Israeli rule brought improved health care and education for Palestinians in Gaza and the West Bank, the lives of many Palestinians, especially those living in the refugee camps, remained miserable. This was most notable in the Gaza Strip, an area of only 360 square kilometres with one of the highest birth rates in the world. By late 1987, 10 per cent of West Bank Palestinians and 25 per cent of Gazans lived in refugee camps, enduring overcrowding, no running water, and sewage flowing openly in the streets.

In 1987, over half the male workers in the Gaza Strip and about a third in the West Bank were employed in Israel, where they saw a much higher standard of living than at home. Paid less than Israelis, they were often employed in menial jobs. Whilst income from jobs in Israel financed a university education for some Palestinians, there were few available jobs once they graduated, due to the high rate of unemployment.

## A future of 'no hope'

By the mid 1980s, more than half of the population in Gaza and the West Bank was aged under fifteen. One-third of the population was aged between fifteen and thirty-four. Without hope that the Arab states would, or could, defeat Israel, most Palestinians also considered the PLO leaders to be far removed from the harsh realities of the territories, living extravagantly in their villas in distant Tunisia.

Many Palestinians concluded that the only way to 'shake off' Israeli rule was to act themselves, rather than rely any longer on the PLO and the Arab states.

## The outbreak of the first intifada December 1987

Violence in the territories had been escalating rapidly from the beginning of 1987.

- In February and March, stone-throwing at Israeli soldiers and settlers led to the deportation of a number of Palestinians.
- In April, a Jewish settler died when his car was firebombed; the major Palestinian university in the West Bank, Bir Zeit, was temporarily closed; and 80 Palestinians from Gaza were arrested.
- In June, Jewish settlers from Kiryat Arba (near Hebron) attacked the Dheisheh refugee camp near Bethlehem.
- In July, when the commander of the Israeli military police in Gaza was killed, the entire Strip was placed under curfew.

**Figure 10.5** Rafah refugee camp in Gaza, 1987.

- In October, seven Palestinians were killed during clashes with the Israeli police and army in two separate incidents and an Israeli settler shot a Palestinian teenager.
- In November, a lone Palestinian gunman on a hang-glider flew into northern Israel from Lebanon and killed six Israeli soldiers. By the end of the month, daily riots were occurring throughout the occupied territories and were particularly severe in the Gaza Strip.

The event that eventually triggered the intifada occurred on 9 December, when an Israeli tank transport vehicle accidentally collided with Palestinian workers' cars at the military checkpoint in northern Gaza, killing four Palestinians and seriously injuring seven. Rumours spread rapidly falsely claiming that the collision was a deliberate act of revenge for the killing of an Israeli in Gaza a few days before. The funerals for those killed turned into mass demonstrations against the occupation. They turned violent the next day and the uprising quickly spread to the West Bank.

## The national leadership of the uprising (UNLU)

The PLO leaders were caught off guard by the outbreak of the intifada. They first heard about it, one report claimed, on their televisions in Tunis. But they quickly attempted to take control, increasing the PLO's presence in the territories and establishing in January 1988, *al-Qiyada al-Wataniyya al-Muwahhida li'l-Intifada* (the 'Unified National Leadership of the Uprising' – UNLU).

The UNLU brought together the four largest nationalist groups then active in the territories: Fatah, the PFLP, the DFLP and the Palestinian Communist Party. They organised general strikes, demonstrations and other forms of civil disobedience, by the regular publication of numbered communiqués. The pamphlets also promoted the (false) claim that the PLO had organised the intifada, reaffirming it as the sole representative of the Palestinian people.

The communiqués articulated the PLO's goals for the uprising:

**Long-term objective:**

To bring about the end of Israeli rule and to establish a democratic Palestinian state. This would be achieved by means of a long struggle.

**Short-term objectives:**

1. To draw the world's attention to the urgent need for a solution, to be achieved by using the mass media, particularly television.

2. To involve the maximum number of Palestinians in the uprising to assure its indefinite continuation.

3. To obtain the release of detainees, the closure of detention camps, cessation of torture and the demolition of houses.

4. To foment comprehensive civil disobedience, such as a halt to the payment of taxes.

5. To discourage residents in the territories from working in Israel.

6. To establish local Palestinian administrative bodies to replace Israeli civil authorities.

7. To encourage world opinion to put pressure on Israel:
   (a) to stop building settlements in the territories, and
   (b) to attend an international peace conference, with the PLO providing a separate delegation as the 'sole legitimate representative' of the Palestinians.

The PLO's claim to leadership of the intifada was immediately challenged by Islamist groups that had, by 1988, established an extensive, grassroots support base in the occupied territories. The 'Islamisation' of Palestinian nationalism provided an alternative ideology to the PLO's secular nationalism. This distinctive feature of the first intifada would have a long-term impact on Palestinian politics and the Israeli-Palestinian conflict.

# Key features of the first Palestinian intifada

## The rise of Islamist movements as an expression of Palestinian nationalism

Throughout the 1980s, the Egyptian-based Muslim Brotherhood established Islamist groups in both Gaza and the West Bank. When the intifada began in 1987, two important movements emerged, the larger being *Harkhat al Muqawama al-Islamiyya* ('the Islamic Resistance Movement'), known by its acronym, Hamas (which means 'zeal' in Arabic). The smaller group was *Harakat al-Jihād al-Islāmi al-Filastīn* ('Palestinian Islamic Jihad Movement').

### Key concept: Islamism, Islamist

Islamism is a set of political ideologies that view Islam not only as a religion, but also as a political system that should govern all spheres of legal, cultural, social and political life. Islamist movements seek to change the political system of a state and the foundations of society by implementing a conservative version of *Sharia* (Islamic law).

Islamists do not all hold identical views. For example, they differentiate between what is referred to as 'Islamism from above' and 'Islamism from below'. In the first version, the priority is to overthrow the state through violent action and to impose *Sharia* by force (as happened in Iran in 1979, and as attempted by groups like al-Qaeda). In the second version, Islamists attempt to establish and organise what are referred to as 'Islamised spaces' in society, to 'change society from within' using non-violent means, that is, to build an Islamist society 'from the ground up'.

People belonging to an Islamist group call themselves, and are called by other Islamists, '*islaamiyy* for men and '*islaamiyya* for women. Both men and women are called Islamists in English.

## The Islamic Resistance Movement: Hamas

The Islamist groups established in Gaza and the West Bank by the Muslim Brotherhood aimed primarily to establish there an Islamist Palestinian society. Despite their radically anti-Israel and anti-Jewish rhetoric, the Brotherhood did not openly confront Israeli forces during the decade before the intifada. The one exception was Sheikh Ahmad Yassin, founder of the most important network of Islamist groups in Gaza. Before 1987, he had already been arrested and convicted by Israel for establishing an armed cell to destroy Israel.

**Figure 10.6** Hamas founder: Ahmad Yassin (c.1937-2004).

When the intifada began in December 1987, Yassin quickly established Hamas to coordinate the activities of the various Muslim Brotherhood groups and to promote the uprising. Hamas published its own communiqué in opposition to those of the UNLU, providing a precise timetable for general strikes, fasting periods, and direct confrontation with Israeli forces.

Hamas' attempt to take control of the intifada coincided with efforts to 'Islamise' the population. It published pamphlets promoting religious sentiment and organised religious education in the mosques. Hamas also issued warnings to shopkeepers not to exploit Palestinians involved in resistance and threatened Palestinians who 'collaborated with the enemy'. Beatings were used as a warning. Many suspected collaborators were killed.

Yassin also established a network of military cells and prisoner committees responsible for collecting information about the IDF, training recruits in military tactics and organising operations.

In August 1988, Hamas published its Charter, a 40-page text divided into 36 articles, setting out its beliefs and objectives. Establishing its nationalist credentials, the Hamas Charter declares that '*wataniyya* (patriotism) is an integral part of the profession of faith.' Based on the belief that Palestine has been an Islamic *waqf* since its Muslim conquest and 'will be until the day of Judgement', *jihad* (holy war) is asserted to be a religious duty and the only way to victory. Thus the primary objective of the organisation is 'to unfurl the banner of Allah over every inch of Palestine', namely, the West Bank, Gaza and the territory of Israel. In its statements about the Jews, some of the Charter's provisions are openly racist, such as Articles 7 and 32.

**Figure 10.7** Hamas logo.

# Palestinian Islamic Jihad Movement

The Palestinian Islamic Jihad was formed in Gaza during the 1970s by Fathi Shaqaqi as a branch of the Egyptian Islamic Jihad, the group responsible for assassinating Egyptian President Anwar Sadat in 1981. That year the group became more publicly active in Gaza. Its political platform made jihad against Israel a *fard 'ayn* ('religious duty'). The name 'Islamic Jihad' (IJ) became generic for all groups embracing this principle.

**Figure 10.8** Islamic Jihad logo.

For IJ, destruction of Israel is obligatory for the successful Islamisation of Muslim society in general, and Palestine in particular. The liberation of Palestine, IJ argues, is a religious duty that concerns the entire Islamic community. According to IJ, the main challenge of the present times for Muslims is to protect Islam from the 'West's repeated attacks', which Israel spearheads 'against the Muslim world'. It is therefore imperative to 'annihilate the Western menace by destroying the Jewish entity.'

Islamic Jihad is much smaller than Hamas, and lacks its wide social network. However, its commitment to ongoing violence played an important role when the intifada began. When Israel attempted to destroy the organisation, IJ relocated its headquarters to Damascus in Syria as a base for operations against both the IDF and Israeli civilians.

## Israel's initial support for the Islamist groups

Throughout the 1980s, while the Islamist networks were establishing themselves, focusing primarily on reconstructing Palestinian society based on *Sharia*, Israel viewed them as a non-violent alternative to the PLO leadership. Further, Israelis saw the Muslim Brotherhood's charity work as a means of pacifying the Palestinian population. Israel changed its views of the Islamist organisations once the intifada began and Hamas and IJ declared publicly their mission to destroy Israel through jihad.

**In The Name Of The Most Merciful Allah**

Israel will exist and will continue to exist until Islam will obliterate it, just as it obliterated others before it ...

**Article 1:** The Islamic Resistance Movement: The Movement's program is Islam. From it, it draws its ideas, ways of thinking and understanding of the universe, life and man. It resorts to it for judgement in all its conduct, and it is inspired by it for guidance of its steps.

**Article 2:** The Islamic Resistance Movement is one of the wings of Muslim Brotherhood in Palestine. Muslim Brotherhood Movement is a universal organisation which constitutes the largest Islamic movement in modern times. It is characterised by its deep understanding, accurate comprehension and its complete embrace of all Islamic concepts of all aspects of life, culture, creed, politics, economics, education, society, justice and judgement, the spreading of Islam, education, art, information, science of the occult and conversion to Islam ...

**Article 6:** The Islamic Resistance Movement is a distinguished Palestinian movement, whose allegiance is to Allah, and whose way of life is Islam. It strives to raise the banner of Allah over every inch of Palestine, for under the wing of Islam followers of all religions can coexist in security and safety where their lives, possessions and rights are concerned. In the absence of Islam, strife will be rife, oppression spreads, evil prevails and schisms and wars will break out.

**Article 7:** ... The Islamic Resistance Movement is one of the links in the chain of the struggle against the Zionist invaders. It goes back to 1939, to the emergence of the martyr Izz al-Din al-Kassam and his brethren the fighters, members of Muslim Brotherhood. It goes on to reach out and become one with another chain that includes the struggle of the Palestinians and Muslim Brotherhood in the 1948 war and the Jihad operations of the Muslim Brotherhood in 1968 and after. ... the Islamic Resistance Movement aspires to the realisation of Allah's promise, no matter how long that should take. The Prophet, Allah bless him and grant him salvation, has said: 'The Day of Judgement will not come about until Muslims fight the Jews, when the Jew will hide behind stones and trees. The stones and trees will say O Muslims, O Abdulla, there is a Jew behind me, come and kill him. Only the Gharkad tree would not do that because it is one of the trees of the Jews.'

**Article 8:** Allah is its target, the Prophet is its model, the Koran its constitution: Jihad is its path and death for the sake of Allah is the loftiest of its wishes ...

**Article 11:** The Islamic Resistance Movement believes that the land of Palestine is an Islamic *Waqf* consecrated for future Muslim generations until Judgement Day. It, or any part of it, should not be squandered: it, or any part of it, should not be given up. Neither a single Arab country nor all Arab countries, neither any king or president, nor all the kings and presidents, neither any organisation nor all of them, be they Palestinian or Arab, possess the right to do that ...

**Article 13:** Initiatives, and so-called peaceful solutions and international conferences, are in contradiction to the principles of the Islamic Resistance Movement. Abusing any part of Palestine is abuse directed against part of the religion. Nationalism of the Islamic Resistance Movement is part of its religion. ... There is no solution for the Palestinian question except through Jihad. Initiatives, proposals and international conferences are all a waste of time and vain endeavours. The Palestinian people know better than to consent to having their future, rights and fate toyed with.

**Article 27:** The Palestine Liberation Organisation is the closest to the heart of the Islamic Resistance Movement. It contains the father and the brother, the next of kin and the friend. The Muslim does not estrange himself from his father, brother, next of kin or friend. Our homeland is one, our situation is one, our fate is one and the enemy is a joint enemy to all of us. ... [However] we are unable to exchange the present or future Islamic Palestine with the secular idea. The Islamic nature of Palestine is part of our religion and whoever takes his religion lightly is a loser. ... The day the Palestine Liberation Organisation adopts Islam as its way of life, we will become its soldiers, and fuel for its fire that will burn the enemies ...

**Article 32:** ... The Zionist plan is limitless. After Palestine, the Zionists aspire to expand from the Nile to the Euphrates. When they will have digested the region they overtook, they will aspire to further expansion, and so on. Their plan is embodied in the 'Protocols of the Elders of Zion', and their present conduct is the best proof of what we are saying ...

## The *Shibab* and 'low-tech' violence

Another feature of the intifada was the central role played by young Palestinians known as the *shibab*. From the outset, the uprising was conducted in the streets of the refugee camps where the *shibab* carried out ambushes of IDF patrols and then engaged with them in street fighting, showering Israeli troops with rocks and stones, petrol bombs ('Molotov cocktails') and grenades. Of those Palestinians who were killed in clashes with Israeli troops, 23 per cent were under the age of sixteen.

Palestinians also blocked roads into Arab villages using either stones or burning tyres. After 1991, stabbings of Israeli civilians in urban areas also became more frequent.

## Civil disobedience and low-level violence

In addition to violence against the Israeli army and settlers, many Palestinians also supported the intifada through non-violent means, engaging in what is called 'civil disobedience'. This took the form of general strikes, and the resignation of most Palestinian policemen who had previously helped to maintain order in the major Palestinian population areas. Political graffiti also became a popular means of protest.

In 1988, the Palestinians began withholding taxes used by Israel for the territories' administration. When prison did not stop the activists, Israel attempted to crush the boycott by heavy fines, seizing equipment and goods from local stores, factories, and even homes.

**Figure 10.9** Palestinian youths throwing stones at IDF.

Further non-violent action by Palestinians during the intifada involved dissolution of Village League branches set up by Israel to facilitate its rule. When regular schools were closed, underground schools were also established.

## Widespread international media coverage

World media coverage of Palestinian youths throwing objects at Israeli tanks became another feature of the intifada, winning sympathy for the Palestinian cause. In the 1967 War, Israel had been portrayed in the international media as the 'underdog', surrounded by bellicose Arab states; however, during the intifada, the Palestinians were portrayed as underdogs and Israel as the oppressor.

## Israel's military response: Continuing the 'Iron Fist' policy

The Israeli authorities, like the PLO, did not foresee the intifada. Their immediate response was to try and crush the uprising by harsh, swift retaliation. Rabin's 'Iron Fist' policy, first instituted in the mid 1980s, was reintroduced. Rubber bullets and tear gas were used against crowds of demonstrators.

Curfews were imposed to keep demonstrators off the streets, and universities closed to minimise nationalist agitation. Thousands of Palestinians were imprisoned and prisoners were routinely beaten, as were Palestinians stopped by IDF patrols. Homes of hundreds of leading activists were either sealed or blown up to deter further rebellion. Houses located next to stone-throwing sites were routinely vandalised and tear-gassed, affecting also people who had not participated in the stone-throwing.

By December 1989, the end of the second year of the intifada, an estimated 626 Palestinians and 43 Israelis had been killed. 37 439 Palestinians were wounded, and between 35 000 and 40 000 arrested. Instead of crushing the uprising, Israel's reprisals heightened Palestinian nationalist feeling.

All the while, both domestic and international pressure mounted against Israel's 'Iron Fist' policy. America, too, urged Israel to change its policies. In September 1988, US Secretary of State, George Shultz, stated:

> The status quo between the Arabs and Israelis does not work. It is not viable. It is dangerous. Israel's security is paramount, but Palestinian political rights must also be recognised and addressed. The principle must be land for peace, and negotiations between Israel and the Palestinians.

Within Israel, the IDF took legal action against Israeli soldiers charged with exceeding their orders. Their defence, that they were following orders from superiors, including Defence Minister Yitzhak Rabin, was disallowed by the Israeli courts.

## Israel's political response: The 1989 'Shamir Plan'

While Israel's unity government agreed on its military response to the intifada, its political response reflected diametrically opposed views held by the two key coalition parties, Labor and Likud.

- The *Labor Party* had been committed since 1967 to the principle of 'land for peace', involving Israel's withdrawal from the West Bank and Gaza Strip in exchange for peace with the Palestinians and the Jordanians. It was intended, though, that the West Bank would form part of a Palestinian/Jordanian federation, the 'Jordanian Option'.

- The *Likud Party*, on the other hand, opposed giving any territory to Jordan or the Palestinians, maintaining that Palestinian autonomy in the West Bank and Gaza Strip would not occur under a Palestinian government or within a Jordanian federation.

In May 1989, the government compromised, approving a 20-point plan for Palestinian autonomy in the occupied territories.

Known as the 'Shamir Plan', after Israel's Prime Minister Yitzhak Shamir, its key points were:

1. The continuation of the political process by direct negotiations based on the principles of the Camp David Accords.

2. Opposition to the establishment of an 'additional Palestinian state in the Gaza district and in the area between Israel and Jordan.

3. No negotiations with the PLO.

4. Democratic elections among the Palestinians in the territories to be held 'in an atmosphere devoid of violence, threats, and terror'. Those elected would negotiate with Israel and Jordan a five-year transitional period of self-rule (Stage A); and eventually 'a permanent solution' for peace between Israel and Jordan (Stage B).

5. During the transitional period of Palestinian self-rule, Israel would continue to be responsible for security, foreign affairs and all matters concerning Israeli citizens.

Arafat responded to the Shamir Plan by insisting that the PLO was the only legitimate representative of the Palestinian people with whom Israel must negotiate. However, he also declared that the PLO supported elections in the territories, though only after Israel had withdrawn from *all* of the West Bank and Gaza. Hamas dismissed the entire plan. It was committed to the destruction of Israel and hence refused to negotiate with it.

## Competing Palestinian leaderships

As the uprising progressed, the PLO lost ground to Islamist organisations in the territories, especially to Hamas. Hamas was bolder in its resistance to the occupation, but equally harsh towards internal rivals and the wider Palestinian population. While the Tunis-based PLO leadership focused primarily on the national struggle, Hamas also had a social and religious agenda.

In an effort to regain popularity among Palestinians and to take advantage of international media coverage of the intifada, Arafat followed the advice of his deputy, Mahmoud Abbas (Abu Mazen), to announce in June 1988 that he was ready to make several important concessions in an effort to resolve the conflict.

## The PLO's diplomatic initiative: The declaration of a Palestinian State and recognition of Israel

At an Arab League meeting in June 1988, Bassam Abu Sharif, a close adviser to Arafat, set out a plan for a 'two-state solution' to the Israeli-Palestinian conflict. Central to the plan would be PLO-Israeli negotiations under UN supervision. In November, the proposal was endorsed at the 19th Palestine National Council meeting in Algiers. On 15 November, at the PNC's closing session, Arafat declared the establishment of the independent State of Palestine in the West Bank and Gaza Strip, for which he received a standing ovation. But it was a 'state' that controlled neither its territory nor its people, a state in name only.

The new PLO political program went further, accepting for the first time UN resolutions 242 and 338. It condemned terrorism outside Israel and the occupied territories, and endorsed the UN's partition plan of 1947, as set out in UN Resolution 181. Significantly, the PLO was now publicly committed to the idea of Israel and a Palestinian state coexisting between the Jordan River and the Mediterranean Sea.

After the PLO's announcements, Arafat addressed the UN General Assembly in Geneva on 14 December 1988, where he declared 'the right of all parties concerned in the Middle East conflict to exist in peace and security, including the State of Palestine, Israel and their neighbours.' This historic announcement was favourably received. The General Assembly adopted a resolution calling for an international conference with PLO representation. UN delegates also 'recognised the declaration of the State of Palestine' and approved changing the name of the PLO's observer delegation to 'Palestine'. Following Arafat's public renunciation of violence, the US also, for the first time, opened formal talks with the PLO. These began on 16 December.

The PLO's 1988 initiative was an important turning point in the Arab-Israeli conflict. Through it, the Palestinian leadership set aside its traditional strategy of violence and armed struggle to bring about the destruction of Israel, the hallmark of its national movement since 1968.

In response, Israel argued that the PLO's call for a two-state solution was insincere since its charter still called for the destruction of Israel. Until this changed, and the PLO stopped sponsoring terrorist acts against Israeli citizens, Israel would not negotiate with the organisation.

## King Hussein relinquishes Jordan's claim to the West Bank

Another important development in 1988 impacted significantly on the local conflict. By July, King Hussein had recognised the shifts that had begun to emerge in PLO policy in response to the intifada, and their potential impact upon the attitudes of his own population. He therefore announced that Jordan no longer claimed sovereignty over the West Bank, reversing a policy established many decades earlier by Hussein's grandfather, King Abdullah I. It also left the Israeli Labor Party (and the US) without a 'Jordanian Option' for the resolution of the Israeli-Palestinian conflict. Now all that remained was a 'Palestinian Option'. With the withdrawal of Hussein's claim to the West Bank, only Israel and the Palestinians remained as contenders for sovereignty over this territory.

In August 1988, Jordan took further steps to sever its legal, administrative, and financial links with the West Bank. The West Bank Development Plan was cancelled, and Jordan's Ministry of the Occupied Lands' Affairs was replaced by a political department within the Ministry of Foreign Affairs. Approximately 21 000 Jordanian civil servants and employees were fired. Some members of the Jordanian Parliament's Upper House of Palestinian origin were also dismissed. Residents of the West Bank and Gaza Strip lost their Jordanian citizenship, their passports becoming identification documents only.

However, Hussein maintained control of the Islamic *Waqf* which was responsible for Islamic courts and Muslim holy sites in Jerusalem. This reflected the King's intention to maintain his custodianship of those sites, a policy later enshrined in the 1994 peace treaty between Jordan and Israel.

## The impact of the first Palestinian intifada

The intifada impacted significantly on the Arab-Israel conflict, bringing the 'Palestine Question' back to centre stage, as it had been before 1948.

For Palestinians, resistance to occupation had come at a high cost. Between December 1987 and the end of 1993, some 1100 were killed by Israeli security forces. A further 500 Palestinians accused of collaborating with Israel were killed by other Palestinians. An estimated 2000 Palestinian homes were destroyed, and about 175 000 Palestinians were jailed, 23 000 of whom were subjected to 'harsh interrogation', according to Israeli human rights organisations.

Hundreds of thousands of Palestinians were also indirectly affected by intifada-related violence, as the occupied territories generally suffered from an estimated 40 per cent decline in living standards by the end of the uprising.

As for Israel, whilst its superior force succeeded in containing the intifada, the uprising highlighted numerous IDF operational and tactical shortcomings, and general problems arising from Israel's prolonged control of the Palestinian territories. Israel's ongoing occupation was widely criticised, both in international forums (in particular, when humanitarian questions arose), and by Israel's own public. Among Israelis, the intifada exacerbated the political divisions between those who held onto the hope that Israeli military rule over millions of Palestinians in Gaza and the West Bank could become permanent, and those who argued that the occupation could not and should not continue, and that it was time to negotiate with the Palestinian leadership. Critical of the tactics used to suppress the Palestinian uprising, a small number of Israeli soldiers refused service in the territories while others sought exemption.

Despite mounting opposition in Israel, Prime Minister Yitzhak Shamir refused to alter his government's policies or to contemplate negotiations with the Palestinians based on the principle of 'land for peace'. When elections were held in 1992, a majority of Israelis voted a new government into power.

In the meantime, the local and regional levels of the Arab-Israeli conflict were affected by events further afield, including the collapse of Soviet power in 1991, and the 1990-91 Gulf War.

# The collapse of the Soviet Union and the end of the Cold War: Impact and effects on the Arab-Israeli conflict

The bipolar world of international relations that had emerged at the end of World War II, characterised by decades of East-West confrontation (the Cold War), came to an end in the late 1980s and early 1990s. The final collapse of the Soviet Union in 1991 was the culmination of a series of dramatic developments. These included Soviet domestic reforms known as *glasnost* (openness) and *perestroika* (reconstruction), the political revolutions in Eastern Europe in 1989, the reunification of Germany in October 1990, and the formal end of the Warsaw Pact.

## The impact of *glasnost* and *perestroika* on Soviet Jewry and immigration to Israel

For decades, Jews had been refused permission to leave the Soviet Union. Those who applied to leave were known as 'refuseniks'. They lost their jobs, were subjected to harassment from the secret police and in some cases were arrested, imprisoned without trial and tortured. In spite of the restrictions and persecution, a small number of Jews emigrated from the USSR in the early and late 1970s, the majority of whom went to live in Israel.

By 1989 Gorbachev's policies of *glasnost* and *perestroika* had removed obstacles to emigration, but could not stave off a period of severe economic deterioration throughout the Soviet Union and a concomitant rise in antisemitism. Strongly nationalistic organisations, like *Pamyat*, disseminated anti-Jewish propaganda and violently attacked Jews and their property. These factors motivated hundreds of thousands of Soviet Jews to seek a better life elsewhere. Many sought a new home in Israel, the largest numbers arriving between 1989 and 1991. In 1990, up to 30 000 new immigrants arrived in Israel every month.

This significant infusion of people placed a tremendous strain on Israel's infrastructure. Thirteen new towns were built between 1990 and 1991 alone. Unemployment among the new arrivals was also high. Education and health-care facilities were stretched to their limits.

In time, Russian immigrants developed their own political organisations and in 1995, led by a famous 'refusenik', Natan Sharansky, formed the *Yisrael b'Aliyah* (Israel on the Rise) Party. Originally a 'centrist' party, *Yisrael b'Aliyah* moved to the political right, adopting a position on the occupied territories aligned with the Likud Party, with whom *Yisrael b'Aliyah* merged in 2003.

Previous Soviet confrontation with America was replaced by Russian dependence on US diplomatic and economic support. This transition impacted significantly on regional conflicts, including those in the Middle East. By this time, too, US dependence on Middle Eastern

## Immigration of Ethiopian Jews (the Falasha) to Israel

**Figure 10.10** Ethiopian Jews leaving Addis Ababa for Israel, 1991.

In 1977, during the civil war in Ethiopia, Ethiopian Jews fled the fighting for refugee camps in Sudan. By 1984, thousands were without sufficient food or medical care and feared for their lives. Between 21 November 1984 and 5 January 1985, 7500 Ethiopian Jews were airlifted to Israel in a secret rescue mission called 'Operation Moses'. In May 1991, another Israeli rescue operation, 'Operation Solomon', saw a further 14 200 Ethiopian Jews airlifted to Israel. On this occasion, they were brought from the Ethiopian capital, Addis Ababa where 20 000 Jews lived in overcrowded conditions.

oil had begun to decrease but stability in the region remained central to its foreign policy objectives. That stability was directly challenged by the development of a new crisis in the Middle East in 1990.

# The 1990-1991 Gulf War

On 2 August 1990, several divisions of the Iraqi army invaded neighbouring Kuwait. Within days, what had begun as an interstate dispute over war debts, boundary demarcation and oil prices, turned into a conflict of global proportions.

## Events leading to Iraq's invasion of Kuwait

The first Gulf War between Iran and Iraq from 1980 to 1988 had left the Iraqi economy in tatters. At the May 1990 Arab League summit held in Baghdad, Iraq's President, Saddam Hussein, demanded that the Arab states should cancel all Iraqi debts, including its debt of US\$26 billion to Saudi Arabia. Iraq's demand was rejected. Later, at an Arab oil producers meeting in July 1990, the Iraqi representative accused Kuwait and the United Arab Emirates (UAE) of crippling Iraq's oil-dependent economy by flooding the oil market and reducing the oil price. He also accused Kuwait of stealing Iraq's oil by illegally 'slant drilling' across Iraq's border, and demanded compensation of US\$2.4 billion, the cancellation of all Iraq's war debts to Kuwait, and control of the Kuwaiti islands of Bubiyan and Warba. Kuwait rejected Iraq's accusations and demands.

Adding to the tensions among the Arab Gulf states, Saddam Hussein revived the claim, made intermittently since Iraq's independence in 1933, that Kuwait is an illegitimate entity and that its territory rightly belongs to Iraq. The Kuwaiti government rejected the claim as a threat to Kuwaiti sovereignty and a violation of previous treaties between the two countries.

On 2 August 1990, Iraqi troops invaded Kuwait. The Iraqi government announced the formal annexation by Iraq of Kuwait in its entirety, and began massing troops along the Saudi Arabian border.

## The regional and international responses to the invasion

On 6 August the UN Security Council passed Resolution 660, which condemned Iraq's invasion of Kuwait as an act of aggression, and Resolution 661, which imposed economic sanctions upon Iraq until it withdrew its forces. Among Arab League members, only Algeria, Jordan, Yemen and the PLO, supported Iraq's invasion.

## Operation Desert Shield

In response, Iraq continued massing troops along the Saudi border and threatened to invade, firing Scud missiles into Saudi territory. Saddam's threat was heightened by Iraq's previous use of chemical weapons against Iran during the 1980-88 Gulf War, and against Iraq's own Kurdish population at various times during the 1980s. On the same day that UN SC Resolution 660 was passed, US Secretary of Defence, Dick Cheney, offered the Saudi government US military support. With Iraqi troops on the Saudi border, and fearing the same fate as Kuwait, Saudi King Fahd accepted America's offer of military assistance. Thus began Operation Desert Shield, in which the US and its allies sent air, ground and naval forces to Saudi Arabia to prevent an Iraqi invasion.

In the months following, various peace proposals failed. The UN insisted on Iraq's full and unconditional withdrawal from Kuwait. In response, Saddam Hussein demanded that Iraq's withdrawal from Kuwait be linked to simultaneous withdrawals of Syrian troops from Lebanon and Israeli troops from all the occupied territories. While Morocco and Jordan supported this plan, Syria, Israel and the US-led coalition dismissed it as an attempted distraction from the Kuwait issue.

## Operation Desert Storm

When Iraq failed to comply with Resolutions 660 and 661, the Security Council passed Resolution 678, authorising UN member states to use 'all necessary means to uphold and implement Resolution 660', a diplomatic formulation authorising the use of force to compel Iraq to withdraw from Kuwait. The deadline for Iraq's compliance expired on 15 January 1991, and two days later, US-led military forces commenced Operation Desert Storm, a massive aerial bombing campaign against Iraqi forces in Kuwait and Iraq.

## Operation Desert Sabre

On 24 February, the coalition forces launched their ground force offensive, Operation Desert Sword (later renamed Desert Sabre), made up of personnel from 28 countries, including troops from Qatar and Syria. However, fighting

was limited as the Iraqi troops surrendered or fled back to Iraq. Within 48 hours, the US-led coalition forces had routed the Iraqi army, defeating 42 Iraqi divisions, and liberated Kuwait. On 28 February, the Iraqi Foreign Minister, Tariq Aziz, informed the United Nations that Iraq was ready to 'comply fully with Resolution 660 and all UN resolutions on Kuwait'.

However, before fleeing Kuwait, Iraqi forces set fire to most operating oil wells, blew up or set fire to major buildings in Kuwait City, and destroyed power-generating plants.

## Israel and the 1990-91 Gulf War

One day after Operation Desert Storm began, Iraq fired Scud missiles into Israel, even though Israel was not part of the anti-Iraq coalition. Saddam Hussein hoped to provoke an Israeli response to unravel the alliance of Arab and non-Arab forces. Iraq's attacks also avenged Israel's destruction of Iraq's nuclear reactor at Osiraq in 1981.

In all, Iraqi forces fired 39 Scud missiles into Israel, aimed primarily at civilians in large coastal centres, such as Tel Aviv and Haifa. The worst attack came on 22 January, when 90 were injured and 3 died from related heart attacks. However, Israel decided not to counterattack when America provided it with Patriot antimissile batteries and promised to guarantee loans to Israel to the value of US$10 billion (thereby allowing Israel to obtain the benefit of much lower interest rates).

Interestingly, Syria responded to the Scud attacks by announcing that Israel had a right to defend itself against Iraqi aggression. This was significant in the light of Syria's long-standing animosity towards Israel, but reflected Syria's desire to curry favour with America and its allies so as to leave Syria with a free hand to continue its domination of Lebanon.

## The Palestinians and the 1990-91 Gulf War

Following Iraq's invasion of Kuwait on 2 August 1990, PLO Chairman Yasser Arafat publicly supported the Iraqi leader. The Palestinians celebrated Saddam

Hussein's challenge to America and the Gulf oil-producing states, hoping it might alter the regional status quo and focus attention on their plight. A prominent Palestinian spokesperson, Dr Hanan Ashrawi, declared in January 1991 that people would see Saddam Hussein as 'a leader who has stood up for Arab pride.'

Palestinians throughout the occupied territories and in Jordan expressed solidarity with Iraq. Newspaper articles and mass rallies reflected popular support, while Palestinian spokespeople denounced UN-authorised measures to restore Kuwait's sovereignty as 'foreign intervention' in the region. As Scud missiles flew over the West Bank towards Tel Aviv, international television coverage showed Palestinians dancing on their rooftops in celebration.

# The impact of the 1990-91 Gulf War on the Arab-Israeli conflict

## A shift in Syrian policy

A precondition for some Arab states to join the anti-Iraq coalition had been a US commitment to renew efforts to resolve the Arab-Israeli conflict after the war. Syria was one state that had made this demand, representing a shift in Syrian policy following a number of changes that had occurred in the broader international arena. From the 1970s, Syria had been the USSR's main Middle Eastern ally, both countries having signed a Friendship and Cooperation Treaty in October 1980. The decline in Soviet power and a significant reduction in Soviet foreign aid meant that Syria could no longer rely on its old Cold War patron, and the pursuit of strategic parity

**Figure 10.11** Yasser Arafat and Iraqi President Saddam Hussein in Baghdad, Iraq.

with Israel was no longer possible. With the Soviets applying pressure on Syria to abandon war and seek a peace settlement with Israel, Syria found itself isolated in the region.

As early as 1990, Syria had shown signs of softening its position towards America and its Arab allies. US Secretary of State James Baker visited Damascus in September 1990, and in November, US President Bush and Syrian President Hafez al-Assad met in Geneva. Syria re-established full diplomatic relations with Egypt (which had been severed following the 1979 Egyptian-Israeli Peace Treaty), and on 6 March 1991, Syria and Egypt signed the 'Declaration of Damascus' with the six members of the Gulf Cooperation Council (GCC). It included a proposal to convene an international conference under UN auspices to resolve the Arab-Israeli and Israeli-Palestinian conflicts.

## Israeli-US relations

Another important shift in regional politics following the 1990-91 Gulf War was a cooling in relations between America and Israel. When the Bush Administration asked Israel to end settlement activity in the West Bank to demonstrate its commitment to a resolution of the Arab-Israel conflict, Prime Minister Shamir refused. In response, the US reneged on its promise to provide US$10 billion worth of loan guarantees to Israel.

## A shift in focus from Tunis to the Palestinian territories

The Palestinian leadership's decision to support Saddam Hussein was a strategic disaster for the PLO and the Palestinian people. After the war, Yasser Arafat's solidarity with Saddam Hussein was condemned internationally as well as by the majority of Arab states. The PLO was diplomatically isolated, with Kuwait and Saudi Arabia cutting financial support to the PLO, significantly reducing the organisation's income. Arab oil-producing states expelled Palestinian residents and some 250 000 Palestinian workers, resulting in a substantial loss of income for Palestinians and causing a humanitarian crisis in Jordan where many of those expelled were forced to flee.

These events significantly affected the Palestinian nationalist movement. The shift in leadership from Tunis to the occupied territories, which had begun following the outbreak of the intifada in 1987, now accelerated. In almost all elections held for professional associations and trade unions in the first years after the war, Hamas won between 40 per cent and 60 per cent of the votes respectively.

# The Madrid Peace Conference and historic negotiations

Although the international community rejected Saddam Hussein's attempt to link Iraq's invasion of Kuwait to Israel's occupation of Gaza and the West Bank, renewed efforts to resolve the Arab-Israeli conflict were high on the coalition's postwar agenda. America was now the world's only superpower, and wielded significant influence in the region. Accordingly, US Secretary of State Baker initiated an international peace conference in October 1991, held in Madrid, Spain.

Syrian President Assad agreed to send a Syrian delegation to attend the conference, hoping to negotiate a return to Syria of the Golan Heights. The Lebanese government and King Hussein of Jordan also accepted the invitation. Israeli Prime Minister Shamir agreed to attend on the condition that the PLO be excluded from the talks and that Palestinian statehood not be directly addressed. With the PLO 'in disgrace' for supporting Iraq's invasion of Kuwait, America and the Arab participants accepted Shamir's conditions. Instead, a number of Palestinians from the West Bank and Gaza joined the Jordanian delegation.

The Jordanian-Palestinian delegation included prominent Palestinian figures such as Dr Haidar Abdel-Shafi from Gaza and Faisal al-Husseini from Jerusalem. Though not ideal for the PLO, Arafat endorsed the arrangement, while the PFLP, DFLP and Hamas issued a joint statement condemning Arafat's willingness to approve Palestinian participation.

During the conference, the Palestinian delegation maintained regular telephone contact with the PLO leadership in Tunis, allowing Arafat indirectly to repair damaged relations with key regional and international players. One of the Palestinian delegates, Ghassan al-Khattib, noted Arafat's success in this endeavour:

The Gulf War left us in a miserable situation, politically isolated, our morale low, our image distorted, and facing economic disaster. But now the Saudis are [again] ... willing to pay, our image has improved dramatically, and our morale is up.

## The Madrid Conference

The historic summit in Madrid, jointly sponsored by America and Russia, began on 30 October and ended on 1 November 1991. For the first time, representatives from Israel, Syria, Lebanon and Jordan, as well as Palestinian representatives from Gaza and the West Bank, met at an international conference aimed to end the decades long Arab-Israeli conflict. During the proceedings, the US adopted an even-handed approach and pledged to promote a settlement to provide security for Israel and justice for the Palestinians. Negotiations were to be based on the principle of 'land for peace' enshrined in UN Resolutions 242 and 338.

## The 'Madrid Talks'

The first face-to-face negotiations began immediately after the formal conference had ended, based on the 'parallel track' framework agreed upon at the conference, namely, bilateral and multilateral negotiations. The teams established at Madrid were as follows:

The Bilateral Negotiation Teams:
- Israel and the Palestinians
- Israel and Jordan
- Israel and Syria
- Israel and Lebanon

The Multilateral Working Group Teams:
- Economic Cooperation and Development (chaired by the European Union)
- The Environment (chaired by Japan)
- Water (chaired by the United States)
- Refugees (chaired by Canada)
- Arms Control and Regional Security (chaired by Russia and the United States)

The 'Madrid Talks' included several rounds of negotiations from October 1991 to mid 1993.

## The Washington Talks

Following the Madrid Conference, a series of bilateral talks took place in Washington, hosted by the US Department of State. However, talks between the Israelis and Syrians faltered as each side clung to its starting position, Syria requiring Israel to withdraw unilaterally from the entire Golan Heights before any peace negotiations, and Israel refusing to withdraw other than in the context of an overall peace agreement. Israeli-Lebanese negotiations concerning Israel's withdrawal from southern Lebanon also broke down.

The talks between Israel and Jordan were the most successful after the Madrid Conference. They continued for almost two years, during which negotiators drafted a peace accord. A formal peace treaty between Israel and Jordan was signed in 1994, after progress had taken place on the Israeli-Palestinian track.

As for the immediate negotiations between Israel and the Palestinians, Shamir had announced after the first round that his government would not give up any of the West Bank or Gaza Strip, claiming, 'In this small area, there is no room for two states, and therefore no Palestinian state will be established here.' Instead, he stated that his government's strategy was to build more settlements so that an independent Palestinian state would be impossible.

In June 1992, Shamir's Likud Party lost the general election and a new Labor government came to power in Israel, led by Yitzhak Rabin. The consensus in the country was that it was time for a change in policy towards the Palestinians and the occupied territories.

# Summary

In December 1987, after decades of empty promises from the Arab states and the PLO to liberate Palestine, the first Palestinian intifada began as a spontaneous, grassroots uprising to 'shake off' Israeli occupation, during which Islamist groups emerged to challenge the PLO's hold over the Palestinian nationalist movement. To regain the initiative, the PLO reversed its 20-year policy of armed struggle to liberate all of the former Mandatory territory of Palestine. In 1988, Arafat announced that the PLO would now accept a 'two state' solution to the Israeli-Palestinian conflict on the basis of UN Resolution 181, and declared the independence of the State of Palestine in Gaza and the West Bank.

The PLO's moderation briefly won it international acceptance. However, in 1990 when Arafat and other PLO officials supported Saddam Hussein's invasion of Kuwait, they were ostracised regionally and internationally. At the local level of Palestinian politics, the position of Hamas and Islamic Jihad was further enhanced. So, too, was their commitment to violent jihad to 'shake off' Israeli rule. This meant that by the end of the intifada, the culture of violence first adopted by the PLO in its struggle from 'the outside', now became part of the Palestinian culture from 'the inside'.

Israel responded harshly to the intifada, believing that a show of superior force would crush it. This was a serious miscalculation, as the use of force and harsh tactics only heightened the Palestinians' determination to end the occupation and preparedness to use violence to achieve this aim.

The opportunity for diplomatic negotiations to end the Arab-Israeli and Israeli-Palestinian conflicts arose in the wake of the 1990-91 Gulf War. Peace talks were launched at the US-Soviet sponsored Madrid Peace Conference in October 1991. While the Israeli-Jordanian track showed progress, Likud's uncompromising position regarding the occupied territories proved an insurmountable obstacle on the Israeli-Palestinian track. Israeli-Syrian negotiations foundered as neither side was prepared to renounce their interpretation of UN Resolution 242.

When Israelis voted in national elections in June 1992, Shamir and the Likud Party were clearly out of step with the consensus that demanded change in Israel's Palestinian policy. Since the 1967 War, Israeli academic Itamar Rabinovich explains, the 'Palestinians had failed to devise an effective strategy for their struggle against Israel, and whenever Israeli society weighed the costs of keeping the status quo or working out a new compromise, the balance had tilted towards maintaining the status quo'.[1] But by 1992, the majority of Israelis were ready for a new strategy.

The events which led to mutual recognition between Israel and the PLO and the Israeli-Palestinian peace process that followed are examined in the next chapter.

# Review and research questions

1. Outline the political, economic and social reasons for the first Palestinian intifada.

2. Account for the establishment and rise in popularity of Hamas during the period of the intifada.

3. Research the personal background of Sheikh Ahmad Yassin. What were his values and attitudes influencing his relations with the Palestinians, the PLO and Israel? What were the major events in which he was involved that impacted on the Israeli-Palestinian conflict? How would you assess his contribution to this history?

4. Compare the objectives and methodologies of the Palestinian nationalist movement headed by the PLO and those of Hamas and Islamic Jihad. What are the similarities and differences?

5. Evaluate Israel's policies in response to the intifada.

6. What impact did the intifada have on Palestinian politics and society?

7. What impact did the intifada have on Israeli politics and society?

8. Assess the impact of the 1990-91 Gulf War on the Arab-Israeli conflict.

9. What objectives did the US pursue in co-sponsoring the Madrid Peace Process?

## Discussion question

1. What role have religious groups played in the Israeli-Palestinian conflict since the 1967 War? In your opinion, does religion serve to lessen or intensify the conflict? Give your reasons.

# 11 The Peace Process 1993-1999

By the end of this chapter you will be familiar with the:

- Oslo Peace Process
- Israeli-Jordanian Peace Treaty
- successes and setbacks in the peace process from 1993 to 1999
- attitudes towards the peace process among Israelis and Palestinians
- effect on the peace process of the assassination of Yitzhak Rabin and the election of Benjamin Netanyahu as Prime Minister of Israel.

In 1992, Israelis went to the polls and, tired of what the majority viewed as Likud's rejectionist policies, voted Yitzhak Rabin's Labor-led coalition into power. In early 1993, secret negotiations began in Oslo, Norway, between Israeli and PLO officials, culminating in the historic 'Declaration of Principles' of September 1993.

Initially, there was wide support among Israelis and Palestinians for the agreements. Arafat arrived in Gaza on 1 July 1994, greeted by hundreds of thousands of Palestinians, and established the Palestinian National Authority (PA). In 1994-95, Israel redeployed its troops from Gaza and major towns in the West Bank and the PA took control of civil and security affairs. In January 1996, Arafat was elected President of the Palestinian National Authority.

However, from the outset there were opponents of the peace process on both sides. Some used violence to try to derail the negotiations. Hamas unleashed a terrorist bombing campaign in 1994, following an attack on the Ibrahim Mosque in Hebron by an Israeli terrorist. In November 1995, days after Israeli and Palestinian negotiators had completed a draft 'final status' agreement, a Jewish extremist assassinated Yitzhak Rabin. Shimon Peres became caretaker Prime Minister and in the May 1996 election lost narrowly to the Likud leader, Benjamin (Bibi) Netanyahu, against the backdrop of a Hamas bombing campaign.

The events of the peace process between Israel, the Palestinians and the Arab states, from 1993 to 1999, provide the focus of this chapter.

| Timeline | Event |
|---|---|
| June 1992 | Yitzhak Rabin forms a new Labor-led government in Israel. |
| December 1992 | Knesset passes bill approving official contacts with the PLO. |
| January 1993 | Secret talks between Israeli and Palestinian representatives in Oslo, Norway. |
| August 1993 | Israeli-Palestinian Declaration of Principles initialled in Oslo. |
| 10 September 1993 | Israel and PLO exchange letters formally recognising each other. |
| 13 September 1993 | Yitzhak Rabin, Shimon Peres and Yasser Arafat officially sign the Declaration of Principles (Oslo Accords) at the White House in Washington. |
| February 1994 | An Israeli terrorist massacres 29 Palestinians at the Mosque of Ibrahim in Hebron, wounding over 100. |
| April 1994 | A Hamas terrorist drives a car bomb into a bus stop in Afula, Israel, killing 8 and injuring 51. |
| May 1994 | The 'Gaza-Jericho First Agreement' is signed, marking the beginning of Palestinian self-rule. |
| September 1994 | The 'Interim Agreement on the West Bank and the Gaza Strip' (Oslo II) is signed. |
| October 1994 | Hamas terrorist blows himself up in Tel Aviv killing 22 Israelis, wounding 50. Israel and Jordan sign a peace treaty. |
| August 1995 | Two Hamas terrorists blow themselves up, killing 10 Israelis and wounding over 100. |
| 4 November 1995 | Yitzhak Rabin is assassinated by an Israeli right-wing extremist. Shimon Peres becomes Prime Minister. |
| December 1995 | Israeli forces withdraw from major West Bank towns as stipulated in Oslo II. |
| 5 January 1996 | Israel assassinates Yahya Ayyash, Hamas' bomb maker. |
| 20 January 1996 | Palestinians hold their first national elections to choose representatives of the Palestinian Self-Governing Authority; Yasser Arafat elected as President. |
| March to February 1996 | Four Hamas terrorists blow themselves up, killing 59 Israelis and wounding over 200. |
| March to April 1996 | Israel's 'Operation Grapes of Wrath' against Hizballah bases in south Lebanon. |
| April 1996 | First PNC vote to remove anti-Israel clauses from the PLO Charter. |
| May 1996 | Under new electoral law, Bibi Netanyahu is elected Prime Minister of Israel. |
| June 1996 | Bibi Netanyahu forms a new Likud-led government in Israel. |
| September 1996 | Exit to Hasmonean Tunnel is opened, igniting major clashes between Israeli and Palestinian security forces. |
| January 1997 | Hebron Redeployment Agreement signed between Israel and the PLO. |
| October 1998 | Wye Memorandum signed between Israel and the PLO. |
| December 1998 | Second PNC vote to remove anti-Israel clauses from the PLO. |
| 18 May 1999 | The 'One Israel' Party (which includes Labor) forms a new government in Israel with Ehud Barak as Prime Minister. |

# Labor-led coalition returns to government in Israel

During the 1992 election campaign, Labor leader Yitzhak Rabin distinguished his party's policy on the Palestinians from Likud's Yitzhak Shamir as follows: 'In a nutshell, I am unwilling to give up a single inch of Israel's security, but I am willing to give up many inches of ... territories – as well as 1 700 000 Arab inhabitants – for the sake of peace ... We seek a territorial compromise which will bring peace and security.' Rabin recommitted to the 1978 Camp David Accords with Egypt, as a starting point for negotiations. Labor won the largest number of Knesset seats in the June election and formed a coalition government with the left-wing *Meretz* Party, which also proposed territorial compromise with the Palestinians.

Rabin's new government demonstrated it had changed Israel's priorities by placing a freeze on new settlements in the occupied territories (although it permitted the expansion of existing ones). America responded by endorsing loan guarantees previously denied to Likud.

Rabin initiated bilateral negotiations with Jordan, Syria and the Palestinians, but in December 1992, talks with the Palestinians were halted following the kidnapping and murder of an Israeli border guard.

## Secret talks in Norway

In early 1992, Terje Roed-Larsen of the Norwegian Institute for Applied Social Science, contacted Yossi Beilin, a close adviser of Shimon Peres, reporting that the PLO wanted to pursue negotiations through a confidential but direct Israeli-PLO channel in order to break the two-year-old deadlock in the formal peace negotiations.

Following his appointment as Deputy Foreign Minister in Rabin's government, Beilin sent two Israeli academics to Oslo, Norway, to negotiate 'unofficially' with the PLO. Arafat, encouraged by his deputy, Mahmoud Abbas, dispatched PLO Minister of Finance, Ahmad Qurei (Abu Ala) to negotiate on his behalf. Both parties agreed that strict secrecy was necessary if negotiations were to succeed.

Negotiations began in January 1993, with the aim of reaching an 'interim accord' that would provide the Palestinians with civil responsibilities and police powers in those parts of the occupied territories where they were most heavily concentrated. Although this fell far short of Palestinian statehood, it provided mutual recognition and a starting point for a comprehensive settlement.

Egyptian President Hosni Mubarak, incoming US President, Bill Clinton, and his Secretary of State, Warren Christopher, were informed of the secret Oslo negotiations. Christopher sent his Middle East negotiator, Daniel Kurtzer, to shuttle between Tunis and Jerusalem, seeking to close the differences between the PLO and Israel.

In May 1993, Israel and the PLO upgraded their Oslo representatives to 'official' status, although strict secrecy was maintained. The most difficult issues were left for future discussions, and negotiations centred on protecting Israel's security needs and the Palestinians' requirements for limited self-government. By August, an agreed draft of a 'Declaration of Principles on Interim Self-Government Arrangements' (DOP) had been formulated, which was provisionally signed by Israel and the PLO.

## Mutual recognition between Israel and the PLO

Before the DOP was signed, letters were exchanged between Arafat and Rabin, in which the PLO acknowledged Israel's right to exist in peace and security, renounced the use of terrorism and violence, and pledged to amend 'those articles of the Palestinian Covenant which deny Israel's right to exist.' Rabin's letter to Arafat stated that 'Israel has decided to recognise the PLO as the representative of the Palestinian people and to commence negotiations with the PLO within the Middle East peace process.' Without this mutual recognition between Israel and the PLO, no meaningful agreement would have been possible.

## The Declaration of Principles on Interim Self-Government Agreements (DOP/Oslo Accords)

On 13 September 1993, Arafat, Rabin and Peres signed the 'Declaration of Principles on Interim Self-Government Agreements' (the DOP or 'Oslo Accords') at the White House in Washington, sponsored by President Clinton.

The signing of the Oslo Accords marked another watershed in Israeli-Palestinian relations. During his speech at the signing ceremony, Rabin declared:

> Let me say to you, the Palestinians, we are destined to live together on the same soil in the same land. We, the soldiers who have returned from battles stained with blood; we who have seen our relatives and friends killed before our eyes; we who have attended their funerals and cannot look into the eyes of their parents; we who have come from a land where parents bury their children; we who have fought against you, the Palestinians, we, say to you today in a loud and clear voice, enough of blood and tears. Enough!

In Arafat's speech, he promised 'to implement all aspects of UN Resolutions 242 and 338', and that 'the right to [Palestinian] self-determination' would not 'violate the rights of their neighbours or infringe on their security.' Following the speeches, Arafat offered his hand to Rabin and they shook hands. It was a historic moment, for which they were awarded the 1994 Nobel Peace Prize, along with Shimon Peres.

The DOP consisted of 23 pages of basic text, four annexes and agreed minutes, and the 'Letters of Mutual Recognition' between Arafat and Rabin of 9-10 September.

**Figure 11.1** After signing the Oslo Accords, Israeli Prime Minister Yitzhak Rabin (left) shakes hands with PLO Chairman Yasser Arafat (right), with US President Bill Clinton (centre).

The agreement's spirit and historical significance are captured in these extracts:

**Opening Statement**

The Government of the State of Israel and the PLO team representing the Palestinian people, agree that it is time to put an end to decades of confrontation and conflict, recognise their mutual legitimate and political rights, and strive to live in peaceful coexistence and mutual dignity and security and achieve a just, lasting and comprehensive peace settlement and historic reconciliation through the agreed political process. Accordingly, the two sides agree to the following principles:

**Article 1: Aim of the Negotiations**

The aim of the Israeli-Palestinian negotiations within the current Middle East peace process is, among other things, to establish a Palestinian Interim Self-Government Authority, the elected Council (the 'Council'), for the Palestinian people in the West Bank and the Gaza Strip, for a transitional period not exceeding five years, leading to a permanent settlement based on Security Council Resolutions 242 and 338.

It is understood that the interim arrangements are an integral part of the whole peace process and that the negotiations on permanent status will lead to the implementation of Security Council Resolutions 242 and 338.

In essence, the DOP was an agenda for negotiations, with a specific timetable for a five-year interim period of Palestinian self-government, during which a 'final status' agreement would be negotiated, involving the most difficult issues at the heart of the conflict.

Israel's obligations in the interim period included withdrawing from the Gaza Strip, except for Israeli settlements, and a phased withdrawal from major Palestinian towns in the West Bank. Israel's military administration would be replaced by a Palestinian National Authority (PA), created for the purpose of self-rule. Until the final status of the Palestinian territories was agreed, the West Bank and Gaza would be divided into three zones:

- Area A – under full control of the Palestinian Authority.
- Area B – under Palestinian civil control and Israeli military control.
- Area C – under full Israeli control (where Israeli settlements were located).

The DOP left five issues for further negotiation during the following five years: Jerusalem; refugees; Israeli settlements; final borders; and the final status of the Palestinian 'entity' (i.e. autonomy under the PA or a sovereign state). Arafat claimed that the DOP ultimately required Palestinian sovereignty, while Rabin insisted this was only one of several possibilities. It was intended that these issues would be agreed in final status talks to begin no later than May 1996.

## The significance of the DOP

The DOP created a framework for a peace treaty between Israel and the PLO and for an independent Palestinian state. A key objective was to initiate confidence-building measures to create trust as an essential precondition for the compromises each side would need to make to achieve a final settlement. Both sides committed to ending violence to resolve disputes and instead to use negotiations.

The DOP was criticised for deferring the 'final status' issues, but most Israelis and Palestinians were prepared to give it a chance to develop into a peaceful resolution. The signing of the DOP officially ended the Palestinian intifada.

# The peace process unfolds

## The Gaza-Jericho First Agreement 4 May 1994

The first phase to be implemented was the Israeli withdrawal from Gaza and from Jericho (and surrounding area) in the West Bank. The details were set out in Article 2 of the 'Agreement on the Gaza Strip and the Jericho Area', a follow-up to the DOP, which was signed in Cairo on 4 May 1994. It is known as 'the Gaza-Jericho First Agreement' (Figure 11.2).

In addition to Israel's military withdrawal, the document required both sides to contribute to confidence-building measures, as set out in Articles 9 and 14.

**Article 9** stipulated that: 'Israel and the Palestinian Authority shall seek to foster mutual understanding and tolerance and shall accordingly abstain from incitement, including hostile propaganda, against each other and, without derogating from the principle of freedom of expression, shall take legal measures to prevent such incitement by any organisations, groups or individuals within their jurisdiction.'

**Article 14** of the agreement committed both sides to treat the other's population humanely and 'with due regard to internationally-accepted norms and principles of human rights and the rule of law.'

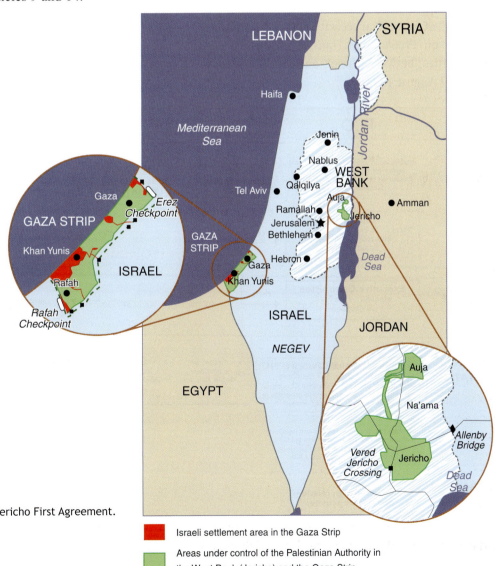

**Figure 11.2** The Gaza-Jericho First Agreement.

Israeli settlement area in the Gaza Strip

Areas under control of the Palestinian Authority in the West Bank (Jericho) and the Gaza Strip

## Establishment of the Palestinian National Authority

Article 5 of the Gaza-Jericho First Agreement provided for a Palestinian National Authority (PA) to be established by the PLO, with legislative, executive and judicial powers and responsibilities similar to those of a sovereign state.

However, the PA did not control external security or 'internal security and public order' over Israeli settlements. Nor did it have jurisdiction over foreign relations, which remained Israel's sole responsibility. Article 8 of the Gaza-Jericho Agreement required the PA to establish 'a strong police force' to maintain internal security and domestic order. A joint Israeli-Palestinian 'Coordination and Cooperation Committee' was established for mutual security purposes. A further 'Agreement on Preparatory Transfer of Powers and Responsibilities between Israel and the PLO' was signed on 29 August 1994.

Disagreements soon emerged over interpretation of the agreements and whether each side was fulfilling its obligations. This resulted in Israel halting further withdrawals from the West Bank. The parties signed a further agreement in September 1995 to try to move the process along and accelerate the transfer of powers to the PA.

## Interim Agreement on the West Bank and the Gaza Strip (Oslo II) 28 September 1995

This second major agreement was signed between Israel and the PLO on 28 September 1995, and is called the 'Interim Agreement on the West Bank and the Gaza Strip' or 'Oslo II'. The agreement expanded Area A in the West Bank from where Israeli troops were to be withdrawn, extending Palestinian self-rule to Bethlehem, Hebron, Jenin, Nablus, Qalqilya, Ramallah, Tulkarm, and some 450 villages. Israel was required to withdraw its forces from some (though not all) of these areas by 31 December 1995.

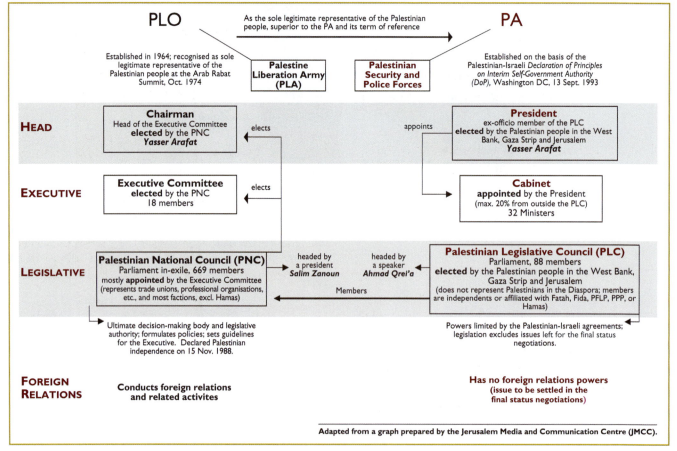

**Figure 11.3** The PLO and its relationship to the PA.

## The 'Abu Mazen-Beilin Plan' for a final status agreement

Parallel to official negotiations between Israel and the PLO, unofficial secret talks were held in Stockholm, Sweden, to try to reach an agreement on the 'final status' issues and to prepare for a permanent peace agreement. The talks were closely monitored by Israel's Deputy Foreign Minister, Yossi Beilin, and the PLO's Mahmoud Abbas. At the end of October 1995, the negotiators produced a working paper as the basis of the 'Framework for the Conclusion of a Final Status Agreement Between Israel and the PLO', or the 'Abu Mazen-Beilin Plan'. Before Beilin could present it, Rabin was assassinated.

## The Israel-Syria Track

The bilateral talks between Israel and Syria begun following the Madrid Conference were continued by the Rabin government. During the negotiations, the Syrians demanded that Israel fully withdraw from the Golan Heights, up to the 1967 armistice line. Israel argued for withdrawal to the 1923 International border, which was slightly more favourable to it. Further, Israel required normalisation of relations, strict security arrangements, and a staged withdrawal conditional upon Syria meeting its commitments.

Although Israel and Syria made considerable progress, they did not reach final agreement.

## The Jordan-Israel Peace Treaty 26 October 1994

On 14 September 1993, the day after Israel and the PLO signed the DOP, Jordan and Israel signed a preliminary peace document, called the 'Israel-Jordan Common Agenda', which listed their mutual objectives concerning security, water sharing, refugees and displaced persons, and to establish a permanent border 'with reference to the boundary definition under the [British] Mandate, without prejudice to the status of the territories presently under Israeli military government control'.

On 25 July 1994, King Hussein and Prime Minister Rabin signed the 'Washington Declaration', establishing a solid framework for Israeli-Jordanian cooperation in political, economic, and cultural areas.

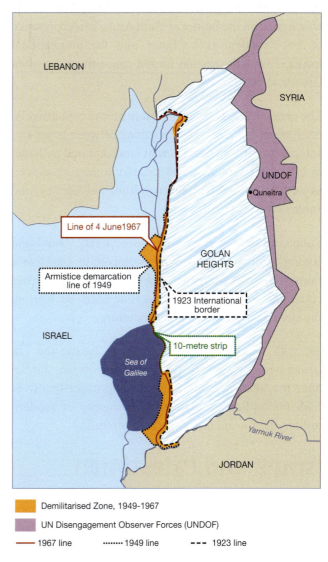

**Figure 11.4** The 1923 International border between Mandatory Palestine and Syria, and the 1967 armistice line between Israel and Syria.

## The Israeli-Jordanian Peace Treaty 26 October 1994

These preliminary agreements culminated in a formal Israeli-Jordanian peace treaty on 26 October 1994. It was signed on the border at Wadi Araba in the presence of US President Bill Clinton and the international media. It was the second formal peace treaty between Israel and an Arab state.

The treaty defined Jordan's western border conclusively, established full diplomatic relations between Israel and Jordan, guaranteed the return of land captured by Israel in 1967 (approximately 380 square kilometres), as well as an equitable share of water from the Yarmuk and Jordan rivers.

Following the signing of the peace treaty, Israel and Jordan negotiated a series of protocols to establish a framework for relations in trade, transportation, tourism, communications, energy, culture, science, navigation, the environment, health and agriculture.

As with the Egyptian-Israeli Peace Treaty, the US committed substantial financial support to Jordan once the treaty was signed, including cancelling over US$700 million of debt and the supply of modern military hardware, including F-16 aircraft.

# Israeli and Palestinian responses to the peace process

The signing of the Oslo Declaration of Principles in September 1993 and Israel's subsequent withdrawal from parts of the occupied territories exposed deep divisions among Israeli and Palestinian societies about the very idea of peaceful compromise.

## Israeli responses to the peace process

Israelis debated the Palestinians' sincerity towards their commitments under the DOP and subsequent agreements. Many on the Left argued there were enough Palestinians willing to live permanently in peace with Israel to bring the rest with them. Those on the Right maintained that the Palestinians would never reconcile themselves to a Jewish state situated in the heart of the Arab-Muslim world. They pointed out that Palestinian violence against Israelis continued after the DOP, despite the formal end of the intifada. They pointed, for example, to the April 1994 Hamas car bombing in Afula, which killed 8 Israelis and injured 51; and the Hamas bomber who blew himself up in Tel Aviv in October, killing 22 and wounding 50. However, the majority of Israelis supported the peace process and the West Bank withdrawals, at least for a period.

The most vocal opponents of the peace process were extremist, religious Jews who claimed that it was a grave sin to abandon territory in the 'Greater Land of Israel' that God had promised to the Jewish people. They also accused Rabin of abandoning 120 000 settlers. On 25 February 1994, an Israeli terrorist, Baruch Goldstein from the settlement of Kiryat Arba, entered the Mosque of Ibrahim in Hebron and shot dead 29 Palestinians, wounding over 100 others, before he was killed. Revenge came on 6 April 1994 when a Hamas terrorist carried out the Afula car bombing.

Then, in an unprecedented event, an Israeli fundamentalist assassinated Prime Minister Rabin on 4 November 1995 at a peace rally in Tel Aviv. The assassin, Yigal Amir, belonged to an extremist religious organisation that considered Rabin to be a traitor to Israel.

Rabin's assassination shocked Israelis, including many of his critics within the Knesset. Many supporters of the peace process rallied behind Rabin's successor, Shimon Peres. An opinion poll taken shortly after Rabin's assassination showed that 70 per cent of Israelis continued to support the peace process with the Palestinians.

One of Peres' first acts as Prime Minister was to order Israeli troop withdrawals from the West Bank, as stipulated in the Oslo II agreement, including from major towns like Bethlehem, Tulkarem, Nablus, Qalqilya and Ramallah. By the end of 1995, the only major Palestinian population centre from which Israel had not withdrawn was Hebron, a place holy to both Jews and Muslims.

**Figure 11.5** King Hussein of Jordan (left) and Israeli Prime Minister Yitzhak Rabin (right) shake hands after signing a joint declaration at the White House, ending 46 years of hostilities between the two countries.

## Palestinian responses to the peace process

When the DOP was signed in September 1993, polls showed about 75 per cent of Palestinians in the occupied territories supported the peace process. Support for Hamas' military campaign for a 'one state' solution dropped to about 8 per cent. Hamas and other Islamist groups therefore embarked on a violent campaign to undermine the Oslo Accords. For the Islamists, all of Palestine had been entrusted by God for exclusive Muslim rule. Like Israeli religious extremists, they were committed to reversing the peace process and ending negotiations for a two-state solution to the conflict.

The Islamists' strategy was twofold: to carry out bomb attacks against Israeli civilians; and when Israel responded by assassinating Islamist leaders, to carry out further attacks against Israelis. Hamas and IJ calculated that by targeting civilians at 'strategic moments', they would discredit the peace process among Israelis and provoke responses that would in turn discredit Arafat among Palestinians. The aim was to maintain a level of violence that would make a peace agreement unachievable.

## 'Homicide'/'suicide' bomb attacks or 'martyrdom operations'

In the post-Oslo years, Palestinian Islamists have used a particular type of terrorist attack against Israeli civilians. Typically, the terrorist detonates explosives attached to her/his body, or contained within a vehicle. In the Western press, these are referred to as 'suicide bombings', a term that reflects the intention of the bomber to die while killing or maiming as many civilians as possible.

Many Muslims condemn such actions as a violation of Islam's strict prohibitions against murder and suicide. However, Islamists who plan and carry out these attacks argue that these are not acts of *intihar* (suicide), but an *istishhad* ('martyrdom operation') and that the bomber is a *shahid* ('martyr'), who has died to prove her/his faith in Allah.

The Hamas bombing campaign against Israeli civilians began three months before Israel's 1996 general election. By killing Israeli civilians Hamas hoped to discredit the Labor government, bringing Likud back to power and end the peace process. On 25 February, terrorist bombers on buses in Jerusalem and in the coastal city of Ashkelon killed 25 Israeli passengers and injured 77. A week later, another bomber killed 12 Israeli shoppers in Tel Aviv and wounded 126.

By this time, the peace process had also suffered another severe blow when Arafat made public statements indicating that he saw the Oslo process as a temporary measure to extract concessions from Israel and that, despite his solemn commitments, he, too, sought Israel's ultimate destruction. Shortly after he signed the DOP in September 1993, Arafat explained his 'strategy of stages' on Jordanian television:

> Since we cannot defeat Israel in war, we do this in stages. We take any and every territory we can of Palestine … and use it as a springboard to take more. When the time comes, we can get the Arab nations to join us for the final blow against Israel.

**Figure 11.6** Rabin's funeral was attended by over 4000 dignitaries, including Egyptian President Hosni Mubarak (third from left), US President Bill Clinton (centre) and King Hussein of Jordan (right).

Area A: Full Palestinian civil and security control

Area B: Palestinian civil control, Israeli security control

Area C: Israeli civil and security control

**Figure 11.7** Areas A, B, and C in the West Bank and Gaza Strip at the end of 1995.

Again Arafat restated what was the PLO's 1974 'strategy of stages' in a speech in South Africa on 10 May 1994:

I am not considering it [the Oslo Accords] more than the agreement which had been signed between our Prophet Muhammad and Quraish [which Muhammad had abrogated when his forces became stronger]. And you remember that the Caliph Omar had refused this agreement, considering it a despicable truce. But Muhammad accepted it and we are accepting now this peace offer … Peace for us means the destruction of Israel. We are preparing for an all-out war.

Later that year, Arafat wrote to Palestinian groups in neighbouring states, including the DFLP and the PFLP:

In order to obtain the goal of returning to Palestine, all of us sometimes have to grit our teeth. But it is forbidden that this harm the continued struggle against the Zionist enemy. Cooperation and understanding between the PLO and the rejectionist organisations is what will lead to the speedy retreat of Israel from the occupied territories in the first stage, until the establishment of a Palestinian state with its capital in Jerusalem. Only a state like that can then continue the struggle to remove the enemy from all Palestinian lands.

These statements by Arafat were made in Arabic, and contradicted his public statements made in English, in which he claimed that he and the PLO were ready for peace. This fact was highlighted by Israeli opponents of the peace process, especially Likud and other right-wing parties. Israeli sceptics of the peace process also pointed to Palestinian school books teaching hatred towards Jews and characterising Israel as an illegitimate and illegal state.

While among the Palestinians Arafat promoted the ongoing struggle against Zionism and Israel, he also cracked down on his Islamist opponents, particularly in Gaza, Hamas' stronghold. In 1994, Arafat appointed Muhammad Dahlan to head the Preventative Security Service in Gaza, the purpose of which was to, among other things, restrict Hamas and IJ operations.

In 1995, Dahlan disarmed and jailed about 2000 Hamas members following their bombing campaign against Israelis. Dahlan shaved off their beards and allegedly tortured some of them. Dahlan's police also closed Islamic charities, schools and mosques and in 1996, again moved against Hamas following another bombing campaign. At this time, Palestinians generally supported Dahlan's actions and the peace process. This changed following the Israeli election that returned Likud to government.

Figure 11.8 Hamas member marches wearing a bomb belt and holding a copy of the Koran.

## Israel's responses to Hamas' terrorist bombings

On 5 January 1996, Hamas' master bomb maker, Yahya Ayyash ('The Engineer') was killed in Gaza by a booby-trapped mobile phone. Israel's General Security Service, *Shabak*, was believed to have planned and carried out the assassination. Ayyash had masterminded Hamas' 1995 terrorist bombings in which 50 Israelis has been killed and scores wounded. Hamas claimed revenge when it began its February 1996 'anti-Oslo' bombing campaign, following which Peres closed the territories and hundreds of Hamas members were arrested and the homes of the bombers were bulldozed.

Opinion polls showed that Israelis' support for Peres declined dramatically after Hamas' February bombing campaign, while Israel's reprisals angered Palestinians who believed they were 'collective punishment' for the actions of the extremists.

## The first Palestinian national elections 20 January 1996

When the PA was established in 1994, Arafat became its Chairman and appointed all other members. Elections for the 88-member Palestinian Legislative Council (PLC) and PA President were held for the first time on 20 January 1996. Arafat was elected President with 88.2 per cent of the vote, and gained the new title of *Ra'is* (Head). Fifty of the 88 Legislative Council seats were won by Arafat's Fatah movement, with most of the remaining seats going to parties also loyal to Arafat.

Arafat was now the undisputed leader of the Palestinian nationalist movement, Chairman of the PLO, head of Fatah (with the majority of seats in both the PLO and the PLC), and President of the PA, all positions which he retained until his death in 2004. He also now controlled the finances of both the PLO and the PA, and all ministerial and judicial appointments.

## The PA's finances and aid from abroad

After the signing of the DOP, the international community committed billions of dollars to the fledgling Palestinian Authority for infrastructure development projects. By 1998 US$2.5 billion had been disbursed to the PA: 38% from Europe, 14% from the US, 13% from Japan, and 8.59% from Arab states.

Despite this aid, the PA remained poor. The main reasons for this were (i) mismanagement (ii) corruption and (iii) the failure to build a viable Palestinian economy. In May 1997,

the Palestinian comptroller's report stated that US$326 million of the PA's annual budget of US$800 million (37%) had been lost to corruption or mismanagement.

The PA's income was also affected by Israeli closures of PA-ruled areas following acts of violence and, as a consequence, by frequent fluctuations in the number of Palestinian workers employed in Israel. This reduced the amount of taxes the PA could collect. Declining remittances from the Palestinian diaspora also hurt the economy.

## The PLO votes to alter its charter

The DOP had committed the PLO to convene the Palestinian National Council (PNC) to amend its 1968 Charter by removing all provisions calling for Israel's destruction. The 1995 Oslo II agreement made this a specific requirement as it had not been fulfilled following the signing of the 1993 Oslo Accords.

On 26 April 1996, the PNC considered the issue and adopted the following by a vote of 504 to 54:

A. The Palestinian National Charter is hereby amended by cancelling the articles that are contrary to the letters exchanged by the PLO and the Government of Israel on 9-10 September 1993.

B. Assigns its legal committee with the task of redrafting the Palestinian National Charter in order to present it to the first session of the Palestinian Central Council.

**Figure  11.9**   The remains of a Jerusalem bus following a Hamas bombing, February 1996.

## The Wye Memorandum 23 October 1998

The October 1998 peace summit was hosted by the US at the Aspen Institute's Wye River Conference Centre in Maryland. The summit's first priority was to agree on how to implement the Interim Agreement on the West Bank and Gaza Strip of September 1995 (Oslo II). The result was the Wye Memorandum, which dealt with issues of redeployment and security in the West Bank, the rewriting of the PLO Charter (which still had not been amended despite the PNC vote), and economic cooperation between Israel and the Palestinians. Despite acrimony over Jewish settlements and Palestinian terror attacks, Arafat and Netanyahu reached their agreement after a final 21-hour session, brokered by President Clinton and Jordan's King Hussein.

The Wye Memorandum was little more than a commitment by both sides to fulfil unmet obligations from previously signed agreements, but was significant because it ended a long stalemate in the peace process.

In response, Hamas carried out a terrorist attack on 6 November 1998, in which two bombers blew themselves up in a car in a crowded Jerusalem market, seriously injuring many Israelis.

On 20 November, Netanyahu complied with Stage 1 of the Wye Memorandum's 12-week planned redeployment by ordering the agreed upon withdrawal. This expanded Area A in the West Bank to 18 per cent and Area B to 21.7 per cent. A further redeployment was scheduled for June 2000.

The agreement and subsequent Israeli redeployment triggered a revolt in Netanyahu's government whereby his right-wing coalition partners eventually left the government. In December 1998, Netanyahu failed to win a confidence vote forcing early elections in May 1999.

For the next five months, the peace process stalled and Israeli scepticism grew at the prospects of a lasting peace with the Palestinians. Arafat, PA officials and religious figures employed by the PA, redoubled their propaganda, teaching hatred of Jews and promised the eventual destruction of Israel. On 3 May 1999,

for example, a religious sermon broadcast on the PA's official radio 'Voice of Palestine' asserted that recognition of Israel's right to exist was forbidden by Muslim religious law: 'The land of Muslim Palestine is a single unit which cannot be divided ... There is no difference between Haifa and Nablus, between Lod and Ramallah, between Jerusalem and Nazareth. The division of the land of Palestine into cantons and the recognition of the occupation is forbidden by religious law, since the land of Palestine is sacred *Waqf* land for the benefit of all Muslims, east and west. No one has the right to divide it or give up any of it.'

Among Palestinians, there was ever-increasing scepticism about Israel's commitment to the basic principle of 'land for peace' as Jewish settlements expanded in the West Bank.

## Summary

The DOP signed in September 1993 promised to set in motion a process to end Israeli rule over two million Palestinians living in the Gaza Strip and the West Bank. Despite its limitations and ambiguities, it marked a major breakthrough in the century-old conflict between Arabs and Jews over Israel/Palestine. The clash between Jewish and Palestinian nationalisms had always been at the heart of the conflict, each side denying the other's legitimacy and right to sovereignty in the land between the Jordan River and the Mediterranean Sea. The DOP and the letters which accompanied it replaced mutual denial with mutual recognition. The handshake between two previously sworn enemies, Arafat and Rabin, on the White House lawn on 13 September 1993 was a powerful symbol of the willingness of the two peoples to accommodate each other's aspirations.

The agreement was based on a historic territorial compromise to partition the land of Israel/Palestine. Ideology was replaced by pragmatism when each side concluded that it could not impose by force its own vision on the other. But not all Israelis and Palestinians were ready or willing to compromise. On both sides, opponents of reconciliation and territorial compromise accused their leaders of treason. The climax of the anti-Rabin campaign was his assassination by a religious-nationalist fanatic.

When Shimon Peres lost the next election and instead one of Rabin's most vocal opponents, Bibi Netanyahu, became Israel's Prime Minister, supporters of the peace process viewed his two and a half years in power as a 'relentless attempt to arrest, freeze and subvert the Oslo Accords.' Netanyahu's coalition government believed the Oslo Accords were a bad deal for Israel and sought to avoid their further implementation from the moment they came to power in June 1996. The situation was summarised by Israeli historian, Yoram Meital:

> In political deliberations, in cabinet and government decisions, and even in Knesset votes the government remained true to the cause, playing havoc with implementation schedules, adopting unilateral decisions, and exploiting the Palestinian leadership's inability to staunch violence and terror.[1]

However, those Israelis and Palestinians opposed to the peace process were disappointed that the peace process, while bruised and battered, was still breathing at the end of Netanyahu's term. During his troubled period of office, countless regional and international attempts had tried to keep negotiations going, mostly in vain. There were two important exceptions, being the Hebron Agreement of January 1997, providing for a new redeployment scheme for the disputed city; and the Wye Memorandum of October 1998, providing for further Israeli troop withdrawals from the West Bank in exchange for the PA implementing previously agreed security measures. These agreements formalised the Likud leader's retreat from the party's long-held expansionist position.

**Figure 11.10** PLO Chairman Yasser Arafat (left), US President Bill Clinton and Israeli Prime Minister Bibi Netanyahu (right) sign the Wye River Agreement as Jordan's King Hussein looks on.

Those who point to Netanyahu as causing the downfall of the Oslo peace process argue that peace would have been possible if Likud had not reneged on Israel's side of the deal. In particular, Netanyahu's policy of expanding settlements in the West Bank prevented the emergence of a viable Palestinian state, without which there can be no end to the conflict.

The contrary view is that the peace process was fatally undermined by the continuation of Palestinian terrorism after the DOP, despite the intifada's ostensible ending. This view holds Yasser Arafat primarily responsible, especially his practice of speaking peace in English and calling for war in Arabic. The Palestinians' continuing resort to violence meant Israelis lost their trust in the peace process, without which progress was impossible.

Another reason why the Oslo peace process broke down is that the DOP and subsequent agreements sought to build peace step by step by focusing on what was achievable at any given time, and deferring the most difficult issues to the end. These issues were, and remain, the Palestinian refugees, a Palestinian state with Jerusalem as it capital, the final borders between Israel and Palestine, and Israeli settlements. It is argued that the DOP created irreconcilable expectations among Israelis and Palestinians about the eventual resolution of these issues.

The Israeli and Palestinian architects of the DOP believed that including these contentious issues would have prevented an initial agreement to commence the peace process. Perhaps they were right, as evidenced by the events of 2000, when Israel and the PLO attempted to reach a final status agreement. The factors that led to the final collapse of the Israeli-Palestinian peace process are summarised in the final chapter.

# Review and research questions

1. Review the events that led to the signing of the Declaration of Principles in September 1993. How would you account for the success of this process?

2. Compare and contrast the policies of the Israeli Labor and Likud parties in regard to the Palestinians and the occupied territories between 1967 and 1999. Account for the similarities and differences. What impact did these policies have on the peace process?

3. Compare and contrast the policies of the PLO and Hamas in regard to Israel and the peace process between 1988 and 1999. Account for the similarities and differences. What impact did these policies have on the peace process?

4. Evaluate the events that led to the signing of the Israeli-Jordanian Peace Treaty in 1994. Do you think that the timing of this event was important? Give reasons for your answer.

5. Investigate the negotiations between Israel and Syria from 1991 to 1999. Analyse the demands made by each side. How do these reflect the different perspectives on 'peace' held by the two countries' leadership?

6. What impact did Yitzhak Rabin's assassination have on the peace process?

7. Evaluate the successes and setbacks of the peace process from 1991 to 1996.

8. How do you explain the fluctuations in attitudes of Israelis and Palestinians towards the peace process from 1991 to 1996?

9. Account for and assess the different perspectives and interpretations of the conflict among and between Israelis and Palestinians.

10. Research the personal background of Benjamin Netanyahu. What were his values and attitudes influencing his relations with the Palestinians and wider Arab world?

11. In the Preamble to the 'Israeli-Palestinian Interim Agreement on the West Bank and the Gaza Strip' (Oslo II), signed in Washington on 28 September 1995, it is recorded:

    The Government of the State of Israel and the Palestine Liberation Organisation, the representative of the Palestinian people; ...

    [Recognise] that the peace process and the new era that it created, as well as the new relationship established between the two Parties above, are irreversible, and the determination of the two Parties to maintain, sustain and continue the peace process ...

    In the light of this claim, assess the impact that Arafat and Netanyahu (and his coalition government) had on the Israeli-Palestinian peace process from 1996 to 1999.

12. Assess the role that the US played in the peace process from 1993 to 1999.

13. Investigate the personal accounts of Israelis and Palestinians who were involved in the peace process from 1991 to 1999. In the light of these accounts, assess the following quote from Dennis Ross, chief US negotiator during the 1991 to 2000 Arab-Israeli peace process:

> Over time, the negotiations that emerged from the Madrid and Oslo processes were very detailed on all issues. But the points of departure were very different. The Arabs and Palestinians always sought acceptance of their principles while the Israelis always sought recognition of the practicalities. The gaps on the issues bore not just disagreements but very different attitudes about the negotiations, their purpose, and the tactics that should be employed.[2]

14. Evaluate the impact that terrorism had on the Israeli-Palestinian peace process from 1993 to 1999.

1.    Read the poems below. The first, *Magash HaKesef* ('The Silver Platter') was written by well-known Israeli poet, Natan Alterman, and published around 1948. The second, *Bitaqati Hawiya* ('Identity Card') was written by well-known Palestinian poet, Mahmoud Darwish, and published in 1964. Assess and account for the different perspectives and interpretations of the Israeli-Palestinian conflict captured by these poems.

## *Magash HaKesef* (The Silver Platter)

By Natan Alterman (1948)

Translated from the Hebrew by Esther Raizen

'A State is not served to a people on a silver platter' – Chaim Weizmann

The land is hushed, a reddening sun
Slowly dims
Over smoking borders.
And a Nation stands – heart-torn yet alive –
To encounter the miracle
The only miracle.

In preparation for ceremony she rises athwart the moon's crescent
And stands, before daybreak, swathed in celebration and awe.
Then from afar come
A maid and a youth
And slowly, slowly they pace towards the Nation.

Clad in ordinary attire but with military harness and heavy-booted,
In the path they proceed,
Advancing without speaking.
They have not changed their clothing nor yet laved-away with water
The marks of the day of toil and the night in the line of fire.

Infinitely weary, withdrawn from rest,
Dripping with the dew of Hebrew youth -
Quietly the two approach
Then stand motionless,
And there is no sign whether they live or have been shot.

Then the Nation asks, flooded by tears and wonderment,
Who are you? And the two softly
Answer her: We are the silver platter
Upon which was served to you the Jewish state.

Thus they say, and fall at her feet, shrouded with shadow.
And the rest shall be told in the history of Israel.

## *Bitaqati Hawiya* (Identity Card)

By Mahmoud Darwish (1964)
Translated from the Arabic by Naseer Aruri and Edmund Ghareeb

Record!
I am an Arab
and my Identity Card
is number fifty thousand
I have eight children
and the ninth
is coming midsummer
Will you be angry?

Record!
I am an Arab
employed with fellow workers
at a quarry
I have eight children

to get them bread
garments
and books
from the rocks –
I do not supplicate charity
at your doors
Nor do I belittle myself
at the footsteps of your chamber
So will you be angry?

Record!
I am an Arab
without a name – without title
patient in a country
with people enraged
My roots –
were entrenched before the birth of time
and before the opening of the eras
before the olive trees, the pines and grass
My father –
descends from the family of the plough
not from a privileged class
And my grandfather –
was a farmer
neither well-bred, nor well-born
And my house –
is like a watchman's hut
made of branches and cane
This is my status

Does it satisfy you?
I have a name but no title.

Record!
I am an Arab
The colour of my hair – black
The colour of my eyes – brown
And my distinctive features:
The headdress is *hatta wi'gal*
And the hand is solid like a rock
My favourite meal
is olive oil and *zatar*
And my address:
A village – isolated and deserted
where the streets have no names
and the men – work in the fields and quarries

They like socialism
Will you be angry?

Record!
I am an Arab
You have stolen the orchards
of my ancestors
and the land
which I cultivated
Along with my children
And you left us with those rocks
So will the State take them
as it has been said?

Therefore!
Record on top of the first page:
I do not hate man
Nor do I encroach
But if I become hungry
The usurper's flesh will be my food
Beware – beware – of my hunger
and my anger!

# 12 Epilogue: Into the 21st Century

By the end of this chapter you will be familiar with the:

- unilateral withdrawal of Israel from southern Lebanon
- Israeli-Palestinian attempts to negotiate a 'final status' agreement
- the second Palestinian intifada and Israel's response
- Israel's unilateral withdrawal from the Gaza Strip
- biography of Yasser Arafat.

William Quandt, an American official present during the 1978 Camp David talks between Egypt and Israel, said:

During the 1990s, the peace process between Israel and the Palestinians was something like a roller-coaster. Moments of despair and violence alternated with moments of hope and creativity. Issues that had long been avoided were tackled with an unprecedented degree of seriousness. At the same time, however, old suspicions lingered, distrust was never far from the surface, and radicals in both camps were prepared to do all they could to undermine the hard work of the more moderate leaders who had decided to gamble on peace.[1]

This analysis is especially applicable to the 15-month term of Israeli Prime Minister Ehud Barak. Elected Prime Minister of Israel in May 1999, Barak ordered the unilateral withdrawal of Israeli troops from Lebanon and engaged in intensive peace negotiations with the PLO. Nevertheless, by the end of his term in office, the Oslo peace process was dead and a second intifada had erupted.

## Israeli-Palestinian peace process resumes

Labor leader Ehud Barak was elected Prime Minister on 19 May 1999, defeating Likud incumbent Bibi Netanyahu. Barak campaigned as the bearer of Rabin's legacy, committed to withdrawing Israel's troops from Lebanon within a year, and to a two-state solution to the conflict with the Palestinians.

In September 1999, Arafat and Barak signed the 'The Sharm el-Sheikh Memorandum', promising to implement their respective commitments outstanding from the 1998 Wye Memorandum, and to resume 'final status' negotiations which, under the 1993 DOP, were due to have been concluded in September 1998. In November 1999, final status talks began between Israel and the PLO and in March 2000, Israeli troops withdrew from further West Bank areas, as had been agreed in the Sharm el-Sheikh Memorandum. Progress in the peace process seemed slow but at least measurable.

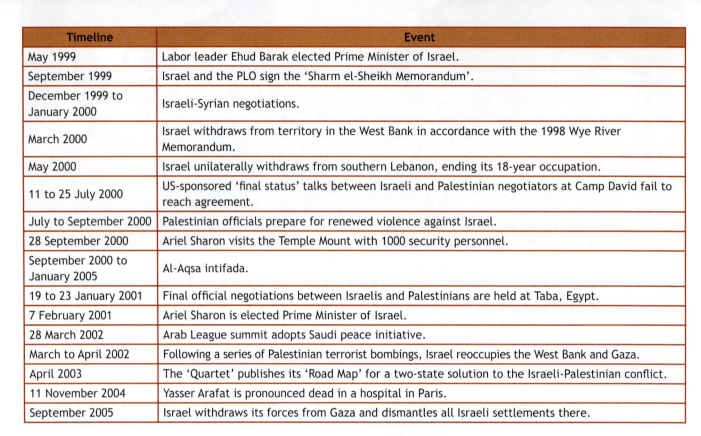

| Timeline | Event |
|---|---|
| May 1999 | Labor leader Ehud Barak elected Prime Minister of Israel. |
| September 1999 | Israel and the PLO sign the 'Sharm el-Sheikh Memorandum'. |
| December 1999 to January 2000 | Israeli-Syrian negotiations. |
| March 2000 | Israel withdraws from territory in the West Bank in accordance with the 1998 Wye River Memorandum. |
| May 2000 | Israel unilaterally withdraws from southern Lebanon, ending its 18-year occupation. |
| 11 to 25 July 2000 | US-sponsored 'final status' talks between Israeli and Palestinian negotiators at Camp David fail to reach agreement. |
| July to September 2000 | Palestinian officials prepare for renewed violence against Israel. |
| 28 September 2000 | Ariel Sharon visits the Temple Mount with 1000 security personnel. |
| September 2000 to January 2005 | Al-Aqsa intifada. |
| 19 to 23 January 2001 | Final official negotiations between Israelis and Palestinians are held at Taba, Egypt. |
| 7 February 2001 | Ariel Sharon is elected Prime Minister of Israel. |
| 28 March 2002 | Arab League summit adopts Saudi peace initiative. |
| March to April 2002 | Following a series of Palestinian terrorist bombings, Israel reoccupies the West Bank and Gaza. |
| April 2003 | The 'Quartet' publishes its 'Road Map' for a two-state solution to the Israeli-Palestinian conflict. |
| 11 November 2004 | Yasser Arafat is pronounced dead in a hospital in Paris. |
| September 2005 | Israel withdraws its forces from Gaza and dismantles all Israeli settlements there. |

## Negotiations between Israel and Syria

In December 1999, Israel and Syria began negotiations to end the state of war between the two countries. In early January 2000, a 'working draft' of a peace treaty was presented to their respective governments for further consultation. Despite agreement that negotiations would resume on 17 January 2000, the parties differed on key issues and further talks never eventuated.

The main areas of disagreement concerned interpretation of UN Resolution 242, the site and size of the demilitarised zone between the two states, and the location of the border at the Sea of Galilee. While Syria insisted that discussion of security arrangements depended on Israel agreeing unconditionally, in advance, to withdraw to the pre-1967 lines, Israel required any agreement on territory to be part of a comprehensive peace treaty also dealing with security and access to water. Similar issues had undermined earlier negotiations following the 1991 Madrid Conference.

Formal negotiations between Israel and Syria thus came to an end.

**Figure 12.1** Areas A, B and C in the West Bank as at the end of 2000.

## Israel withdraws from southern Lebanon

On 23 May 2000, Barak ordered the unilateral withdrawal of Israeli forces from southern Lebanon. The end of Israel's occupation of Lebanon was verified by UN officials and accepted in Security Council Resolution 1310, confirming the Secretary-General's statement that 'Israel had removed all violations of the withdrawal line.' This was contested by Lebanon and Syria, who claim that the Sheba'a Farms area is part of Lebanon. However, the Sheb'a Farms area was captured by Israel from Syria in 1967, not from Lebanon. The claim that the area is part of Lebanon was therefore rejected by UN officials and by the Security Council. Regardless, it has provided Hizballah – backed by both Iran and Syria – with a pretext to fire rockets at towns in northern Israel. Hizballah and Iran remain openly committed to destroying Israel.

# The July 2000 Camp David talks and their aftermath

After withdrawing from Lebanon, Barak returned to negotiations with the Palestinians in an effort to resolve the final status issues that had been deferred in the original 1993 DOP and to reach a permanent peace settlement. US President Clinton agreed to sponsor a summit between Arafat and Barak at the Camp David Presidential retreat. Arafat accepted the invitation with hesitation, saying the Palestinians needed more time to prepare for the negotiations.

Talks began on 11 July 2000, but ended on 25 July without a formal agreement. The major points of dispute were the final borders between Israel and the future State of Palestine, limitations on Palestinian control in East Jerusalem, and the Palestinians' claim to a 'right of return' to Israel for all Palestinian refugees and their descendants (some 4 million people). The talks ended when Arafat rejected Barak's proposals without putting forward counterproposals.

In the absence of an official report of what Barak proposed and what Arafat rejected at Camp David, each side has made claims as to who caused the talks to fail. When Clinton joined the debate, he publicly blamed Arafat for not being willing to make the compromises necessary to end the conflict. Palestinian spokespeople argued that they had compromised enough by accepting defeat in their struggle for the liberation of all of (Mandatory) Palestine and accepting an Israeli state in 78 per cent of that territory.

In Israel, the media reported that at Camp David Barak had offered the Palestinians 'Religious Sovereignty' over the Temple Mount (*al-Haram al-Sharif*) in Jerusalem. The issue was hotly debated as most Israelis believed that Jerusalem should remain united under Israeli sovereignty.

## The al-Aqsa intifada

Since Israel's unilateral withdrawal from Lebanon in May 2000, Hizballah had broadcast the message to the Palestinians that when negotiations fail, 'violence pays'. In the wake of the Camp David summit, whilst some in the Palestinian leadership argued that real progress had been made on final status issues and negotiations should continue, others argued that its failure required a return to armed struggle. Marwan Barghouti, a PA official and founder of the *Tanzim* (Fatah's military wing operating in Gaza and the West Bank), supported the latter view. In the wake of the failed Camp David talks, he argued that:

> Experience teaches us that negotiation without struggle in the field is beggary and humiliation ... [Israel] will not listen to us except when there is struggle on the ground. The goal of [such a struggle] is not to destroy the peace process. But rather to rebuild it on new foundations that include the UN resolutions setting the time table for new negotiations while ending the US monopoly on the peace process and the inclusion of active international forces such as China, the EU, Russia and various Arab parties.

Arafat was of the same view and in the month following his return from Camp David, he directed preparations for a new intifada. To this end, PA officials published statements in the Palestinian press that the PA would soon declare an 'intifada for Jerusalem' and that 'the Palestinian people are willing to sacrifice even 5000 casualties'. Simultaneously, PA security forces began paramilitary training in the Gaza Strip while Force 17 (Arafat's elite presidential guard) reinforced their positions with trenches and sandbags. By September 2000, most PA police stations and bases had been transformed into military bases.

Israel's Chief of Staff, Shaul Mofaz, responded by warning that Israel would 'use tanks and jets if the Palestinians launched an armed offensive'. In turn, PA security officials predicted an Israeli defeat if it attempted to reoccupy the West Bank and Gaza Strip.

Amid this heightened tension Ariel Sharon, in his campaign to contest the Likud leadership, visited the Temple Mount on 28 September 2000, hoping to win the support of voters who felt that Barak had been prepared to concede too much on the Jerusalem issue. His visit, accompanied by 1000 security personnel, offended and provoked Palestinians to violent demonstrations. It was the 'straw that broke the camel's back', igniting a second uprising, the al-Aqsa Intifada. Palestinian Legislative Council member, Hussam Khadhr, explained the circumstances at the time:

I think that Sharon made his visit to al-Aqsa for political reasons and against the backdrop of the internal conflict in the Likud, as well as the historical struggle with the Labor Party. He wanted to embarrass Barak's government. ... This intifada, however, with this high level of violence and sacrifice, did not come about solely because of Sharon's encroachment of Al-Aqsa. ... [It] was merely the spark that ignited the explosion. We had seven dry years of political activity and negotiations with the enemy, which culminated in a negative effect on the public. The Palestinian public was also frustrated with the future of the peace process. Additionally, the citizens feel that [civil] institutions are not being built and there is no struggle against corruption. These feelings led to an accumulation of [tension] which was unloaded in the struggle against the occupation.

Israelis blamed Arafat for the violence saying that he had planned it before Sharon's visit to pressure Israel into making more concessions. Palestinians viewed the intifada as the response of an occupied people, daily provoked and humiliated by Israeli soldiers and settlers.

## Final Israeli-Palestinian negotiations

Talks held between Israeli and Palestinian negotiators at Sharm el-Sheikh in November 2000 resulted in a short-term cease-fire. But when violence resumed, Barak was pressured to call new elections. He resigned as Prime Minister in December and elections were scheduled for February 2001.

Before the elections, two further rounds of Israeli-Palestinian negotiations took place in an effort to reach a final status agreement. The first were held in Washington in late December 2000, hosted by President Clinton, who presented the parties with what became known as the 'Clinton Proposal'. This became the basis for the final round of talks in Taba, Egypt, in January 2001, sponsored by Egyptian President Hosni Mubarak.

Although the Taba negotiations ended without a final agreement, a significant outcome was the joint statement issued by Israelis and Palestinians at the conclusion of the talks:

The Israeli and Palestinian delegations conducted during the last six days serious, deep and practical talks with the aim of reaching a permanent and stable agreement between the two parties.

The Taba talks were unprecedented in their positive atmosphere and expression of mutual willingness to meet the national, security and existential needs of each side. ...

The negotiation teams discussed four main themes: refugees, security, borders and Jerusalem, with a goal to reach a permanent agreement that will bring an end to the conflict between them and provide peace to both people. ...

On all these issues there was substantial progress in the understanding of the other side's positions and in some of them the two sides grew closer.

**[T]he political timetable prevented reaching an agreement on all the issues. However, in light of the significant progress in narrowing the differences between the sides, the two sides are convinced that in a short period of time and given an intensive effort and the acknowledgement of the essential and urgent nature of reaching an agreement, it will be possible to bridge the differences remaining and attain a permanent settlement of peace between them.**

In this respect, the two sides are confident that they can begin and move forward in this process at the earliest practical opportunity.

The Taba talks conclude an extensive phase in the Israeli-Palestinian permanent status negotiations with a sense of having succeeded in rebuilding trust between the sides and with the notion that **they were never closer in reaching an agreement between them than today. ...**

(*Emphasis added*)

**Figure 12.2** Israeli Prime Minister Ehud Barak (left), Bill Clinton, Yasser Arafat, and Egyptian President Hosni Mubarak (right), at the peace summit in Sharm el-Sheikh, Egypt, November 2000.

Nevertheless, the intifada continued with Arafat apparently powerless to stop it. At elections for Israel's Prime Minister held on 7 February 2001, Sharon defeated Barak by a margin of more than 20 per cent. Sharon's platform was for 'Peace with Security', meaning that peace would only be achieved once security was assured. He accused Arafat of reneging on the Oslo Accords, and promised a new approach to the conflict with the Palestinians. Once in office, Sharon announced that Israel would engage in no further negotiations with the PLO until violence ended.

# The end of the peace process

Although Israel and the PLO had come close to reaching agreement at Taba, throughout 2001 and 2002, Hamas, Islamic Jihad, the PFLP, and Fatah's al-Aqsa Brigades (established at the beginning of the intifada) continued terrorist attacks against Israeli civilians. Their operatives blew themselves up on Israeli buses and in cafes, restaurants and shopping malls. The IDF responded by raiding Palestinian self-rule areas, demolishing property of those involved in the bombings, and sealing off land and sea access to the Palestinian territories. Helicopter gunships were used to assassinate militant leaders, at times resulting in civilian deaths.

Through the 'Mitchell Plan', 'Zinni Plan' and 'Tenet Plan', America tried unsuccessfully to bring the parties back to negotiations. Saudi's Crown Prince (later King) Abdullah also proposed a peace initiative which he presented to the 2002 Arab League Summit in Beirut. It was adopted, with some modifications, on 28 March 2002. The initiative proposed security for Israel and normalisation of its relations with Arab states in exchange for its withdrawal from all territories occupied since 1967, creation of an independent Palestinian state with *al-Quds al-Sharif* (East Jerusalem) as its capital, and the right of Palestinian refugees (and their descendants) to return to Israel.

In the same month, the UN Security Council passed Resolution 1397, affirming the need to end the al-Aqsa intifada and to realise Palestinian statehood. By this time, the intifada death toll stood at 1169 Palestinians and 339 Israelis. Israeli and Palestinian officials supported the resolution, but no progress was made in brokering a cease-fire. Instead, the violence intensified.

On 27 March 2002, a Palestinian bomber blew himself up at a Jewish Passover function at the Park Hotel in Netanya, north of Tel Aviv, killing 30 Israelis, including three generations of an entire family. The next day, Prime Minister Sharon ordered Israel's military forces to reoccupy Gaza and the West Bank in order to destroy all terrorist bases. The operation, beginning on 29 March, reversed all prior Israeli withdrawals from the Palestinian territories since 1994. In the process, a pitched battle with Palestinian forces in the Jenin refugee camp resulted in the deaths of 52 Palestinians and 23 Israelis. (Initial reports of a massacre of Palestinians were discredited by the UN and human rights groups.) Israel imprisoned Fatah's *Tanzim* leader, Marwan Barghouti, and Arafat's Ramallah compound, the *Muqata'a*, was besieged. Palestinian gunmen occupied the Church of the Nativity in Bethlehem for five weeks before they were exiled overseas.

As a result of Israel's reoccupation of areas that had previously been relinquished to the PA, intifada-related violence abated. However, Palestinians now faced increased hardships as the IDF regularly raided their towns and cities looking for terrorists, and imposed extended curfews. Lengthy delays at checkpoints, and humiliating searches became a perennial source of resentment among the Palestinian population.

## The West Bank separation barrier

On 19 May 2002, a member of the PFLP blew himself up in the local market in Netanya, Israel, killing 3 Israelis and injuring another 59. The following day, Sharon announced that Israel would build a separation (security) barrier between Israel and the West Bank. Construction began that year, scheduled for completion in 2007.

Unlike the Gaza Strip separation barrier built by the Rabin government in 1994, the West Bank barrier does not strictly follow the pre-1967 armistice line (the so-called 'Green Line'). Although 95 per cent of the barrier is a wire fence, some sections (5 per cent) consist of high concrete walls and parts cut into the West Bank, completely surrounding a number of Palestinian towns and Israeli settlements.

The majority of Israelis support the construction of the barrier because it has resulted in the reduction of Israeli casualties by 90 per cent. However, Israeli settlers living on the Palestinian side oppose it. Palestinians, too, are totally opposed to the barrier as it has significantly reduced their freedom of movement and caused them loss of land and economic decline. According to a March 2005 UN report:

> The route inside the West Bank severs communities, people's access to services, livelihoods and religious and cultural amenities. In addition, plans for the Barrier's exact route and crossing points through it are often not fully revealed until days before construction commences. This has led to considerable anxiety amongst Palestinians about how their future lives will be impacted ... The land between the Barrier and the Green Line constitutes some of the most fertile in the West Bank. It is currently the home for 49 400 West Bank Palestinians living in 38 villages and towns.

In December 2003, the UN General Assembly passed a resolution requesting an advisory opinion from the International Court of Justice (ICJ) on the 'legal consequences of the wall'. In 2004, the ICJ published its opinion (by 14 votes to 1) that the separation barrier violates international law and should be removed. Israel rejected the advisory opinion, highlighting that it was not legally binding, and it had failed to consider Israel's security needs or the human rights of Israeli citizens, including their fundamental right to life.

In June 2004, the Israeli Supreme Court ruled that a section of the barrier near Jerusalem disproportionately violated Palestinian human rights. The Court ordered 30 km of the existing and planned barrier to be

re-routed. The Israeli Government therefore approved a new route in February 2005, which would leave 7 per cent of the territory of the West Bank and 10 000 Palestinians on the Israeli side.

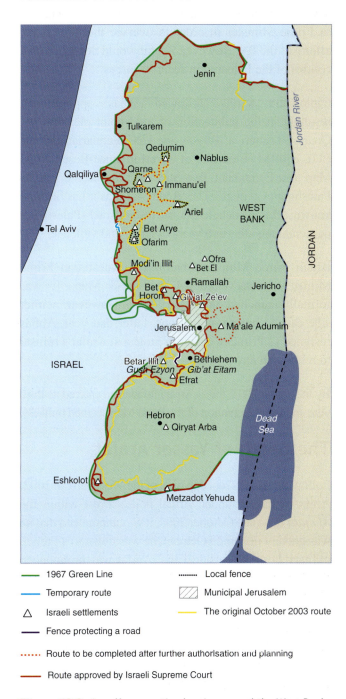

**Figure 12.3** Israel's separation barrier around the West Bank, as of September 2005.

## The Quartet's Road Map

In March 2003, in response to ongoing pressure from within the PA and from America and the EU, Arafat agreed to appoint Mahmoud Abbas (Abu Mazen) as Prime Minister in order to oversee the day-to-day affairs of the PA. However, Arafat would not relinquish control of the Palestinian security forces.

Diplomatic activity followed Abbas' appointment, resulting in the publication of a 43-point plan by 'the Quartet' (America, Russia, the UN Secretariat and the EU), entitled 'Elements of a Performance-Based Road Map to a Permanent Two-State Solution to the Israeli-Palestinian Conflict'. The 'Road Map', as it has become known, offered a detailed plan to restart Israeli-Palestinian peacemaking after two years of terror and violence.

Israeli Prime Minister Sharon and Palestinian Prime Minister Abbas endorsed the Road Map. It was formally launched on 30 April 2003. However, neither side carried out its obligations. Later that year, Abbas resigned as Prime Minister in protest at Arafat's refusal to relinquish any power.

By the end of 2003, the al-Aqsa intifada had entered its third year and implementation of the Road Map seemed unlikely.

## The death of Yasser Arafat

Following Israel's reoccupation of the West Bank in 2002, Arafat remained under virtual house arrest within the *Muqata'a*. In late October 2004, it was announced that he was gravely ill. On 29 October, he was flown to a French military hospital outside Paris. Arafat was pronounced dead on 11 November. His body was flown to Cairo for a state funeral, and then to Ramallah for burial.

### 'Unofficial' attempts at Israeli-Palestinian peacemaking

After the last official negotiations between Israel and the PLO at Taba in January 2001, two important 'unofficial' proposals were negotiated by Israelis and Palestinians. The first was the 'Nusseibeh-Ayalon Agreement' of September 2002. The second was the 'Geneva Accords' of October 2003. The documents recommend similar solutions. These include:

- Territory occupied in the West Bank by the major Israeli settlement blocs near the pre-1967 armistice line would become part of Israel. In return, an equivalent amount of Israeli territory would be ceded to the State of Palestine to be established in the Gaza Strip and remaining West Bank, where all Jewish settlements would be dismantled.

- The two states would share sovereignty over the Temple Mount/*Haram al-Sharif*.

- The Jewish and Arab parts of Jerusalem would become part of the states of Israel and Palestine respectively. There would be a symbolic 'right of return' of Palestinian refugees to Israel, limited to a maximum of 50 000 of the original 1948 refugees who are still alive and wish to become Israeli citizens. All other Palestinian refugees would have the right to live as citizens in Palestine.

**Figure 12.4** Final borders of Israel and Palestine according to the unofficial Geneva Peace Accords.

## Sharon announces 'disengagement' from Gaza

During a speech in Jerusalem on 18 December 2003, Sharon shocked many inside and outside of Israel by announcing his plan for unilateral disengagement from Gaza and some of the settlements in the north of the West Bank near Jenin. A year later, the Knesset endorsed the plan and in September 2005, all Israeli military personnel and settlers were withdrawn from the Gaza Strip and the settlements demolished.

## Mahmoud Abbas becomes Palestinian President

Following Arafat's death, the Palestinians went to the polls in January 2005 to elect a new President of the PA. Mahmoud Abbas won 62 per cent of the vote after campaigning on a platform of security. Immediately calling for an end to the al-Aqsa intifada, he outlined his strategy for a negotiated settlement with Israel and the establishment of a Palestinian state. With support from the Palestinians, Abbas was able to negotiate an informal *hudna* (cease-fire) with Hamas to end its terrorist attacks against Israel, though not with Islamic Jihad and the PFLP who continued their attacks.

Since his election, Abbas has presided over increasing lawlessness in Gaza and the West Bank. Causes include the limited capability of the PA, which lacks legitimacy and popular support, and the weakness of the Palestinian security forces, despite having more than 60 000 personnel. When the al-Aqsa intifada began, PA security forces participated in the violence, resulting in Israel systematically destroying much of the capacity and infrastructure of the PA security forces. Israel continues to refuse to allow the PA to procure all the weapons and ammunition that its security forces say they need to maintain order among their people. The vacuum has been filled by armed gangs loyal to competing militant groups. These include the al-Aqsa Brigades, Hamas, and the PFLP.

# Conclusion

At the end of 2005, what might be said concerning the prospects for peace between Israelis and Palestinians? Firstly, the Arab-Israeli conflict, which has taken many twists and turns over more than a century, has still not run its course. Secondly, although both parties signed the Quartet's Road Map in 2003, subsequent progress along the 'road' to peace has been minimal, with no official agreement about the details of the peace that lies at the end of the 'road'.

However, one thing is certain: although withdrawal from territory can be achieved unilaterally, peace cannot. Peace will require Israelis and Palestinians to formulate a final status agreement that both peoples can live with, even if it falls short of all their expectations. This will require each side to accept the sovereign rights of the other to part of the land. Another imperative will be for the leaders on each side to be convinced of the seriousness of their counterparts' intention to negotiate and abide by a permanent peace.

Despite these apparent obstacles, Israelis and Palestinians came very close to agreement on many key issues at Taba in January 2001. Two detailed blueprints for a peace agreement have since been proposed by 'unofficial' Israeli and Palestinian negotiators. This gives reason to hope that the Arab-Israeli conflict will be the last chapter in the seemingly timeless struggle for the land of Israel/Palestine. It takes courage to admit that one's enemy has legitimate claims. The goal of a just and lasting peace is within reach, if and when leaders on both sides find that courage.

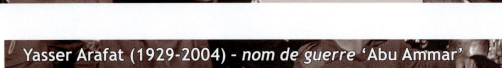

## Yasser Arafat (1929-2004) - *nom de guerre* 'Abu Ammar'

**Figure 12.5**   Yasser Arafat (1929-2004).

| Timeline | Event |
|---|---|
| 24 August 1929 | Abdul Rahman Abdul Ra'uf Arafat Al-Qudwa Al-Husseini (Yasser Arafat) is born in Cairo, Egypt. |
| 1933 to 1937 | After mother dies, sent with brother Fathi to live for four years with an uncle in Jerusalem. |
| 1946 to 1956 | Studies civil engineering at King Fuad I University in Cairo, graduating in 1956.<br>• In 1948, fights in Gaza during the First Arab-Israeli War.<br>• In 1952, founds the General Union of Palestinian Students (GUPS) in Cairo and remains President until 1957.<br>• In 1956, is founder and chairman of the Union of Palestinian Graduates in Cairo. |
| 1957 | After a short time in the Egyptian army, moves to Kuwait.  While there establishes a successful engineering company. |
| 1958 | Co-founds (with Abu Iyad and Abu Jihad) the first Fatah cell. |
| January 1959 | Co-founds Fatah Party, which remains the largest faction within the Palestine Liberation Organisation (PLO). |
| 1964 | Moves to Jordan to head up Fatah's attacks on Israel. |
| March 1964 | Is a member of the first Palestinian delegation to China to confer with Premier Chou-En-Lai. |
| January 1965 | Plans first sabotage mission inside Israel, targeting its National Water Carrier. |

| March 1968 | Fights in the battle of Karameh which he claims as a Palestinian victory, resulting in significant increase in Fatah's membership. |
| --- | --- |
| February 1969 | Elected Chairman of the PLO's Executive Committee; changes the focus of the PLO from pan-Arabism to the Palestinian national cause. |
| September 1970 | Appointed Commander-in-Chief of the Palestine Liberation Army (PLA). |
| 1974 | At Palestine National Council (PNC) Conference, sets out change in PLO strategy to 'liberate Palestine by stages' rather than by single conquest. |
| 13 November 1974 | Addresses the UN General Assembly for the first time. |
| 1978 | Rejects the Egyptian-Israeli Camp David Accords. |
| June 1982 | Flees Beirut for Syria when Israel invades Lebanon to crush and evict the PLO. |
| 1983 | Battles Syrian-backed PLO forces in Lebanon and following defeat, relocates PLO command in Tunis, Tunisia. |
| February 1985 | Signs the 'Amman Accords' with King Hussein of Jordan encompassing plans for a Palestinian-Jordanian confederation; agreement abrogated by King Hussein in 1986 when Arafat fails to condemn a PLO terrorist attack on the *Achille Lauro* cruise ship. |
| October 1985 | Narrowly escapes death in an Israeli air raid on PLO headquarters in Tunis. |
| November 1988 | Recognises Israel, renounces terrorism and proclaims an independent Palestinian state. |
| 2 April 1989 | Elected by the PLO Central Council as the first President of the State of Palestine. |
| August 1990 | Endorses Iraq's invasion and occupation of Kuwait. |
| November 1991 | Secretly marries Suha Tawil; announces marriage in February 1992. |
| April 1992 | Survives plane crash-landing in the Libyan desert, but suffers serious head injury requiring surgery to drain blood clots. |
| 13 September 1993 | Signs the Oslo Declaration of Principles with Israeli Prime Minister Yitzhak Rabin and Foreign Minister Shimon Peres, marking the beginning of the Israeli-Palestinian peace process. |
| May 1994 | Signs 'Gaza-Jericho First' agreement (Oslo II). |
| 1 July 1994 | Triumphantly returns to Gaza to head up the interim Palestinian National Authority (PA). |
| December 1994 | Wins Nobel Peace Prize, along with Rabin and Peres. |
| July 1995 | Daughter, Zahwa, is born in Paris, France. |
| November 1995 | Makes his first (secret) visit to Israel following assassination of Israeli Prime Minister Yitzhak Rabin to offer condolences to Leah Rabin. |
| 20 January 1996 | Elected Chairman (*Ra'is*) of the PA in the first Palestinian national elections. |
| January 1997 | Signs Hebron Agreement with Likud Prime Minister Benjamin Netanyahu. |
| October 1998 | Signs Wye Memorandum with Netanyahu. |
| September 1999 | Signs Sharm el-Sheikh Agreement with Labor Prime Minister Ehud Barak. |
| July 2000 | Attends Camp David Summit with Barak, hosted by US President Bill Clinton; taking a firm stand on Palestinian refugees, rejects Barak's offer for a 'final status' agreement but does not provide counterproposal. |
| August to October 2000 | Prepares his people for a second intifada, which is sparked by visit to *Haram al-Sharif* by Ariel Sharon on 28 September; forms Al-Aqsa Martyr Brigades. |
| March 2002 | Ramallah compound, the *Muqata'a*, is besieged by Israeli tanks. |
| February, October 2003 | Appoints Mahmoud Abbas as first Palestinian Prime Minister; Abbas resigns due to Arafat's refusal to relinquish power; Arafat appoints Ahmed Qrei'a as new PM in October 2003. |
| 29 October 2004 | Flown to military hospital outside Paris suffering from an unspecified condition. |
| 11 November 2004 | Pronounced dead. |

[Arafat] did not win military battles, neither in the homeland nor in the diaspora. But he did win the battle of defending our national existence. He placed the Palestinian question squarely on the regional and international political map. He gave shape to the national identity of the Palestinian refugee, lost and forgotten at the edges of oblivion. He caused the Palestinian reality to take root in the human consciousness and succeeded in convincing the world that war starts in Palestine and peace starts in Palestine. Yasser Arafat's kufiya, folded and fixed in place with symbolic and folkloric importance, became the moral and political guide to Palestine.

From Mahmoud Darwish's 'Farewell Arafat.'[2]

It might be argued that the most important Arab figure in the Arab-Israeli conflict from the late 1960s until his death in 2004 was Yasser Arafat. His actions certainly influenced the lives of millions of people. As detailed in Chapter 9 and following, the political career of the Palestinian leader began in earnest with the founding of Fatah, through which he eventually took control of the PLO in 1969. He led the PLO through the Jordanian and Lebanese civil wars, the Israeli-Palestinian peace process and its subsequent collapse, and the years of the second Palestinian intifada. Assessments concerning the role of Arafat in the history of the Palestinian people specifically, and the Arab-Israel conflict more generally, are far from unanimous. To Arafat's supporters he was 'Mr Palestine', the embodiment of Palestinian nationalism and the person who placed the Palestinian cause on the world stage. To his detractors, Arafat was a corrupt and unscrupulous dictator, an unrelenting terrorist responsible for the murders of thousands of innocent civilians. Others believe there is a significant kernel of truth in both viewpoints.

For four decades Arafat's name made headlines and his face was a familiar one in the international media. He was the subject of thousands of commentaries and analyses in books, journals and newspapers for which he gave hundreds of interviews. Yet in spite of this uninterrupted flow of information and opinion, even a cursory reading of the many (unofficial) biographies of Arafat reveals conflicting stories concerning key events in his life. This, according to one writer, is because Arafat was 'a grand obfuscator – right down to the small details of his life'.[3] Whilst Arafat cooperated with several biographers, such as Alan Hart and Rasheda Mahran, he provided them with contradictory information and he never recorded his own life story. Hence titles of Arafat biographies contain words such as 'mystery' or 'myth', while details are qualified by phrases such as 'hard to explain'.

Arafat's life begins with the 'myth' of his birthplace and ends with the 'mystery' of the cause of his death.

## Family background

Yasser Arafat was born Abdul Rahman Abdul Ra'uf Arafat Al-Qudwa Al-Husseini on 24 August 1929 in Cairo, Egypt. He was one of seven children born to Abdul-Raouf Arafat (from the Al-Qudwah family of Gaza and Khan Younis), and Zahwa (from the Abu Al-Saoud family of Jerusalem). Arafat later insisted that he was born in Palestine (either in Jerusalem or Gaza) and then brought to Egypt. However, Arafat's birth certificate gives Cairo as his place of birth, as do his university records. Cairo was where his father, a textile merchant, had moved the family in 1927.

Arafat's mother died when he was four, and his father sent him and his brother Fathi to live with a maternal uncle in Jerusalem. He returned to Cairo in 1937. Back in Egypt, Arafat gained the nickname 'Yasser', which means 'easy' in Arabic. Arafat biographer, Said Aburish, also reports that he ran a 'gang of neighbourhood children' which he 'bullied and organised', 'taking pleasure in ordering them around and marching them up and down the streets while hectoring them like a tough, rough-speaking sergeant from the films of that time'.[4]

However, it was his four years in Jerusalem that Arafat later adopted as the reference point for his family background, along with the (false) claim that his mother was a relative of the famous al-Husseini family. Aburish explains:

... when the young Arafat sought to establish his Palestinian credentials and promote his eventual claim to leadership, he could not afford to admit any facts which might reduce his Palestinian identity. Indeed, that is why he dramatised it by describing himself as 'the son of Jerusalem'. ... [this] was probably a wise move. Admitting his Egyptian birth, and that his father was half Egyptian, could have affected his chances of success, particularly during periods when the Palestinians were inclined to separate themselves from the rest of the Arabs, whose efforts on their behalf had disappointed them. ... [Thus] Arafat insistently perpetuated the legend that he had been born in Jerusalem and was related to the important Husseini clan of that city, the leading political family in Palestine and claimants to a lineage that stretched back to the prophet Muhammad. [5]

**Figure 12.6** Young Arafat.

## Early student activism in Cairo

During his teens Arafat developed a passion for politics and, like many in Egypt at the time, a keen interest in the conflict in Palestine. When Hajj Amin al-Husseini, the exiled head of the Palestinian Arab Higher Committee, arrived in Cairo in 1946, Arafat became a volunteer assistant to Hajj Amin's chief advisor, Sheikh Hassan Abdul Saoud, who was a distant relative. In this role, he became involved in the purchase of weapons that were smuggled from Egypt into Palestine for use by the 'Holy Strugglers', Arab irregulars who were fighting against the British and the Jews.

In 1947 Arafat entered King Fuad I University (now Cairo University) to study civil engineering. While at university, he became a committed student activist for the Palestinian nationalist movement.

When the British left Palestine in May 1948, Arafat went to Gaza to fight in the First Arab-Israeli War. Some reports state that when he reached Gaza, he was disarmed and turned back by Egyptian military forces. Arafat later claimed that this was another act of betrayal by the Arab regimes. However, other reports record that Arafat successfully entered Gaza and fought there with irregulars from the Egyptian Muslim Brotherhood who had been dispatched 'to retrieve and protect Muslim rights and honour in Palestine'.

According to Aburish, this brief experience of fighting in Palestine had a long-term impact on Arafat who became convinced that the Arab governments who fought the Israelis had lost 'because of corrupt and incompetent leadership and that, left alone, the Palestinians would have won the war. It was these two beliefs which propelled him forward and which, because he was reluctant to admit other influences, many accept as the basis of his political philosophy' to the end of his days.[6] He was also deeply affected by the onset of the Palestinian refugee problem, claiming later in his life that he was a refugee from the 1948 War.

In 1949, back at university in Cairo, Arafat continued his student activism. He became a member of the Egyptian Union of Students and the Federation of Palestinian Students, and published a magazine, *The Voice of Palestine*, which called on Arabs to fight 'the Zionist entity, the cancer in our midst, the agent of imperialism'. It was also during this period that he befriended Salah Khalaf (Abu Iyad) who would later become a prominent member of Fatah.

Before graduating in 1956, Arafat was elected chairperson of the General Union of Palestinian Students (GUPS), a position he held until he left Egypt in 1957. He also founded the Union of Palestinian Graduates in 1956 and in August that year, attended an international student congress in Prague, Czechoslovakia, his debut on the international scene where he donned a white *kufiyeh* (male Arab headdress). In time, the black and white *kufiyeh* would become his trademark.

Reflecting on Arafat's success in student politics, Aburish identifies certain traits that set him apart from other activists of the day, in particular, his single-mindedness'. 'It is true' says Aburish, that Arafat 'was a chameleon, but he was never subservient and made a virtue out of being stubborn and uncompromising; on occasion he resorted to browbeating people, while others found him actually using his fists.' But he was also 'a great storyteller' and although not a public speaker, he was 'endowed with that rare quality of being able to talk people into following him and doing his bidding.'[9] Arafat was known for these traits throughout his entire life.

Arafat finally graduated from university in 1956 with a Bachelor's degree in civil engineering. Soon afterwards, he entered the Egyptian army and was trained as a bomb disposal officer, reaching the rank of first lieutenant. Some reports say that he fought in the 1956 Suez War, although this is contested. However, at some time during the mid 1950s, Arafat spent time in Gaza fighting alongside the Palestinian *fedayeen* during their raids into Israel.

It was in Gaza that Arafat met Khalid al-Wazir (Abu Jihad), a member of the Palestinian Muslim Brotherhood, who would later co-found Fatah. Both men were frustrated when, in the wake of the 1956 Suez War, the UNEF were stationed in Gaza as a condition of Israel's withdrawal. Arafat blamed Egyptian President Nasser for thwarting the activities of the Palestinian nationalists and for attempting to keep the *fedayeen* in Gaza 'on a tight leash for fear of Israeli reprisals'. This, according to Aburish, had

a profound impact on Arafat: by deciding 'to place the interests of Egypt first' and exercise strict control over the *fedayeen* to limit their effectiveness, Nasser 'forced a Palestinian identity on Arafat'.[10] It was at this point that he became convinced that the Palestinians needed to act independently of the Arab states.

Back in Cairo at the beginning of 1957, Arafat and some of those who would become his most senior colleagues, including al-Wazir and Khalaf, began to consider their next move. According to al-Wazir, three lines of thinking emerged from the discussion:

> [One] current emerged among a number of youths in Cairo calling for the assembly of certain Palestinian leaders and for prompting them to form a defined structure to lead our Palestinian people. … [but this led] to a dead end. … [A] second group saw a need to announce a Palestinian government-in-exile on the foundations of the All Palestine Government, in order to represent our Palestinian people and lead the struggle for the restoration of Palestinian rights. But this attempt too met Arab official refusal and the obstacles set by Arab agencies and leaders.
>
> There was a third current, which believed that existing Arab reality would never allow even the establishment of a Palestinian organisation, and so there was no alternative for the Palestinians but to go underground and adopt absolute secrecy in their organisation, until it could impose itself on that reality and force recognition. [11]

Over the years, Arafat carefully crafted an image of himself that came to bear much of the symbolism of the Palestinian nationalist movement. His khaki uniform affirmed his belief in armed struggle as the method to achieve national liberation, while his *kufiyeh* differentiated the Palestinian nationalist movement from all others. He was often asked about his attire in interviews and on one occasion, in response to a question concerning his uniform, he answered: 'Don't forget that I am the supreme commander of the Palestinian forces. I cannot change my skin. I am not a chameleon. I also said to President Reagan, if you give me a country, I am ready to wear a tuxedo and bow tie.'

But it was Arafat's *kufiyeh*, in particular, that became a potent symbol of Palestinian nationalism. Historically, the black and white *kufiyeh*, or *hatta*, was the popular headdress of the *fellaheen*, thus signifying a lower social status and a rural background. However, during the 1936-39 Arab revolt against the British, those who took an active part in the uprising wore a *kufiyeh*, regardless of social status, 'thus creating a national symbol of resistance and solidarity that superseded other differences'. By donning the popular black and white *kufiyeh* (early pictures show Arafat wearing a plain white *kufiyeh*, which was traditionally worn by Arab notables), Arafat symbolised the popular nature of Fatah's struggle and directly linked his movement with the 1936 uprising. He also paid careful attention to the way in which he arranged the fabric on his head and shoulders, as journalist Amina Elbendary explains:

> Legends surround Arafat's kufiyeh and the distinctive style in which he donned it, the carefully hemmed crease in the middle of his forehead, its twist and toss in a particular manner to the right of his face in the shape, many insist, of the map of Palestine. … Over the years the khakis and the kufiyeh remained the emblems of the man and his struggle. During the hype that surrounded the signing of the Oslo Accords and the White House lawn celebration in 1993, Western media wondered whether Arafat would shun his gun and khakis now that the struggle – they insinuated – was over. But Arafat did not. He arrived on the White House lawn, all smiles and hugs, in his pseudo-military uniform and his kufiyeh.[7]

Thus every detail of Arafat's outward appearance was symbolic, even his characteristic unshaven face. When asked about this in an interview, Arafat would answer either that he did not want to waste time on shaving that he could be dedicating to the Palestinian nation, or that the conditions of his life did not allow luxuries such as shaving.

The names Arafat assumed were also highly symbolic, such as the *teknonym* he adopted as his *nom de guerre*, 'Abu Ammar' (father of Ammar). (The practice of *teknonymy* is common in Arab culture whereby a parent is designated by the name of her/his oldest son, hence 'father of _' or 'mother of_'). Arafat adopted this *nom de guerre* when he co-founded Fatah. He did not have any children, and so chose a name that had an allusion to Yasser ibn Ammar, one of the companions of the Prophet Muhammad.

Whilst his people most often referred to Arafat as Abu Ammar, his other names included *al-Khetyar* (the old man), representing the perception of Arafat as the patriarch of the Palestinian people, the 'father of the nation' as some have called him. TIME reporter Tony Karon comments on this further:

> The 'father of the nation' appellation is not simply a product of Arafat's 35 years at the helm of the Palestine Liberation Organisation (PLO), or his half-century in charge of the secular-nationalist Fatah movement he founded in 1956 [sic], and which remains the single largest party in Palestinian politics. It derives from the fact that Arafat's ascent in the national movement epitomised a Palestinian declaration of independence. Before Arafat and his comrades took charge of the PLO in 1968, the very term 'Palestinian' hardly existed in the international lexicon. The fate of the Arab residents of what had once been British-mandate Palestine was viewed by the West, Israel and the Arab world as properly the responsibility of the Arab regimes. But with their failed military campaigns to destroy the Jewish State in 1948, 1967 and 1973 leaving the vast majority of Palestinians living either as refugees in the Arab world or under Israeli occupation in the West Bank and Gaza, Arafat personified a determination among Palestinians to take charge of their own fate.[8]

Arafat, al-Wazir and Khalaf belonged to this latter group and set to the task of creating new underground political cells and uniting existing ones wherever there was a Palestinian community. While al-Wazir returned to Gaza to establish his base, Arafat remained in Cairo. In both locations, student organisations were used as a cover for their work. The clandestine nature of their activity, explains biographer Alan Hart, was necessary 'because no Arab regime wanted to see the emergence of an independent Palestinian movement.'[12]

Arafat's efforts were quickly frustrated by the Egyptian intelligence agency which applied pressure on him to leave Cairo. Forced to look elsewhere for a livelihood, he applied for a position in Saudi Arabia, but before his papers were cleared, he accepted a job as a civil engineer with the government of Kuwait. The latter country was still a British protectorate (until 1961), and relatively unaffected by the politics of pan-Arabism.

# Arafat's rise to prominence

Arafat prospered in Kuwait, becoming a successful engineer and wealthy building contractor, owning two and three cars at a time (his favourite was a Ford Thunderbird). Years later, TIME reporter Lisa Beyer wrote that, Arafat 'would design his own bomb shelter outside his residence in Lebanon and would boast that despite Israeli bombings, it held up while the one beside it, built by a big commercial firm, collapsed.'[13]

## Foundation of Fatah

Although he worked hard in his business, politics remained Arafat's passion. Soon after arriving in Kuwait in 1957, he was joined by al-Wazir, who took a job as a school teacher. Here the two activists were able to organise more freely. Later that year, along with three (some sources say four) other Palestinians, they agreed to establish a clandestine Palestinian nationalist organisation. The first cell was formed during the following year. (There are a number of dates given for the official formation of Fatah, including October 1959 and January 1965.) In order to avoid detection by the Arab and British intelligence services, each member adopted a *nom de guerre,* Arafat taking the name Abu Ammar. A formal name for the organisation was not agreed upon until the end of 1958. The name *Harakat al-Tahrir al-Watani al-Filastini* ('The Palestinian National Liberation Movement'), is better known by its reverse acronym, *Fatah* (also spelt *Fateh* or *Feteh*, meaning 'conquest' in Arabic).

Some 500 new members joined the group in 1959, the most prominent of whom was Salah Khalaf (Abu Iyad). In that same year, Fatah began its own publication, *Nida al-Hayat – Filastinuna* ('The Call of Life – Our Palestine'), which first appeared in Beirut. Between 1959 and 1964, some 40 issues of *Filastinuna* were published – several articles carrying Arafat's initials – which set out the basic principles of Fatah's ideology: 'war should be waged relentlessly against Israel, political deals that left Israel in existence should be rejected, the Arab governments were not to be trusted and their attempts at hegemony or tutelage should be resisted, and, above all, the people of Palestine should take their fate into their own hands and unite all their resources in the armed struggle.'[14] Beyond these principles, Fatah intended to 'keep the pot boiling and to provoke a war between the Arabs and Israel which, they believed, the Arabs were bound to win.' This remained the basis of Arafat's thinking for the next decade, until, as Hart states, 'the Arabs lost the war that had to be won if the strategy was to be justified.'[15]

Concerning Arafat's personal ideology, almost all of his biographers agree that, unlike other leaders who considered themselves 'revolutionary', he did not have a guiding vision of a better society, or a grand strategy for social transformation, like Marxism or Islamism. Instead, Arafat's central belief was that his national group had a superior claim to the land of Palestine and must defeat those he viewed as usurpers. There was no room for compromise or coexistence. According to Arafat, this would require overcoming a series of tactical challenges through

'armed struggle', by which he meant military action, in particular, sabotage and terrorism. 'Military action', Arafat believed, 'was necessary to fix the Palestinian identity.' This became his slogan.

However, in the early period of the group's development, Arafat's argument that Fatah needed to engage immediately in guerilla warfare and terrorism was not supported by all its members. Two factions thus emerged. Arafat's group, which was referred to as the 'mad ones', urged Fatah to armed action. The other group, the so-called 'sane ones', argued that before any military action was taken, the infant organisation needed to win over the wider Palestinian population, which could not be done by engaging only in guerilla and terrorist warfare.

Arafat's hope that the first Fatah cell would be the nucleus of a rapidly expanding network of similar cells throughout the Arab world and beyond was slow to be realised. It would be seven years before Fatah emerged from the underground. There were a number of reasons for this. Firstly, until the 1967 'Six-Day War', the majority of Palestinians continued to pin their hopes for national salvation on Nasser, who had emerged from the 1956 War as a pan-Arab hero. Further, Fatah could not publicly reveal its strategy of pushing the Arab states into a war with Israel – a war which the regimes certainly did not want. Finally, Arafat's call for Palestinians to liberate their homeland through armed struggle relying on their own efforts, was considered by most Palestinians to be 'ludicrous'.

But within a decade, Fatah, with Arafat as its declared leader, had been catapulted from obscurity to overall leadership of the Palestinian people. The process began in 1963, when Fatah was transformed from a clandestine cell to a more permanent organisation with a central committee responsible for directing the organisation and its membership. Ultimate power was held by Arafat, with al-Wazir as deputy.

The following year, Arafat left Kuwait for Jordan where he planned to become a 'full-time revolutionary', organising Fatah raids into Israel. The first of these came in 1965. Arafat sent a team of Fatah guerillas under the name al-Assifa ('The Storm') to place explosives in the Beit Netopha canal, a section of Israel's National Water Carrier then under construction. Although their efforts were unsuccessful (Israelis discovered and dismantled the bomb before its timer was set to go off), the attack was publicised by the Israelis, as were a number of subsequent al-Assifa infiltrations. These actions by an underground group willing to confront 'the enemy' directly and carry out acts of violence in Israel, captured the attention and respect of the Palestinians around the Arab world. By mid 1967, al-Assifa, now openly recognised as the military arm of Fatah, had undertaken nearly 100 acts of sabotage in Israel, killing 11 Israelis and wounding over 60.

The next step in Arafat's rise to prominence came in the wake of the Arab states' humiliating defeat in the June 1967 War. The catalyst for this came in March 1968, when Fatah, with Jordanian army support, battled with the IDF at the Palestinian refugee camp at Karameh, located on the Jordanian side of the West Bank border (the camp was Fatah's major training and supply headquarters). Whilst the battle was an Israeli victory, a number of Israeli soldiers were killed and some tanks and armoured vehicles destroyed by Jordanian artillery. After the Israelis withdrew, their disabled vehicles were paraded by Fatah through the streets of Amman and Arafat claimed victory for having held out, even if briefly, against the 'invincible' IDF. This was a cause for much celebration among Palestinians everywhere, many of whom had lost hope in Nasser's pan-Arab message in the wake of the 1967 defeat. In the weeks and months following, thousands of Palestinians signed up to join *Fatah*, propelling the organisation and its leader to the top of the Palestinian national movement.

Arafat's next move was to take control of the Palestine Liberation Organisation (PLO). This was perhaps his most far-reaching political achievement.

## Leadership of the PLO

Within a year of the Karameh battle, Fatah had successfully moved to take control of half the seats of the Palestine National Council, the PLO's emerging parliament-in-exile. The organisation was reconstituted as a roof body for all Palestinian guerilla groups and its charter was revised to reflect Fatah's vision of the liberation of Palestine by armed struggle alone.

At the Fifth Palestine National Congress in February 1969, Arafat was elected Chairman of the PLO's 15-member Executive Committee, which Fatah now controlled, and in September 1970, he became Commander-in-Chief of the Palestinian Liberation Army (PLA), the regular military force of the PLO which numbered some 15 000 men. Arafat continued to hold these positions until his death in 2004. As chief architect, Arafat rapidly transformed the PLO from a feeble association of small guerilla bands into a wealthy, multibranched establishment conducting military, economic-financial, social, medical and educational operations. Large sums of money were put at Arafat's disposal, mainly by the rich Arab oil-producing states.

Under Arafat's leadership, the PLO ceased to be subordinate to the pan-Arabist movement and gave priority to Palestinian liberation. Compromise with the Jews was not an option as Israel's destruction was seen as the only solution. 'Revolutionary armed struggle', explained Arafat's close colleague Salah Khalaf, was the strategy to be employed. The PLO and its leadership 'had no right to negotiate a settlement but must keep struggling, even if they cannot liberate a single inch, in order to preserve the option to regain all of Palestine someday. … Our steadfastness and our adherence to our land is our only card … We would rather be frozen for ten more years than move toward treason.' Arafat would use this same terminology in speeches in 1977 and again, more significantly, in 1988.

In his capacity as Chairman of the PLO's Executive Committee, Arafat came to be recognised by the Arab regimes as the top leader of the Palestinians. At the 1974 Arab League summit in Rabat, Morocco, the PLO was recognised by the League as 'the sole legitimate representative of the Palestinians'.

Arafat's new status was similarly recognised by leaders of the non-aligned states and Islamic organisations. On 13 November 1974, with backing from the Arab League, Arafat was invited to address the UN General Assembly, the first head of a non-governmental organisation to do so. During his speech, whilst condemning Zionism he also made the famous statement: 'Today I have come bearing an olive branch and a freedom fighter's gun. Do not let the olive branch fall from my hand.' Following his address, the General Assembly granted the PLO observer status. Two years later, the PLO was admitted to full membership in the Arab League from which time Arafat attended Arab League summits and maintained regular contact with Arab heads of state.

## Development of the terrorism campaign

Even before Arafat assumed the leadership of the PLO, he had organised numerous Fatah attacks on Israeli infrastructure and terrorist attacks against its civilians. Once in control of the PLO, he was engaged directly or indirectly in a long campaign of terrorism against Israelis at home and abroad, and against the international air transportation system.

PLO terrorist attacks throughout the 1970s and 1980s included the first hijacking of an Israeli (El Al) airliner in 1968; the hijacking in 1970 of a SwissAir flight bound for Tel Aviv, which was bombed in mid-flight, killing 47; the September 1970 hijacking of planes that were blown up in Jordan, which sparked the Jordanian-PLO civil war; the attack in 1970 on an Israeli school bus during which 9 children and 3 teachers were shot and killed; the murder of 11 Israeli athletes at the 1972 Olympic Games in Munich, Germany; the machine-gun attack in 1972 at Lod Airport in Tel Aviv, killing

27 tourists; the 1973 bombing of a Pan Am office at Fiumicino Airport in Rome which killed 32; the murder in 1973 of two US diplomats in Sudan; the 1974 attack on an Israeli apartment block in Kiryat Shmona, during which 18 were killed including 8 children; the attack in 1974 on an Israeli school bus in Ma'alot resulting in 20 children killed; the 1975 attack on the Tel Aviv seafront during which hostages were taken and 3 civilians killed; the 1976 attack on an Israeli bus killing 26 passengers; the hijacking in 1976 of an Air France airliner which was flown to Entebbe in Uganda where 3 were killed; the 1985 hijacking of the *Achille Lauro* cruise ship which resulted in the murder of a wheelchair-bound passenger; and also in 1985, the attack on an Israeli yacht off the coast of Cyprus resulting in 3 deaths.

Under Arafat's leadership, terrorism became the major tool of the PLO's efforts to keep the Palestinian quest for sovereignty on the front pages of the international media. Israeli civilians – so-called soft targets – were the primary target.

But there was another reason for this choice of tactic, as Salah Khalaf explained in his 1981 autobiography:

Fatah's young men [who were] unable to wage classic guerilla warfare across Israel's borders … insisted on carrying out a revolutionary violence of another kind, commonly known elsewhere as 'terrorism'. They wanted to wreak vengeance not only on the Zionist enemy, but also on the Arab murderers and traitors who had made themselves Israel's accomplices. To keep the violence from taking an individualistic and anarchic form, there was no other way than to channel the wave of anger, to structure it and give it a political content. [16]

Whilst terrorist attacks attracted international attention for the Palestinian cause, they also drew condemnation in many quarters for the wanton spilling of innocent blood.

**Figure 12.7** Arafat addressing the UN General Assembly, November 1974.

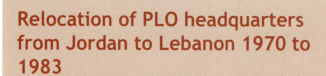

# Relocation of PLO headquarters from Jordan to Lebanon 1970 to 1983

From his command base in Jordan, Arafat built the PLO into a formidable force, able to operate within the country as a 'state within a state'. By the late 1960s, heavily armed Palestinian *fedayeen* had taken control of areas where refugee camps were located as well as several strategic positions, including the oil refinery near Az Zarq. Tensions steadily mounted as King Hussein came to view Arafat and the PLO as a threat to Jordan's sovereignty. Open fighting erupted in June 1970.

Conflict between Jordanian and Palestinian forces came to a head three months later, when on 12 September, PLO terrorists flew three hijacked civilian planes to Jordan where they blew them up. This was of great embarrassment to the King who, four days later, declared martial law. On the same day Arafat became commander of the Palestine Liberation Army (PLA). After secretly securing support from Israel and the US if required, Hussein ordered his forces to take action to regain control of his country. The PLO responded by attempting a *coup* at which point civil war erupted between the PLO and the Jordanian army.

Initially the PLO was supported by Syria, which invaded Jordan with a force of around 200 tanks. However, the Syrians retreated when a squadron of Israeli jet fighters flew over the Syrian forces and the US dispatched its Sixth Fleet to the eastern Mediterranean. By 24 September the Jordanian army had defeated the Palestinian forces, with many thousands killed. Arafat, disguised as a Kuwaiti official (some reports say as a bedouin woman), fled first to Syria, and then to Lebanon, together with most of the remaining PLO leadership.

Once in Lebanon, Arafat rebuilt his command in Beirut, while using the Palestinian refugee camps in the south of the country as bases from which to attack northern Israel. More broadly, due to Lebanon's weak central government, the PLO was able to develop as a 'state within a state', as it had in Jordan. Clashes between Arafat's men and the Lebanese security forces became common place, causing many deaths, government crises and serious divisions within a county whose political structure was already weakened by sectarian divisions.

In 1975, fighting between the PLO and Lebanon's Christian forces sparked a 15-year civil war during which brutal acts of murder, rape and revenge were carried out by the PLO against Lebanese Christian civilians and by Lebanese Christian forces against Palestinian refugees.

A year after the war began, Arafat also found himself at war with Syria, whose army was sent into Lebanon by President Asad, in part to prevent a PLO victory. Asad biographer, Patrick Seale, explains:

> The war in Lebanon brought to the surface the essential irreconcilability of the interests of the Arab states and those of the [PLO] guerillas. The Palestinians yearned for freedom to decide their own strategies, but such independence could be had only at the expense of the security of the Arab states. In 1975-6 Asad woke up to the fact that the Palestinians held the key to Lebanon's sovereignty: the power of decision over peace and war. This was the crux of his conflict with them.[17]

During the course of the civil war, Israel invaded Lebanon twice in an effort to end PLO attacks on Israel's northern towns and villages and to destroy the PLO infrastructure. As a result of the 1982 invasion, the PLO command and the majority of its forces were expelled from south Lebanon and evacuated from west Beirut. Arafat fled to Syria and from there, was able to control small bases in the Syrian-occupied Biqa Valley (in east Lebanon) and in Tripoli (in north Lebanon on the Mediterranean coast).

## Relocation of PLO headquarters from Lebanon to Tunis 1983-1993

In June 1983, the Syrians expelled Arafat and sponsored an anti-Arafat rebellion among the remaining Fatah and PLO forces in Lebanon. Arafat headed to Tripoli to rally his forces there and in the Palestinian camps around the city. Fierce fighting between the various PLO factions followed. After fighting Israel, Jordan, Syria and the Lebanese, in August 1983 Arafat and his loyalists were now fighting fellow Palestinians. By the end of the year, Arafat and the *fedayeen* loyal to him had been defeated by the Syrian-backed Palestinian forces. They were evacuated to Tunis, the capital of Tunisia in North Africa.

This was the second time Arafat had lost a battle against Arab forces. Indeed, the Arab states were both a blessing and a curse for Arafat. On the one hand, the Arab League had provided legitimacy for the PLO and Arafat's leadership of the Palestinian movement in 1974. Some Arab states, in particular, Saudi Arabia, provided funding for the organisation and for Arafat's personal expenditure. (Most other states who pledged money did not pay up.) On the other hand, some Arab leaders had sought to dominate the PLO and injure Arafat, if not have him killed. As Palestinian scholar Yezid Sayigh put it, 'virtually every Arab state has stabbed [the Palestinians] in the back at one point or another.' The Arab states have been responsible for the deaths of approximately three-quarters of the Palestinians killed in the Arab-Israeli conflict. [18]

Once in Tunis Arafat re-established the political and administrative headquarters of the PLO, which remained his centre of operations until 1993. From here he dispersed military commands and operational departments in various other Arab countries,

**Figure 12.8   In 1990, Arafat married Suha Tawil, who had worked on his personal staff in Tunis.** At the time, Arafat was 61 and Suha 28.  The marriage was kept secret until February 1992.  In July 1995, Suha had a daughter who was named Zawha, after Arafat's mother. When the second Palestinian intifada began, Suha moved to Paris to live with her mother and daughter.

supported financially by Iraq and Saudi Arabia. He also made every effort to travel as often as possible to Arab and other world capitals in an effort to keep the Palestinian cause at the forefront of regional and international politics.

During his years in Tunis, Arafat survived a number of 'near death' experiences – both physical and political. In 1985, following the terrorist attack on an Israeli yacht carried out by Fatah's elite squad, 'Force 17' (which is responsible for the protection of top PLO figures), Israel responded by bombing Arafat's headquarters in Tunis. More than 60 PLO and Force 17 members were killed in the attack, but Arafat survived as he was out jogging at the time.

Then in April 1992, Arafat again escaped death when his plane crash-landed in the Libyan desert during a sandstorm. While others were killed, Afatat survived, though with several broken bones and a serious head injury which required surgery to drain blood clots.

Arafat also survived many challenges to his leadership from within the PLO. The 1983 rebellion in Lebanon had caused a deep, if not irreversible split within the PLO. Afterwards, the rebels and their supporters, such as the Abu Nidal group, demanded that Arafat resign from his position as PLO Chairman. They boycotted all meetings and sessions held by Arafat loyalists, including a 1984 session of the PLO National Council which endorsed Arafat's policies and ongoing leadership.

Arafat had achieved reconciliation with many of the PLO rebels by 1987, though not with those aligned with Syria. Unity became all the more critical at this time because at the year's end, the first Palestinian intifada began. The uprising came at a low period for the PLO after its expulsion from Lebanon. It thus provided Arafat with the opportunity to refocus world attention to the difficult plight of the Palestinians.

## Change from terrorism to diplomacy

In the mid 1970s Arafat began to make public statements in which he condemned the hijacking of foreign aircraft and emphasised the need for political solutions to the conflict with Israel. Some saw this as a shift in Arafat's long-held belief that armed struggle alone, through military attacks and terrorism, would realise Palestinian national aspirations. He spoke, for example, of joining international efforts to negotiate a settlement, as long as the creation of an independent Palestinian state was an intended outcome of the negotiations. Accordingly, Arafat rejected the 1978 Egyptian-Israeli Camp David Accords because they gave no role to the PLO in future negotiations and the proposed model of Palestinian autonomy fell far short of the Palestinians' aspiration for statehood. However, he did not object to the 'all-Arab' peace plan proposed by Crown Prince Fahd of Saudi Arabia in 1981, which was adopted with amendments by the Arab League in 1982.

But suspicions concerning Arafat's true motives persisted, particularly among Israelis, who pointed to the PLO's 1974 'Phases Plan' as evidence that the organisation and its leaders still sought Israel's destruction. While the plan represented a shift in PLO policy, in so far as it was willing to establish a 'national authority' in any part of Palestine, side by side with Israel, the document also made clear that this was merely an initial step required 'to complete the liberation of all Palestinian soil'. This latter aim was reaffirmed by the Fourth Fatah Conference in 1980, which also confirmed the group's commitment to 'popular armed revolution' and 'armed struggle', to be 'carried on without interruption until the annihilation of the Zionist entity and the liberation of Palestine are achieved.' Further, Arafat failed to condemn ongoing terrorism perpetrated by PLO member groups, such as Black September, the DFLP and the PFLP.

Following the PLO's expulsion from Lebanon in 1982, a clearer shift in policy 'from terrorism to diplomacy' seemed to emerge as Arafat sought to mend relations

with Jordan in the hope that the PLO might be able to re-establish a base there. His negotiations with King Hussein focused on two main issues: a confederation between a future Palestinian state and Jordan; and a joint Palestinian-Jordanian policy towards a peace settlement with Israel, including a possible joint negotiating team. The two leaders reached an agreement in February 1985, called the Amman Accords, but final negotiations failed to resolve differences over the PLO's refusal to recognise Israel and Arafat's ambiguity regarding terrorism. The 1985 agreement was abrogated by King Hussein in 1986 when Arafat failed to condemn the Palestinian hijacking of the *Achille Lauro* cruise ship. In the decades that followed, Arafat continued to preside over the PLO's Executive Committee, members of which were actively involved in terrorism, as were members of Fatah and 'Force 17'.

A significant shift in Arafat's diplomacy did come a year after the onset of the first Palestinian intifada, by which time the Islamist opposition group, Hamas, had risen to challenge the leadership of the PLO and Arafat in particular. In November 1988, during his speech at the 19th Palestine National Council, Arafat attempted to return the Palestinian cause to the international stage by proclaiming a 'State of Palestine'. This was despite the fact that no government-in-exile or administration had been set up and the new 'state' had no control over any territory or people. In the same speech, Arafat renounced terrorism and publicly accepted UN Resolution 242 as the basis for a negotiated peace between Israel and the PLO. He repeated these same statements at a special UN session held in Geneva, Switzerland, on 13 December 1988, when he declared that the PLO renounced 'terrorism in all its forms, including state terrorism', and supported 'the right of all parties concerned in the Middle East conflict to live in peace and security, including the state of Palestine, Israel and other neighbours'.

However, in less public statements following both declarations, Arafat affirmed the continuing relevance of the 1968 PLO Charter, the aims of which were contrary to the new policy, and he insisted on the PLO's right to continue to conduct 'military'

operations against Israel. As far as Arafat was concerned, this meant ongoing support for attacks on Israeli targets – combatants and non-combatants – as he did not accept that any form of PLO attacks against Israelis constituted terrorism.

Nevertheless, Arafat's symbolic declaration of Palestinian statehood was recognised by more than 90 countries and on 2 April 1989, Arafat was elected the first President of the State of Palestine by the PLO's Central Council. America, too, agreed to hold a dialogue with the PLO in Tunis. But in June 1990, when Arafat did not denounce an attempted terrorist act (foiled by Israel), the US suspended the dialogue. In his defence, Arafat's supporters argued that he was caught between 'a rock and hard place': while attempting to cooperate with the international community, he also needed to appease his critics within his own party. These included the 'rejectionist' factions within the PLO who refused to contemplate any form of accommodation with Israel and viewed killing Israelis as 'legitimate'.

Arafat's support within the wider international community plummeted in August 1990 when he publicly endorsed Iraq's invasion and occupation of Kuwait and denounced the US-led coalition which was sent to liberate Kuwait. His actions antagonised not only the leaders of the US, Europe and the Soviet Union, but also the majority of the Arab leaders, including those of Egypt and Syria, and all of the Gulf states. Consequently, the PLO was isolated regionally and internationally and hundreds of thousands of Palestinians were evicted from their homes and jobs in the Gulf states.

## Role in the peace process

As a result of Arafat's support for Saddam Hussein and the Iraqi military takeover of Kuwait, he was not invited to participate in the Madrid Peace Conference, co-sponsored by America and Russia in October 1991. Instead, residents of the Palestinian territories (Gaza and the West Bank) conducted negotiations with Israel as a part of the Jordanian delegation, although all were affiliated with the PLO and maintained contact

with Tunis throughout the conference. Whilst the conference represented the first formal negotiations between Israelis and Palestinians, no breakthrough was expected in view of the intransigent position of Israel's Prime Minister Yitzhak Shamir, who considered the West Bank to be a part of the Biblical 'Land of Israel' to remain under Israeli occupation.

The political situation changed significantly following the 1992 elections in Israel which brought a Labor-led government to power that was willing to negotiate with the PLO, although secretly at first. On the Palestinian side, Arafat was encouraged to reciprocate by his deputy Mahmoud Abbas (Abu Mazen). Shortly thereafter, Israelis and PLO officials began secret negotiations in Oslo, Norway.

The negotiators in Oslo laid the foundations for an agreement to give the Palestinians self-rule in Gaza and Jericho (in the West Bank) to be followed by autonomy in other parts of the West Bank. Arafat and Israeli Prime Minister Yitzhak Rabin signed the Oslo Declaration of Principles (DOP) in September 1993. The ceremony took place at the White House in Washington. The agreements were accompanied by an exchange of letters between Arafat and Rabin in which the PLO and Israel recognised each other.

Although some analysts argue that the peace process that emerged from Oslo was Arafat's greatest diplomatic triumph, it is important to note that he had negotiated with Israel from a position of weakness, due to his previous support for Saddam Hussein. One result was that fundamental issues such as Jewish settlements and the future of Jerusalem were deferred, for which Arafat was criticised by many Palestinians. In response, Arafat explained in interviews with the Arab media and in talks given to Muslim groups abroad that he regarded the Oslo agreements, which he referred to as the 'Peace of the Brave', to be comparable to the 'Hudaybiyeh Agreement'. This agreement was a ten-year truce signed between Muhammad and the Qureish tribe in 637 CE. Muhammad reneged on the agreement after only 18 months, massacring the tribe and conquering Mecca.

The DOP made provision for the establishment of a Palestinian National Authority (PA) with offices in Gaza City and Ramallah in the West Bank. In July 1994, Arafat arrived in Gaza to take up the position of acting head of the PA. Also in 1994, he shared the Nobel Peace Prize with Yitzhak Rabin and Shimon Peres. Thus within four years, Arafat moved from a disgraced national leader to Nobel Peace Prize winner and respected international statesman.

Elections for a Palestinian Legislative Council (the governing body of the PA) and PA Chairperson were held in January 1996. Arafat was elected Chairman with 87.3 per cent of the vote. Among the Palestinians, he assumed the title President, or *Ra'is* in Arabic. Arafat's Fatah Party won the majority of seats in the Legislative Council. There were no further elections until after Arafat died.

Arafat's peace partner, Yitzhak Rabin, was assassinated by a Jewish extremist in November 1995. In the Israeli elections which followed in May 1996, a right-wing government came to power and soon after, the peace process slowed down considerably. Over the next three years, Israeli-Palestinian relations grew hostile and tensions mounted. Against a backdrop of terrorist bombings by Islamist groups Hamas and Islamic Jihad, the Israeli Prime Minister Benjamin Netanyahu blamed Arafat for the slowdown as he refused to fulfil the PA's obligations to halt Palestinian violence under the DOP and subsequent agreements. In response, Arafat blamed Netanyahu and his government for not fulfilling Israel's obligations and for not withdrawing from more territory in the West Bank.

In 1998, US President Clinton intervened by arranging meetings between the two leaders. The result was the Wye River Memorandum of 23 October, which detailed steps to be taken by the Israeli government and the PA to complete the peace process. This was a significant agreement in the history of the peace process, as Arafat acknowledged the following month at Fatah's Conference in Ramallah: 'By signing the Wye Plantation Agreement with the Israeli Likud government, we managed to shatter the slogan of

the Israeli extremists regarding 'the Greater land of Israel'. [It] put an end to this expansionist dream and to the false Israeli claims that the land of Israel spreads from the Nile to the Euphrates.'

Regardless, little progress was made and both sides failed to fulfil their obligations under the new agreement.

In 1999, a left-wing government was elected to power in Israel, with Ehud Barak as Prime Minister. He was committed to reaching a final settlement between Israel and the PLO. (The PLO remained the official body negotiating with Israel, not the PA.) Barak was prepared to agree to the establishment of an independent Palestinian state in the West Bank and Gaza Strip. He requested Clinton to host a summit between Israel and the PLO to resolve all outstanding matters. The talks took place at Camp David, the US Presidential retreat in Maryland, in July 2000.

In the early days of negotiations, Barak offered Arafat a Palestinian state in Gaza and most of the territory of the West Bank (90-91%), with its capital to be located in an outlying suburb of East Jerusalem. Under the Israeli proposal, Israel would annex 9-10% of the West Bank encompassing large settlement blocs, in exchange for Israeli land in the Negev, contiguous with the southern area of the West Bank. Arafat rejected the offer saying it did not include the 'right of return' for Palestinian refugees to Israel and Palestinian sovereignty over all of East Jerusalem (including the Old City). For Arafat, the right of return for the Palestinian refugees was sacred and fundamental to any final status agreement with Israel.

Negotiations broke down when Arafat made no counteroffer. After the summit, Barak and Clinton blamed Arafat for its failure, pointing to the absence of a Palestinian counterproposal to that put forward by Barak. Palestinians and their supporters argued that not only was Arafat justified in rejecting Barak's offer, but by doing so, he proved that he remained committed to securing the aspirations of the Palestinian people. So argued Hani Shukrallah, the editor of Egypt's *Al-Ahram* newspaper:

> The Palestinian leader's moment of truth came in the final status negotiations at Camp David in the summer of 2000. And there Arafat was faced with his most historic choice: had he gone far enough for him to forsake for good the Palestinian people's aspirations, agreeing to preside over a truncated and Bantustanised Israeli protectorate, or would his love of homeland and intimate connection with his people prevail? He chose. Still bungling, still manoeuvring, still speaking out of both sides of his mouth, but he chose to live his last years on the side of his people.[19]

Nevertheless, no definitive explanation has been given as to why Arafat did not put forward his own detailed counterproposals.

Arafat had warned of a second Palestinian intifada for some time before it finally erupted in October 2000. Upon his return from Camp David, Arafat spoke publicly of the need to return 'to the gun' if diplomacy failed to achieve Palestinian aspirations. The event which precipitated what became known as the al-Aqsa Intifada was Ariel Sharon's visit to the Temple Mount (*Haram al-Sharif*) on 28 September 2000. (The ill-planned visit was part of Sharon's challenge to Netanyahu for the leadership of the Likud Party.)

In January 2001, the final month of Barak's Prime Ministership, Israel and the PLO again tried to reach a final settlement, at Taba in Egypt. After the talks, both sides declared that they had come 'very close' to reaching an agreement. However, Barak lost the election in the following month and his successor, Ariel Sharon, refused to continue negotiations with Arafat and the PLO while the intifada continued. This remained the status quo until Arafat died nearly four years later.

During this period, Arafat was implicated in the renewed campaign of Palestinian terrorism due to his establishment of Fatah's Al-Aqsa Brigades, one of the groups responsible for terrorist attacks during the second intifada.

Sharon ensured that Arafat spent the last three years of his life under virtual house arrest in his presidential compound in Ramallah called the *Muqata'a*.

On 29 October 2004, suffering from an illness that was not made public, the 75-year-old Arafat was taken to Percy Military Hospital in Paris, where he was pronounced dead on 11 November. The cause of death was never announced, and to this day it remains a 'mystery'. Claims that Arafat had AIDS, or was poisoned by Israeli agents, have been denied by his former aides. It is not inconceivable that the brain injury Arafat suffered in the 1992 air crash in Libya was a contributing factor in his death in 2004.

After his death, Arafat's body was flown from Paris to Cairo, where a ceremony was held in his honour, attended by many foreign dignitaries. Arafat's remains were then flown to Ramallah, inside the *Muqata'a*, where he was buried with soil brought from *Haram al-Sharif* in Jerusalem. Thousands of Palestinians attended the ceremony, mourning the loss of their leader who, for nearly four decades, had kept their plight in the world spotlight.

# Significance and evaluation

Arafat's leadership was the outcome of a complex historical process, played out during some of the most difficult days in recent Arab history. As in Syria and Iraq, the Palestinian sense of nationhood developed during the interwar period during the struggle against Western imperialist rule. But unlike other Arab peoples Palestinian national unity was shattered following the creation of Israel in 1948 and the Arab defeat of 1967. Fatah's, and the PLO's, struggle for Palestinian liberation and independence helped to revive the national identity of a people more than half of whom were scattered outside the homeland. Arafat, as the leader of both Fatah and the PLO, came to symbolise the re-emergence of the Palestinians as a nation and not as refugees. His deep understanding of the strong association between the Palestinian cause and the Arab situation secured for him a leading position in the Arab political arena.[20]

**Figure 12.9** Thousands of Palestinian mourners at Yasser Arafat's burial.

# Autocratic style of leadership and its effects on the Palestinian cause

Even from a young age, Aburish records, Arafat was 'a natural publicist and a workaholic', but one who had an obsessive desire to be leader of the pack and to get his way. Indeed, Arafat's style of leadership enabled him, more than any other person, to chart the course of Palestinian history and politics over the past 40 years. It was also the case that the decision-making processes of both the PLO and the PA, and the lines of command and financial institutions of both organisations were moulded to suit his temperament, work rhythm and style of leadership.

*Decision making:* As early as 1959, when Fatah was established in Kuwait, Arafat only paid lip service to the idea of collective leadership and within a short period of time, his associates noticed how he 'exercised total control over the Fatah war chest and how he bribed people to join him.' While showing similar traits as leader of the PLO, this job was not so easily centralised. Many PLO groups were dispersed throughout the Arab world where their loyalty was given first to their Arab host. Unable to achieve direct control over the entire organisation, Arafat developed a style of leadership that was suited to these circumstances, as biographer Barry Rubin explains: '[C]onstantly indecisive and refusing to impose his power on the many Palestinian groups and factions, Arafat was the very opposite of a dictator giving orders and enforcing discipline with an iron fist. Ironically, though, this style also helped preserve a loose but overriding sense of unity while also ensuring his own popularity and legitimacy across the political spectrum.'[21] When a decision was required by the PLO's executive, he would only seek support when he knew it was ensured.

Arafat's leadership of the PA, established as a part of the peace process in 1994, took on a more centralised and autocratic form. As a 'one man show', he was responsible for almost every decision as well as personally selecting each appointee to important PA positions. He favoured the politics of patronage, and was able to maintain loyalty by his control and personal use of the PA's finances, and by imprisoning those who opposed him. The latter also faced sanctions against their businesses, families, and career prospects, while PA judges with independent views were sacked.

Even Arafat's supporters criticised his autocratic leadership style. Decisions made by the Palestinian Legislative Council were ignored and he made every effort to undermine attempts at democratic reform within the PA. He was also able to limit public opposition to his rule through his control of the media in Gaza and the West Bank – radio, print and television.

*Chain of command:* As Rubin points out, 'Arafat's three decades of virtually unchallenged leadership and status as founding father of the Palestinian-state-in-the-making [was] an enormous political asset for him, making Arafat the only imaginable Palestinian leader. His role as the PA's chief executive further entrenched him. And, of course, his recognition as Palestinian leader and diplomatic partner by Israel, the United States, and Arab states further reinforced this primacy.'

Nevertheless, Arafat felt threatened by potential successors. He refused to appoint a successor or an effective chain of command. To avoid any official becoming too powerful within the PA, Arafat created a multitude of government ministries, most with overlapping responsibilities, all reporting directly to him. If he considered a PA official to be threatening to him in any way, the official would be replaced.

He also established a number of competing security organisations. The most important and effective of these were in turn divided further so that one half of their leaders would be in Gaza and the other half in the West Bank, to ensure that no security personnel gained too much power or influence. The end result was, as one Palestinian commentator put it 'a wasteland of a national bureaucracy … consisting of overlapping, inefficient, undemocratic structures, dependent upon Gulf petrodollars, and with little sense of direction as to how liberation could be achieved.'

Arafat's autocratic style was also evident in his approach to negotiations with Israel during the peace process. When it began, Arafat refused to delegate, fearing that a successful negotiator could represent a threat to his leadership. In 2003, the US intervened directly in internal PA politics by pressuring Arafat to appoint a Prime Minister. Arafat complied by first appointing Mahmoud Abbas and then Ahmed Qrei'a when Abbas resigned. Neither succeeded in wresting any power from the *Ra'is*.

In the latter years of Arafat's rule, particularly from the onset of the second Palestinian intifada in 2000, opposition to his autocracy and corruption became more public, particularly among the so-called 'young guard' who demanded a change in the status quo. They claimed Arafat had lost sight of the people's nationalist aspirations and was no longer equipped for leadership. Opinion polls showed that his popularity had decreased from 47% before the intifada to 35% by the end of 2003. Occasionally his popularity rating reached about 50%, but this was only when Israel threatened to kill or expel him.

*Financial management:* Another characteristic of Arafat's autocratic style of leadership was his tight control of the finances of Fatah, the PLO, and the PA. He was the only person who knew the location of all the so-called 'secret funds', which included accounts that were at the disposal of Arafat for his sole discretion and for which he was the sole signatory.

In view of the significant amount of Palestinian money at Arafat's personal disposal, it is not surprising that there were many reports of his inappropriate and corrupt use of funds. These include the claims made by Jaweed Al-Ghussein, treasurer of the PLO's National Fund (PNF) from 1984 to 1996. According to Al-Ghussein, Arafat 'enriched a privileged inner circle of cronies and salted away billions of dollars in secret bank accounts' and was in personal receipt every month from the PNF of a cheque for US$10.25m, which amounted to US$123m (A$165m) every year. Arafat's system of patronage included handing 'bodyguards wads of cash from a briefcase he kept in his office and instructing them to take it to individuals he had decided to help. Each day the briefcase would be refilled from bank accounts that Arafat controlled.' In the absence of auditing, there was no record of who had sent money to Arafat or how it was spent. The same lack of financial transparency was evident when Arafat and the PA began to receive donations from the EU, the US and other states. The result, concluded Al-Ghussein, was that Arafat's control and use of money did not serve any purpose for the Palestinian people, but only lined 'the pockets of his cronies.'[22]

Al-Ghussein's claims were substantiated in 2003 when the International Monetary Fund (IMF) conducted an audit of the PA during which it was discovered that Arafat had diverted US$900 million in public funds to a special bank account which he alone controlled. In that same year, Forbes ranked Arafat sixth on its list of 'Kings, Queens and Despots', estimating his personal wealth at a minimum of US$300 million. Others view this as a conservative estimate, estimating Arafat's personal wealth to have between US$1 and 3 billion. [23]

## Aims and methods used to achieve Palestinian goals

By insisting on independence from the leaders of the Arab states, who either ignored or repressed Palestinians, Arafat laid the vital framework for recognition of his people by the world and, ultimately, by their neighbours in the Middle East. As biographers Barry Rubin and Judith Colp Rubin state: 'Forged in a tumultuous era of competing traditionalism, radicalism, Arab nationalism, and Islamist forces, the Palestinian movement was almost entirely Arafat's creation, and he became its leader at an early age. Arafat took it through a dizzying series of crises and defeats, often of his own making, yet also ensured that it survived, grew, and gained influence.' [24]

For his admirers, Yasser Arafat was without doubt a 'larger-than-life figure'. Among many of the obituaries following his death, one Palestinian wrote: 'No one who followed the man's life, comments,

transformations, and public appearances could deny he possessed charisma and an ability to connect with Palestinians of all classes, religions, and ideological currents, even after a series of miscalculations on his part that damaged his credibility among Arabs in general and Palestinians in particular.' To Palestinians, Yasser Arafat embodied the Palestinian nationalist movement. Under his leadership the plight of the Palestinians and their quest for statehood first made an impact on Western public opinion. As Afif Safieh, Palestinian General Delegate to the UK and the Holy See, put it, 'For me, Yasser Arafat was the Palestinian De Gaulle, the architect of the resurrection of our national movement in the mid 1960s, and its locomotive for almost 40 years.' [25]

However, Arafat's maximalist aims could never be realised in the face of superior Israeli military capability. And even when he shifted publicly to a more minimalist position in an effort to achieve a diplomatic outcome, to non-Western audiences, particularly to his own people, he continued to call for Israel's destruction and the esablishment of a Palestinian state in all of what was once Mandatory Palestine.

Arafat's methods thus presented a 'catch-22': while the extreme nature of PLO violence brought the plight of the Palestinians to the attention of the world, it unified and strengthened the Israelis, against whose superior military force the PLO would never be victorious.

By the time of his passing, Arafat had achieved limited Palestinian goals: his people's nationalist rights and their struggle for self-determination had been recognised regionally, internationally, and by the majority of Israelis; and he had ruled over an autonomous entity in Gaza and parts of the West Bank (before Israel reoccupied these areas following the onset of the second intifada).

But even for these limited outcomes, concludes Yezid Sayigh, the Palestinians paid a high cost:

Arafat succeeded, but he did so in a manner that exaggerated the material costs to his people at virtually every stage. His jealous grip on power and reliance on planned corruption prevented rational planning, minimised learning and accumulation of experience, and impeded coordination of resources. The result was to reduce the political utility of sacrifices and strategic opportunities, and ultimately to bring diminishing returns. Just how much of the bloodshed after the start of the Camp David process at the end of 1978, or at least after the Israeli invasion of Lebanon in 1982, was unavoidable is a moot point. The PLO under Arafat finally accepted limited autonomy in the West Bank and Gaza at a moment when fundamental changes in states and societies throughout the Middle East threatened to relegate the Palestine cause to the back of domestic, regional, and international concerns. The armed struggle probably could have achieved no more, at any time, than the offer of transitional autonomy made in 1978. It is unlikely that better organisation and a different style of politics and leadership could have altered the outcome in any fundamental way, given the objective reality of divergent Arab priorities, Israeli power, Soviet diffidence, and US hostility. There can be no doubt that the final gains, however modest, were purchased at tremendous cost to the Palestinians and their Arab hosts. Their eventual success in establishing an autonomous entity in the West Bank and Gaza was partly due to Arafat, and partly in spite of him. The armed struggle had taken the Palestinians this far, but the future of their attempt to build a sovereign state amidst severe external constraints [will] depend largely on their success in transforming their internal politics and organisational dynamics.[26]

# The Two Yasser Arafats

**Leanne Piggott** on why the Palestinian leader could not deliver statehood for his people

To Palestinians, Yasser Arafat was 'Mr Palestine', a historical figure who embodied the Palestinian nationalist movement. It was only under his leadership of the Palestine Liberation Organisation that the plight of the Palestinians and their quest for statehood first made an impact on Western public opinion. Their enduring memory will be of a benign, grandfatherly figure blowing kisses to his people.

Yet for all those who admire Arafat, there are many who revile him. Israelis, Christian Maronites and others who were his victims will remember above all the furtive mendacity of the man who preached peace while his hands dripped with blood.

There have been two main phases in Arafat's career as the Palestinians' recognised leader. The first phase began in 1969, when Arafat assumed the leadership of the PLO.

He tirelessly promoted the Palestinian cause and became a perennial focus of media interest.

Through spectacular acts of terrorism – including the hijacking of aircraft, the massacre of 11 Israeli Olympic athletes at Munich in 1972 and the targeted killing of Israeli school children and other civilians at Ma'alot and Kiryat Shmona in the mid 1970s – Arafat ensured that the Palestinian cause regularly made the headlines.

Under his leadership, the PLO was granted observer status at the UN. It is a mark of Arafat's success that the General Assembly has passed more resolutions against Israel than any other member state. Other stateless nations, such as the Kurds and Tibetans, greatly outnumber the Palestinians. But they have

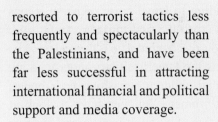

resorted to terrorist tactics less frequently and spectacularly than the Palestinians, and have been far less successful in attracting international financial and political support and media coverage.

The second significant phase of Arafat's career began in 1993 when he signed the Oslo Declaration of Principles with Israeli prime minister Yitzhak Rabin, for which they were both awarded the Nobel Peace Prize. The Israelis recognised the PLO and agreed to negotiate a gradual transition to Palestinian independence. The PLO recognised Israel and renounced violence as a political tool.

After Arafat made a triumphant return to the Gaza Strip in 1994, he assumed the leadership of the newly established Palestinian Authority. Arafat's responsibility was to prepare the way for Palestinian statehood by creating authentic state institutions and encouraging the development of a viable economy and civil society.

Instead, he gave priority to maintaining his political pre-eminence among Palestinians. Although the Palestinians had many of the forms of democratic governance – elections in 1996, a parliament, a cabinet and a judiciary – the substance was conspicuously lacking. Arafat remained a virtual dictator, as he had always been as head of the PLO.

Despite his peace prize, Arafat also kept the violence simmering against his enemies, internal and external, and in 2000 he unleashed the al-Aqsa intifada.

Palestinians saw his duplicity as a necessary strategy and admired Arafat's steadfast refusal to compromise on key issues such as the status of East Jerusalem and the demand that Palestinian refugees be allowed to return to what is now Israel. Arafat's supporters believed that his unbending stance on these issues would eventually result in a better deal for the Palestinians. It didn't.

Arafat's opponents likened him to a compulsive gambler who kept raising the stakes, and losing. His rigid adherence to a hard line on basic issues might have been popular with his people but achieved nothing. By pandering to extremists instead of bringing them into line, Arafat forfeited several opportunities to achieve statehood for his people and most, if not all, of their demands.

In truth, Arafat never quite made the transition from independence fighter-terrorist to nation-builder. After 10 years, the Palestinian Authority has no proper system for controlling and managing its financial accounts. Hundreds of millions of dollars entrusted personally to Arafat have never been accounted for. Maintaining a monopoly over the money and the coercive apparatus of the PA was part of Arafat's survival strategy, as was his refusal to appoint a clear successor.

These deficiencies are as much a part of Arafat's legacy as his successes in placing the Palestinian cause on the world stage. Perhaps Arafat's funeral will provide an opportunity for the gathered representatives of the world to salvage the lost hopes of peace. To quote US Secretary of State Colin Powell, 'We stand ready to move forward'. History's assessment of Arafat will depend on how effective his successors will be in achieving the goals that ultimately eluded him.

Op Ed From *The Australian*, 12 November 2004

# Evaluation: Terrorist or peacemaker?

Arafat viewed himself as a modern-day Saladin. His aim was to drive the Jews from the Holy Land and return the holy places in Jerusalem to the bosom of the Arab nation. He wanted to be remembered as the 'Father of the Palestinian Revolution', the man who founded and established the Palestinian movement. He also sought the role of the founder and President of a Palestinian state, the man who started with a small organisation and succeeded in establishing an independent state, recognised by all.

To achieve these objectives, Arafat first pursued a campaign of violence against Israel. When violence alone proved unsuccessful, he turned to diplomacy. When diplomacy was tried and failed, he returned to violence. Thus he died a hero among many, and a villain among as many again.

Was Arafat a terrorist? Yes. While disavowing terrorism repeatedly, he also practised it constantly. Was Arafat a peacemaker? Yes. After years of devotion to armed struggle, Arafat made a dramatic peace agreement with Israel that let him return to his claimed homeland and transformed him into a ruler of a fledgling state-in-the making, although that state is yet to be established.

## Arafat quotes

In an interview with TIME magazine in November 1974, Arafat stated: 'Palestine is the cement that holds the Arab world together, or it is the explosive that blows it apart.'

During his 13 November 1974 speech at the UN, Arafat made the famous comment: 'I have come bearing an olive branch and a freedom fighter's gun. Do not let the olive branch fall from my hand.'

In 1980, Arafat frankly stated: 'Peace for us means the destruction of Israel. We are preparing for an all-out war, a war which will last for generations.'

In 1988, responding to Israel's use of harsh tactics in an attempt to crush the first intifada, Arafat said: 'Everyone has now discovered who is the real terrorist organisation: It is the Israeli military junta who are killing women and children, smashing their bones, killing pregnant women. You just have to look at television to see this. So now it is clear and obvious who the terrorists are.'

In 1993, upon signing the Oslo Declaration of Principles (DOP) with Israeli Prime Minister Yitzhak Rabin, Arafat described the process as 'the peace of the brave', that 'the battle for peace is the most difficult battle of our lives.'

Later the same day, in an interview on Jordanian television, Arafat explained his reason for signing the DOP: 'Since we cannot defeat Israel in war we do this in stages. We take any and every territory that we can of Palestine, and establish sovereignty there and we use it as a springboard to take more. When the time comes, we can get the Arab nations to join us for the final blow against Israel.'

In a speech given on 6 August 1995 at a party to celebrate the birth of his daughter, Arafat stated: 'The Israelis are mistaken if they think we do not have an alternative to negotiations. By Allah I swear they are wrong. The Palestinian people are prepared to sacrifice until either the last boy and the last girl raise the Palestinian flag over the walls, the churches and the mosques of Jerusalem.'

On the Voice of Palestine Radio, on 11 November 1995, Arafat proclaimed, 'The struggle will continue until all of Palestine is liberated.'

To an Arab audience in Stockholm, Sweden, in 1996, Arafat declared: 'We plan to eliminate the state of Israel and establish a purely Palestinian state. We will make life unbearable for Jews by psychological warfare and population explosion. … We Palestinians will take over everything, including all of Jerusalem.'

At the 1998 Fatah Conference held in Ramallah, he declared: 'The Right of Return is sacred and the heated battle over it is fundamental and important... 55% of our people are refugees and I am one of them.'

On 21 January 2002, Arafat stated: 'I swear to God, I will see [the Palestinian state], whether as a martyr or alive. Please, God, give me the honour of becoming a martyr in the fight for Jerusalem.'

In a March 2002 interview with *Al-Jazeera* television, while under siege by Israeli forces at his *Muqata'a*, Arafat said: 'They either want to kill me, or capture me, or expel me. I hope I will be a martyr in the Holy Land. I have chosen this path and if I fall, one day a Palestinian child will raise the Palestinian flag above our mosques and churches.'

## Extract from a script prepared by BBC World journalist Jon Leyne in the week preceding Arafat's death, November 2004

'I love my running, and there's no better place for it than the lovely hills on the western edge of Jerusalem.

Whenever I am in the city I do my best to join my friends at the local running club, for their Saturday morning run there. From the Holocaust Museum, the route winds up into the hills. First it goes through some of Jerusalem's most pleasant suburban neighbourhoods, silent with sleep as we set off early in the morning.

Then it plunges down along a gravelly track into the sweet-smelling woods. Next there's the testing climb up to the Kennedy memorial. At the top, the prize of a clear, still morning view over the lush green slopes. When I am up there I always think – this really is the land of milk and honey.

As we run together, it's a great opportunity to find out what average Israelis think of the latest developments I have been sent to report on. I remember vividly a conversation I had with a fellow runner nearly four years ago, a few months after the start of the current round of violence. At that time a Labor government headed by the Prime Minister Ehud Barak, was futilely trying to tackle the latest unrest. 'I am a lifelong Labor supporter', explained one fellow runner to me, 'if I forget Labor, let my right hand lose its cunning. 'But', he said, 'this time I am backing Ariel Sharon as the only man who can provide us with security.'

It was a sentiment that captured the mood of a good part of the nation, and probably still does.

So when I was out running last weekend I asked another runner what he thought of Yasser Arafat. Without a trace of bitterness he replied simply: 'I think he has been responsible for the death of many Israelis.' Surely, again, the judgement of most people in Israel.

On the run back down through the hills I spotted some disused terracing. That's the way the Palestinians prepare the hillsides for agriculture. There are no Palestinians left in this rich Jewish suburb now. So even this idyllic corner of Israel seems to have had a troubled history.

Just two days later I visited a Palestinian refugee camp in neighbouring Jordan. One hundred and twenty thousand Palestinians live there, packed into its squalid streets. Some of them, like 70-year-old Aida, have been refugees since the war of 1948.

My ears picked up when Aida said she used to live in a village on the outskirts of Jerusalem. How ironic, I thought, if she'd lived in the area I'd been running through the previous weekend.

Aida couldn't explain exactly where her village was, and I couldn't find the name on the map. Perhaps it no longer exists. But her description sounded just like that lovely spot outside Jerusalem. She was only a young girl when she left and she hasn't been back in half a century. But she still remembers the taste of the olives, the ripe oranges they could eat straight from the trees. Even the lentils had a richer smell there, she recalls.

Aida says her family fled in the middle of the night, under an Israeli air raid. She's dreamt of returning ever since. Now she says she would like to go back, even if she only lives to see her village for one day, so she can be buried there.

In a way, Yasser Arafat failed her almost as badly as he failed the Israelis. The Oslo peace accords didn't bring the prospect of a return to her beloved village one tiny step closer. And Mr Arafat never had the courage to tell the brutal truth to Aida and her fellow exiles – that they are almost certainly never going to see their promised land.

Yet Aida loves Arafat. She talks about him with a smile on her face and a chuckle. 'He tried his best to get us back to our homeland,' she said, 'but nothing is in his hands. Now he is dying and he is still fighting to the last breath.'

For the younger generation of Palestinians, that mystique may no longer exist. And it was noticeable that I did not see any photos of Arafat in the refugee camp that I visited. But for Aida, with no country of her own, no capital, and no passport, that strange gnarled face of Yasser Arafat is perhaps her last link, her only symbol of national identity.

# Review and research questions

1. Evaluate efforts to resolve the Israeli-Syrian and Israeli-Palestinian conflicts from 1999 to 2005.

2. Research the details of the 'Nusseibeh-Ayalon Agreement' of September 2002 and the 'Geneva Accords' of October 2003. Assess whether a permanent peace settlement between Israelis and Palestinians along the lines stipulated by these agreements would be achievable.

3. Describe and evaluate the roles of Ariel Sharon and Mahmoud Abbas during the conflict.

4. Research the personal background of Yasser Arafat and consider the historical context in which he lived. Examine his rise to prominence through the foundation of Fatah and leadership in the PLO; his role in PLO terrorism; his use of diplomacy in the effort to achieve Palestinian self-determination; his involvement in the Jordanian and Lebanese civil wars; and his role in the Oslo peace process. What were the major events in which he was involved that impacted upon the Arab-Israeli and Israeli-Palestinian conflicts? Assess his leadership style and how this impacted on the Palestinian cause. In the context of your assessment of Arafat's aims and the methods he used to achieve his goals and those of the Palestinian people, do you consider him to have been 'an unrelenting terrorist', a 'peacemaker', or both? Do you think he achieved his dying wish to be 'a martyr in the Holy Land'? Give reasons for your answers.

## Discussion questions

1. Israeli and Palestinian negotiators agree that they came very close to agreeing on a permanent peace settlement at Taba in January 2001. In your view, will the Israelis and Palestinians reach a point of workable 'conflict management' that might one day lead to a final resolution of the conflict?

2. Consider Israeli writer Amos Oz's argument as to why he believes in the 'separation' rather than the 'reconciliation' of Israelis and Palestinians:

'(The Israeli-Palestinian conflict is) not a war of cultures, nor one of religions, even if certain people wish it were. It all revolves around the simple question: *Who owns the land?* Our country is tiny. Both peoples have a right to be there. How could anyone dispute the fact that it's the home to the Palestinians? Which it is, just as Holland is home of the Dutch. And equally who would question the Jews' right to the land? Historically it's clear this is the only homeland they have, there's never been another. In this situation there's no good and bad as (some) often like to believe. It's not a western film; it's not a fight between good and evil. It's a real tragedy because it amounts to the conflict between two rights of entitlement!' Translated from *L'Express*, 27 March 2006.

# Glossary

Arabic words are denoted by (A), Hebrew words by (H) and Turkish by (T)

**A**

**Aliyah (s.), Aliyot (pl.) (H)** – Literally 'to ascend', is a wave of Jewish immigration to Palestine and later Israel.

**Anti-Semitism** – a form of racism consisting of hatred of, and/or prejudice against Jews as a group.

**Ashkenazi (s.) Ashkenazim (pl.) (H)** – Jew of European background.

**HaAvoda (Mifleget haAvodah haYisra'elit) (H)** – The Israeli Labor Party, formed in 1968 following the merger of Mapai and two other left-wing parties, Ahdut HaAvoda and Rafi.  In 1969, Labor formed a voting alliance with Mapam, called Ma'arach (Labor Alliance), which lasted until 1984.

**Awqaf (A)** – Ministry of Islamic endowments or trusts

**A'yan (A)** – Literally 'eyes', refers to Muslim urban notables.

**B**

**Ba'ath (A)** – Literally 'renaissance', refers to the pan-Arab Renaissance (Ba'ath) Party in Iraq and Syria.

**Bayat al-Maqdis (A)** – The House of Sanctity, a Muslim name for Jerusalem.

**B'nei Yisra'el (H)** – The Children of Israel.

**Bilad al-Sham (A)** – Literally 'Land of the Sun' or 'Land of the Dignity', refers to 'Greater Syria' incorporating Jordan, Lebanon, and Israel/Palestine.

**D**

**Dar al-Islam (A)** – the Realm of Islam.

**Dhimmi (s.) ahl al-dhimma (pl.) (A)** – non-Muslim having protected (and inferior) status under Sharia.  Refers mainly to Christians and Jews.

**Diaspora** – Literally 'dispersion', places to which a people have been dispersed outside their homeland.

**Druze (s.) Druzes (pl.) (A)** – sect of Shia Islam, dating to 11th century.

**E**

**Emir (A)** – Arab prince, chieftain or governor.

**Eretz Yisra'el (H)** – The Land of Israel, traditional name for the land where Jews had lived and been sovereign in ancient times.

**Eretz Yisra'el Ha'Shlema (H)** – The Greater Land of Israel, refers to Israel together with Judaea and Samaria (the West Bank).

**F**

**Fard 'ayn (A)** – Muslim religious duty.

**Fatah (A)** – Literally 'conquest', is the reversed acronym of Harakat al-Tahrir al-Watani al-Filastini, the Palestinian National Liberation Movement.

**Feday (s.), Fedayeen (pl.) (A)** – guerilla fighter.

**Fellah (s.), Fellaheen (pl.) (A)** – peasant farmer.

**Filastin (A)** – Palestine.

**G**

**Galut (H)** – Jewish Diaspora.

**Ghurba (A)** – Palestinian Diaspora.

**Gulf Cooperation Council (GCC)** – formed in May 1981 by United Arab Emirates, State of Bahrain, Kingdom of Saudi Arabia, Sultanate of Oman, State of Qatar and State of Kuwait.

**H**

**Haganah (H)** – Literally 'defence', refers to the Yishuv's largest militia.

**Haj (A)** – pilgrimage to Mecca, one of the five pillars of Islam.

**Hamas (A)** – Literally 'zeal' or 'courage', is the acronym of Harakat al-Muqawama al-Islamiyyah, the Islamic Resistance Movement, (Palestinian branch of the Muslim Brotherhood).

**al-Haram al-Sharif (A)** – The Noble Precinct (location of the al-Aqsa Mosque and the Dome of the Rock).

**Har haBayit (H)** – The Temple Mount, site of the First and Second Jewish Temples in ancient times.

**Herut (H)** – Literally 'freedom', is the party headed by Menachem Begin following 1948, became Likud in 1973.

**Hijra (A)** – Literally, 'withdrawal', refers to Muhammad's move from Mecca to Medina in 622 and marks the beginning of the Muslim calendar.

**Histadrut (H)** – Jewish Workers' Organisation, or Labour Federation.

**Hityashvut (H)** – 'Settling the land', a pillar of Zionism in the pre-state period.

**Hizb al-Istiqlal (A)** – The (Palestinian) Independence Party.

**Hizballah (A)** – The Party of God, is the major Shia party in Lebanon.

**Hovevei Zion (H)** – 'Lovers of Zion'.

**Hudna (A)** – cease-fire

**I**

**al-Ikhwan al-Muslimun (A)** – The Muslim Brotherhood.

**Imam (A)** – Muslim religious leader, also a prayer leader.

**Intifada (A)** – Literally 'shaking off', refers to the two Palestinian uprisings (1987-1993; 2000-2005) in the occupied territories.

**Irgun (Irgun Tzvai Leumi) (H)** – The National Military Organisation (acronyms Etzel, IZLI), military wing of the Yishuv's Revisionist Party.

**J**

**Jewish Agency** – established in 1929 by the World Zionist Organisation as the representative of the Yishuv to the British Mandatory authority.

**Jihad (A)** – Literally 'to strive' or 'to struggle', term used by Muslims for 'holy war'.

**Jund Filastin (A)** – Province of Palestine

**K**

**Ka'aba (A)** – The holiest shrine of Islam located in Mecca, Saudi Arabia.

**Keren Kayemeth LeYisrael (H)** – Jewish National Fund.

**Kevutzah (s.), Kevutzot (pl.) (H),** – Literally 'group', refers to early Yishuv agricultural cooperatives.

**Khalifate (Caliphate) (A)** – Islamic State or Empire.

**Kibbutz (s.) kibbutzim (pl.) (H)** – agricultural community with common ownership of land.

**Knesset (H)** – Pre-1948, the Yishuv's National Assembly; post-independence, Israel's Parliament.

**Kotel (Kotel ha'Ma'aravi) (H)** – The Western Wall of the Jews' Second Temple.

**L**

**Labor Party (Israeli)** – see under Ha'Avoda.

**Likud (H)** – Literally 'unity', is a right wing Israeli political party formed in 1973, winning government for the first time in 1977.

**Lohamei Herut Yisrael (H)** – acronym Lehi, also known as the Stern Gang, a pre-state Jewish militant group which split from the Irgun.

**M**

**Madinat an Nabi (A)** – The Prophet's City (Medina)

**Majlis (A)** – Supreme Muslim Sharia Council.

**Makkah al Mukarramah (A)** – Mecca The Blessed.

**Mapai (Mifleget Poalei Eretz Ysra'el) (H)** – Worker's Party of the Land of Israel, a Labour Zionist party that dominated the politics of the Yishuv and post-independence Israel until 1977. In 1968 it merged with other left wing parties to form Ha'Avoda (The Labor Party).

**Maronites** – largest Christian group in Lebanon

**Masjid al Aqsa (A)** – The Al Aqsa Mosque.

**Medinat Yisra'el (H)** – The State of Israel

**Milchemet Ha'Atzma'ut (H)** –War of Independence, refers to the 1948 War.

**Mizrachi (H)** – from merkaz ruhani, 'spiritual centre', refers to the Mizrachi Party, a religious Zionist party.

**Moshav (s.) moshavim (pl.) (H)** – cooperative agricultural community with individual ownership of land.

**Mufti (A)** – Muslim scholar and leader.

**Mutasarriflik (T)** –subdivision of a vilayet.

**Muqata'a (A)** – Yasser Arafat's compound in Ramallah.

**N**

**Al-Nakbah (A)** – Literally 'The Disaster', refers to the 1948 War.

**Al-Naksah (A)** – Literally 'The Setback', refers to the 1967 War.

**O**

**Olim (H)** – Jewish immigrants.

**P**

**Palmach (H)** – (from Plugot Mahatz) – The Haganah's special 'Strike Force'.

**Pelishtim (H)** – Philistines.

**Poalei Zion (H)** – Workers of Zion.

**haPoel haZair (H)** – The Young Worker.

**Pogrom** – violent attack on a Jewish community.

**Q**

**Qawmiyya** – Loyalty to the 'Arab Nation' (pan-Arabism, as distinct from wataniyya, local nationalism).

**Qibla (A)** – The direction of Muslim prayer.

**Qubbat as-Sakhrah (A)** – Dome of the Rock.

**al-Quds (A)** – a Muslim name for Jerusalem.

**R**

**Ramadan (A)** – the Muslim holy month.

**S**

**Sanjak (T)** – administrative district within the Ottoman Empire.

**Sephardi (s.) Sephardim (pl.) (H)** – Jews who came from Spain (Sepharad) and other countries under Muslim rule.

**Sharia (A)** – Islamic religious law.

**Sharif (A)** –a descendant of Muhammad through his grandson Hasan, and custodian of Makkah al Mukarramah (the holy city of Mecca), hence the title, 'Sharif of Mecca'.

**Sheikh (A)** – tribal leader, also used as a title of honour.

**Shi'ah (A)** – Literally 'factions' or 'party' from shi'at Ali (the Party of Ali), refers to those who follow the Imam Ali and his family, representing about 10% of Muslims.

**Shibab (A)** – Literally 'young boys', refers to the youth who played a prominent role in the first Palestinian intifada.

**haShomer (H)** – The Watchmen, the first defence group established by the Yishuv.

**Stern Gang** – see Lehi

**Sunni, Ahl ul-Sunna (A)** – Literally 'People of the Tradition', refers to the largest Muslim group.

**Supreme Muslim Council** - highest body in charge of Muslim community affairs in Palestine during the Mandate period.

**Syria-Palaestina** – Roman (Latin) name given to Judaea following the destruction of Jerusalem and the expulsion of the Jews in 70 CE.

**T**

**Tanzim (A)** – Fatah militants under command of Marwan Barghouti.

**Tanzimat (T)** – Ottoman reforms.

**Tochnit Dalet (H)** – Plan D.

**Torah (H)** – the first five books of the Hebrew Bible.

**U**

**Umma (A)** – Muslim community

**V**

**Va'ad Leumi (H)** – National Executive of the Knesset.

**Vilayet (T)** – Province of the Ottoman Empire.

**W**

**Wali (T)** – governor.

**al-Watan al-Arabi (A)** – The Arab Nation or Arab Fatherland.

**Waqf (s.) awqaf (pl.) (A)** – Islamic endowment or trust, including land.

**Wataniyya (A)** – Loyalty to one's local territory and people (as distinct from qawmiyya).

**White Paper** – a document issued by a government to explain or discuss policy matters.

**Y**

**Yerushalayim (H)** – Jerusalem.

**Yishuv (H)** – Literally 'settled community', refers to the Jewish community living in Palestine before 1948.

**Yisra'el (H)** – Israel.

**Yom Kippur (H)** – The Day of Atonement, a Jewish fast day.

**Z**

**Zion (H)** – a name for both Jerusalem and the wider area of historic Eretz Yisra'el.

# References

## Chapter 1

1. Darby, J. 1991, *What's Wrong with Conflict?* Centre for the Study of Conflict, University of Ulster, Coleraine. [Online] http://cain.ulst.ac.uk/csc/reports/conflict.htm

2. Taylor, A. R. 1970, *Prelude to Israel: An Analysis of Zionist Diplomacy, 1897-1947*, Institute for Palestine Studies, Beirut, p xi.

3. Ross, D. 2004, *The Missing Peace: The Inside Story of the Fight for Middle East Peace*, Farrar, Straus and Giroux, New York, p. 15.

4. Ibn Khaldun. 1967, *The Muqaddimah: An Introduction to History*, trans. F. Rosenthal, ed. N. J. Dawood, Princeton University Press, Princeton.

## Chapter 2

1. Said, E. W. 1992, *The Question of Palestine*, Vintage Books, New York, p. 11.

## Chapter 3

1. Herzl, T. 1959, 'The Jewish State (1896)' in A. Hertzberg (ed.), *The Zionist Idea: A Historical Analysis and Reader*, Antheneum, New York, pp 204-226.

2. Lossin, Y. 1997, *Pillar of Fire: the Rebirth of Israel – A Visual History*, Shikmona Publishing Company Ltd, Jerusalem, p.33.

3. Ben-Gurion, D. 1959, 'The Imperatives of the Jewish Revolution' in A. Hertzberg (ed.), *The Zionist Idea: A Historical Analysis and Reader*, Anthenum, New York, pp 606-619.

4. Quoted in Mandel, N. 1976, *The Arabs and Zionism before World War I*, University of California Press, Berkeley, p. 45.

5. Quoted in Mandel, N. 1976, *The Arabs and Zionism before World War I*, University of California Press, Berkeley, p. 89.

6. 'Program of the League of the Arab Fatherland' in Laqueur, W. and Rubin, B. (eds). 2001, *The Israel-Arab Reader: A Documentary History of the Middle East Conflict*, 6th edn, Penguin, New York, p. 5.

7. Gorny, Y. 1987, *Zionism and the Arabs 1882-1948: A Study of Ideology*, Clarendon Press, Oxford.

## Chapter 4

1. Cohn-Sherbok, D. and El-Alami, D. 2001, *The Palestine-Israeli Conflict: A Beginner's Guide*, Oneworld, Oxford, p. 104

2. Muslih, M. Y.1988, *The Origins of Palestinian Nationalism*, Columbia University Press, New York , p. x.

3. Quoted in Khalidi, R. 1997, *Palestinian Identity: The Construction of Modern National Consciousness*, Columbia University Press, New York, p. 158.

4. Gelvin, J. 2005, *The Israel-Palestine Conflict: One Hundred Years of War*, Cambridge University Press, Cambridge, p. 93

## Chapter 5

1. Smith, C. 2004, *Palestine and the Arab-Israeli Conflict*, 5th edn, Bedford/St. Martin's, Boston, p. 108.

2. Quoted in Eban, A. 1992, *Personal Witness: Israel Through My Eyes*, G. P. Putnam's Sons, New York, pp 108-9.

## Chapter 6

1. Quoted in Shlaim, A. 1988, *Collusion Across the Jordan: King Abdullah, the Zionist Movement and the Partition of Palestine*, Clarendon, Oxford, p. 142.

2. Zweig, R. W. 1991, 'Israeli–Diaspora Relations in the Early Years of the State' in Silberstein (ed.), *New Perspectives on Israeli History*, New York University Press, New York, p. 258.

3. Segev, T., 1986, *1949: The First Israelis*, Henry Holt and Company, New York, p. viii.

4. Sayigh, Y. 1997, *Armed Struggle and the Search for a State: The Palestinian National Movement, 1949-1993*, Oxford University Press, Oxford, p. 14.

5. Morris, B. 2004, *The Birth of the Palestinian Refugee Problem Revisited*, Cambridge University Press, Cambridge, p.164.

6. Bregman A. and el-Tahri, J. 1998, *The Fifty Years War: Israel and the Arabs*, BBC Books, London, p. 33.

7. Dawisha, A. 2003, *Arab Nationalism in the Twentieth Century: From Triumph to Despair*, Princeton University Press, Princeton, p. 129.

8. Khalaf, I. 1991, *Politics in Palestine: Arab Factionalism and Social Disintegration 1939-1948*, State University of New York Press, Albany, pp 1-2.

9. Jamal, A. 2005, *The Palestinian Nationalist Movement: Politics of Contention, 1967-2005*, Indiana University Press, Bloomington, p. 1.

10. Khalidi, R. 2001 'The Palestinians and 1948: The Underlying Causes of Failure,' in Rogan and Shlaim (eds), *The War for Palestine: Rewriting the History of 1948*, Cambridge University Press, Cambridge, pp 12-13.

11. Morris, B. 2001, 'Revisiting the Palestinian Exodus of 1948' in E. Rogan and A. Shlaim (eds.), *The War for Palestine: Rewriting the History of 1948*, Cambridge University Press, Cambridge, pp 37-38.

12. Quoted in Segev, T. 2000, *One Palestine, Complete: Jews and Arabs Under the British Mandate*, Henry Holt and Company, New York, p. 506.

13. Said, E. 2001, 'Afterword' in E. Rogan and A. Shlaim (eds.), *The War for Palestine: Rewriting the History of 1948*, Cambridge University Press, Cambridge, p. 209.

## Chapter 7

1. Kerr, M. H. 1971, *The Arab Cold War: Gamal 'Abd al-Nair and His Rivals, 1958-1970*, 3rd edn, Oxford University Press, Oxford, p. 126.

## Chapter 8

1. Interview with US President Jimmy Carter with The Academy of Achievement, 25 October, 1991. [Online] http://www.achievement.org/autodoc/page/car0int-2

2. Shlaim, A. 2000, *The Iron Wall: Israel and the Arab World*, New York, W. W. Norton & Company, p. 352.

## Chapter 9

1. Khalidi, R. 1997, *Palestinian Identity: The Construction of Modern National Consciousness*, Columbia University Press, New York, p. 197.

## Chapter 10

1. Rabinovich, I. 2004, *Waging Peace: Israel and the Arabs 1948-2003*, Princeton University Press, Princeton, p. 34.

## Chapter 11

1. Meital, Y. 2005, *Peace in Tatters: Israel, Palestine, and the Middle East*, Lynne Rienner, Boulder, p. 49.

2. Ross, D. 2004, *The Missing Peace: The Inside Story of the Fight for Middle East Peace*, Farrar, Straus and Giroux, New York, pp 44-5.

## Chapter 12

1. Quandt, W. 2005, 'Israeli-Palestinian Peace Talks: From Oslo to Camp David II' in T. Cofman Wittes (ed.), *How Israelis and Palestinians Negotiate A Cross-Cultural Analysis of the Oslo Peace Process*, United States Institute of Peace Press, Washington, p. 13.

2. Darwish, M. 2004, 'Farewell Arafat', *Al-Ahram Weekly*, 18-24 November [Online] http://weekly.ahram.org.eg/2004/717/sc81.htm.

3. Beyer, L. 2004, 'A Life in Retrospect: Yasser Arafat', TIME, 12 Novermber [Online] http://www.time.com/time/world/article/0,8599,781566-1,00.html

4. Aburish, S. 1998, *Arafat From Defender to Dictator*, Bloomsbury, London, pp 13-14.

5. Aburish, p. 8.

6. Aburish, p. 19.

7. Elbendary, A. 2004, 'The Portrait of a Leader', *Al-Ahram* Weekly, 18-24 November [Online] http://weekly.ahram.org.eg/2004/717/sc82.htm

8. Karon, T. 2004, 'Arafat's Ambiguous Legacy', *TIME*, 11 November [Online] http://www.time.com/time/world/article/0,8599,780282,00.html

9. Aburish, pp 24, 25.

10. Aburish, p. 30.

11. Sayigh, Y. 1997, *Armed Struggle and the Search for a State: The Palestinian National Movement, 1949-1993*, Oxford University Press, Oxford, pp 83-4.

12. Hart, A. 1994, *Arafat: A Political Biography*, Sidgwick & Jackson, London, p. 118.

13. Beyer, 2004.

14. Sayigh, pp 84-5.

15. Hart, pp 124.

16. Abu Iyad. 1981, *My Home, My Land*, Times Books, New York, pp 188-89.

17. Seale, P. 1988, *Asad of Syria: The Struggle for the Middle East*, I.B. Tauris & Co Ltd, London, p. 282.

18. Sayigh, Y. 1984, 'Fatah: the First Twenty Years', Journal of Palestine Studies, vol. 13, no. 4, p.115.

19. Shukrallah, H. 2004, 'The Phoenix always rises' *Al-Ahram Weekly*, 18-24 November [Online] http://weekly.ahram.org.eg/2004/717/sc11.htm

20. Nafie, B. M. 2004, 'The imperatives of continuity', *Al-Ahram Weekly*, 18-24 November, [Online] http://weekly.ahram.org.eg/2004/717/sc11.htm

21. Rubin, B. 1998, 'After Arafat: Succession and Stability in Palestinian Politics', *MERIA*, vol. 2, no. 1 [Online] http://meria.idc.ac.il/journal/1998/issue1/jv2n1a4.html

22. Sparks, J. and Walker, T. 2004, 'Arafat 'heaped cash' on cronies', *The Sunday Times*, 15 August, [Online] http://www.timesonline.co.uk/article/0,,2089-1217133,00.html

23. CBS, 2003, 'Arafat's Billions', *60 Minutes*, 9 November [Online] http://www.cbsnews.com/stories/2003/11/07/60minutes/main582487.shtml

24. Rubin, B. and Colp Rubin, J. 2003, *Yasir Arafat: A Political Biography*, Oxford University Press, Oxford.

25. Safieh, A. 2004, 'Our Own Palestinian De Gaulle', *The Guardian*, 12 November.

26. Sayigh, pp 691-2.

# Further Reading

(Texts in the References list are not repeated here and texts listed for one chapter will often be of value for another but are not repeated.)

## Chapter 2

Ben-Sasson, H. H. (ed.). 1985, *A History of the Jewish People*, Harvard University Press, Cambridge, Mass.

Esposito, J. 1998, Islam: *The Straight Path*, Oxford University Press, Oxford.

Hitti, P. and Khalidi, W. 2002, *History of the Arabs*, 10th edn, Palgrave Macmillan, Basingstoke.

Lewis, B. 1997, *The Middle East*, Scribner, New York.

Telushkin, J. 1991, *Jewish Literacy: The Most Important Things to Know About the Jewish Religion, Its People, and Its History*, William Morrow and Company, New York.

## Chapter 3

Avineri, S. 1981, *The Making of Modern Zionism: the Intellectual Origins of the Jewish State*, Basic Books, New York.

Choueiri, Y. M. 2000, *Arab Nationalism: A History. Nation and State in the Arab World*, Blackwell Publishers, Oxford.

Gershoni, I. and Jankowski, J. 1997, *Rethinking Nationalism in the Arab Middle East*, Columbia University Press, New York.

Hertzberg, A. (ed.). 1984, *The Zionist Idea: A Historical Analysis and Reader*, 2nd edn, Atheneum, New York.

Khalidi, R. et al. 1993, *The Origins of Arab Nationalism*, Columbia University Press, New York.

Laqueur, W. 1976, *A History of Zionism*, Schocken Books, New York.

Wistrich, R. S. 1995, *Antisemitism: the Longest Hatred*, Thames Mandarin, London.

## Chapter 4

Antonious, G. 1969, *The Arab Awakening: The Story of the Arab Nationalist Movement*, Librairie du Liban, Beirut.

Ayyad, A. A. 1999, *Arab Nationalism and the Palestinians: 1850-1939*, Birzeit University Press, Birzeit.

Kimmerling, B., and Migdal, J. 1994, *Palestinians: The Making of a People*, Harvard University Press, Cambridge Mass.

O'Brien, C. C. 1988, *The Siege: The Saga of Israel and Zionism*, Paladin Grafton Books, London.

Sachar, H. M. 1996, *A History of Israel: From the Rise of Zionism to Our Time*, Alfred A. Knopf, New York.

Weizmann, C. 1971, *Trial and Error*, Greenwood Press, Westport.

## Chapter 5

Abboushi, W. F. 1977, 'Road to Rebellion: Arab Palestine in 1930s', *Journal of Palestine Studies*, vol. 6, no. 3, pp 23-46.

Bethel, N. 1979, *The Palestine Triangle: the Struggle between the British, the Jews and the Arabs 1935-48*, Andre Deutsch, London.

Farsoun, S. K and Zacharia, C. 1997, *Palestine and the Palestinians*, Westview Press, Boulder.

Porath, Y. 1974, *The Emergence of the Palestinian Arab National Movement*, Frank Cass, London.

Quandt, W. et al, (eds.). 1973, *The Politics of Palestinian Nationalism*, University of California Press, Berkeley.

Stookey, R. W. (eds.). 1986, *The End of the Palestine Mandate*, I.B. Tauris & Co, London.

Tessler, M. 1994, *A History of the Israeli-Palestinian Conflict*, Indiana University Press, Bloomington.

## Chapter 6

Bar-Joseph, U. 1987, *The Best of Enemies: Israel and Transjordan in the War of 1948*, Frank Cass, London.

Flapan, S. 1987, *The Birth of Israel: Myths and Realities*, Pantheon, New York.

Gilbert, M. 1998, *Israel: A History*, Doubleday, London.

Karsh, E. 1997, *Fabricating Israeli History: The 'New Historians'*, Frank Cass, London.

Morris, B. 1987, *The Birth of the Palestinian Refugee Problem, 1947-1949*, Cambridge University Press, Cambridge.

Pappé, I. 1992, *The Making of the Arab–Israeli Conflict 1947-1951*, I.B. Tauris, London.

Rogan, E. and Shalaim, A. (eds.). 2001, *The War for Palestine: Rewriting the History of 1948*, Cambridge University Press, Cambridge.

**Chapter 7**

Abu Lughod, I. (ed.) 1970, *The Arab-Israeli Confrontation of June 1967: an Arab Perspective*, Northwestern University Press, Evanston.

Ajami, F. 1992, *The Arab Predicament: Arab Political Thought and practice Since 1967*, Cambridge University Press, New York.

Bar-Siman-Tov, Y. 1980, *The Israeli-Egyptian War of Attrition, 1969-1970: A Case Study of a Limited War*, Columbia University Press, New York.

Cohen, A. 1998, *Israel and the Bomb*, Columbia University Press, New York.

Fawzi, M. 1986, *Suez 1956: An Egyptian Perspective*, Shorouk International, London.

Harkabi, Y. 1972, *Arab Attitudes to Israel, trans. by Misha Louvish*, Valentine, London.

Heikal, M. 1978, *The Sphinx and the Commissar: The Rise and Fall of Soviet Influence in the Middle East*, Harper & Row, New York.

Herzog, C. 1982, *The Arab-Israeli Wars: War and Peace in the Middle East*, Random House, New York.

Oren, M. 2002, *The Six Days of War: June 1967 and the Making of the Modern Middle East*, Oxford University Press, Oxford.

Parker, R. B. 1993, *The Politics of Miscalculation in the Middle East*, Indiana University Press, Bloomington.

Troen, I. 1996, 'The Protocol of Sèvres: British/French/Israeli Collusion Against Egypt, 1956', *Israel Studies* vol. 1, no. 2, pp 122-139.

**Chapter 8**

Blum, H. 2003, *On the Eve of Destruction: The Untold Story of the Yom Kippur War*, Harper Collins Publishers, New York.

Dayan, M. 1981, *Breakthrough: A Personal Account of the Egypt-Israel Peace Negotiations*, Weidenfeld and Nicolson, London.

Kamil, M. 1986, *The Camp David Accords: a Testimony*, Routledge & Kegan Paul, London.

Meir, G. 1973, *A Land of Our Own*, Weidenfeld & Nicolson, London.

Meir, G. 1975, *My Life*, G.P. Putman's Sons, New York.

Meir, M. 1983, *My Mother Golda Meir: A Son's Evocation of Life with Golda Meir*, Arbor House Publishing Company, New York.

Quandt, W. B, 2001, *Peace Process: American Diplomacy and the Arab-Israeli Conflict Since 1967*, Brookings Institution, Washington.

Rabinovich, A. 2004, *The Yom Kippur War: The Epic Encounter that Transformed the Middle East*, Schocken Books, New York.

Rubin, B., Ginat, J. and Ma'oz, M. (eds.) 1994, *From War to Peace: Arab-Israeli Relations 1973-1993*, Sussex Academic Press, Brighton.

Sela, A. 1998, *The Decline of the Arab-Israeli Conflict: Middle East Politics and the Quest for Regional Order*, State University of New York Press, Albany.

Stein, K. W. 1999, *Heroic Diplomacy: Sadat, Kissinger, Carter, Begin and the Quest for Arab-Israeli Peace*, Routledge, New York.

**Chapter 9**

Cobban, H. 1984, *The Palestine Liberation Organisation: People, Power, and Politics*, Cambridge University Press, New York.

Deeb, M. 1980, *The Lebanese Civil War*, Praeger Publishers, Westport.

Khalidi, R. 1986, *Under Siege: PLO Decision-making in the 1982 War*, Columbia University Press, New York.

Muslih, M. 1988, *The Origins of Palestinian Nationalism*, Columbia University Press, New York.

Sahliyeh, E. 1986, *The PLO after the Lebanon War*, Westview Press, Boulder.

Rabinovich, I. 1985, *The War for Lebanon, 1970-1983*, Cornell University Press, Ithaca.

Rubin, B. 1981, *The Arab States and the Palestine Conflict*, Syracuse University Press, Syracuse.

## Chapter 10

Abu-Amr, Z. 1994, *Islamic Fundamentalism in the West Bank and Gaza*, Indiana University Press, Bloomington.

Hroub, K. 2000, *Hamas: Political Thought and practice*, Institute for Palestine Studies, Washington.

Litvak, M. *The Islamization of Palestinian Identity: the Case of Hamas* [Online] http://www.tau.ac.il/dayancenter/d&a-hamas-litvak.htm

Peretz, D. 1990, *Intifada: The Palestinian Uprising*, Westview Press,.

Schiff, Z. and Ya'ari, E. 1989, *Intifada – The Palestinian Uprising: Israel's Third Front*, Simon and Schuster, New York.

Nasser, J. and Heacock, R. (eds). *1990, Intifada: Palestine at the Crossroads*, Praeger, New York.

## Chapter 11

Abbas, M. 1997, *Through Secret Channels: the Secret Road to Oslo*, Garnet Publishing, Reading.

Freedman, R. (ed) 1995, *Israel under Rabin*, Westview Press, Boulder.

Makovsky, D. 1996, *Making Peace with the PLO: The Rabin Government's Road to the Oslo Accord*, Westview Press, Boulder.

Quandt, W. B. 2001, *Peace Process: American Diplomacy and the Arab-Israeli Conflict since 1967*, Brookings Institute, Washington.

Said, E. W. 1995, *Peace and Its Discontent: Essays on Palestine in the Middle East Process*, Vintage, New York.

Savir, U. 1998, *The Process: 1,100 Days That Changed the Middle East*, Random House, New York.

## Chapter 12

BBC News. 2004, *'Profile: Yasser Arafat'* [Online] http://news.bbc.co.uk/2/hi/middle_east/3102112.stm

Gowers, A. and Walker, T. 1990, *Behind the Myth: Yasser Arafat and the Palestinian Revolution*, W H Allen, London.

Karsh, E. 2003, *Arafat's War: The Man and his Battle for Israeli Conquest*, Grove Press, New York.

Nobel e-Museum. 1994, *'Yasser Arafat – Biography'* [Online] http://nobelprize.org/peace/laureates/1994/arafat-bio.html

Nofal, M. 2006, *'Yasir Arafat, the Political Player: A Mixed Legacy'*, Journal of Palestine Studies, vol. 35, no. 2, pp. 23-37.

PASSIA, 2004, *'Yasser Arafat Photo Album'* [Online] http://www.passia.org/Arafat/images2/pages/AraNew_img_000.html

Rubinstein, D. 1995, *The Mystery of Arafat*, Steerforth Press, Hanover.

Walker, T. & Gowers, A. 2005, *Arafat: The Biography*, Virgin Books, London.

Wallach, J. & Wallach, J. 1990, *Arafat: In the Eyes of the Beholder*, Lyle Stuart, New York.

# Index